No Child
Left
Behind?

No Child Left Behind?

The Politics and Practice of School Accountability

Paul E. Peterson
Martin R. West
Editors

BROOKINGS INSTITUTION PRESS
Washington, D.C.

ABOUT BROOKINGS

The Brookings Institution is a private nonprofit organization devoted to research, education, and publication on important issues of domestic and foreign policy. Its principal purpose is to bring knowledge to bear on current and emerging policy problems. The Institution maintains a position of neutrality on issues of public policy. Interpretations or conclusions in Brookings publications should be understood to be solely those of the authors.

Library of Congress Cataloging-in-Publication data

No child left behind? : the politics and practice of school accountability / Paul E. Peterson, Martin R. West, editors.
     p.   cm.
Includes bibliographical references and index.
   ISBN 0-8157-7028-6 (cloth : alk. paper)
   ISBN 0-8157-7029-4 (paper : alk. paper)
   1. Educational accountability—Law and legislation—United States.   2. Education—Standards—United States.   3. Federal aid to education—United States.   4. Education—United States.   I. Peterson, Paul E.   II. West, Martin R.
   KF4125.N6   2003
   379.1'58'0973—dc22   2003020782

9 8 7 6 5 4 3

The paper used in this publication meets minimum requirements of the American National Standard for Information Sciences—Permanence of Paper for Printed Library Materials: ANSI Z39.48-1992.

Typeset in Adobe Garamond

Composition by Betsy Kulamer
Washington, D.C.

Printed by R. R. Donnelley
Harrisonburg, Virginia

Contents

Preface

W̲ell before the No Child Left Behind Act was passed by Congress and signed into law by President George W. Bush, it was clear that a strikingly new education initiative would be enacted. Both the president and Al Gore, his Democratic opponent in the 2000 election campaign, had called for stronger accountability, and the idea had strong, bipartisan support on Capitol Hill. For a moment, it seemed that the events of September 11, 2001, might slow the process, but, if anything, the national spirit evoked by those harrowing moments only convinced members of Congress to put group and partisan considerations to one side, speeding the course of the legislation.

Anticipating the law's enactment, Harvard University's Program on Education Policy and Governance (PEPG) decided in the spring of 2001 to bring together the nation's leading scholars on the politics and practice of accountability. The result is the first comprehensive scholarly assessment of the issues to be faced as No Child Left Behind is implemented by states and localities. After our introductory essay, part 1 of the book examines the politics surrounding passage of the legislation, as well as the political challenges looming ahead for states and localities as they attempt to comply with the rules and regulations stipulated by the Department of Education. In parts 2 and 3 of the volume, authors look at the impact of existing accountability schemes in various states and localities and abroad. Taken as a whole, the collected essays suggest that the pressures to weaken the force of the legislation will be powerful. Yet even partial measures—soft accountability, as it were—may have a positive impact on American education. One thing is missing in the legislation, however. It requires little in the way of student accountability, even though students themselves are most central to the learning process.

The preparation of these essays has taken more than two years. Authors were given considerable time to prepare their papers. The conference itself was held in June 2002 at Harvard's Kennedy School of Government. Each essay was critically discussed by scholars and practitioners knowledgeable about issues of research design and interpretation, then subjected to conferencewide discussion. Following the conference, authors were asked to revise their papers in light of the discussion and additional comments from the editors. A second round of revisions occurred following the peer review process conducted by the Brookings Institution Press.

The revised and edited papers appear in the pages that follow. Inasmuch as both editors were equally engaged in all stages of the volume's preparation, the title page follows conventional practice and lists their names alphabetically. The ordering of the names is reversed for the introductory chapter, another joint product to which both editors contributed equally.

Many people assisted us in the preparation of the volume. In addition to the authors of the chapters, conference participants were Alan Altshuler, Dale Ballou, John Bishop, Robert Costrell, Denis Doyle, Ronald Ferguson, Ted Hershberg, Caroline M. Hoxby, William Howell, Susan Mayer, Donald McAdams, James Peyser, Michael Podgursky, Andrew Rotherham, Kathryn Schiller, Robert Schwartz, and Herbert Walberg. These participants and the many others in attendance had the opportunity to hear the Bush administration's perspective on the legislation from Secretary of Education Rod Paige, who was introduced by Harvard president Lawrence Summers.

Financial support for the conference was provided by a grant from the John M. Olin Foundation and from the funds of the Taubman Center on State and Local Government at the Kennedy School of Government. The Program on Education Policy and Governance is part of the Taubman Center on State and Local Government and the Center for American Political Studies in Harvard's Department of Government. Alan Altshuler, director of the Taubman Center, provided the editors with extensive help and guidance.

Antonio Wendland, the associate director of PEPG, provided invaluable assistance with the organization of the conference and the preparation of the volume. Thomas Polseno and Mark Linnen also contributed to this effort.

Susan Woollen handled cover design with her usual skillfulness and care, while Colleen McGuiness edited the manuscript carefully. Finally, we are especially grateful to Robert L. Faherty, director of the Brookings Institution Press, and Christopher Kelaher, acquisitions editor, for their sustained commitment to timely and readable academic books.

PAUL E. PETERSON
MARTIN R. WEST

1

The Politics and Practice of Accountability

MARTIN R. WEST AND PAUL E. PETERSON

As a path breaker, No Child Left Behind (NCLB), the federal legislation signed into law in January 2002, stands alongside the pioneering compensatory and special education laws enacted in 1965 and 1974. In the words of political analyst David S. Broder, NCLB "may well be the most important piece of federal education legislation in thirty-five years."[1] The crucial aspect of all three pieces of legislation is not so much the money authorized as the policy framework imposed. Compensatory education and special education laws have never provided more than a fraction of the real cost of educating those they professed to serve. Similarly, NCLB increased the federal share of the country's total school funding by barely 1 percentage point. The federal government's fiscal role in education has always been small, in recent years hovering around 7 to 8 percent of all public funding of elementary and secondary education, with the balance being covered by local and, to an increasing extent, state revenues.

No, it is not the federal dollar contribution but the direction given to all school spending—whether federal, state, or local—that is key. Just as the 1965 compensatory education law sensitized the country to the needs of minority and low-income students, and just as the 1974 special education law guaranteed for the first time free, appropriate, education to disabled students, so the 2002 legislation redirects educational thinking along new channels. Under its terms, every state, to receive federal aid, must put into place a set of standards together with a detailed testing plan designed to make sure the standards are being met. Students at schools that fail to measure up may leave for other schools in the same district, and, if a school persistently fails to make adequate progress toward full proficiency, it becomes subject to corrective action.

The new law will not transform American schools overnight. Just as it took decades before compensatory education and special education laws altered American educational practice, so NCLB will only gradually take hold in states and localities across the country. Although a few parents were almost immediately given the right to move their children from failing schools into another public school within the same school district, substantial delay is written into the law in many different ways. Its most strenuous provision—school reconstitution—does not take effect for at least five years, by which time the legislation will already need to be renewed.

The earlier laws also demonstrate how federal intervention can alter school practice in unexpected—and potentially unintended—ways. Compensatory education accelerated school desegregation in the South, enhancing the educational experiences of many African American students. Yet many compensatory education programs also left localities burdened with rules and regulations that may have diminished their educational effectiveness. Similarly, special education has had ambiguous consequences. On the one hand, it opened the door to educational and medical services previously denied to disabled children. On the other hand, the procedures used to define those in need of special education stigmatized many students, minorities in particular, as special when all they needed was a more appropriate classroom climate. In the same vein, NCLB will undoubtedly reshape the focus of public schools in ways yet unforeseen.

The law's arrival on the educational scene raises many questions. How did its passage come about? What were the educational, social, and political forces that gave it shape? What issues will arise in its implementation? What are its likely consequences? Full and complete answers to these questions cannot yet be given. But enough is known—both about the enactment of NCLB and about the workings of precursor accountability policies—that these topics can be explored in an informed and deliberative way.

In part 1 of the collection of essays that follows, four political scientists examine the process leading up to the passage of the legislation, the issues that can be expected to arise in the course of its implementation, and the nature of the political struggle that can be expected to ensue. In part 2, policy analysts explore the practice of school accountability, offering an early assessment of its effectiveness and valuable advice for state policymakers attempting to achieve compliance in the manner most beneficial for students. Although the accountability provisions of NCLB apply exclusively to schools, some existing rules instead hold individual students accountable. Part 3 examines the issue of student accountability through the lenses of the minimum competency testing and course graduation requirement policies of the 1970s and 1980s, the accountability system erected in Chicago in the 1990s, and curriculum-based exams administered before the completion of high school in many nations around the globe.

The Origins of Accountability

The accountability movement has its origins in long-standing efforts to measure cognitive aptitude and ability. It is premised on the notion that standardized tests can and do measure an important dimension of educational quality. Such a position is increasingly uncontroversial, as evidence mounts that student achievement as measured by standardized tests is strongly associated with both individual and aggregate economic success.[2] However, broad support for the use of standardized tests as measures of both student cognitive ability and school quality developed only after many years of academic research and trial-and-error application.

Major steps toward more precise measurement of cognitive ability performance occurred during World Wars I and II, when psychometricians, in their search for the best American soldiers, developed tests used to predict performance in a variety of military-related tasks. Testing instruments were further refined during peacetime in the expectation that they could help identify those best suited for further education and high-skilled employment. Over the course of the 1950s, the Scholastic Aptitude Test (SAT), a product of these efforts, was identified as a useful admissions tool by an ever-increasing number of colleges and universities. Soon, college-bound students in most regions of the country felt they had to take the exam.

Although the SAT was originally designed as a curriculum-free device for identifying talented individuals, it gradually came to be seen as a useful tool for measuring the quality of public schooling. When SAT scores began to fall during the 1960s and 1970s, critics of American schools had a quantitative measure to justify their concerns. Between 1967 and 1982, SAT test scores went down by no less than 0.3 standard deviations.

A decline of this magnitude is no trivial matter. A standard deviation is a statistical unit that measures how much scores are spread around their average, facilitating comparisons from one test to another. In terms of test score performance, a difference of a full standard deviation is generally considered very large. For example, the long-standing difference in average math scores of black and white students in American schools—the much noted black-white test score gap—is approximately 1.0 standard deviation, as is the performance difference between typical fourth and eighth graders. A full standard deviation is also the size of the difference in the math performance of students in the United States and Japan, a difference large enough to have led many scholars abroad to try their hand at explaining the difference. Although only about a third the size of these differences, the decline in SAT scores in the fifteen years preceding 1982 this period was large enough to cause many people to question the direction in which American education was headed.

Before SAT scores began their slide, most Americans thought their schools, which they usually regarded as the best in the world, were continually getting better. The United States was the first country to achieve universal elementary education, the leader in the expansion of secondary education, the earliest to create comprehensive schools that combined students from all backgrounds into a common institutional framework, and a trailblazer in the area of higher education. After World War II, the baby boom accelerated the demand for quality schools. New and attractive buildings were constructed, teacher salaries rose, the numbers of students per classroom steadily declined, and state and local commitments to education deepened. Not only were Americans proud of what their schools had already accomplished, but education also came to be seen as the solution to almost all the country's ailments. It was expected to solve problems associated with civil rights, hunger and malnutrition, immigration, crime, teenage drug use, economic inequality, and other issues too numerous to mention.

As early as the 1950s, a few elitist curmudgeons objected to the quality of instruction in America's schools. A small back-to-basics movement complained about progressive education, the growing number of life-experience courses, the paucity of attention paid to the "great books," and slipping academic standards. Hardly anyone had paid attention to these malcontents, however, until SAT scores began their slide. Some said the fall was simply the result of more students taking the SAT, itself a sign of progress, but others showed this factor could not account for the bulk of the decline.[3]

Because the SAT was being taken only by juniors and seniors bound for selective colleges, and therefore did not provide a comprehensive picture of overall student performance, the federal government, in the late sixties, funded a new test, the National Assessment of Educational Progress (NAEP), to be administered to a random sample of all students at ages nine, thirteen, and seventeen. By testing a sample of all students at these ages, NAEP results were expected to provide more complete information. Promoters of NAEP overcame resistance from school officials by making it clear that the test was only a yardstick, not a program designed to hold local schools accountable. The sponsors of the test, the Education Commission of the States (an institution governed by representatives from state governments), foreswore providing any information about student performance for any particular state or locality. (NAEP was even designed so that no one student took the entire test, effectively making it impossible to calculate results for any particular individual or school.) Specific information about particular places would be misleading, it was argued, because student performance may reflect family background and other factors beyond state or local control. Instead, only national results, broken out by ethnic group, region, and community size, would be reported. But even though it was designed so as not to inform anyone about how individual schools were doing, NAEP, ironically, would prove to be a key mechanism in hastening the accountability movement forward.

Many expected that NAEP would prove the SAT wrong, that it would show that the country was progressing after all, just as the P in the acronym promised. Unfortunately, NAEP, by revealing more losses than gains in student test performance, only confirmed what the SAT had suggested. Between 1970 and 1982, the performance of seventeen-year-old students on the science examination fell by 0.4 standard deviations. In math, the drop was 0.2 standard deviations. Only the reading scores increased—and these only by a hairbreadth. The trends were not as disappointing for younger students (those age nine and thirteen), but even here NAEP revealed more stagnation than progress.

Concern intensified when Americans discovered further that the United States lagged behind many countries it thought it had left behind. Well-regarded international surveys of educational achievement routinely revealed that U.S. students trailed their peers abroad. The situation deteriorated the longer students remained in school. Among nine-year-olds, U.S. students performed in math and science among the top tier of nations, if not at the very highest levels attained by some Asian nations. By age thirteen, U.S. students had fallen below the international average in these subjects, and by age seventeen, they trailed all the other industrial countries in the world, remaining ahead of only such nations as Lithuania, Cypress, and South Africa.[4]

A decade or more passed before these trends had clear political consequences. But, in 1982, unexpectedly, the Reagan administration made education reform a top political priority. A national commission, appointed by Secretary of Education Terrel H. Bell, issued a report claiming that the quality of America's schools was leaving the country endangered by foreign competition. Released in 1983, *A Nation at Risk* called for a wide range of reforms that it hoped would reverse the downward trend. Students needed to be given more challenging tasks; teachers needed to be better paid and better trained in the subject matter they taught; states needed to extend the school day and the school year; parents needed to expect more of their children; and a commitment to quality needed to be affirmed by all those responsible for training the young.[5]

That all this should happen during the Reagan years ran contrary to any reasonable expectation. After all, as a candidate for the presidency in 1980, Reagan had called for the disestablishment of the Department of Education that the Carter administration had successfully urged upon Congress just two years earlier. In the view of the early Reagan administration, most of the department's functions should have been turned back to states and localities. Consistent with this perspective, Reagan originally refused to appoint a presidential commission on education, thereby limiting Bell's commission to mere departmental status. Yet when the same commission's report was welcomed with great applause, the Reagan administration reversed course. It dropped all plans to shut down the Department of Education and even increased the level of federal funding. By 1985 the president had appointed William Bennett, an articulate and outspoken educational reformer, as his secretary of education. Still, the call for reform was not backed up by any clearly defined accountability scheme. It would take nearly two decades before another Republican administration would move beyond rhetoric and prompt a real intervention.

Even so, *A Nation at Risk* pushed the nation further toward accountability, principally by raising educational issues higher on state political agendas. In many states, especially in the South, governors saw political profit in making school reform a key plank in their governing platform. Voting rights legislation had made African Americans a significant bloc within the southern electorate, forcing gubernatorial candidates to find ways of garnering support from black and white voters alike. Increased school spending, coupled with accountability requirements, proved useful in this regard. Governors could call for more educational spending to upgrade predominantly black schools. At the same time, they could balance their liberal, pro-spending proposals with a more conservative insistence that stringent requirements accompany the new money, thus ensuring the support of business leaders concerned about the quality of the work force. Pioneering efforts were initiated by governors in Tennessee (under future Republican secretary of education Lamar Alexander), in South Carolina (under future Democratic secretary of education Richard W. Riley), in Arkansas (under Bill Clinton), and, most comprehensively, in North Carolina (under another Democratic presidential hopeful, James B. Hunt Jr.). That these governors found accountability an issue that helped elevate them to the national scene was not lost on their peers in other states.

The most significant story was unfolding in Texas. Businessman and future presidential candidate H. Ross Perot, as head of a state education commission, first called for tough requirements that would hold schools and students accountable. Perot captured national attention by requiring that athletes earn C's in class to be eligible to play on varsity teams. More important, in 1993 the Texas legislature heeded his call for testing procedures that would monitor the annual progress of students in each school. Perot's proposals had broad public support and bipartisan appeal. Both Democratic governor Ann Richards and her Republican successor, George W. Bush, embraced the idea, ensuring continuity down to the present time. And when a high-profile study of state NAEP results suggested that, as a result, test scores in Texas and North Carolina were rising faster than scores in other states, the finding helped set the stage for a national intervention.[6]

Initial federal efforts to promote accountability—both those promulgated by the George H. W. Bush administration and by the Clinton administration during its first days in office—had relied on voluntary cooperation from state and local officials. But in 1994, at the prodding of the Clinton administration, Congress imposed the first accountability mandate on the states. It ostensibly required local schools to show, by means of tests, annual student progress toward a state-designated standard of educational proficiency. In short, the core idea underlying NCLB had been conceived.

The pregnancy would prove elephantine. The 1994 law was vague, federal enforcement was lax, many of the state accountability plans were poorly designed, and progress was uneven. Yet the passage of the 1994 law signaled bipartisan support for school accountability. Just as governors found that accountability, coupled with increased expenditure, had an appeal across the political spectrum, so members of Congress—and presidential candidates—found it attractive to hoist their flag on a similar podium. Both George W. Bush and Al Gore embraced accountability in the 2000 presidential campaign.

Despite bipartisan support for the concept, it remained unclear whether the idea would reach infancy. Congress had been unable to agree on new federal education legislation during the waning days of the Clinton administration, and the disputed conclusion to the presidential 2000 election left both Democrats and Republicans embittered. After control of the Senate shifted to the Democrats, continued stalemate seemed as likely as not. Yet politicians often find ways of overcoming their grievances when failure to do so puts them on the wrong side of a popular issue. George W. Bush needed concrete evidence that he was a compassionate conservative, and Democrats on Capitol Hill could not afford to obstruct passage of a law addressing an issue listed among the top items of voter concern, especially after a coming together of Americans in the wake of the September 11, 2001, terrorist attacks. Predictably, centrist Democrats played a key role in shaping compromises. More surprisingly, President Bush and Sen. Edward M. Kennedy, D-Mass., found it relatively easy to work with one another. For their efforts, they were rewarded with a school accountability law passed by a large, bipartisan majority, which the president signed in January 2002.

The key provisions of the law are well described in Andrew Rudalevige's thorough account of the legislation's origins and of the political process that led to its passage. Briefly, the law requires states to assess the performance of all students in grades three through eight in math and reading each year, with an additional test administered at some point during grades ten to twelve. Test results are to be released to the public. Each year, every school will need to show that students (as well as students within each ethnic subgroup of significant size) are making, on average, adequate progress toward full educational proficiency. Schools that do not measure up to standard will be identified as "in need of improvement," and their parents will have the option to place their child in another public school within the same district. Schools that fail to improve after five years will be "restructured" by the district, with new personnel in charge. States must take an analogous approach with persistently underperforming districts.

The Politics of Accountability

These sweeping new requirements imposed tough mandates on states, localities, and schools. Still, as the Rudalevige essay reveals, the need to achieve a legislative consensus ensured that many aspects of the accountability regime remained unspecified, leaving them to be resolved by the federal Department of Education responsible for its implementation. As a result, some have wondered whether the law would prove to be as influential as many analysts initially expected. It is still too soon to tell, but signs already are evident that the law will not have the force its passage seemed to foreshadow. Here are some of the law's chief limitations:

—Congress left to the states the precise standards to be set, the specific design of their testing instruments, and the administration of their accountability systems. Although all states must administer the NAEP, this national test need not be used as a standard of performance. As a result, standards actually have been lowered in some states.

—If a school fails, parents have the right to send their children only to those nonfailing public schools located within the same school district. States may leave the administration of this requirement to districts, which have scant incentive to ensure that they provide parents with meaningful choice. Evidence is already mounting of districts making it difficult for parents to find an alternative.[7]

—Although annual progress toward full proficiency is required, schools have twelve years to reach this target, and the specific amount of progress required each year is not stated. At least two states have already exploited this loophole by submitting accountability plans that postpone the bulk of the necessary improvements to the end of this twelve-year period.

—The toughest requirements in the legislation do not take effect for several years, opening up the possibility that a subsequent Congress will revise them before they are enforced. For example, a school must fail to make progress for each of five years before the restructuring requirement comes into play.

—Students themselves face neither sanctions nor rewards based on their performance. States need not establish high school graduation requirements—nor standards that govern promotion from one grade to the next. While schools are held strictly accountable, students are not.

In short, the legislation's impact will be highly dependent upon the way it is administered by the states and on the specific strategies they devise to promote improvement. If states establish and maintain high standards, if they develop precise measurement tools that accurately identify both excellent schools and those in need of improvement, if they ask students to pass tests to reach the next grade level and to graduate from high school, if they take action when signs of low performance are evident, if they dismiss principals and teachers who are low-performing, and if these rules are put into place promptly and decisively, then NCLB may have dramatic consequences. But if standards are low, measurement weak, students exempted, few consequences imposed, and implementation postponed, then its influence will be more limited.

Perhaps the best guide to future state behavior is the way states have approached accountability in the past. In this regard, Frederick M. Hess's essay on the politics of accountability at the state level is particularly instructive. He distinguishes between tough, coercive high-stakes accountability, on the one hand, and soft, nice, low-stakes accountability, on the other. The former sets high standards, imposes rigorous testing, and specifies clear consequences. The latter has low standards and few penalties. In his review of state practices thus far, Hess finds a tendency for state accountability systems to drift from a tough approach toward a softer one. As popular as tough accountability is when first announced, it encounters political opposition as time goes by. Tough accountability has vague, general support from broad constituencies, but, as its coercive teeth begin to bite, the individuals and groups most directly affected complain bitterly. To ease political opposition, standards are lowered, exceptions granted, and penalties postponed.

The pattern is the same for students, teachers, and schools alike. Student accountability is particularly challenging, because rigorous standards will keep underperforming students from advancing to the next grade level with their peers and may discourage some from completing their secondary education. The appearance of punishing students let down by a school system in which few have confidence makes strict accountability for students difficult to sustain.

It would seem easier to hold teachers accountable, if their students underperform. But it is unlikely that many teachers will lose their jobs simply because students in their classes are failing to learn. As Terry M. Moe explains in his penetrating analysis of the role that teacher unions can be expected to play in the implementation of high-stakes accountability arrangements, the unions have a duty to protect the job security of their members, even the weakest ones. In pursuit of this objective, unions have negotiated contracts with school boards that require extensive grievance procedures before an employee can be dismissed. Unions are likely to find mitigating circumstances whenever students' performance falters. Attributing results to the work of a specific teacher will be virtually impossible.

Admittedly, teacher unions have, on occasion, embraced laws requiring high standards. As Jennifer Hochschild recounts in her essay on accountability politics, former president of the American Federation of Teachers Albert Shanker was a particularly forceful proponent of such standards at a time when the accountability movement was just beginning. Similarly, Robert Chase, former president of the National Education Association (NEA), called for reform-minded unions as a supplement to the "bread-and-butter unionism" that focused solely on wages and job protection. But, Hochschild also notes, with the passage of NCLB, the union mood has altered. Those campaigning for NEA leadership in 2002 denounced the new law, calling its title "another empty phrase." Even Chase, in his farewell address, complained that accountability tests "have little or no use in pinpointing the learning problems of students."

Teacher opposition threatens the viability of any accountability scheme, simply because their unions are well poised to shape educational policy, especially at state and local levels. Whereas unions are only one of many participants in national education debates, they are often the dominant players at the state and local level. They are heavy contributors in school board and state elections. Their expertise is taken seriously in public debates. They employ many full-time group representatives in state capitols. Their members vote more frequently than the average citizen. According to some analysts, they are the single most influential lobby in state government. In many states, all of this political power is backed up with the right to strike, a power that comes into play any time a teacher's job is on the line.

But if teachers cannot be held accountable, can schools be? According to NCLB, a school is to be reconstituted if students do not make annual progress in any one of five years. It is not clear whether this provision will ever be invoked. Depending on how this clause is interpreted, even the poorest of schools could slip through its loopholes. As Thomas J. Kane and his colleagues have shown, test scores can fluctuate randomly in ways that have nothing to do with student progress.[8] For any year with a bounce downward, chances are good the next year will see a bounce upward. If so, it will be difficult for a school to avoid showing progress in at least one of five years. It remains to be seen whether state accountability machinery will deal adequately with meaningless annual fluctuation in test scores. Moreover, even if persistently failing schools are reconstituted, nothing in the law prevents the same personnel from being reassigned to other schools. NCLB does nothing to relieve school districts of union-negotiated constraints on the dismissal of teachers. Shifting ineffective personnel from one school to the next will not enhance overall educational quality.

Finally, many will argue that schools cannot be held accountable unless they are given more resources. Many of the first state accountability programs were a product of political bargains that gave educators additional resources in exchange for increased accountability for results. As NCLB is being implemented, however, states and localities are experiencing major budgetary shortfalls, which have already forced cutbacks in school expenditures. Teacher organizations and local officials will argue that resource constraints limit their capacity to meet the law's objectives. Indeed, in July 2003 the NEA announced plans to file a lawsuit claiming that NCLB imposed unfunded federal mandates on local schools.

The argument that additional resources are needed may seem odd, given that the cost of designing and implementing a comprehensive accountability system is tiny, dwarfed by the huge cost of other reform strategies, such as class-size reduction or increases in teacher salaries.[9] Moreover, the 15 percent increase in school expenditures during the 1990s—per pupil public expenditure in real dollars increased in the United States from around $8,000 in

1990 to more than $9,200 in 2000—was not accompanied by any noticeable improvement in student performance.[10] Nor have most of the more closely calibrated studies of school expenditure found much connection between dollars spent and learning gained, a sign that greater accountability may be just what is needed to ensure that resources are used effectively.[11] But if studies show little effect of resources on school performance, most voters think otherwise. Thus the lack of resources will be invoked as still another reason to slow the application of accountability provisions.

Fortunately, the more persuasively this argument is made, the greater the likelihood that existing resource disparities among schools will decline. Especially where schools are low-performing, states and localities will be asked to see whether performance levels are a consequence of resource limitations. In this regard, Julian R. Betts and Anne Danenberg's analysis of the impact of California's accountability program on resource distribution within the state is encouraging. In contrast to the state's class-size reduction policy, which seems to have adversely affected the quality of the resources available to low-performing school districts, California's accountability law had no such negative impact.

In short, student, teacher, and school accountability all pose major challenges. Keeping intact the necessary political will over the long run is likely to be highly problematic. Hess, Moe, and Hochschild all emphasize that high standards and tough enforcement depend upon the continuous involvement of political leaders responsive to the broad constituencies that support such policies. If authentic accountability is to be established, presidents, governors, and mayors, backed by a well-organized business community, need to remain committed to the effort. Yet such leaders, with their numerous responsibilities, are easily distracted. Fighting wars, preventing terrorism, maintaining economic growth, balancing budgets, and many other issues, too unpredictable to anticipate, can easily shift educational accountability to the back burner. When that happens, well-organized, narrow interests gain the upper hand. All in all, there is every reason to believe that tough, coercive accountability will gradually evolve into something softer, nicer, more acceptable to those directly affected.

The Practice of School Accountability

If No Child Left Behind will be implemented less vigorously than some might wish, it may still constitute a landmark piece of legislation. If a highly coercive accountability system is politically infeasible, a softer version may be enough to prod the American education system forward, though perhaps only gradually and to a lesser extent than otherwise. Soft accountability may be conceived of as something akin to transparency, the simple reporting of facts about student performance in specific grades at individual schools. Increasingly, this kind of soft accountability is becoming commonplace to American education. Under NCLB, with its requirement that all students in grades three through eight be tested annually, many more parents will have more detailed information about what children are learning at their child's school.

Two consequences flow from this new transparency. First, parents can be expected to express concerns about low or falling test scores to school officials. The bland satisfaction most parents currently express concerning their child's school may already be in jeopardy. Still, it is difficult for parents to organize effectively vis-à-vis well-entrenched bureaucrats, who can bring the full weight of their official authority and educational expertise to bear on the deliberations. For transparency to translate into effective change, it will take more than just political action.

Fortunately, in many parts of the country, parents can influence school policy through a second channel: They can leave communities whose schools are ineffective. Even without well-defined testing systems, parents have long been using available information to distinguish good schools from bad. The better the school, the larger the number of parents who want their child attending that school. As demand grows, property values in the area served by the school increase. When property values increase, the whole community—parents and other property owners alike—prospers accordingly. If the local property tax finances the school, more money becomes available to the school board. On the tide of rising test scores floats the entire community. Conversely, a communitywide ebb tide often accompanies falling test scores, making more than just individual parents unhappy. When property values are adversely affected, transparency can pressure schools to improve even in the absence of explicitly coercive accountability policies. Accountability via transparency works best in suburban areas with multiple school districts, especially where most parents have the financial resources to purchase homes in neighborhoods with first-rate schools. Unfortunately, it is less effective in holding schools accountable in urban districts attended by large numbers of low-income, minority families.

Self-enforcing accountability of this kind may already have arrived in many states. In their essay opening part 2 of this collection, Eric A. Hanushek and Margaret E. Raymond report that by 2001 thirty-one states had accountability arrangements of one form or another. It is true that many of them were of the soft variety. The measuring sticks used by many states were flawed, their enforcement mechanisms weak, and their standards not particularly high. Some merely reported test results, depending exclusively on transparency as the mechanism for improvement. But despite these apparent limitations, Hanushek and Raymond find that NAEP scores rose more rapidly during the 1990s in the states that had accountability arrangements than in states that did not. Hanushek and Raymond are the first to say their results are preliminary. Nevertheless early signals suggest that soft accountability is moving many schools in the right direction.

Other essays in this section explore specific aspects of school accountability in greater depth. Thomas J. Kane and Douglas O. Staiger consider an oddity of accountability plans that ask schools to ensure that students from all ethnic backgrounds make test score gains. Such rules appear to penalize integrated schools, even when they are doing as well as more segregated ones, because the multiple categories within which progress needs to be made increase the risk that random fluctuation will wrongly make them appear ineffectual. Kane and Staiger accordingly recommend that schools be judged by their performance as a whole, not by group-specific performances. Tom Loveless next points out that many state accountability schemes provide misleading information about the performance of charter schools, especially small ones and those that serve at-risk populations. He foresees adverse consequences of NCLB—unless consideration is given to the smaller size of charter schools, their relatively disadvantaged student populations, and the fact that many will have formed only recently.

If these essays suggest that much remains to be sorted out, another suggests that school accountability has already had positive effects. Julian Betts and Anne Danenberg evaluate a voluntary intervention program for underperforming schools in California in which the state gave schools additional resources if they agreed to stiff sanctions when students failed to improve. A larger number of underperforming schools applied than could be funded, so participants were selected by lottery, making it possible for the authors to conduct the first randomized field trial of an accountability scheme. When Betts and Danenberg compare the test scores of participating schools with those who applied for the program but were not selected, positive differences are observed. If these results hold elsewhere, school accountability may work after all.

Student Accountability: What Works?

If No Child Left Behind is designed to hold schools accountable, it places no direct burdens on students themselves. It does not require standards for high school graduation or levels of performance for passing from one grade to the next. Although nothing in the legislation prevents states from instituting such standards on their own, they are under no federal mandate to do so. Yet the student is the learner, the one person whose engagement in the educational process is essential to the enterprise. If a student is attentive, curious, enthusiastic, committed, and hardworking, much can be accomplished—even with limited resources. Abraham Lincoln, raised by a stepmother and near illiterate father (of whom he seems not to have been particularly fond), managed to write the Gettysburg Address, arguably the finest piece of American prose ever written, even though he had less than a year's worth of formal schooling. Lincoln educated himself by reading—and rereading—Shakespeare, the Bible, and a few classics neighbors loaned him. Not every student can be as resourceful as "Honest Abe," but systems that try to get teachers to work harder will not have much effect if students are unresponsive.

However essential student engagement may be, it is easy to see why NCLB dodged this issue. Consider the requirement that students pass an examination to graduate from high school. If the standard is set too high, many students will fail, provoking an outcry among parents and educators. As Frederick Hess points out in his essay on accountability politics, tough initial requirements are eventually relaxed—by stretching out the compliance period, lowering the passing standard, and permitting students to have a second chance. If the standard emerging from this process is too low, nearly every one passes easily, and the signal goes out that not much is required to obtain a high school diploma. The policy has an effect precisely the opposite of what is intended.

Such may have happened during the 1970s when many states set minimum competency standards for graduation. Precursors to the contemporary accountability movement, minimum competency laws were the first to mandate that students achieve a certain level of test performance, if they were to graduate. The tests proved a very soft form of accountability. States set passing grades at a level almost every high school graduate could achieve, allowing minimum competency to live up to its name. Nearly everyone who tried seems to have eventually passed. As Hess points out, the requirement became so bland it faded into the educational woodwork, eclipsed by the educational excellence approach endorsed by *A Nation at Risk*, an approach that rejected these minimalist reforms as hopelessly inadequate.

The first paper in this collection's third section, which focuses on student accountability, offers the first rigorous assessment of the long-term impacts of minimum competence tests. In 1990 the U.S. Bureau of the Census asked 5 percent of all households a detailed set of questions about their members' education, income, place of residence, and many other matters. Using this resource, Thomas Dee has devised a sophisticated way of estimating the effect of state-level reform programs. He examines course taking in high school, high school graduation rates, college attendance rates, employment in 1990, and wages in 1990 for those affected by the reforms, as compared with those who completed their schooling before the reforms took effect. Controlling for other factors, he offers the best available estimate of the long-term impact of the early effort to hold students minimally accountable.

For high school students taken as a whole, the tests had little impact, one way or another. Apparently the standards were so minimal they did not deter high school graduation, but neither did they stimulate more learning that would pay off in higher levels of college attendance, dependable employment, or higher wages. Their only significant effect seems to have been to reduce the number of math and science courses students took, perhaps because the undemanding nature of the tests implied that such courses were unnecessary. But for two groups, the minimum competency movement had broader effects. African American male students, who, on average, score much lower on these kinds of tests, had modestly lower high school graduation rates after the tests were introduced. Despite these lower graduation rates, the tests had a positive impact on future black male employment. For black males as a whole, then, very soft accountability seems to have had a modestly positive long-term impact. White females had slightly lower employment rates, a result difficult to interpret, inasmuch as no other effects were detected for this subgroup.

Dee also considers the impact of increasing the number of academically oriented courses required of students, a central component of the states' response to *A Nation at Risk*. In many states, students were expected to take additional courses that offered at least nominally academic instruction in English, science, math, and so forth. Once again, the reform was softened by the fact that principals, department heads, and teachers could decide what was to be taught under the academic label. Dee nonetheless finds that the new course requirements for graduation had noticeable effects. Not surprisingly, the clearest impact was on the type of courses a student took. After the reforms, many more students took courses that were at least apparently academic in content. Turing to long-term outcomes, Dee finds more diverse impacts. On the one hand, the reforms depressed high school graduation rates, presumably because some students found such courses not to their liking. On the other hand, they had positive effects on future employment, both overall and especially for black males. Academic courses in high school seem to make for more productive workers later in life.

More recently, student accountability has been given a serious trial in Chicago. In 1995 Mayor Richard Daley appointed Paul Vallas as superintendent of Chicago's schools and gave full backing to the superintendent's efforts to raise student performance by imposing a new set of requirements on students. Tougher high school graduation requirements were put into place, and students in grades three, six, eight, and nine were expected to pass a test, if they were to advance to the next grade. Students who failed to pass the test could get a second chance if they went to summer school. Although Chicago's plan also included school accountability measures similar to those mandated by NCLB, as of spring 2003 the district had yet to subject any elementary or middle school to this penalty.

Two essays in part 3 assess the impact of this, the longest running student accountability scheme to have been closely examined by the scholarly community. Their analyses reveal just how hard it is in the near term to draw firm conclusions about the impact of accountability policies, especially on the basis of the aggregate evidence typically available. At first glance the reform seems to have boosted test scores dramatically, by as much as half a standard deviation (approximately half the black-white test score gap). But at least some of this gain is more apparent than real. As Anthony S. Bryk points out, more students were being retained in their previous class for a year, more were assigned to special and bilingual education programs (exempting them from testing), and the test day was shifted back a month, allowing for additional instruction. All of these moves helped lift the test score average, even without any real improvement in the quality of instruction.

Fortunately, in the case of Chicago, the availability of rich student-level data allows statistical adjustments to be made for most of these factors. When that is done, the gains are less remarkable. But both Bryk and Brian A. Jacob, in a second analysis, identify a noticeable improvement in performance after the city's reform plan, with its heavy emphasis on student accountability, was put into place. Jacob also analyzes performance on individual exam questions to evaluate the meaningfulness of changes in test scores, showing that they reflect a genuine increase in skills. Less clear is whether these underlying gains constitute a one-time impact or whether they are evidence of a more productive school system.

Economist Ludger Wößmann considers an older, more enduring accountability system that has been practiced worldwide and remains intact in many nations: curriculum-based examinations offered to students in their final year of high school, examinations whose results are given great weight by universi-

ties and employers when students leave secondary school. These exams are
generally offered in a variety of subject areas, and students can pass them at
different levels. As such, they can challenge even the most able students,
while remaining within reach of less talented ones. Although virtually
unheard of in the United States, such exams are a prominent instrument of
educational accountability in numerous school systems around the world.
Well-known examples include the General Certificate of Secondary Education in Britain, the Baccalaureate in France, the Abitur in some German Län-
der, and the Hesanchi in Japan.

Wößmann's magisterial paper provides the best estimates to date of the
effects of curriculum-based graduation examinations on student achievement. Because these exams are generally administered on a nationwide basis,
estimating their effects requires data on student performance from many
countries. Wößmann examines results from the math and science tests
administered by the International Education Association to seventh- and
eighth-grade students in thirty-nine countries in 1995 and, again, in thirty-
eight countries in 1999. Using state-of-the-art econometric techniques, he
adjusts for other differences between countries to isolate the independent
effect of curriculum-based graduation examinations. Results are consistent
for the two, separate administrations of these tests. Overall, he provides con-
vincing evidence that students in middle school perform at a higher level in
math and science when the prospect of a demanding examination at the close
of high school awaits them.

Wößmann further advances the literature on this subject by offering a
comprehensive theoretical rationale for why curriculum-based examinations
should prove effective. They provide a clear, external standard, outside the
school, against which student performance can be measured. Performance
has real consequences for a student's future. The student does not simply pass
or fail; instead, the exams challenge students across the ability spectrum. As
an external standard, it motivates peers to work together, teachers to coach
students in their lessons, and parents to ensure their children are receiving
the best possible education. Armed with reliable information about student
performance, each of these stakeholders is well equipped to pursue these
goals effectively. Consistent with this logic, Wößmann provides evidence that
external exams are most beneficial when teachers have the most flexibility
and autonomy. Apparently, teachers left to their own devices can find the
best learning solutions when external exams hold their students accountable.
The United States might well give further thought to an accountability system other countries have had in place for nearly a century.

Conclusions

Much can be learned from reading the essays that follow. Though No Child Left Behind is undoubtedly the most important piece of education legislation in thirty-five years, it does more to initiate a political process than to decide it. So much has been left to state and local governments, the most important political battles are more likely to be waged at these levels than in Washington. As much as political leaders may insist that they have established clear standards of performance and have ended what presidential candidate George W. Bush called "the soft bigotry of low expectations," much remains to be decided.

If the past is any guide to what will happen in the next few years, softer forms of accountability are likely to be the norm. NCLB itself leans in this direction. Although it requires annual testing, annual progress, parental choice, and, in the extreme, school reorganization, close inspection of these requirements reveals many gaps. The annual testing is only for those in elementary and secondary school. No high school graduation test is required. Exactly how much annual progress toward what standard is left unspecified—until twelve years are up (a date far enough in the future that new legislation could easily supersede this rule). Parental choice is limited to nonfailing public schools within the same school district. School reorganization is not to be posed for five years, and the exact conditions that warrant this intervention—and just how draconian it will turn out to be—are left unstated.

Given the flexibility in the law, it will be up to states and localities to interpret its terms. The process will be political, heavily influenced by the teacher unions whose members are subject to its provisions. They will press for softer rules—weaker standards, postponed deadlines, and minimal consequences for teachers. Unless governors and mayors take strong stands on the other side, the union position will carry great weight.

But if soft accountability is to be expected, it may be sufficient to make a difference. If student performance is transparent to parents and community residents, this by itself will place new pressure on schools, which will then expect more of their students. Still, one element is missing in the national legislation. Too little attention has been given to holding students accountable, despite accumulating evidence that this is where the greatest immediate gains could be achieved. The lost opportunities that result may weigh most heavily in the nation's distressed urban school districts, where transparency alone is least likely to stimulate improvement. States that take the initiative to experiment with curriculum-based examinations administered before graduation may be positioning themselves as leaders in the next generation of accountability.

Notes

1. David S. Broder, "Long Road to Reform: Negotiators Forge Education Legislation," *Washington Post*, December 17, 2001, p. A1.

2. For a recent review of this evidence, see Eric A. Hanushek, "The Failure of Input-Based Schooling Policies," *Economic Journal*, vol. 113, no. 485 (February 2003), pp. F64–F66.

3. Diane Ravitch, *National Standards in American Education: A Citizen's Guide* (Brookings, 1995), pp. 64–70.

4. Erik A. Hanushek, "The Seeds of Growth," *Education Next*, vol. 2, no. 3 (Fall 2002), p. 15.

5. National Commission on Excellence in Education, *A Nation at Risk: The Imperative for Educational Reform* (Department of Education, 1983).

6. David W. Grissmer and others, *Improving Student Achievement: What NAEP State Test Scores Tell Us* (Santa Monica, Calif.: RAND Corporation, 2000), pp. 55, 99–100.

7. Ron Brownstein, "Locked Down," *Education Next*, vol. 3, no. 4 (Spring 2004), pp. 40–46.

8. Thomas J. Kane and Douglas O. Staiger. "The Promise and Pitfalls of Using Imprecise School Accountability Measures," *Journal of Economic Perspectives*, vol. 16, no. 4 (Fall 2002), pp. 91–114; and Thomas J. Kane, Douglas O. Staiger, and Jeffrey Geppert, "Randomly Accountable," *Education Next*, vol. 2, no. 1 (Spring 2002), pp. 57–61.

9. Caroline M. Hoxby, "The Cost of Accountability," NBER Working Paper (Cambridge, Mass.: National Bureau of Economic Research, March 2002). See also General Accounting Office, *Title I: Characteristics of Tests Will Influence Expenses; Information Sharing May Help States Realize Efficiencies* (May 2003).

10. On the increase in per pupil expenditures, see Caroline M. Hoxby, "What Has Changed and What Has Not," in Paul E. Peterson, ed., *Our Schools, Our Future: Are We Still at Risk?* (Stanford, Calif.: Hoover Institution Press, 2003), pp. 101–02. On performance, see Paul E. Peterson, "Stagnant Schools," in Peterson, ed., *Our Schools, Our Future: Are We Still at Risk?* pp. 39–72.

11. Hanushek, "The Failure of Input-Based Schooling Policies," pp. F64–F98.

PART 1

The Politics of
Accountability

2

No Child Left Behind: Forging a Congressional Compromise

ANDREW RUDALEVIGE

The scene was a civics text come to life. Flanked by jubilant members of Congress, cheered on by a young crowd, President George W. Bush declared the start of a "new era" in American public education. "As of this hour," said the president, "America's schools will be on a new path of reform, and a new path of results." With a presidential smile and signature, the No Child Left Behind Act (NCLB) of 2001, a sweeping six-year reauthorization of the Elementary and Secondary Education Act (ESEA), became law.[1]

Bush's upbeat assessment was not unique. Press accounts were largely favorable, judging No Child Left Behind the most important piece of federal education legislation since the original ESEA in 1965. The leaders of the large bipartisan legislative coalition behind the act (it had passed the Senate 87-10 and the House 381-41) also agreed. John A. Boehner, R-Ohio, chair of the House Education and the Workforce Committee, said it was his "proudest achievement" in two decades of congressional service. Rep. George Miller of California, the committee's ranking Democrat, said it comprised

Thanks to Dickinson College, the Dana Foundation, and Harvard University's Program on Education Policy and Governance for support of this research; to Audrey Rose and Tim Sidore for research assistance; and to Marty West, Paul Peterson, Don McAdams, Andrew Rotherham, Rusty Silverstein, and several anonymous reviewers for their helpful comments. Special appreciation goes to the members of the education community in and out of government; their insights (and hard work) drive this narrative.

"fundamental, unprecedented reforms." Sen. Judd Gregg, R-N.H., called it "an exceptional piece of legislation," while Edward M. Kennedy, D-Mass., went even further. "This is a defining issue about the future of our Nation and about the future of democracy, the future of liberty, and the future of the United States in leading the free world," the Senate icon said. "No piece of legislation will have a greater impact or influence on that."[2]

Florid rhetoric is no stranger to the ESEA. "We called ours sweeping," said Clinton administration education secretary Richard W. Riley of the 1994 version; "Whoever passes the next reauthorization will call it sweeping." Still, the plaudits of 2001 and 2002 had a new theme: the central place of accountability in the law. As its proponents stressed, the No Child Left Behind Act mandated that schools achieve measurable improvement in the academic performance of their students, or face the consequences. "Accountability is the cornerstone of reform," Bush said as he sent his bill to Congress; and in his signing statement he called it "the first principle" of the new law. Boehner echoed, "States have accepted billions in federal education aid but have never been held accountable for improving student achievement. Until now." NCLB marks an important extension of federal authority over states and local schools, imposing new requirements for annual testing of students while sanctioning districts and schools whose student populations, even in part, do not meet specific measures of annual progress on those tests.[3]

This chapter will trace the legislative history of NCLB's accountability provisions, with an eye toward the relationship of that story to its sequel: the effects of the law in practice. It centers on several themes worth highlighting at the start.

First, the accountability measures in the law were not, for the most part, newly formulated in 2001. NCLB collected and encompassed proposals advanced in theory and substance for years, accreting Ronald Reagan–, George H. W. Bush–, and Bill Clinton–era initiatives into a single bill. These were, to be sure, combined in a fresh way, with important effect. The most important new ingredient, perhaps, was President George W. Bush. Bush persuaded some Republicans to accept proposals they had rejected just one session of Congress earlier, and he tacked with Democrats toward common ground.

Second, though, in so doing, agreements of principle sometimes papered over real differences in policy preference. The new statute made many of ESEA's demands more specific than ever before. But the key term *accountability* itself was a variable used in different ways by different actors throughout the process. Reaching bipartisan agreement required appealing to ambiguity and deferring specific questions of function and funding.

This meant, finally, that many key issues were postponed to the implementation process. For all the sound and occasional fury over the new law,
for all the hours of work put into its legislative formulation by hundreds of
people, the ultimate meaning of the act will be defined in practice. The rulemaking process began in early 2002, with the first wave of final regulations
issued in late November. States filed preliminary plans for compliance with
the Department of Education at the end of January 2003. The outcome of
departmental and peer review—and how the scope and stricture of testing
and sanction are ultimately defined—are vital to how seriously states and
schools will take the new requirements and how much the education of children heretofore left behind will improve. So far the department has been
more strict, and the states less evasive, than many observers had feared. But
the process is still in its early stages and is caught up in the sticky residue of
federalism. After all, the federal government is a "seven percent investor" in a
huge company owned by someone else, as Bush education adviser Alexander
"Sandy" Kress put it, referring to the 93 percent of education costs paid at
the state and local level. Is that enough to leverage change?

Thus, while skirting policy disagreement was critical to ensuring legislative consensus in a narrowly divided Congress, the result was to raise the
stakes of what followed. Rep. Tim Roemer, D-Ind., an active participant in
the bill's formulation, praised the NCLB as "a legislative success." However,
he cautioned, "the jury is still out on whether it's a substantive success."[4]

Accountability in No Child Left Behind

Accountability in education has been described as a "tripod" made up of
standards, tests that measure whether those standards have been reached, and
penalties or rewards linked to performance on the tests. Bush adviser Kress
picked up this refrain when he defined "real robust accountability" as "high
standards, annual testing, and . . . real consequences that flow from the
measurement."[5]

On these three fronts, what does NCLB require? While the act is hugely
complex, covering 681 finely printed pages, the provisions most relevant to
accountability are highlighted here.[6]

Title I (specifically Title I, Part A) dates from the 1965 ESEA and directs
resources to economically disadvantaged children. Title I is the centerpiece of
federal aid to education. In fiscal 2001, before the passage of NCLB, it
accounted for close to $9 billion in distributions to 90 percent of school dis-
tricts in the United States. In fiscal 2003, $11.8 billion was appropriated.

States may opt out of the NCLB requirements by refusing to accept Title I funding, but none has.

Most broadly, NCLB requires that states receiving Title I money develop "challenging," "coherent and rigorous" academic standards and that all students be judged at least "proficient" with regard to those standards in reading and math within twelve years. Students must be tested in reading and math every year from grades three through eight, and again in high school, later adding science to the mix. Test results must be reported in the aggregate but also broken down by categories such as race, ethnicity, economic status, and disability, to identify schools where high overall averages hide pockets of failing students. At least 95 percent of pupils in each group must be assessed.

States must participate in the National Assessment of Educational Progress (NAEP) tests in two grades every other year as an informal check on the rigor of the state tests. "Report cards" detailing the performance of each student subgroup by state and school each year must be distributed. Crucially, that performance must make "adequate yearly progress" (AYP) toward the twelve-year deadline of universal proficiency. The specifics of the process are left to the states to develop, with federal approval; this was a contentious issue in both the legislative and rulemaking processes.

Finally, NCLB imposes a series of corrective actions on schools and districts when they fail to make AYP for two or more consecutive years. From the outset, students in such schools must be offered the chance to attend another public school within the district. Students in schools failing to make progress for three years must also be provided with Title I–funded "supplemental services" such as tutoring, for which they can choose private vendors. Broader consequences range from technical assistance to the school in question (after two years) to a range of options including the replacement of staff or curriculum (after four years) to the restructuring of the school (after five years)—by state takeover, for example, or by turning it into a charter school or one run by a private company.

In return for these mandates, the law gives states some new flexibility in how they spend federal monies. The number of ESEA programs was reduced slightly from fifty-seven to forty-five, and its categorical strings were loosened somewhat. All districts may transfer about half of certain funds between spending categories, and in a few (covering seven states and 150 school districts) federal funds are transformed into a broad block grant, contingent on meeting performance standards. Authorized spending is increased and better targeted toward needy districts.[7]

Overall, the provisions mix so-called coercive accountability (where student performance is measured across schools on a standardized basis) with a dash of free-market accountability (where parents and students can freely choose schools and force competition).[8] During congressional debate, the term *accountability* covered each of these options, allowing legislators to draw different policy conclusions using the same vocabulary. In at least two areas the resultant compromise limited aspects of each. On the one hand, national standards are absent. NAEP results are not officially linked to the progress measured by state tests; and states themselves are not penalized for failure to make adequate progress. On the other hand, the free-market approach was de-emphasized when true Title I "portability" allowing students to use their share of Title I funds to attend any school they wished, public or private, was removed from the bill in its early stages and when block grant approaches to funding were limited.

NCLB accountability thus centers in two areas: in the requirements that must be met in return for federal money and in creating information that can drive parental demands of, and choice within, the public schools. As the law leaves it to the states to define standards, tests, and AYP, the detailed reporting mandates in the law are a critical means of shaming them into ensuring those standards are in fact "challenging."

Creating NCLB: Shopping for Ingredients

In large part, the provisions of NCLB were assembled from various proposals offered up by members of the education issue community over time, floating in what John Kingdon has called the "policy primeval soup."[9] The result was a legislative blend, its ingredients drawn from divergent sources in a process that built cumulative momentum over a period of years (see table 2-1).

The stress on standards, for example, derives from the 1980s, but most immediately from the 1994 reauthorization of ESEA and its companion legislation that year, the Goals 2000 Act. School choice has been on the national agenda since at least the Reagan administration. It reemerged in 1991 and 1994, and it took firm hold in the legislative debates of 1999. Likewise, the flexibility, assessment, and consequence language of NCLB has clear antecedents in the Clinton-era debates over ESEA and especially the effort to reauthorize it in 1999–2000. Mandatory annual testing was added by George W. Bush on the 2000 presidential campaign trail.

The Basic Blend: 1983–97

Previous reauthorizations of ESEA, along with other education proposals, created the basic recipe for the NCLB process. Standards, assessments, and

Table 2-1. *Federal Accountability Legislation Leading to No Child Left Behind*

Legislative goal	Ronald Reagan/ George H.W. Bush (1981–93)	103d Congress (1993–94)	106th Congress (1999–2000)	George W. Bush campaign (2000)	No Child Left Behind (2001)
Standards established					
Standards	Voluntary standards	Yes[a]	Proposed[b,c]	Yes[b]	Yes, mandatory
Deadline for proficiency	—	—	Proposed[c, d]	—	Yes, twelve years
Disaggregation	—	—	Proposed[c]	Partial	Yes
Assessment					
State testing	—	Yes[e]	Yes[e]	Yes[f]	Yes[f]
High-stakes national testing	Proposed[g]	—	Proposed[h]	Yes[g]	Partial[i]
Adequate yearly progress (AYP)	—	Yes, but vague	Proposed[c]	Yes	Yes
Sanctions					
Improvement plans	—	Yes	Proposed[c]	Yes	Yes
Restructuring	—	—	Proposed[c]	Yes	Yes
Choice	Proposed[j]	—	Proposed[j]	Yes	Partial[k]
State flexibility					
Block grants	—	Yes, Ed-Flex	Proposed[c, l]	Yes	Partial[m]
Grant consolidation	—	—	Proposed[n]	Yes	Partial
Targeting	—	—	Proposed	—	Yes

Note: No Child Left Behind, P.L. 107-110; Ed-Flex = Education Flexibility Partnership.

a. Mandatory for Title I students.
b. Mandatory for all students.
c. Passed House.
d. Ten years.
e. Three tests between grades three and twelve.
f. Annual, grades three through eight, plus one in high school.
g. National Assessment of Educational Progress (NAEP) as benchmark.
h. Voluntary; implementation banned.
i. NAEP required but not linked to funding.
j. Tuition tax credits, Title I vouchers.
k. Some intradistrict choice and supplemental services vouchers.
l. Academic Achievement for All Act.
m. Charter states.
n. Public Education Reinvestment, Reinvention, and Responsibility.

consequences had been part of the national education debate for nearly two decades.

STANDARDS. The rise of the standards-based reform movement dates most prominently to the 1983 *A Nation at Risk* report prepared by Reagan administration education secretary Terrel H. Bell's National Commission on Excellence in Education. President George H. W. Bush's 1989 education summit with the nation's governors in Charlottesville, Virginia, set broad performance goals for American schools and students. During the 1980s the process was largely state-driven. But, in 1991, President Bush's America 2000 legislation included voluntary national testing tied to "world-class" standards, a provision that abetted the bill's demise.

In 1993 President Bill Clinton—who as governor of Arkansas helped lead the Charlottesville meeting—proposed a broad system of grants for developing state-level content standards in various subjects. This, too, was a voluntary system. The final terms of the Goals 2000 law passed in 1994 (P.L. 103-227) spoke generally of "strategies or standards." The new National Education Standards and Improvement Council authorized to draft national standards in various subjects was never formed.[10]

However, later in 1994 came the reauthorization of ESEA, the Improving America's Schools Act (IASA). IASA tied Title I funding to the creation of content and performance standards for students receiving such aid, to be just as rigorous as a state's overall standards. Both were new and important developments. So was the related notion of adequate yearly progress, though at this stage no deadline was set to attain proficiency. In IASA, AYP represented "continuous and substantial yearly improvement . . . sufficient to achieve the goal of all children under this part meeting the State's proficient and advanced levels of performance."[11]

ASSESSMENTS AND CONSEQUENCES. Academic progress in the 1994 IASA was linked "primarily" to tests measuring proficiency levels for all students in subjects of the state's choosing. One test was to be held sometime during grades three to five, a second during grades six to nine, and a third in grades ten to twelve. States had a good deal of flexibility in setting their standards and in developing their assessments, and this work progressed very slowly (see chapter 3 in this volume).[12] In his 1997 and 1998 State of the Union addresses, President Clinton urged the creation of voluntary national tests to serve as a quality benchmark for state tests. However, Congress forbade it. The chief reason was Republican opposition to a national curriculum. (The GOP also was not pleased with its usual allies in the business community who broke ranks to support the plan.) However, many Democrats did not feel it was fair to assess schools that lacked the financial resources to come up to par. Others worried about classroom time spent "teaching to the test." As education analyst Chester E. Finn Jr. observed at the time, "Republicans don't like 'national,' Democrats don't like 'test.' "[13]

Neither side liked consequences much, either. State standards were to be in place by the 1997–98 school year; assessments and final definitions of AYP, by 2000–01. But the Education Department never withheld Title I aid from states that failed to meet these timelines. Nor were school districts compelled to take action against schools failing to make AYP (presuming AYP had been defined). The Clinton administration, concerned that cracking down would rile the Republican Congress, focused on providing states with technical assistance to aid the development process.[14] As of the original 1997 deadline, the American Federation of Teachers found that just seventeen states had "clear and specific standards" in English, math, social studies, and science. Fewer than half the states had created the unified accountability systems for both Title I and non–Title I students foreseen by IASA. While forty-six states claimed to be aligning their assessments with their standards, without strong standards this did not mean much.[15]

Consequences grounded in competition made similarly small headway. The idea of programs mandating school choice, usually using private schools to provide it via a system of vouchers, had a long history in academic debate. The Reagan administration had pressed unsuccessfully in the early 1980s for tax credits to subsidize private school tuition and to allow Title I students to use their funds where they chose, and Bush provided for vouchers in his 1991 legislation. But while a few locales (Milwaukee, Wisconsin; Cleveland, Ohio; Florida) experimented with school choice, at the federal level the issue proved hugely partisan whenever it arose. Each party was allied with one pole of the debate: Democrats with the teachers and administrators who saw vouchers as destructive to public education (and their jobs), and Republicans with the conservatives who sought to avoid funding the educational establishment from which they had opted out. This latter group was particularly successful in the 1990s at keeping the legislative focus on social issues (school prayer, homeschoolers' rights) tangential to reform.

The creation of the Education Flexibility Partnership (Ed-Flex) in 1994 did allow nine states to waive many statutory and regulatory education requirements for five years in exchange for an approved comprehensive improvement plan.[16] Further, districts were allowed (though not required) to let students at failing schools move to other public schools within the district. Grant programs were established to underwrite public school choice through charter and magnet schools, again on a voluntary basis, with $5 million appropriated for charter school start-up costs.

By the mid-1990s, then, many of the themes of NCLB were already on the table, albeit in different form. Because IASA was to expire in 2000, the 106th Congress provided a natural forum for variations on those themes. Congressional debate as early as 1998 provided much of the terminology, and even the specific legislative language, utilized in 2001.

Add New Proposals, New Democrats: 1998–2000

As the states dragged their collective feet on standards and assessments, education analysts across the ideological spectrum converged on the conclusion that federal dollars needed to be tied more explicitly to measurable improvements in student performance. This served as the basis for a series of bipartisan gatherings in 1998 sponsored by Sens. Slade Gorton, R-Wash., and Joseph I. Lieberman, D-Conn. The "think group" meetings—by most accounts more turbulent than that phrase suggests—ultimately included a wide range of organizations and scholars.[17]

The participants in those meetings agreed strongly on two things: (1) that states needed to be more accountable for their ESEA dollars and (2) that a focus on funding inputs and regulatory compliance needed to be augmented with a focus on outputs; that is, on student performance. However, they disagreed about the mechanisms to accomplish this. One core difference was over whether federal funding should be targeted and how much flexibility states and districts should have in spending it.

Lieberman's centrist New Democratic allies tended to feel that more funding was needed, but that it should be better aimed at needy districts.[18] Accreted federal mandates had diffused spending. New Democrats argued these should be swept away, refocusing ESEA on its primary goal of improving economically disadvantaged students' academic performance. In April 1999 Andrew Rotherham of the Democratic Leadership Council (DLC) Progressive Policy Institute (PPI) summed up the key elements of this view in an influential white paper. He argued that achieving educational equity meant equalizing not the dollars spent on education but its quality, as measured by the results students achieved. The federal government "should play the role of investor and catalyst rather than 'command and control' manager," focusing on the poorest school districts and using tough national standards and testing to enforce results. To rectify Title I's status as "an undertaking without consequences" for everyone except students, Congress should set performance benchmarks and terminate aid to districts that failed to meet them. ESEA's fifty-plus categorical grants would be reduced to five broad "performance-based grants" based on Title I, teacher quality, English proficiency, public school choice, and innovation.[19]

Conservatives in the group bought the premise of state flexibility with an ex post federal check, but they wanted a broader, purer plan. By September 1998 Republicans had pushed the Dollars to the Classroom bill through the House. The legislation combined thirty-one programs into a $2.74 billion block grant, building on the pilot Ed-Flex provisions. Nina Shokraii Rees and Kirk A. Johnson of the Heritage Foundation called on the Senate to enlarge this into a "Super Ed-Flex" program, dramatically revamping ESEA's categorical grant programs. States would have substantial discretion over spending so long as their academic performance met a standard jointly agreed to by the state and the federal government.[20]

Democrats tended to oppose broad block grants, because such grants threatened categorical requirements they held dear, or the grants undercut targeting within Title I, or both. In any case President Clinton was pushing a different set of issues—class-size reduction, teacher training, and school construction and renovation. While the president did win additional funding for these through astute veto bargaining, the 1998 session ended with little resolved.

But all of these approaches surfaced again in the 106th Congress. Republicans in both chambers pushed the block grant approach as part of a bill called the Academic Achievement for All Act (Straight A's, for short). A version limited to ten states squeaked through the House in October 1999. Despite a veto threat, the House also approved a second bill merging teacher training and class-size reduction funds into a second block grant.

A third bill reauthorized Title I of ESEA. Entitled the Student Results Act (H.R. 2), it contained more than a kernel of the language that would find its way into NCLB two years later.

The key player on H.R. 2 was Rep. George Miller, who worked with the Republican leadership to give the bill real bipartisan appeal (the October 1999 vote was 358-67).[21] While states could still determine what constituted adequate yearly progress, H.R. 2 required that the state plan compare separately "the performance and progress of students" by disaggregated subgroups (race, income, and so on) and "include annual numerical goals for improving the performance of all groups and narrowing gaps in [their] performance." Not only that, the state plan had to ensure that each group of students would be proficient on each state assessment within ten years. Both schools and states were required to produce annual report cards detailing the results.[22]

Under the House plan, if a school did not make AYP for two consecutive years, it was identified for "school improvement" and given two additional years to improve. At that point districts were to take more direct corrective action: withholding funds, running the school from the district level, making "alternative governance arrangements" (such as reopening the school as a public charter school), revamping the curriculum, or firing the staff. School choice and charter schools were options on which schools or districts could spend Title I money at any time. If a school was the target of corrective action, and public school choice was part of the correction, the district had to pick up transportation costs as well.[23]

The Senate tweaked portions of the three House bills into an omnibus measure in early March 2000. Despite the reluctance of Health, Education, Labor, and Pensions (HELP) Committee chair Jim Jeffords, R-Vt., S. 2 slightly expanded the Straight A's program from ten to fifteen states. It also strengthened the public school choice program, requiring it (including transportation) in any school identified as needing improvement—after two years of failure to make AYP, then, instead of four as in the House.

This latter language on choice would surface again in 2001, but the bill as a whole wound up satisfying no one. Liberal Democrats sought a substitute amendment protecting extant categorical programs and pushing the class size–school construction–teacher training triumvirate. Judd Gregg and other conservative Republicans demanded a far larger Straight A's block grant and a broader voucher program. New Democrats, led by Lieberman, pushed the "Three R's" (for Public Education Reinvestment, Reinvention, and Responsibility). Like the PPI proposal, it created five major grants, raised overall funding by $35 billion over five years (again, targeting poor school districts), kept the class-size reduction program, and added $100 million for public school choice. Three R's took its accountability and AYP language largely from H.R. 2, which Sen. Jeff Bingaman, D-N.M., pushed separately but failed to get through HELP's partisan buzzsaw.

In the end no agreement was reached. Old and New Democrats clashed over the latter's defection; "You'd have thought we had launched a grenade in the caucus," one aide recalled. The Republicans insisted on Title I vouchers, dooming potential compromise with the New Democrats (though the idea used in 2001 allowing the portability of supplemental services money emerged during these talks). The Three R's amendment ultimately got just thirteen votes. And as a long list of riders on unrelated issues such as gun control bogged down floor debate, both sides decided to take their chances on the imminent presidential election.

Thus, for the first time in its history, ESEA was not reauthorized. Funding for its extant programs was simply rolled over for an additional year.[24] PPI's Rotherham complained, "At the national level, the debate about how to address education has broken down along predictable and partisan lines." He urged that the New Democratic proposal be the basis for the new administration's first move on education reform.[25] Surprisingly, in a way it was.

Add: One "Compassionate Conservative"

As 1999 progressed, Gov. George W. Bush of Texas was on the presidential campaign trail, pitching himself as a "compassionate conservative." The compassion was for students hampered by rigid school bureaucracies and what Bush frequently called "the soft bigotry of low expectations." The conservatism lay in maximizing parental choice and local spending flexibility. However, Bush also envisioned a strong national role in education policy. This put him at odds with Republicans who cared mainly about keeping the national government out of local schools. Bush had to lobby to eliminate language calling for the abolition of the Department of Education from the 2000 Republican platform.[26]

For Bush, focusing on education had potential risks, given its association with voters as a Democratic issue. In July 1999, for example, a Pew Research Center poll found that, by a margin of 52 to 29 percent, voters trusted Democrats to do a better job on education. The very title of the Bush campaign position paper on the topic, "No Child Left Behind," was cribbed from the liberal Children's Defense Fund.[27]

However, education reform was a major issue in Texas and Bush felt strongly about it. As governor, he had built on his predecessors' policies to annualize testing in reading and math in grades three through eight. Students could not graduate high school without passing Texas Assessment of Academic Skills (TAAS) exams, while teachers and administrators saw their own careers tied to student performance. In the 1990s TAAS scores had risen among all students, but particularly for blacks and Latinos. Some observers were skeptical of those findings, or of whether Governor Bush could take credit. On the campaign trail, though, the stress on education seemed to work, as polls found no statistical difference between voters' assessments of Bush and Vice President Al Gore, the Democratic presidential candidate, on this issue.[28]

Developing these themes for the campaign was a small policy staff that included Bush's education adviser in Texas, Margaret La Montagne, and Sandy Kress.[29] Kress was a Dallas attorney, a school board member who had worked with Bush on Texas's accountability statutes, and, as Bush liked to point out, a Democrat and DLC member. As such, Kress was familiar with Rotherham's PPI paper and the various 1999 bills, and he borrowed widely from them.

The result was a polygamous marriage. Consolidation and performance-based funding were wed to Texas's annualized testing and to a voucher program similar to that passed under Gov. Jeb Bush in Florida. To a predominantly Latino audience in Los Angeles, George W. Bush argued that Title I programs had failed poor and minority students and that diverting funds to parents would force schools to improve. In another major speech, Bush argued for the emergence of an "age of accountability." He proposed that sixty ESEA grant categories be narrowed to five, slightly differently defined than in the New Democrats' plan.[30] Annual testing, he reiterated at every campaign stop, was vital. And while those tests would be locally developed and under local control, Bush also proposed that the federal government should pay for states to participate in NAEP as one of several ways to verify performance on state assessments.[31]

Even before Bush's electoral victory was finalized by the U.S. Supreme Court decision on December 12, 2000, privately funded transition work had begun in Washington.[32] Later that month the president-elect invited about twenty members of Congress to Austin to discuss education policy. Along with Republican leaders—Boehner, Gregg, Jeffords—New Democrats such as Evan Bayh, D-Ind., Tim Roemer, and Zell Miller, D-Ga., were prominently featured. So was George Miller, whom Boehner urged Bush to court and whom the president was soon calling "Big George." Senator Kennedy was conspicuously absent, illuminating the president's intention to seek a Republican-New Democrat coalition. Warned that pushing hard on private school vouchers would end that prospect, Bush gave his reassurances: Vouchers were not make-or-break. Democrats were "satisfied, if not exuberant." Common ground seemed possible.[33]

As January began, and with it the 107th Congress, No Child Left Behind emerged, not as a piece of draft legislation but as a thirty-page legislative blueprint. The proposal, released just three days after the inauguration, closely tracked Bush's campaign agenda. It included his version of categorical grant consolidation; a broad block grant program providing new spending flexibility to "charter states"; new content standards in history and science; grade three through eight annual testing; fourth- and eighth-grade NAEP participation each year; state and school report cards disaggregated by subgroup; and a requirement that adequate yearly progress be made by the "disadvantaged" students within any school receiving Title I funds. Requirements for "corrective action" when a school or district identified as failing continued to fail were not fully specified, but public school choice and, later, "exit vouchers" toward private school tuition or for supplemental services were to be included. Schools and states that succeeded "in closing the achievement gap" would receive funding bonuses from the federal government; those that did not would lose administrative funds under Title I.[34]

The blueprint, in short, provided for the consolidation elements of the Three R's, plus much of the House's 1999 language on accountability and AYP, the Senate's 2000 school choice provisions, Straight A's, vouchers, Bush's annual testing, and a NAEP benchmark. Bush "essentially plagiarized our plan," said one Lieberman aide, but others in Congress could have made the same claim.[35] As a result, the response on Capitol Hill was generally positive.

The Blueprint Goes to Congress

In Texas, Governor Bush had found success in producing broad statements of principle instead of legislative drafts.[36] Perhaps remembering the 1993 health care debate—when majority Democrats insisted the Clintons produce a complete bill, then sniped at its fine print until it sank—Republicans in the 107th Congress did not demand more. Because the White House gauged it had enough friends in the House and Senate to get a satisfactory bill to the floor, the blueprint approach left ample room for flexible collaboration. If the bill died, the fingerprints on the body would be congressional—and, with luck, Democratic.

The president's core accountability priority was annual testing. What was in the tests, and how they were used, was less critical. Vouchers were less critical still. In a January 2001 interview, Kress stressed that Bush would not move away from "flexibility" and "accountability" but did not define those terms.[37] The administration had thus set itself up to claim credit at the end of the process while Congress squabbled over the specifics. As one Democratic staffer put it, "This was great political strategy. When you put out legislation, then you're fighting for colons and sentences and subheadings. The White House had orders: don't get bogged down in details."

Lawmaking, in Three Movements

Lawmakers thrive on detail, notwithstanding the devil's reputed place of residence. But as the stalemate in the 106th Congress made clear, reauthorizing ESEA would require building bipartisan coalitions. After all, the 107th Congress was even more closely divided.

Enough legislators wanted passage to make that coalition building possible. But because different actors had different reasons for joining ranks, in both the House and Senate the pursuit of bipartisanship meant that agreement on broad principle trumped policy specifics. The same flag of "accountability" flew over different camps—which bartered forward progress across common ground by postponing conflict, ultimately to the implementation process itself.

ALLIANCE POLITICS IN THE SENATE. Conservatives such as Judd Gregg, no fan of the Senate HELP Committee's 2000 bill, feared Chairman Jim Jeffords would again ally with ranking Democrat Kennedy and other liberals in 2001. In the short run, committee unity was maintained by delay, as choices regarding vouchers, state spending flexibility, and funding levels were put off to the Senate floor.[38]

But the formal committee process proved tangential. This development reflected a shrewd brand of alliance politics on the part of the White House. On the one hand, Kress dealt mainly with Gregg, who clearly called the Republican shots (backed up, in staff-level meetings, by staffers to Majority Leader Trent Lott, R-Miss.). On the other hand, he cultivated the New Democrats, using those discussions to lure Kennedy to the table. After all, thirteen Democratic votes had not done much in 2000, but added to fifty Republicans, they reached the Senate's magic threshold of sixty (the number of votes needed to defeat a filibuster). While Kennedy had been left out of the Austin summit in December, the senior senator was a consummate deal-maker, expert in the issues and perturbed by the prospects of a major bill in his jurisdiction moving forward without him. Bush and Kress began to woo him. Kennedy, for his part, "bought himself into the game," according to a Senate staffer, by agreeing that some form of program consolidation and block grant flexibility, along with supplemental services portability, could be part of the Senate bill.

The result was a three-way coalition among conservative Republicans, New Democrats, and the Democratic regulars that worked to draw up a substitute amendment for the truncated committee version. Jeffords's momentous decision in late May to quit the Republican caucus, throwing the Senate to the Democrats, had little impact on the education bill. Kennedy's decision to deal with the White House had made him a major player already.[39]

The coalition was almost derailed in late April over the definition of adequate yearly progress, prompting what one Senate staffer colorfully called "hell week." Governors had been pressuring the White House to weaken the bill's AYP requirements. As it stood, the Senate language required annual progress by each individual subgroup, such that all became proficient within ten years. But states were worried that too many schools would be identified as failing—an expensive, and embarrassing, label. Jeffords's staff fueled this with analyses claiming a majority of schools, even wealthy ones in states that invest heavily in education, would fail under the bill's formula.

Not everyone agreed the charges were accurate. "They were not really reflective of what would happen in the real world," one staffer later argued. Whatever their policy validity, though, they had clear political utility. The governors (and some committee members) leaped at the chance to gut the disaggregation and testing requirements of the bill. And the Bush negotiators seemed surprisingly sympathetic. After cutting out Jeffords for months, "suddenly Kress was backing up Jeffords's staff."[40] The new language, as worked and then reworked for a week by Kress and Senate aides, required at least a 1 percent improvement in test scores each year per group. However, progress would be judged over a three-year period and the scores of the lowest achieving students would be weighted more heavily, giving schools credit for closing the achievement gap.

The new formula was attacked as unworkable by states and unfair by civil rights groups. Senate staff admitted the new wording was "convoluted" but argued it at least left room for rescue in conference. Some said it was actually tougher than the corresponding House language. Kress did not try very hard to defend the compromise, calling it "Rube Goldbergesque"—but settling the AYP debate for the present kept the bill moving forward.[41]

In the meantime, the challenge was largely to hold on to the (newly) majority Democrats who hoped to boost funding. By wide margins senators agreed to $181 billion in special education funding over ten years and to boost authorized spending on Title I by $132 billion over the same period. Ultimately eighty-nine programs were included in the Senate version of ESEA (up from fifty-five in existing law and forty-seven in the House bill), with a price tag of $33 billion (compared with $19 billion in the president's plan and $23 billion in the House's). "A function of being on the floor too long," moaned a GOP aide, as debate reached seven weeks and 150 amendments.

The members of the formulation group, however, had pledged to suppress amendments that went to the heart of the basic deal. The accountability provisions changed little as group members voted no as needed to maintain the committee status quo. For example, a proposal by Sen. Paul Wellstone, D-Minn., to defer the new annual testing requirements unless Title I funding was tripled failed. Kennedy, Lieberman, and Bayh all voted against it. A Christopher J. Dodd, D-Conn., amendment narrowing the Straight A's program by removing the "21st century schools" program was defeated 47-51 with three New Democrats voting no. A small voucher pilot program, covering just ten districts, was defeated 41-58 with eleven Republicans in the negative. And finally, on June 14, the bill was resoundingly approved, 91-8.

COUNTING HEADS IN THE HOUSE. Like Gregg, new Education and the Workforce chair John Boehner was an unlikely convert to an increased federal role in education, having previously urged elimination of the Department of Education. But Boehner was extremely loyal to the new president; he was dedicated to cementing Bush's disputed electoral victory with a legislative success; and he knew how to count. That is, he knew that thirty to forty House Republicans would never support the sort of testing regime Bush had promised, especially without vouchers. Given the slim Republican majority in the House, the need for Democratic votes was simple fact. And for Democrats to support annual testing, the Republicans would need to give ground on vouchers and block grants.

To elaborate that equation, Boehner convened a bipartisan working group outside the normal committee flow.[42] The starting point was again the set of bills discussed in 1999–2000, to which Boehner's first full draft of H.R. 1 added Bush blueprint provisions such as annual testing, Straight A's block grants, and vouchers. With the Senate's "hell week" in full view, House drafters changed the timeline for states to achieve proficiency from ten years to twelve. In general, though, the group was looking ahead. George Miller, for example, pushed to keep strong AYP provisions in the House version of the bill to force the Senate's hand in conference committee and reduce administrative discretion in enforcing the statute later.[43] To attract conservatives nervous about federal invasion of local curricula, H.R. 1 banned the use of ESEA money for national testing and did not require states to use NAEP tests as a benchmark against their own assessments.[44]

The chairman's mark of the bill ultimately distilled elements from H.R. 1, Miller's draft, and the New Democrats' plan. An emblematic compromise created "transferability," which shifted spending discretion across ESEA titles not to states but school districts. No one (outside the New Democrats, who proposed it) truly liked this, but Boehner was worried that planned efforts to add even the Senate's pilot version of Straight A's would scare off Democrats and scuttle the bill. He brought the GOP leadership to meet with the president, who declared, "I'm with Boehner." The amendment was dropped.[45] Thus transferability allowed the chairman's forces to argue that the bill included enhanced flexibility, without losing Democratic support.

The latter was increasingly important as some conservative Republicans grew antsy about the bill. On issues such as block grants and vouchers, one member griped, "Sandy's OK, but he doesn't push those as hard as the testing stuff." The first committee roll-call vote stripped vouchers from the draft. Markup then had to be suspended so that Boehner, with Kress, could hold a closed-door meeting to mollify committee conservatives, promising a floor vote.[46] An amendment to eliminate annual testing, which had both liberal and conservative support, was also deferred to the full House.

Boehner had achieved bipartisanship, as promised—the final committee vote was 41-7—but with a rather Democratic flavor. GOP dissenters complained that "the bill . . . contains very few provisions of the president's original proposals." Boehner distributed a fact sheet entitled "H.R. 1—What's in It for Conservatives?" and Kress contradicted the dissidents by describing the bill as "a manifestation of [Bush's] proposal." In general the president had no desire, as Undersecretary of Education Eugene Hickok later put it, "to sacrifice accountability on the altar of school choice." This naturally upset those who felt that accountability required choice.[47]

The floor debate put those dueling definitions on display. Roemer, for example, stressed the bill's testing and corrective action requirements as he urged members to vote against including a voucher provision. Noting that private schools were exempt from those mandates, he argued, "This amendment has no accountability in it. We take the money with the voucher from the public school to a private school, and then there is no accountability there. No test, no trail, no nothing." Majority Leader Dick Armey, R-Texas, retorted: "We do not ask the Catholic schools to be accountable to the government, we ask them to be accountable to the parents." Peter Hoekstra, R-Mich., added a mild shot at the Bush blueprint: "The president's plan . . . talked about accountability, and the accountability was to the federal government. What this amendment says is that there is another accountability. It is the accountability of schools, teachers, to parents."[48]

The committee bill passed the full House largely intact. The attempts to add vouchers were defeated. So, too, after intensive White House lobbying, was the coalition of the far left and far right (led by Barney Frank, D-Mass., and Hoekstra, respectively) seeking to eliminate annual testing. The ultimate vote on approval on May 23 was lopsided—384-45, with Republicans making up three quarters of the no votes. Still, holding a skittish membership together had been no easy task.[49] And given the different formulations of the House and Senate provisions, particularly as regarded funding levels, flexibility, and AYP, the task was far from over.

CONFERENCE CALLS. During the summer of 2001, NCLB came under fire from all sides. Attacks came from local officials who did not want national norms, teachers unions that did not want mandatory testing, and conservatives who thought that with vouchers dead the rest of the bill might as well be. The National Conference of State Legislatures called the bill's testing provisions "seriously and perhaps irreparably flawed." And new reports argued that both the House and Senate AYP provisions would result in a large number of schools identified as failing. On Capitol Hill, House Republicans had calculated that with a Republican Senate they could gain back their concessions in conference, but now that chance was gone. Democrats began to wonder, too. After all, didn't the president need this bill more than they did?[50]

The conference committee, then, had to repair the bill's bipartisan armor—and bridge some 2,750 divergences between the House and Senate versions. It would not merely revise but rewrite many provisions that had been pushed through with the promise of a later fix, exploiting to the utmost the remarkable degree of discretion delegated to congressional conferees.

During the summer recess, staff members representing all thirty-nine members of the conference—the Senate, to represent its coalition's various blocs, had named no fewer than twenty-five conferees—met daily to hammer out more than two thousand agreements.[51] Even the September 11, 2001, terrorist attacks and the Capitol Hill anthrax scare did not push NCLB off the agenda.

With periodic presidential exhortation, accountability provisions slowly took shape under the watchful eyes of the "Big Four": Boehner, Miller, Kennedy, and Gregg. Language providing additional targeting of Title I funds to poor districts was approved. A pilot Straight A's program was crafted and then grafted to transferability. Final supplemental services language was developed. Extra money for charter schools was found (though money for special education was not; indeed, most of the Senate's funding levels were slashed). Announced last, or nearly so, was AYP. While the conference's basic stance on AYP was in place by late September, shaped by Boehner, Miller, and Jeff Bingaman, this was kept quiet to allow additional tinkering and to avoid interest group pressure.[52]

The final language required all students, in all groups, to reach proficiency within twelve years. However, it allowed districts to average results across three years and provided so-called safe harbor protections that let subgroups not meeting AYP levels to qualify if the number of nonproficient students in that subgroup dropped by at least 10 percent. These changes—though hardly satisfying all critics—made the final version more workable than either the House or Senate versions, following a presidential plea for a "realistic" formula for determining school failure (see chapter 7 in this volume).[53] However, although states had faced penalties and bonuses for their overall performance in both the House and Senate bills, this language was dropped in conference. No punishment would be imposed on states for low test scores. And though Bush endorsed "an objective check on state accountability systems" (specifically naming NAEP), the national testing issue was settled by requiring states to participate biennially in the fourth- and eighth-grade NAEP tests, but prohibiting penalties from being assessed based on NAEP performance.[54]

At once numbingly detailed and comfortably vague, the conference report was adopted by the House on December 13 and the Senate five days later, with opposition limited to an odd amalgam of the discontented far left and far right. The process had "brought the middle together, and held it."[55] An impressive legislative victory was in place.

Assessment and Implementation

What underlay that victory? And with what result?

Why Did NCLB Pass?

Since ESEA authorization had expired in 2000, Congress was under pressure in 2001 to pass *something*. Still, the 107th Congress was even more closely divided than the 106th. Though the major policy ingredients were already on the table, something new was needed—if not substantively then politically. At least four factors are worth mentioning here.

First is the tentative alliance, foreshadowed in 1999–2000, between moderate New Democrats and much of the Republican caucus. This partnership was underwritten by a common belief that federal education policy had not demanded real results in return for the billions of dollars poured into local schools since 1965. Even liberal Democrats such as Kennedy came to believe that dramatic changes were needed, and an appeal to accountability was a powerful lure.

That common ground had been insufficient in 2000. In 2001, however, many of the same proposals began to look better, especially to Republicans, as GOP leaders supported an array of proposals they had previously opposed. For by then, the second factor was on the scene: new president George W. Bush. Many lawmakers wanted the president to succeed (especially on a campaign priority) more than they needed to be faithful to past positions. Referring to the Big Four, one aide noted, "In the 106th Congress, those four people wouldn't even have sat down together." Bush himself made this easier by embracing Democratic positions and leaders.

Republican observers especially stress that the president, as one put it, "added tremendous value" to the process itself. Certainly the president's intense interest in and personal engagement with the issue were crucial to pushing the bill through stasis and stalemate. Even in the weeks after September 11, he continued to make NCLB a priority and thus empowered lawmakers to do the same. Further, Bush, as a Republican pushing a supposedly Democratic issue, gave the narrative a "man bites dog" quality. This guaranteed the issue (and any failure to reach agreement) intense press coverage and thus high salience in members' constituencies.

A third factor was the unorthodox organizational structure utilized for the bill's formulation.[56] In both House and Senate, formal committee structures were evaded. The bipartisan working groups empowered in their stead worked incessantly and built important internal rapport. This made members willing to jettison things only one party liked, whether spending provisions or class size or private school choice, in the name of moving the process forward. Senate staff distinguished between the "ideological ends" and "the legislators"; the latter "made sure it happened."[57]

Conversely, such cooperation was made possible in the first place by the willingness to move past divisive issues—itself possible because, finally, the conversation was newly framed by a common vocabulary centered on accountability. Accountability was hard to be against, but elastic. It served as a way for Democrats to talk about reform without simply talking about increased spending. It also provided a selling point for additional resources, given that Republicans could console themselves that new funds went to a system newly worthy of investment. Given the consensus that the approach to date had not raised student achievement, the accountability regime of standards and tests had real appeal. While it was unproven, no conclusive evidence existed that it did not work; appeals to accountability could not be falsified. In the absence of empiricism, aphorism took hold, as when House floor debate compared the testing regime with swine care ("You do not fatten the pig by weighing the pig"), or in Education Secretary Rod Paige's athletic counterargument: "If you want to win the football game, you have to first keep score."[58] How one defines accountability matters greatly in practice, but it proved to matter far less in politics; that is, to the term's utility in providing a unifying theme for the NCLB debate that could garner broad agreement in principle even when policy specifics proved elusive. The latter could be compromised or, as often happened, deferred from campaign to committee to floor to conference to implementation. But when the bill became law in 2002, specifics could be deferred no longer.

NCLB at the One-Year Mark

The bipartisan focus on accountability carried NCLB through the substantive minefields that had exploded earlier attempts at reform. But accountability must be implemented, and here the legislative consensus version of accountability reaches its natural bounds. After all, some actors in the process simply meant resources, providing "opportunity to learn," hiring better-trained teachers for small classes in new buildings with new technology. Some meant more flexibility with existing resources, requiring results but not restricting the methods used to achieve them. Some meant holding schools to a national standard of performance. Some meant letting the market take over, forcing public schools to compete or close.

All of these views implied different blends of standards, assessments, and consequences. The resultant compromises are all embodied in parts of the new law. There is additional money, much of it targeted to needy districts, and new flexibility for spending it at the local level. There is annual testing to spur all students to proficiency against challenging standards and the requirement that states participate in NAEP every other year. There is public school choice, charter school creation, school restructuring, and the ability for parents to take Title I money to buy supplemental services from a private sector vendor. Given the development of the standards and testing regime throughout the 1990s, the net result is a change in degree instead of in kind. Still, it is farther than federal law has ever gone in this area. It is as far as it could have gone, given the political alignments of 2001.

But if common language did not always mean common ground, will ground be gained at all? Will the intersection of education policy and federalism file down accountability's sharpest tools?

QUESTIONS OF IMPLEMENTATION. The compromises of NCLB avoided both extremes of the policy spectrum. Democrats, for example, resisted granting wide discretion to local districts, on the one hand, and to parents, on the other. The number of categorical programs under ESEA did not diminish significantly. Public school choice is greatly expanded in principle, but it is not clear how much this will serve students in far-flung rural districts or in urban systems where most or all of the public schools are identified as needing improvement. And experimentation with voucher programs will have to await the baby steps of the supplemental services program and continued local efforts, albeit encouraged by the Supreme Court's June 2002 decision in *Zelman* v. *Simmons-Harris*. NCLB's requirements are largely top-down, but much successful change is largely bottom-up (see chapters 3 and 4 in this volume).

For their part Republicans resisted efforts to require strong state accountability to the national government. The first bullet point in the House fact sheet on the NCLB conference report trumpeted "No National Tests" (see chapter 13 in this volume).[59] There is no consequence linked to NAEP performance or for states that fail to attain AYP. The text of the law left states to set their definition of proficiency and use their own assessments to measure it. Will states pick a definition of acceptable achievement that is simply too low? Should the states decide whether state tests are good enough? Will states be allowed to use tests that are too easy or to use a mixture of state and local assessments?[60]

Both sides ducked the fact that only 7 percent of education funding is federal. This simple fact, despite the rhetoric, limits the amount of change the federal government can leverage. Even if willing to use its sticks, the Department of Education has small sticks to brandish. Yet Congress has little incentive to limit its legislative reach, given its potential to reap credit from successful change and ability to blame poor results on the states. By spring 2002 states were already nervous that the toughest specific requirement—that all subgroups of students make measurable progress each year and achieve full proficiency within twelve years—was the least realistic.[61] The titular commitment of the law to the success of every child made it hard to compromise on this point, but this does not make it feasible policy. To prevent states from defining proficiency down, a lower figure (90 percent?) may be substituted at the halfway point of the twelve-year countdown during the next ESEA reauthorization cycle in 2007.

Despite all this, NCLB represents a major opportunity. If the sanctions are mainly moral, the requirements are clear and very public. State flexibility in itself is not a bad thing, especially given the diverse approaches states have already taken to implement the 1994 requirements. The law does provide a good deal of information to parents, administrators, elected officials, and interest groups, making it clear when states have failed to achieve results—and thus politically difficult for states to dumb down or retreat from a standards and testing regime.[62] The various approaches may prove to be congruent and even additive.

THE REGULATORY REGIME. Making it so puts an enormous burden on the Department of Education as it governs the definition of progress and proficiency in the states. Even if "you don't blame the institution of marriage when someone cheats," as one Senate aide commented in defending the NCLB framework, one might still recommend counseling. The therapist here is the department. During the formulation process, Secretary Paige was accused of irrelevance in the face of a domineering White House.[63] But, the production of a final legislative text does not end the story. The regulatory process is also crucial, even determinative. And, here, the secretary and the department are crucial actors. In a series of congressional hearings on implementation throughout 2002, the department touted its progress and promised to hold firm on enforcement in the face of skeptical Democratic questioning. In May 2003 Georgia lost $783,000 in Title I administrative aid because of its delay in implementing tests required by the 1994 IASA. This marked the first such penalty imposed on any state by the department.[64]

State flexibility has been granted in some areas. Draft rules on testing released in March 2002 indicated that states would be allowed to use different tests in different areas, potentially undercutting their comparability. The department also signaled a hands-off stance on judging the quality of state standards and assessments. The rules released in July 2002 after a negotiated rulemaking process allowed states to use either criterion-referenced tests linked to state standards or norm-referenced tests, modified somewhat to reflect state standards, that measure how students perform compared with their peers. In June 2003 the department accepted state plans (such as Iowa's) to utilize commercial exams instead of standard-driven tests. Further, in a move teachers unions opposed, states were allowed to deem "highly qualified" some teachers still in the process of achieving their certification through alternative routes.[65]

This flexibility suited the Bush administration interpretation of the law's intent. In other areas that interpretation was more stringent. In July 2002, for example, the department listed some eighty-six hundred schools that had failed to meet state standards for two consecutive years. Under NCLB, students in those schools were to be offered the chance to attend a better-performing school in the district starting in September. In an October letter to state school chiefs, Paige warned that state plans to "ratchet down their standards in order to remove schools from their lists of low performers" were "nothing less than shameful." And the final rules made clear that lack of school capacity would not be accepted as a reason to deny intradistrict choice.[66]

That set of regulations, nearly four hundred pages in length, was not released until late November 2002 in advance of a January 31, 2003, deadline for the submission of preliminary state plans for achieving AYP toward proficiency. The rules granted little additional leeway on AYP criteria, reflecting the relative specificity of that portion of the statute. The state plans were produced on time (though some incorporated tasks promised but not yet complete). After extensive meetings with individual states, both on site and in Washington, the department approved the plans by the statutory deadline of June 10, 2003. The plans varied wildly. Their specifics depended in large part on how stringently states defined proficiency and how closely the new law tracked existing local requirements. Some states proposed complicated statistical techniques for gauging school progress; many backloaded their predicted progress, with far greater gains toward the end of the twelve-year time-line. In general, the department granted states more leeway than it had earlier signaled; some observers feared the quick deadline for approval had caused the department to give states too much slack. State officials, while cheered by signs of departmental flexibility, still warned that numerous schools would be identified as failing.[67]

The early outcomes of the rulemaking process seemed to indicate the Bush administration was holding the line on its substantive priorities such as choice and assessments, giving the president a clearer legislative victory than it initially appeared. On the law's first anniversary in January 2003, Bush declared, "We can say that the work of reform is well begun." George Miller, however, accused the administration of implementing regulations in a way "inconsistent with the way the law was approved by Congress" (at least by congressional Democrats) and called Bush a "truant from sound education policy." The president's related, repeated push for a tax credit to subsidize private school tuition prompted complaints that he was reneging on his NCLB agreement and may distract attention from implementing the law's other avenues of school choice.[68]

This opening chasm means many questions remain as the story continues. Many NCLB rules are still under negotiation (for example, those governing special education students' inclusion in assessments). Even more important, the approved state plans for AYP are, as of summer 2003, still a work in progress. Negotiations continue on many fronts, and where states promised instead of reported, the elaboration of standards, tests, and consequences must be made real in relatively short order. The department will be under pressure to grant amendments, waivers, and extensions. How the secretary will balance state experimentation with national rigor is far from settled. Budget issues are a prominent part of the equation. While Democrats were satisfied with the funding levels provided in fiscal year 2002, this was not true for fiscal 2003 or 2004. Complicated by revenue shortfalls and budget cutbacks in many states, the funding and mandate balance promises to be an ongoing source of friction. Further, as the scene shifts to the states and the bureaucracies, interest groups—surprisingly dormant so far—may reassert themselves. One target may be the testing regime itself, if states (and key suburban voters) continue to gripe.

Ultimately, then, the textbook tableau of the signing ceremony was a beginning, not an end. For "the laws are a dead letter until an administration begins to carry them into execution."[69] Two hundred years and more after John Adams made that observation, that is how government still works, even in the textbooks. For the students in American public schools, it will determine how government works in real life.

Notes

1. "President Signs Landmark Education Bill," press release, Office of the White House Press Secretary, January 8, 2002; and Elisabeth Busmiller, "Focusing on the Home Front, Bush Signs Education Bill," *New York Times,* January 9, 2002, p. A1. The full title of the law (P.L. 107-110) is "To Close the Achievement Gap with Accountability, Flexibility, and Choice, So That No Child Is Left Behind."

2. In the Senate, the vote on final passage was 44-3 on the Republican side of the aisle and 43-6 on the Democratic; in the House, the tallies were 183-33 and 198-6, respectively. For commentary see, inter alia, David S. Broder, "Long Road to Reform: Negotiators Forge Education Legislation," *Washington Post,* December 17, 2001, p. A1; and Jonathan Alter, "Give the Pols a Gold Star," *Newsweek,* January 21, 2002, p. 45. Legislators are quoted in the *Congressional Record,* daily ed., December 13, 2001 (House), and December 17–18, 2001 (Senate); and George Miller's statement is from his office's "The Leave No Child Behind Act, H.R. 1," February 2002 (edworkforce.house.gov/democrats/hr1report220.html [February 24, 2003]).

3. Richard W. Riley quoted in Erik W. Robelen, "ESEA to Boost Federal Role in Education," *Education Week,* January 9, 2002, p. 1; George W. Bush, in "Remarks Prior to a Meeting with Congressional Education Leaders, January 23," *Weekly Compilation of Presidential Documents* (Government Printing Office, January 29, 2001), p. 217; and John A. Boehner, in "Fact Sheet: H.R. 1 Conference Report Highlights," House Education and the Workforce Committee, December 10, 2001.

4. Interview with Alexander "Sandy" Kress, April 15, 2002; and interview with Tim Roemer, April 23, 2002. More than fifteen interviews with executive branch personnel and members of Congress and their staff (in both House and Senate, and from both sides of the partisan aisle) inform this essay. Anonymity was granted when requested. Any uncited quotes are from those interviews.

5. Chester E. Finn Jr. and Marci Kanstoroom, "State Academic Standards," in Diane Ravitch, ed., *Brookings Papers on Education Policy 2001* (Brookings, 2001), p. 133; and Kress quoted in Siobhan Gorman, "Education: Step One—Grab the Center," *National Journal,* January 27, 2001, pp. 286–87.

6. This page count is from the conference report accompanying H.R. 1, H. Rept. 107-334, December 13, 2001. For the details of No Child Left Behind (NCLB), see the extensive information at www.ed.gov and www.nclb.gov; see, for example, the secretary of education's policy guidance letter of July 24, 2002. See also Wayne Riddle and others, *K-12 Education: Highlights of the No Child Left Behind Act of 2001,* CRS Report RL31284 (Congressional Research Service, February 27, 2002); and "In Summary," *Education Week,* April 3, 2002, p. 24.

7. Conference report accompanying H.R. 1, H. Rept. 107-334, December 13, 2001.

8. Frederick M. Hess, *Revolution at the Margins: The Impact of Competition on Urban School Systems* (Brookings, 2002), pp. 233–37.

9. John Kingdon, *Agendas, Alternatives, and Public Policies*, 2d ed. (HarperCollins, 1995), esp. chap. 6.

10. See Diane Ravitch, *Left Back: A Century of Battles over School Reform* (Simon and Schuster, 2000), chap. 11; Robert B. Schwartz and Marian A. Robinson, "Goals 2000 and the Standards Movement," in Diane Ravitch, ed., *Brookings Papers on Education Policy 2000* (Brookings, 2000), pp. 173–214; and "National Education Goals Set," *1994 Congressional Quarterly Almanac* (Washington: Congressional Quarterly, 1995), pp. 397–99. The National Education Standards and Improvement Council (eliminated by Congress in 1996) was to draft standards in math, science, English, history, geography, foreign languages, and the arts.

11. P.L. 103-382, Section 1111(b). See also "Lawmakers Renew and Revamp 1965 Education Act," *1994 Congressional Quarterly Almanac* (Washington: Congressional Quarterly, 1995), pp. 383–96.

12. Not until April 2002, after NCLB rulemaking was under way, did the Department of Education announce all states were in compliance with the 1994 reauthorization. Even then, more than twenty-five states had been granted timeline waivers. See Eric W. Robelen, "States, Ed. Dept. Reach Accords on 1994 ESEA," *Education Week*, April 17, 2002, p. 1.

13. Quoted in Schwartz and Robinson, "Goals 2000 and the Standards Movement," p. 178.

14. Erik W. Robelen, "States Sluggish on Execution of 1994 ESEA," *Education Week*, November 28, 2001, p. 1; interview with Undersecretary Eugene Hickok, Department of Education, April 10, 2002; and Michael Cohen, "Unruly Crew," *Education Next*, vol. 2 (Fall 2002), pp. 42–47.

15. See Heidi Glidden and others, *Making Standards Matter 1999: An Update on State Activity*, AFT Policy Brief No. 11 (Washington: American Federation of Teachers, November 1999); and Margaret E. Goertz and M. C. Duffy, *Assessment and Accountability Systems in the 50 States: 1999–2000* (University of Pennsylvania Consortium for Policy Research in Education, 2001).

16. Section 311(e) of Goals 2000. In 1996 the number of states eligible was increased to twelve.

17. Including the Heritage Foundation, the Thomas Fordham Foundation, the Progressive Policy Institute, the Education Trust, the Education Leaders Council, and Empower America. Other prominent scholars such as Diane Ravitch and former Clinton aide William Galston also took part. Thanks to William Galston, Nina Rees, Andrew Rotherham, and Sen. Joseph I. Lieberman's staff for information here; see also Lieberman's account in the *Congressional Record*, daily ed., December 17, 2001, pp. S13399ff.

18. Because of efforts to hit as many districts (school and congressional) as possible, pre–NCLB Title I dollars did not reach about 20 percent of poor schools. Eric W. Robelen, "Off Target?" *Education Week*, September 5, 2001, p. 1.

19. Andrew Rotherham, *Toward Performance-Based Federal Education Funding: Reauthorization of the Elementary and Secondary Education Act* (Washington: Progressive Policy Institute, April 1999).

20. Nina Shokraii Rees and Kirk A. Johnson, *Why a 'Super' Ed-Flex Program Is Needed to Boost Academic Achievement: Heritage Foundation Backgrounder 1261* (Washington: Heritage Foundation, March 5, 1999).

21. By now President Bill Clinton also favored performance-based funding (see his 1999 State of the Union address). The language Miller proposed was developed with Sen. Jeff Bingaman, D-N.M., in conjunction with the so-called Title I Coalition of groups led by the Education Trust. Miller first proposed to amend the Academic Achievement for All Act but shifted the language to H.R. 2, a more natural vehicle.

22. H.R. 2 of 1999 as engrossed by the House, Section 1111(b)(2).

23. H.R. 2 of 1999, Section 112. An amendment to create a ten-state pilot program of Title I vouchers failed by more than one hundred votes.

24. "2000 Legislative Summary: ESEA," *CQ Weekly,* December 16, 2000, p. 2899.

25. Andrew Rotherham, "The New Three R's of Education," *Blueprint,* vol. 9 (Winter 2001) (www.ndol.org/blueprint/winter2001/default.html [July 7, 2003]).

26. David Nather, "Finding Education's Center," *CQ Weekly,* January 13, 2001, p. 112. See George W. Bush's August 3, 2000, speech accepting the Republican presidential nomination for a useful summary of his platform.

27. The Children's Defense Fund's stated (and now trademarked) mission is "to leave no child behind." Poll data in John Hassell, "Republicans Try to Shed 'Anti-Education' Image," *New Orleans Times-Picayune*, July 11, 1999, p. A8.

28. The Texas education reform movement dates back at least to the administration of Gov. Mark White (1983–87), who enlisted businessman H. Ross Perot to lead the charge. The administrations of White's successors, Bill Clements and Ann Richards, also played important roles. Kress interview; "Overview, Student Assessment Division," Texas Education Agency, state of Texas (www.tea.state.tx.us/student.assessment/about/overview.html [February 24, 2003]). See also John Mintz, " 'Texas Miracle' Doubted: An Education 'Miracle,' or Mirage?" *Washington Post,* April 21, 2000, p. A1. A study by the RAND Corporation suggesting that national tests revealed far worse performance by Texas students received wide, if not uncontested, play; see Jim Yardley, "Study Casts Doubt on Texas Test Scores, and Gives the Democrats Ammunition," *New York Times,* October 25, 2000, p. A23. For poll, see Dan Balz and Richard Morin, " 'Education Voters' Pose a Tough Test," *Washington Post,* June 30, 2000, p. A1.

29. Kress and La Montagne received crucial staff support from Sarah Youssef, a former Heritage Foundation staffer. Others vetting the proposal included Ravitch and Finn, along with former education secretary William Bennett, Indianapolis mayor Stephen Goldsmith, and a formal education advisory team. See Robert C. Johnston, "Bush Zeroes In on Accountability for Federal K–12 Funds," *Education Week,* September 8, 1999, p. 28.

30. Mark Barabak, "Bush Suggests Stripping Funds from Weak Schools," *Los Angeles Times*, September 3, 1999, p. A3; and George W. Bush, "A Culture of Achievement," October 5, 1999, speech (transcript obtained from the Manhattan Institute).

31. States not making progress over five years would see a small portion of their federal funding redirected into a grant fund for charter schools. Al Gore also discussed using the National Assessment of Educational Progress (NAEP) as a standard of progress, though his plan would have required a large shift in the way it is conducted. Thanks to Sarah Youssef for providing Bush campaign fact sheets. Ronald Brownstein and Edward Chen, "Gore Education Plan Stresses Accountability: Vice President's Initiative Attempts to Counter One Pushed by Bush," *Los Angeles Times*, April 29, 2000, p. A16.

32. Key staff here included Kress, La Montagne, Youssef, Nina Rees of the Heritage Foundation (who joined Vice President Dick Cheney's staff), and Christine Wolfe (a House Education staffer who joined the Education Department in mid-2001), with help from Boehner's chief education aide, Sally Lovejoy. Most political appointees in the department had not yet been named, much less confirmed. Incoming secretary Rod Paige, superintendent of schools in Houston, was not particularly involved in the formulation of the campaign platform or its translation into legislation.

33. Quote from Roemer interview. See Siobhan Gorman, "Education: Behind Bipartisanship," *National Journal*, July 14, 2001, pp. 2228–33; Dana Milbank, "Bush Likely to Drop Vouchers," *Washington Post*, January 2, 2001, p. A1; and Nather, "Finding Education's Center."

34. President George W. Bush, *No Child Left Behind* (The White House, January 23, 2001).

35. Quoted in Milbank, "Bush Likely to Drop Vouchers."

36. Readers seeking additional detail on NCLB formulation and passage are referred to the substantially longer version of this paper entitled "Accountability and Avoidance in the Bush Education Plan," Working Paper PEPG/02-12 (Harvard University, John F. Kennedy School of Government, Program on Education Policy and Governance, June 2002).

37. While Bush endorsed vouchers in his January 23, 2001, remarks introducing the plan, he declined to threaten a veto of a bill that omitted them. Rep. Todd R. Platts, R-Pa., who opposed vouchers, expressed the sense of others interviewed: He received "no real arm-twisting" from the president (interview, February 12, 2002). Kress is quoted in Gorman, "Education: Step One—Grab the Center."

38. On March 8, 2001, the committee voted 20–0 to approve a truncated S. 1. See David Nather, "Panel Easily Approves Education Bill, Deferring Fights on Vouchers and 'Charter States' to Senate Floor," *CQ Weekly*, March 10, 2001, p. 540.

39. Kress's bargaining eventually pushed the Democrats to close ranks, as the separate deals he reached with Edward M. Kennedy and the New Democrats were used to pressure the other side for additional concessions. See Siobhan Gorman, "Biparti-

san Schoolmates," *Education Next,* vol. 2 (Summer 2002), p. 39. Quotation from interviews; see also Broder, "Long Road to Reform"; Gorman, "Education: Behind Bipartisanship"; Siobhan Gorman, "The Making of a Bush Loyalist," *National Journal,* April 28, 2001, pp. 1246–48; David Nather, "Freed of Election-Year Pressures, Education Debate Begins in Earnest," *CQ Weekly,* April 21, 2001, p. 871; and David Nather and Mary Agnes Carey, "Health, Education: Assertive Dealmaker," *CQ Weekly,* May 26, 2001, p. 1230.

40. Interviews; see also Gail R. Chaddock, "Bush Education Plan Meets New Foe: GOP Governors," *Christian Science Monitor,* May 10, 2001, p. 2; and, crucially, Nicholas Lemann, "Testing Limits," *New Yorker,* July 2, 2001, pp. 28–34.

41. Siobhan Gorman, "When the Fine Print Changes," *National Journal.* May 12, 2001, pp. 1418–19; and Kress quoted in Lemann, "Testing Limits," p. 32. See also David Nather, "Despite Senate's Plans to Cut a Deal, ESEA Bill Bogs Down in Details," *CQ Weekly,* April 28, 2001, p. 917; Lynn Olson and Erik W. Robelen, "Defining 'Failure' Critical to Bush Testing Plan," *Education Week,* May 16, 2001, p. 27; and Valerie Strauss, "Lawmakers Struggle to Define Failing Schools," *Washington Post,* August 28, 2001, p. A8.

42. Core members—though others got involved on issues of interest—included about eight members of both parties. Kress and presidential aide Sarah Youssef were normally present, too. Kress's role as special envoy from the president gave the clear sense that he, not the Department of Education, was in charge of the administration's position. For more detail, see Rudalevige, "Accountability and Avoidance in the Bush Education Plan."

43. Interviews. Scenarios analyzed by the Education Trust for Senate Democrats had indicated that reaching proficiency for all students was more plausible across twelve years than ten. See H. Rept. 107-63, Part I, pp. 8–9. The House also allowed different rates of improvement across subgroups, so long as all reached proficiency within the twelve years.

44. However, when H.R. 1 was reported from committee, the administration joined House Democrats to add conditions that made it more difficult for states to evade NAEP. On national testing, see Nather, "Freed of Election-Year Pressures."

45. The Senate language—"Ted Kennedy's Straight A's," as a GOP aide put it— was not deemed worthwhile by conservatives anyway. But Boehner's math was right. Even a small block grant program dubbed "Super Local Flex," aimed at one hundred districts nationwide, barely passed, 217-209. Broder, "Long Road to Reform"; and interviews.

46. David Nather, "Compromises on ESEA Bills May Imperil Republican Strategy," *CQ Weekly,* May 5, 2001, p. 1009. See also Kerry L. Kantin, "House Conservatives Chafe at Compromise on Education Bill," *The Hill,* May 2, 2001; and David Nather, "Democrats Leaving Their Stamp on Bush's Education Bill," *CQ Weekly,* May 12, 2001, p. 1079.

47. Gorman, "Making of a Bush Loyalist"; dissenting views to H. Rept. 107-63, Part I, p. 1246; Nather, "Democrats Leaving Their Stamp on Bush's Education Bill"; and Hickok interview.

48. *Congressional Record*, daily ed., May 23, 2001, pp. H2589–96. Dick Armey, Majority Whip Tom DeLay, R-Texas, and Boehner sponsored the amendment, though Boehner, as even one GOP staffer conceded, did this with "a nod and a wink."

49. See, especially, David Nather, "Education Bill Passes in House with Strong Bipartisan Support," *CQ Weekly*, May 26, 2001, p. 1256.

50. Interviews; David S. Broder, "Education Reform Is Running on Empty," *Boston Sunday Globe*, July 15, 2001, p. D7; Gorman, "Behind Bipartisanship"; Jodi Wilgoren, "State School Chiefs Fret over U.S. Plan to Require Testing," *New York Times*, July 17, 2001, p. A1; and National Education Association resolution of June 2001, urging that parents be allowed to "opt their children out of all mandated standardized tests." National Conference of State Legislatures letter quoted in David Nather, "Conferees on Education Overhaul Dismiss Whispers of 'Next Year,'" *CQ Weekly*, October 27, 2001, p. 2544. Strauss, "Lawmakers Struggle to Define Failing Schools," notes three reports on adequate yearly progress: one by Thomas J. Kane and Douglas O. Staiger; one by Kane, Staiger, and Jeffrey Geppert; and a third by the Congressional Research Service.

51. Interviews; David Nather, "Conferees Make Little Headway on Biggest Issues in Education Bill: Recess Talks Planned on Accountability," *CQ Weekly*, August 4, 2001, p. 1926. Unusually, the Senate delegation included non–Health, Education, Labor, and Pensions (HELP) Committee members Lieberman and Evan Bayh. The House had a delegation of fourteen (eight Republicans and six Democrats).

52. Interviews; and Gorman, "Bipartisan Schoolmates."

53. George W. Bush, "Remarks to 2001 National Urban League Conference," Office of the Press Secretary, White House, August 1, 2001.

54. Bush, "Remarks to 2001 National Urban League Conference"; and "Conference Report to Accompany H.R. 1," H. Rept. 107-334, December 13, 2001, pp. 24ff.

55. Roemer interview.

56. Much of NCLB's legislative process fits the useful framework developed by Barbara Sinclair in *Unorthodox Lawmaking* (Washington: CQ Press, 2000).

57. Interviews; and see Siobhan Gorman, "Schooled in Survival," *National Journal*, December 15, 2001, pp. 3854–55.

58. For the surprisingly extended House exchange, see the *Congressional Record*, daily ed., May 22, 2001, H2526–2531. See also Rod Paige, "Remarks before the American Council on Education," Washington, D.C., February 20, 2001.

59. See Boehner, "Fact Sheet."

60. Lynn Olson, "Testing Systems in Most States Not ESEA-Ready," *Education Week*, January 9, 2002, p. 1.

61. Lynn Olson, "'Inadequate' Yearly Gains Are Predicted," *Education Week*, April 3, 2002, p. 1; Diana Jean Schemo, "Law Overhauling School Standards Seen as Skirted," *New York Times*, October 15, 2002, p. A21; and Wilgoren, "State School Chiefs Fret over U.S. Plan to Require Testing."

62. In January 2003 New York parents sought to enforce the NCLB regime in the courts, claiming school districts had failed to meet the law's intradistrict choice provisions.

63. Noam Scheiber, "Rod Paige Learns the Hard Way," *New Republic,* July 2, 2001, p. 12; and Diana Jean Schemo, "Education Chief Seeks More Visible Role," *New York Times,* August 5, 2001, p. 17. The substance of these articles is fiercely disputed by White House and departmental officials.

64. See, for example, Senate HELP Committee hearing of April 23, 2002; House Committee on Education and the Workforce hearing of July 24, 2002; and Erik Robelen, "Department Levies $783,000 Title I Penalty on Ga.," *Education Week,* May 28, 2003, p. 18.

65. See Hickok's comments in Gorman, "Bipartisan Schoolmates," p. 43; David S. Broder, "Education Reform Controversy Lingers," *Washington Post,* April 7, 2002, p. A5; Lynn Olson, "Testing Rules Would Grant States Leeway," *Education Week,* March 6, 2002, p. 1; Lynn Olson, "Final Rules Give States Direction, Little Flexibility," *Education Week,* December 4, 2002, p. 1; Lynn Olson, "States Strive toward ESEA Compliance," *Education Week,* December 11, 2002, p. 1; and Lynn Olson, "All States Get Federal Nod on Key Plans," *Education Week,* June 18, 2003, p. 1.

66. Rod Paige letter, Department of Education, October 22, 2002; and "No Child Left Behind Act: Summary of Final Regulations," Department of Education, November 26, 2002.

67. "Education Department Issues Final Regulations," Department of Education, November 26, 2002; *Federal Register,* vol. 67 (December 2, 2002), pp. 71709ff.; David Hoff, "States Revise the Meaning of 'Proficient,' " *Education Week,* October 9, 2002, p. 1; Olson, "Final Rules Give States Direction"; Lynn Olson, "Approval of States' ESEA Plans Suggests Flexibility," *Education Week,* January 22, 2003, p. 14; Lynn Olson, "States' Plans Likely to Test ESEA Pliancy," *Education Week,* February 19, 2003, p. 1; Olson, "All States Get Federal Nod on Key Plans"; and see the Education Commission of the States website at www.ecs.org for updated detail on states' compliance efforts.

68. "Remarks by the President on the First Anniversary of the No Child Left Behind Act," Office of the White House Press Secretary, January 8, 2003; George Miller statement, "Press Conference on NCLB One Year Anniversary," House Education and the Workforce Committee Democratic staff, January 8, 2003; and George Miller, "Bush Administration Cuts Public School Funding to Pay for New Private School Voucher Scheme," press release, February 3, 2003.

69. From his 1787 *Defense of the Constitutions of Government of the United States,* in David McCullough, *John Adams* (Simon and Schuster, 2001), p. 378.

3

Refining or Retreating? High-Stakes Accountability in the States

FREDERICK M. HESS

I n January 2002 President George W. Bush signed into law the No Child
Left Behind Act (NCLB) of 2001 and made the national government a
prominent player in the effort to use high-stakes accountability to drive
school improvement. Months of agonizing negotiation produced a consensus
that the Department of Education should require all states to test students
regularly and hold schools and districts accountable for student performance.
The new law required states to test students in grades three through eight
annually and to ensure that graduates pass a high school exit exam, required
states to participate in the National Assessment of Educational Progress
(NAEP) every two years to benchmark their exams, and imposed a series of
corrective actions on schools and districts that fail to demonstrate "adequate
yearly progress" (AYP). (See chapter 2 in this volume for a more extended
discussion of the legislation and the negotiations that produced it.)

The passage of NCLB followed a decade of concerted activity across the
states. These efforts had produced an array of high-stakes accountability systems adopted during the mid- and late 1990s that were gradually grinding
toward implementation. As of mid-2003, the state efforts follow a familiar
trajectory, with abysmal early student scores improving rapidly even as scat-

I would like to thank the Spencer Foundation and the National Academy of Education for
their generous support.

tered opposition begins to coalesce. When opposition reaches a certain level of intensity, officials seek to mollify critics by refining testing systems in ways purported to make them fairer and more rational. The challenge is for public officials to make such revisions without undermining essential elements of accountability. Whether federal involvement is likely to produce meaningful change, or whether the promise of NCLB will prove vulnerable to the same pressures that often weaken state efforts, will prove pivotal in determining its consequences.

As Eric A. Hanushek and Margaret E. Raymond discuss in this volume (see chapter 6), the merits of various accountability systems have occasioned extensive consideration of various tests, measurement techniques, and incentive structures.[1] Receiving far less attention have been the accompanying political tensions, though these are frequently as educationally significant as any technical concerns. Surveying the developments and implementation of high-stakes accountability programs, it can be difficult to determine which programmatic decisions are inspired by educational concerns and which are politically motivated. While high-stakes accountability is appealing in the abstract, implementation produces visible costs that are more politically salient, at least in the short term, than are the diffuse and long-term educational benefits.

The 1970s minimum competency testing (MCT) movement was the first time this struggle played out in the United States, as a flood of states adopted widely supported testing programs that called for students to master particular skills and content before graduating. In almost every case, large numbers of children failed to meet the initial standards but only an invisible handful of children were ever denied diplomas. While proponents hailed this pattern as evidence that testing had driven systemic improvement, a complementary development was a largely unheralded tale of political accommodation and compromise.

This is not to imply that the politics of accountability are static, across either time or place. The past three decades provide strong evidence of a growing social acceptance of substantive accountability in America, a heightened willingness on the part of voters and public officials to accept some of the inequities and concentrated costs that doomed earlier accountability efforts. Nonetheless, key questions regarding the nature and plight of these efforts remain largely unaddressed.

Why do high-stakes accountability systems launched to widespread acclaim meet growing pockets of resistance even as student performance soars? Why are accountability provisions softened or made more flexible in predictable ways? Finally, what are the implications of these issues for the promise of accountability-driven reform? In considering these questions, I draw upon the experiences of the nation's first attempt at substantive accountability (the minimum competency tests of the 1970s) and the more recent experiences of four states at the forefront of national discussion (California, Massachusetts, Texas, and Virginia). My aim is to illustrate the political challenges implicit in any move to high-stakes accountability and the implications for public policy.

The Politics of High-Stakes Accountability

The political challenges are a direct consequence of the educational promise of high-stakes accountability. The allure of standards-based reform is straightforward. It represents a public commitment that schools ought to ensure that all children be taught a discrete body of knowledge and skills to a specified level of mastery. Setting meaningful performance standards, however, makes it inevitable that some students, teachers, and schools will fail to meet those standards. This poses a daunting political challenge in a democratic society where the low-performers have powerful incentives to challenge the legitimacy of the system.

At the outset, it is important to distinguish between high-stakes accountability systems that include sanctions for students, teachers, or both and those nonintrusive standards-based systems that do not. High-stakes accountability systems link incentives to demonstrated student performance to ensure that students master specified content and that educators effectively teach that content. Under such a regime, school improvement no longer rests primarily upon individual volition or intrinsic motivation. Instead, students and teachers are compelled to cooperate through levers such as diplomas and job security. Such transformative systems seek to harness the self-interest of students and educators to refocus schools and redefine the expectations of teachers and learners.[2] A number of reports illustrate how such accountability may spur dramatic improvement in school performance. For instance, in 2000 researchers at the University of Texas intensively studied four high-poverty, high-achieving Texas districts that dramatically boosted student performance after the introduction of the Texas Assessment of Academic Skills (TAAS) and documented how the districts used the high-stakes nature of TAAS as a lever with which to radically change the way teachers and administrators approached teaching and learning.[3]

High-stakes efforts are fundamentally different from these standards-based reforms that reject coercion. Gentler, more suggestive standards-based approaches seek to improve schooling through informal social pressures, by using tests as a diagnostic device, by increasing coordination across schools and classrooms, and by using standardization to permit more efficient use of school resources. Suggestive accountability can produce educational benefits, but such changes tend to be modest and dependent on the ability and inclination of teachers to use the tests as pedagogical tools. Educators themselves are sympathetic toward the notion of accountability, but they are squeamish about the demands visited by coercive accountability. A Texas principal offered an elegant illustration of this tension in a 2002 magazine account, asking, "Do I believe in rigorous standards for student learning and the need to put pressure on schools to improve instruction?" She answered herself:

> Certainly I do, but I question whether high-stakes testing is the only way to create change in schools, and I wonder if this testing will, in the end, serve the best interests of all students. Last year I had to tell a student that she didn't pass the "last chance" TAAS exam administered in May of her senior year; I do not even want to imagine the heartbreak that she and her family felt. I've only had to do this once, but it was one time too many, and I don't know that I have it in me to do it again.[4]

In practice, the two visions of standards constitute two ends of a continuum. Many accountability programs begin with at least a rhetorical commitment to the transformative high-stakes ideal. Over time, however, implementation gradually makes clear the costs implied by such change, eroding support for coercive accountability while opposition coalesces. Opponents of transformative accountability hardly ever suggest that they are opposed to the broader notion of accountability, instead tracing their opposition to the specifics of existing arrangements. Such critics implicitly agree that they will support transformative accountability only if it is stripped of its transformative character. Typical was the January 2001 response to the proposed NCLB legislation proffered by Wayne Johnson, the president of the California Teachers Association. While suggesting that the union was supportive of sound accountability efforts, Johnson reiterated the union's concerns by reasonably arguing, "[Standardized] tests should not be the sole criteria for determining what public school students and teachers are really accomplishing."[5] By the time one had made all of the recommended adjustments, the result would have been a system where clear-cut determinations of performance or competence were no longer feasible.

The Promise of Outcome Accountability

Conventionally, public schools and educators have been judged on the basis of whether or not they comply with regulations and directives, instead of upon student performance or progress. This approach has represented a compromise among policymakers unwilling or unable to resolve disputes regarding what schools should focus on or how school performance ought to be measured.[6] There resulted well-documented problems, prompting responses that often entailed intrusive regulation and micromanagement.

These developments helped give rise to broad support for outcome accountability, the notion that states ought to establish performance criteria and then free educators to achieve them. Conceptually, outcome accountability offers a number of advantages. Specifying what skills and knowledge students are responsible for mastering fosters agreement on educational goals, giving educators clear direction. This enables administrators to more readily gauge teacher effectiveness. They can then take steps to mentor or motivate less effective teachers and to recognize and reward effective ones. Clear expectations and information on performance can ensure that hard-to-educate students are adequately served and make it difficult for schools to casually overlook such students or argue that they are being served adequately. High-stakes accountability can enhance educator professionalism and boost public support for schooling by holding educators to clear standards and sanctioning those who do not meet them.[7]

Such changes may come at a price. High-stakes accountability may adversely alter the culture of schooling, narrow the scope of instruction and services that schools provide, constrain teachers, leave less room for creative engagement, shift educational resources into test-specific preparation, and disproportionately punish some groups of students.[8] These concerns give rise to the politics of accountability-based reform.

The Politics of Accountability

High-stakes accountability requires officials to make five politically sensitive sets of decisions. First, a prescribed body of content and objectives to be tested must be designated. Such a course necessarily marginalizes some of the goals, objectives, content, and skills that are not included. Second, assessments must be imposed that render clear indications as to whether students have or have not mastered the requisite skills and content. Third, such assessment requires policymakers to specify what constitutes mastery. Fourth, designers need to decide what to do with students who fail to demonstrate mastery. Finally, if accountability is to significantly alter educational provision, educators must be rewarded or sanctioned on the basis of student performance. Each decision tends to produce passionate opposition among those who bear the costs. Opponents of coercive accountability seize upon the arbitrary nature of many of these decisions, arguing that they seek only modifications that will increase test validity and reduce any inequities or pernicious effects produced by misuse of assessments.

Resisting the protests of the aggrieved is the central political challenge confronting advocates of high-stakes reform. In the face of heated opposition, proponents often agree to a series of compromises on program design and implementation, eventually undercutting the coercive promise implied by high-stakes testing.[9] By 2002, more than twenty-five states had adopted mandatory graduation exams and more than twenty states offered school incentives linked to test scores.[10] However, phase-in periods and delays in implementation meant that the graduation requirements and the test-based incentives and sanctions for educators had taken effect in only a handful of states. Even leading accountability states such as Massachusetts and Virginia have opted to provide transition rules that permit some students to graduate despite failing to post the minimum scores on required graduation exams.[11] While the delays and adjustments often make educational sense, providing time to design and refine testing systems and curricula and to ensure that neither students nor educators are unfairly penalized, they have also conveniently pushed into the future the real challenges these systems would face.

The politically useful nature of the delays has been made clear as most of the handful of states that have started to approach initial deadlines have blinked and opted to delay the implementation of sanctions.[12] A 2000 analysis found that roughly a third of the states that have adopted high-stakes accountability systems had slowed or scaled back their original efforts.[13] In Arizona, for instance, where more than 80 percent of tenth graders failed the mathematics component of the state test in 1999 and 2000, the board of education and the legislature scrambled to push back the effective date of the graduation requirements to 2006 from the original goal of 2002.[14] Since 2000, other states, including Alabama, Alaska, Delaware, Maryland, North Carolina, and Wyoming, have also decided to scale back testing programs and postpone the date at which high-stakes instruments would take effect. Other states adopted graduation tests but took steps to make certain that even students who did not pass could receive diplomas. For instance, Wisconsin Republican governor Tommy Thompson pushed for a graduation exam in 1999, but union and Parent-Teacher Association (PTA) opposition to a high-stakes instrument ensured that passage would not be required for graduation.[15] In other states, such as Indiana, coercive systems were confronted with fierce legal challenges mounted by advocates for students with special needs.[16]

The Few, the Angry, the Mobilized

Resistance to high-stakes reforms typically emerges among four especially prominent constituencies: educators concerned about their professional autonomy and the specter of sanctions, ethnic and socioeconomic communities in which students are disproportionately sanctioned by tests, communities with well-regarded schools that resent the disruption or reputational threat of testing, and those who find their moral or curricular preferences marginalized by the testing regime in question.

TEACHER OPPOSITION. The most influential opposition to coercive accountability tends to come from teachers and school administrators. Teachers are generally averse to being evaluated or sanctioned on the basis of student performance.[17] It can be difficult for public officials to resist the concerted opposition of teachers, especially given the lack of a natural pro–high-stakes constituency. Aggressively implementing coercive arrangements requires public officials to threaten public educators with accountability that they do not desire. These educators, in turn, are an active and powerful electoral group that will play a large role in determining whether such officials retain their positions through reelection or reappointment (see chapter 4 in this volume).

The opposition of educators is based not only on a reluctance to be monitored, but also on real and defensible concerns about how testing regimes are developed and applied. Children vary in ability and preparation from community to community and school to school, confronting some educators with greater challenges than others. This raises concern over whether officials can equitably determine teacher performance, forcing advocates of high-stakes accountability to defend inequities in the face of heated criticism from teachers and their allies.[18]

Teachers also have a second complaint, one more geared to the culture of schooling. For several decades, the American public education establishment has embraced a vision of professional, autonomous teachers who operate out of a sense of duty and commitment.[19] Whatever the strengths or weaknesses of such a system, it is the one to which current teachers have grown accustomed and in which they have been acculturated. The premise of high-stakes testing challenges this culture by pressing teachers to teach the content and skills mandated by the state, regardless of their personal preferences. Educators have incentives to resist a system that challenges their autonomy, holds them accountable, and forces them to engage in practices they may not favor.

During 2000–01 the Massachusetts Teachers Association (MTA) launched a $600,000 advertising campaign that attacked the "one-size-fits-all, high-stakes, do-or-die MCAS [Massachusetts Comprehensive Assessment System] test." The administration of the state's Republican governor Paul Cellucci responded by directing the state to launch an aggressive, $500,000 television and radio ad campaign on behalf of the exam.[20] The Cellucci administration also proposed a number of modifications for the MCAS that included expanding the allowable testing accommodations for students with special needs, narrowing the world history section to focus on American history, and permitting students who had not passed by the end of twelfth grade to enroll in alternative programs at community colleges.[21] Despite these efforts to assuage the concerns of critics, a spring 2001 poll of three hundred teachers conducted by the Boston Teachers Union found that about 85 percent of the city's public school teachers opposed using the MCAS exam as a graduation requirement. Just 7 percent of teachers backed the requirement.[22]

In 1999 California began providing new funding to low-performing schools and awarding bonuses to high-performing teachers and schools. Perhaps unsurprisingly, given that the state was using the carrot instead of the stick, it was the first time in California's long history of accountability that provisions were rapidly implemented. Nonetheless, even that effort created a backlash from California Teachers Association officials and classroom teachers, who saw the incentives as the leading edge of an effort to sow division among the state's educators.

RACE-BASED AND CLASS-BASED CONCERNS. While accountability may yield significant long-term and systemic benefits, a meaningful high-stakes system will inevitably fail some students and thereby create some clear losers. The current system takes a high toll on students who perform poorly, permitting many students to be promoted without mastering important skills or to graduate with meaningless diplomas.[23] The difference is that existing inequities can be attributed to impersonal social forces, while high-stakes accountability forces public officials to visibly sanction vulnerable children. Those students denied diplomas suffer clear and immediate costs, while the benefits of effective accountability tend to be diffuse and long term. Those who lose out under high-stakes testing, because they have more immediately at stake, will tend to be passionate. The larger mass of winners will find the issue less pressing.[24] Even if disadvantaged children are the primary beneficiaries of accountability systems—as many proponents argue—such benefits are indirect and hard to define. This situation is especially thorny because children in minority and low-income communities are disproportionately likely to fail high-stakes exams, leaving officials vulnerable to charges of callousness and racial bias. As a result, officials will find themselves pressured to reduce the number of failing students or to reduce the consequences of failure. For instance, for nearly a quarter century, the National Association for the Advancement of Colored People (NAACP) has officially opposed decisions to withhold diplomas or grade promotion on the basis of test results, deeming such policies an effort to blame the victim.[25]

In March 2001 California administered its new California Learning Assessment System (CLAS) test to ninth graders for the first time. In March 2001, amid confusion about whether this was a practice run, more than 75 percent of black and Hispanic students tested received a failing score. Superintendent of public instruction Delaine Eastin termed the results "sobering" and acknowledged "the data show that we have a great deal of work to do."[26] In a state where the population was 32 percent Hispanic and 7 percent black, such failure rates among the minority population triggered stirrings of organized unrest. During 2001 the anti-CLAS Coalition for Education Justice sponsored several rallies and teach-ins to protest the test, drawing three hundred people to a Los Angeles rally where educational officials were urged to protect students from "racist and class-biased high-stakes testing."[27]

RESISTANCE IN HIGH-PERFORMING COMMUNITIES. In many of the most highly regarded school systems concern also arises about the impact of high-stakes accountability. In these communities, the parents and educators are less concerned that students will be sanctioned than that an emphasis on state-mandated tests will hurt local schools by forcing them to shift their attention to state-dictated curricula and content. In particular, parents and educators in highly regarded districts fear that the pressure to teach baseline skills and content will disrupt gifted, advanced placement, and International Baccalaureate classrooms. They also worry that the test scores are an inaccurate proxy for the broader quality of schooling and that an emphasis on test scores may have a variety of negative consequences, such as understating school performance, impeding students' college prospects, and reducing local property values. While it can be readily argued that disruptions indicate that all students were previously not mastering necessary skills and content, or that disappointing test scores may suggest that elite districts are not as effective as believed, no natural constituency exists to advance these claims. Meanwhile, the educated, wealthy, and politically involved residents of high-performing suburban districts have a visceral desire to protect the practices and the reputations of their schools.

In Massachusetts, a state with a small and politically weak minority community, the most active opposition to the state's MCAS tests emerged from the wealthy, staunchly liberal communities. Led by activists in Cambridge and the elite Boston suburbs, critics argued that the tests were harming advanced programs, forcing teachers to dumb down material, and provided misleading depictions of school quality. This opposition birthed an array of anti-test organizations. Comparing themselves with the Freedom Riders who resisted Southern segregation laws, a Committee of 100 Massachusetts Parents—composed primarily of Boston-area parents—tried to organize a boycott of the exams. By 2001 other groups such as the Students' Coalition for Alternatives to the MCAS (SCAM) and the Coalition for Authentic Reform in Education (CARE) were also holding rallies around the state, promoting boycotts, and lobbying officials to revise or dismantle the MCAS.[28]

CONCERNS ABOUT BEING MARGINALIZED. Finally, the multiple agendas that coexist within public schooling ensure that the push for high-stakes accountability will provoke conflict from those whose particular agendas will be marginalized. A deep-rooted disagreement is evident in the United States as to what schools are for, what a good education includes, and what skills and content children need to know. This conflict takes two distinct forms. First, there is conflict over how much time to devote to various subjects and areas of study. Because accountability systems tend to refocus schools on skills such as mathematics and reading, they often reduce time devoted to other subjects—especially the arts. This development inspires concern among those who think such instruction an essential part of schooling and those whose livelihood depends on providing or supporting such instruction. Their concern is entirely valid. For example, a 2000 RAND study that examined the effects of accountability-driven reform in Washington State led to increases of 50 percent or more in the percentage of classroom time devoted to reading, writing, and mathematics and declines of 40 percent or more in the amount of time devoted to social studies, science, the arts, and health and fitness.[29]

Second, there is dispute about the nature of the instruction that takes place within a particular subject area. Teachers and instructional materials will emphasize the content for which students are held responsible. If social studies test questions are based on twentieth-century social movements instead of on the founders, instruction will reflect that. The same will be true if questions emphasize the recall of dates and names instead of analytic capacity. Given sharp disagreement over the merits of these various curricular and pedagogical approaches, efforts to impose statewide agreement inevitably offend some constituencies.[30] Oftentimes, the disagreements will overlay religious or race-based concerns regarding appropriate content, aggravating the divide. The aggrieved will frequently challenge the offending decision, while the broader public will generally evince little interest in the issue.

In 1991 California launched the California Learning Assessment System, featuring a series of standardized tests augmented by student portfolios. The design and implementation of CLAS outraged conservative parents concerned about the literacy and history tests. In the spring of 1994 the conflict reached a boiling point when conservative parents launched an organized effort denouncing many of the prompts used in the exam exercises as offensive. These parents cited a number of examples that they regarded as too violent, personal, or political. Representatives of groups of concerned parents wanted access to the questions. The Department of Education, concerned about preserving test confidentiality, denied them access. A court ruling that students could opt out of the tests and the state's decision to make many questions public wounded CLAS's legitimacy.[31]

In 1994 the Virginia Board of Education initiated the development of statewide standards in math, science, English, and history. While crafting the standards in math and science was relatively consensual, there was disagreement over the emphasis that the language arts standards ought to devote to phonics and fierce conflict over the proposed social studies standards.[32] Critics, including the Virginia Education Association (VEA) and the Virginia Association of School Superintendents, accused the Republican administration of having rewritten the standards to reflect a more conservative perspective and of desiring social studies and language arts standards that promoted the "regurgitation of isolated facts" and "lower-level thinking skills."[33]

In each conflict inspired by the introduction of high-stakes accountability, the dynamics are similar. Proponents of standards must marshal diffuse support in response to challenges from passionate, coherent constituencies. The American political system is notoriously bad at pursuing collective goods when it requires imposing concentrated costs on select groups. American government is highly permeable, making it relatively easy for small but passionate factions to block or soften adverse legislative or bureaucratic decisions.[34] The fate of accountability efforts often turns on the size and strength of these interests. In homogeneous states with weak teacher unions, for instance, the pressures on public officials to fundamentally compromise on coercive accountability is likely to be much less severe than in states with a strong union and large, influential minority communities.

Softening the Blow

In the face of such pressure, transformative systems are generally rendered more suggestive in one of five ways. While each can be readily justified on practical or educational grounds, the common thread is the manner in which they ease political resistance by softening the coercive impact of accountability.

One common compromise is to lower the stakes of the tests for students, for educators, or for both. When sanctions are weak or nonexistent, little incentive exists for teachers, low-performing students, or anyone else to worry much about test results.

A second approach is to simply make tests easier, either by lowering content standards or by adopting easier questions. This can be a politically perilous course if it is seen as signaling a public retreat from the notion of school quality. Consequently, this tack is more often taken by a board of education than by a legislature and is more likely to involve technical adjustments or the altering of questions than an outright reduction of the required passing score.

Third, instead of easing the test, officials can leave the tests alone but reduce the thresholds required to pass the accountability assessments. If weakening test content is difficult, the decision to formally lower the score required to pass the tests is at least equally so. Once passing scores are established, officials find lowering the bar immensely difficult. Consequently, the most popular way to ease the threshold is to offer numerous second chances. Giving students a number of retests or schools several years to boost their performance ensures that the law of averages will help a number of moderately low performers to clear the bar. Just as a solid student might fare poorly on a given exam one time out of five, so a mediocre student may score a 70 percent one-fifth of the time.

If officials choose not to weaken the sanctions and find it difficult to dilute content or lower the bar, they may adopt two other accommodations. One is to permit some students to sidestep the required assessment by providing some form of opt-out provision. This can take the form of permitting students at the bottom to receive a basic diploma or completion certificate without passing the exam or that of permitting high-achieving students to substitute advanced tests for basic exams seen as interfering with important instruction. Finally, officials may reduce opposition by delaying the implementation of sanctions. This permits legislators to take strong action, push the day of reckoning into the (sometimes) distant future, and mollify opponents who know that changes in the political climate or turnover among public officials may later provide a chance to modify the proposed program.

Contextual Forces and the Politics of Accountability

The dance of accountability is shaped by political context. High-stakes accountability systems face stiffer challenges in some states than in others. The politics of coercive accountability is a clash between aggrieved groups with concentrated interests and a broader public that stands to reap diffuse benefits. Such fights generally have a predictable calculus, whether in the case of agricultural subsidies or military base closures, with the concentrated interests emerging triumphant. When the aggrieved interests are larger, more influential, or more organized, they will be more successful at fending off efforts to promote coercive accountability. When such groups are weaker or have less purchase on the decisionmakers or when coherent interests emerge to champion accountability programs, coercive programs are more likely to survive largely intact. However, the outcome of any specific conflict depends not only on the strength of the mobilized group, but also on the political context.

Three contextual elements are worth particular attention. The first, and most significant, is the statewide strength of the Democratic Party. Historically, for a variety of reasons, public employee unions and urban and minority voters have been key components of the Democratic base, leaving liberals significantly more disposed to support the most visible victims of coercive accountability. Whereas Republicans and conservatives are sometimes willing to confront public employees or to frontally challenge the civil rights organizations and the national black leadership, few Democratic leaders have an inclination to steer such a course.[35] Consequently, the most ambitious accountability efforts tend to be launched by Republicans or centrist Democrats. Sustaining and implementing coercive accountability in states, such as Texas or Virginia, where Republicans and conservative Democrats hold sway is far easier than in more liberal and predominantly Democratic states, such as California or Massachusetts.

In the 1980s Republicans made substantial gains in the Virginia legislature. By the time Republican George Allen was elected governor in 1993, as the first Republican governor in twelve years, Republicans held more than 40 percent of the seats in the legislature.[36] Whereas Democratic legislators enjoyed substantial support among the groups most likely to critique or oppose high-stakes testing—for instance, the fifty-thousand-member VEA and the NAACP—Republican legislators were more willing to support measures these groups opposed. In 1994 Allen launched the state's heralded push to devise its standards of learning (SOL) accountability system.

A second key contextual variable is the degree to which an active pro-accountability coalition emerges in a state. Generally, citizens have little reason to spontaneously form such a coalition. However, specific entities have an interest in putting resources and energy into backing accountability systems. The most significant of these is the business community, which depends on schools to help lure and retain employees and to train its next generation of employees and customers. In some states, such as Texas, the business community takes an active role in promoting coercive reform, helping to provide counterpressure and resources that may keep officials from accepting compromise measures they might otherwise adopt.

In 1993, under public pressure for enhanced school accountability—especially from influential business groups such as the Texas Business and Education Coalitions—the Texas legislature fought off fierce opposition from public educators and enacted an accountability system that linked school- and district-level incentives to student TAAS performance.[37] Moreover, the legislature ambitiously mandated that student performance data be disaggregated into African American, Hispanic, white, and economically disadvantaged and required schools to perform effectively in each subgroup. Absent the pressure and political support from the state's mobilized business community, such an aggressive accountability system likely would not have seen the light of day.

A third important factor is the degree to which those designing and implementing accountability measures are insulated from the active, irate interests. When state boards of education enjoy significant influence and autonomy, they permit proponents to act aggressively and with much less regard for the political constraints placed on legislators or executive branch officials. While it would be a mistake to think that the members of even largely independent state boards are immune to informal pressure, they have a significant amount of latitude. Consequently, states with relatively autonomous boards that embrace accountability may move with surprising vigor.

Massachusetts first administered the Massachusetts Comprehensive Assessment System in 1998. The test was billed by the board of education as more rigorous than the typical state assessment. When the board set the passing scores required for graduation in January 2000, board members opted for a standard that roughly half of the state's tenth graders had failed to meet just two months before.[38] The board found it much easier to set a high threshold than elected officials would have, especially in the case of Massachusetts, where the leaders of the heavily Democratic House and Senate enjoyed close relationships with the Massachusetts Teachers Association (MTA). As one MTA official noted in a private communication, "We have relatively little influence over the Board of Education, which is appointed, not elected . . . [and] a lot of education policy is made by the board."

Been Here Before: The Case of Minimum Competency Testing

The tensions that beset high-stakes accountability systems work are not new. They accompany any effort to institute high-stakes accountability. Perhaps the most telling experience was that of minimum competency testing in the 1970s, when a wave of states adopted exit tests that became a condition for receiving a high school diploma.

Minimum competency testing proved a mixed success, but one unable to deliver on its ambitious promise. Few students were ever denied diplomas, in part because resources and tutoring were targeted to low-achieving students and more attention was paid to the academic preparation of previously over-looked students. In large part, however, passing rates were boosted by making the tests exceedingly simple, creating a low bar for passage, offering students a number of chances to pass, and exempting categories of low-performing students. The heavily compromised nature of the 1970s push for minimum competency testing would later help to engender support for more rigorous accountability measures in the 1990s.

After minimum competency testing was first introduced in Oregon in 1973, states began to adopt modified versions of the Oregon system. By 1979, spurred by concern that schools were no longer delivering essential instruction and that students were not mastering vital skills, thirty-six states had enacted some form of minimum competency testing.[39] Eighteen states required students to pass the tests for graduation, with almost all of these exclusively targeting reading, writing, and arithmetic. While the National Institute of Education observed that there was no uniform definition of minimum competency testing, such programs all sought to ensure that graduates mastered a small body of essential knowledge and skills.

Proponents effectively framed the question as one of whether or not states ought to demand some degree of educational performance. Because states had no way to ensure that students were mastering essential skills, and because it was easy to argue that literacy and numeracy were skills vital to any child's life chances, few opponents emerged and those that did made little headway. As one critic conceded in 1984, "Promis[ing] a simple remedy for complicated problems of achievement and accountability, MCT has reached almost universal application in less than ten years."[40] By focusing on basic academic subjects on which the public largely agreed about what graduates needed to know, proponents avoided messy debates about how to define essential knowledge or skills.

While minimum competency testing was typically enacted with only modest opposition, implementation would generate serious political and legal controversy. This was not at first apparent. MCT legislation normally stipulated that requirements would not apply to current high school students, creating a lag of at least four years between adoption and full implementation.

When students first took the new exams, significant numbers inevitably failed to achieve the required passing score. Nearly every state that implemented a graduation test first given in the eighth or ninth grade reported an initial failure rate of 30 percent or more.[41] Issues of equal protection and due process sparked concern among leaders of the civil rights community who fretted that the tests would disproportionately deny diplomas to black and low-income students and children in impoverished communities.[42] Black students generally passed the exams at a much lower rate than their white peers.[43] A steady stream of litigation claiming discrimination resulted. Critics also argued that the tests lacked reliability and validity and that graduation was linked to subjective cutoff scores.[44]

Such concerns were ameliorated by the fact that every state reduced its failure rate to less than 5 percent—and almost always to under 1 percent—by the time the first affected cohort graduated.[45] The number of students failing the exams tended to shrink relatively quickly as students were retested.[46] In Maryland, for instance, 75 percent of those who initially failed the test passed on their second try. In North Carolina, the figure was 53 percent.[47]

Observers disagreed about how to interpret this track record. Proponents argued that the pressure produced by MCT programs motivated students, prompted schools and districts to adjust instructional practices, focused resources on oft-overlooked students, and forced teachers to make sure they were effectively teaching basic skills. Researchers found many districts reported modifying curriculum, tutoring low-achieving students in essential skills, holding in-services for teachers on MCT, and administering pretests to students.[48] For the students who failed to meet those relatively lax standards, the most common response was remediation and repeated retesting.[49]

Critics argued that the gains were less substantive than they appeared. For one thing, more than twenty states exempted students with special needs from the requirements. More than half of the MCT states adopted achievement levels at or below the ninth grade as a passing mark for twelfth-grade students. Critics also suggested that apparent growth was largely an artifact of repeated testing. While offering repeated retests seems fair and appropriate, such a process can dilute the value of the exam—especially because many MCT programs used the same test form for each administration, meaning that some gains could be attributed simply to students' increased familiarity with the test items.[50]

In the end, MCT efforts appeared to have mixed effects. On the bright side, they helped to spur an upgrade in the quality of high school curricula and appeared to contribute to heightened post–high school employment. More negatively, they helped reduce high school completion rates, especially among black students, and had a negative impact on the degree to which students read for pleasure. These effects tended to be of a limited nature, befitting the modest scope of most MCT programs. (For a more detailed discussion of the impact of MCT policies, see chapter 10 in this volume.)

Minimum competency testing never went away so much as it gradually dissipated into another ineffectual educational routine. During the next decade, first the National Commission on Education's 1983 report *A Nation at Risk* and then a raft of reformers would demand tougher graduation standards. These reformers dismissed minimum competency tests as irrelevant or counterproductive and called for more rigorous, demanding, systematic approaches to accountability. By the 1990s, efforts to promote substantive testing systems and graduation exams enjoyed widespread success, and surveys suggested that the public claimed to be willing to back stiff sanctions.[51]

Conclusions

It is not clear whether the NCLB legislation and the dozens of independent state efforts to promote accountability will transform the performance of the nation's schools, or whether they will instead produce the kinds of marginal adjustment prompted by the MCT effort three decades ago. Will testing proponents be able to fend off the compromises and challenges posed by groups hostile to coercive accountability? That will depend not only upon the strength and intensity of the opposition to accountability-based reform, but also upon the strength of their legislative allies, the activity of the pro-accountability lobby, and the degree to which implementation of painful measures is insulated from mobilized unrest.

From the inception of high-stakes testing, proponents tend to laud the requisite tests and accompanying systems as clear, scientifically defensible, manageable, and concise. Critics typically attack the tests and systems as unreliable, simplistic, overly focused on trivia, or lacking the necessary curricular and pedagogical support. In truth, both sides are correct. Because proponents find this a tough concession to make, however, they often seek to meet the concerns of critics by trying to tweak systems without refining them into irrelevance.[52] For instance, adjusting required scores or giving students multiple chances to pass the test can be a useful and appropriate exercise, or doing so can risk undermining the very purpose of transformative accountability. Adding essay questions can usefully broaden assessment; it also renders scoring more subjective and can sometimes make the cost of testing prohibitive. Giving students five or eight chances to pass a test can ensure that no one is denied a diploma because of ill fortune and gives students the incentive and opportunity to improve their performance. It can also undermine the system by permitting students to tiptoe through on the basis of the one test they took on which they caught all the breaks.

The effect of such refinements depends largely on the context in which they take place. The crucial component is the willingness of a majority of voters and officials to tolerate state sanctions on students or educators. Building a stable, rigorous accountability system is far easier when the public will shrug off five thousand students denied diplomas or fifty schools reconstituted than when it will accept only a fraction of that number. The effect of public sensitivity is directly analogous to the manner in which the public's willingness to accept military casualties constrains national security officials as they consider military deployment.

At any given level of public resolve (or callousness, depending on one's perspective), behavioral and institutional factors may help or hinder efforts to erect substantive accountability systems. The relative strength of proponents and opposition groups, and the insulation of educational decisionmakers from public opinion, may determine the fate of any given accountability effort.

A tendency exists to recoil from the real costs of high-stakes accountability, thus producing a series of well-intentioned compromises that leave the façade of accountability intact but strip its motive power. Andrew Rudalevige, in chapter 2 of this volume, documents the degree to which this dynamic was on public display during the negotiations over NCLB, as efforts to precisely map testing requirements, performance expectations, and sanctions were repeatedly blunted by demands that legislators avoid draconian measures and devise a flexible system. The compromises produced an impressive-looking bill, but one in which the effects on schools and students depend largely on how the Department of Education chooses to implement the legislation's often ambiguous provisions.

Proponents have difficulty standing firm on the details of any particular accountability system because essential components relating to content, testing, passing scores, and sanctions are inherently arbitrary. The closer one gets to crafting and enforcing standards the less defensible specific program elements can appear. In the end, standards are a useful artifice. Determining what students need to know, when they need to know it, and how well they need to know it is an ambiguous and value-laden exercise. Neither developmental psychologists nor psychometricians can prove that specified content ought to be taught at particular grade levels. Such decisions are imperfect, publicly rendered judgments about the needs and capacities of children. Because public schooling requires public officials to make these judgments and impose them statewide, these difficult questions inevitably become political ones.

While the push for coercive accountability generates fierce opposition, the political dynamic may reverse once these systems are institutionalized. Experience suggests that high-stakes exams, once in place for a sufficient period, become part of the "grammar of schooling" for educators, parents, and voters.[53] The existence of a widely accepted assessment regime can be useful to educators and public officials, permitting schools to concretely demonstrate performance and strengthen their claim on public support and resources. Over time, the diffuse benefits of accountability become more evident. When high-stakes accountability is institutionalized, the tests become accepted as the unquestioned gold standard for measuring performance and all involved parties adjust their behavior accordingly. Then, opponents of high-stakes testing find themselves in the unenviable position of attacking an established system that helps to ensure that students are learning, teachers are teaching, and schools are serving their public purpose.

The result is a cyclical dance, in which reformers race to institutionalize the regime before resistance leads officials to start dismantling it. In this frantic waltz, proponents of high-stakes reform have generally utilized some combination of four approaches to policymaking. The most common approach is to offer compromises and system-softening measures. Reformers can reduce the size and scope of losers by shrinking the number of students, teachers, and schools that will be labeled inadequate by a test, reducing the real consequences of being deemed inadequate, or both. This builds comfort with accountability, but it does so by lowering standards and by rendering them less significant—a price that reformers may not be willing to pay.

Proponents can also seek to set initially low passing thresholds and then gradually ratchet them up. Such an approach gives all parties a chance to gradually become acclimated to standards and can soften the resistance of critics—who find far less to get exercised about in the initial years of reform. By the time that standards are raised to more significant levels, critics may have difficulty overcoming the more accepting position they have staked out. This was the course that Texas adopted, with much success, in its efforts to enhance its much-noted accountability effort in 1990 and in 1993. In 1990, when Texas adopted the TAAS tests, it dropped the required passing score to 60 percent from the 70 percent that had been the norm under the older

Texas Education Assessment of Minimum Skills (TEAMS) system. This ensured that 80–90 percent, not 40–50 percent, of students passed the tests, squelching an anticipated public outcry. In 1993 Texas began to grade schools based on the percentage of students passing the TAAS—but initially required only that 40 percent of students pass for a school to be rated "acceptable." This figure was increased over time, but the low initial requirement helped to dampen opposition. This approach can backfire, however, as proponents who settle for initially weak legislation may have trouble later raising the bar.

A third approach is to seek to make the status quo so frightening that voters will demand change and reward officials who resist efforts to weaken reforms. A number of reformers in various states have sought to employ this *A Nation at Risk* strategy, with mixed success. The approach can alter the terms of the debate, though it is difficult to whip up a widespread sense of crisis or to sustain one for an extended period. This limits the effectiveness of the approach. In Virginia, Republicans used this approach in 1993 to generate support for the measures that would constitute the state's SOL accountability system. Gubernatorial candidate George Allen attacked his predecessor's reform efforts as a value-laden, costly effort to dumb down academic standards and contrasted them with his call for higher standards and more accountability. He pointed to declining NAEP and SAT scores and a high failure rate among sixth graders on the state's Literacy Passport Test to help spur a sense of crisis.[54] This tack, too, can prove hazardous to proponents, as it can be seen as an assault on public education and educators, alienating centrist voters and mobilizing the opposition.

Finally, proponents can seek to make standards more palatable to educators by tamping down the leading source of opposition. One way to do this is to accelerate the turnover of teachers and administrators while ensuring that new personnel are familiarized with standards and high-stakes testing as a condition for their entry into the field. This increases the percentage of teachers trained and acculturated in an environment where high-stakes accountability is the norm. Similarly, encouraging districts to recruit more entrepreneurial administrators and to train them in the strategies of outcome-based management will help to reduce educator opposition to standards, to make the transition to standards-based schools an easier one, and to foster the ranks of public educators who are supportive of transformative accountability.

The effectiveness of high-stakes accountability rests upon the willingness of public officials to institutionalize a number of subjective decisions. Linking meaningful consequences to these decisions has the power to fundamentally transform schooling, especially in those schools where a reliance on educator magnanimity has failed to serve the interests of the students. Such outcomes, however, require standing firm on a series of decisions that will visit harm and inequity upon some students and teachers. The question is whether proponents of high-stakes accountability are willing and able to sustain the support required to institutionalize the proposed reforms.

During the past three decades, voters have evinced a growing willingness to tolerate some of the costs of accountability. This raises the possibility that ongoing efforts will deliver the substantive change that has often proved elusive. While testing regimes have come and gone rapidly, even in states with relatively stable systems, a growing willingness is apparent on the part of voters and public officials to stand fast in the face of inequities and concentrated costs that sank earlier accountability efforts. Public information, political efforts by pro-accountability forces, concern about school performance, a weakening attachment to local control in education, and comfort with increasingly sophisticated testing technologies all appear to be gradually shifting the center of public opinion.

A number of states seem committed to testing all students, even those with special needs. These states appear increasingly willing to deny diplomas to thousands of graduates—whereas earlier accountability efforts faltered when they were on the verge of denying diplomas to mere hundreds. NCLB offers an impersonal club that state officials can point to when making hard decisions and may deliver the authority to sanction schools and districts to national officials more insulated from local unrest than are their state counterparts. Nonetheless, legislators and policymakers have generally tiptoed up to implementation, only to declare a need for delays or further refinement. How effectively reformers in the various states and in Washington will negotiate demands for compromise is a question that can only be answered in the fullness of time.

Notes

1. For a discussion of some of these technical issues and the problems they can present in using accountability assessments as coercive instruments, see Dale Ballou, "Sizing Up Test Scores," *Education Next*, vol. 2, no. 2 (2002), pp. 10–15.

2. For a clear depiction of how coercive accountability is expected to work, see Jay Greene, "The Business Model," *Education Next*, vol. 2, no. 2 (2002), pp. 20–22.

3. Charles A. Dana Center, "Equity-Driven Achievement-Focused School Districts: A Report on Systemic School Success in Four Texas School Districts Serving Diverse Student Populations" (University of Texas at Austin, 2000) (www.utdanacenter.org/research/reports/equitydistricts.pdf [July 10, 2003]).

4. Stela B. Holcombe, "High Stakes: School Leaders Weigh In on Testing, Reform, and the Goal of Educating Every American Child," *Ed.*, vol. 46, no. 1 (2002), p. 20.

5. California Teachers Association, "Bush's Voucher Plan, U.S. High-Stakes Testing Idea Would Hurt California's and Nation's Public Schools," January 24, 2001 (www.cta.org/news/news_archive/bush_voucher.html [April 25, 2002]).

6. For a thoughtful discussion of this tendency for public schools to try to be all things to all people, see Arthur G. Powell, Eleanor Farrar, and David K. Cohen, *The Shopping Mall High School: Winners and Losers in the Educational Marketplace* (Boston: Houghton Mifflin, 1985).

7. Standards may affect curriculum and pedagogy in different ways. Standards presume that curricular content ought to be shaped by statewide officials, not individual classroom teachers. There is no similar presumption requiring the standardization of pedagogy. Instead, accountability systems will likely reward any teacher who is able to produce impressive outcomes. While some pedagogies will prove more effective than others at producing the desired results, effective teachers need not adopt any particular approach so long as they produce acceptable outcomes.

8. For impassioned discussions of the costs linked to high-stakes accountability, see recent books by Alfie Kohn, *The Case against Standardized Testing: Raising the Scores, Ruining the Schools* (Portsmouth, N.H.: Heineman, 2000); Linda M. McNeil, *Contradictions of School Reform: Educational Costs of Standardized Testing* (New York: Routledge, 2000); and Susan Ohanian, *One Size Fits Few: The Folly of Educational Standards* (Portsmouth, N.H.: Heinemann, 1999). For a more nuanced consideration of the ways in which accountability systems may change teacher behavior and classroom practice, see Brian M. Stecher and Laura S. Hamilton, "Putting Theory to the Test: Systems of 'Educational Accountability' Should Be Held Accountable," *RAND Review*, vol. 26, no. 1 (2002), pp. 17–23.

9. Surveys find that adults overwhelmingly support standards and accountability in the abstract but begin to express doubts when it comes to putting high-stakes standards into practice. For instance, Public Agenda has reported that roughly eight in ten Americans believe it wrong to base grade promotion or graduation on standardized tests. This hesitance stems from the fact that two-thirds or more of Americans express concern that some students do not test well, that testing cannot measure all the skills children should learn, and that too much reliance on testing will cause teachers to focus too heavily on tested material. See Public Agenda, *Questionnaire and Fall Survey Results: National Poll of Parents of Public School Students* (New York: Public Agenda Foundation, 2000).

10. Audrey L. Amrein and David C. Berliner, "High-Stakes Testing, Uncertainty, and Student Learning," *Education Policy Analysis Archives*, vol. 10, no. 18 (2002) (epaa.asu.edu/epaa/v10n18/ [May 23, 2002]).

11. Massachusetts Department of Education, "MCAS Appeals Process Unanimously Approved," press release, January 23, 2002; and Christina A. Samuels, "Va. Offers SOL Appeals Process for 3 Classes," *Washington Post*, July 26, 2002, p. B1.

12. Perhaps not surprisingly, legislators have been much more willing to move quickly when implementing systems of rewards for teachers or schools.

13. Jacques Steinberg, "Student Failure Causes States to Retool Testing Programs," *New York Times,* December 22, 2000, p. A1.

14. Darcia Harris Bowman, "Turf War Erupts in Ariz. over Delaying Graduation Test," *Education Week*, April 4, 2001, p. 21.

15. Julie Blair, "Wisconsin Legislators Approve Revised Plan for Graduation Exam," *Education Week*, October 20, 1999, p. 17.

16. Lynn Olson, "Indiana Case Focuses on Special Ed," *Education Week*, May 31, 2000, pp. 1, 14–15.

17. For instance, the delegates to the 2001 National Education Association annual convention voted to oppose mandatory national testing—with or without attached consequences—and to support state legislation that permits parents to let their children skip standardized tests.

18. The value of coercive accountability can be justified despite such concerns, as Jay Greene has argued, but it is neither an easy nor an alluring argument for a public official to make. See Greene, "The Business Model."

19. For the classic treatment of the resultant "school house" culture, see Dan C. Lortie, *Schoolteacher: A Sociological Study* (University of Chicago Press, 1975).

20. Ed Hayward, "State Kicks Off $500G Campaign to Boost Public Support of MCAS," *Boston Herald*, April 4, 2001, p. 12.

21. Lynn Olson, "States Adjust High-Stakes Testing Plans," *Education Week*, January 24, 2001, pp. 1, 18–19.

22. Anand Vaishnav, "Teachers, in Poll, Fault MCAS Mandate," *Boston Globe* April 9, 2001, p. B2.

23. The fact that so many minority and low-income children are ill served by their current schools helps to explain why leaders of these groups emerge on both sides of the high-stakes accountability discussion. While some leaders voice concerns about the inequitable impact of sanctions, others applaud the fact that educators are being forced to effectively serve students they previously overlooked.

24. For a classic discussion, see R. Doug Arnold, *The Logic of Congressional Action* (Yale University Press, 1990).

25. National Research Council, *High Stakes: Testing for Tracking, Promotion, and Graduation* (Washington: National Academy Press, 1999), p. 45.

26. Kathleen Kennedy Manzo, "More Than Half of California 9th Graders Flunk Exit Exam," *Education Week*, June 20, 2001, p. 19.

27. FairTest, "End the Racist Tests, City Schools Deserve the Best," press release, May 8, 2001.

28. Steve Rauscher, "MCAS Opponents Rip Test as 'Arbitrary' at Gathering," *Boston Herald*, March 25, 2001, p. 16.

29. Brian M. Stecher and others, *The Effects of the Washington State Education Reform on Schools and Classrooms: Initial Findings*, RAND/DB–309-EDU (Santa Monica, Calif.: RAND, 2000).

30. For a useful, though ideologically colored, account of how this tension produced conservative backlash against high-stakes accountability in the early 1990s, see FairTest, "Right Wing Attacks Performance Assessment," *Examiner*, vol. 8, no. 3 (Summer 1994), pp. 1, 10–11.

31. Bill Honig and Francie Alexander, 1996, "Re-Writing the Tests: Lessons from the California State Assessment System," in *95th NSSE Yearbook*, part I (University of Chicago Press, 1996), pp. 143–65, esp. pp. 157–59.

32. The social studies standards encompassed the disciplines of civics, geography, economics, and history, but history was the source of most conflict.

33. Teresa Lemons Coleman, "Social Studies: 'A Long Shot,' " *Richmond Times-Dispatch*, June 18, 1995, p. A1.

34. See John E. Chubb and Terry M. Moe, *Politics, Markets, and America's Schools* (Brookings, 1990), pp. 26–47, for a particularly nice discussion of this point in the context of education.

35. As the Republican Party has sought to aggressively court Hispanic voters in recent years, it has grown more sensitive to the displeasure of Hispanic leaders.

36. See Frederick M. Hess and David L. Leal, "Republican Party Growth in Southern Legislative Elections," *Virginia Newsletter*, vol. 75, no. 4 (1999), pp. 1–4.

37. Don McAdams, *Fighting to Save Our Urban Schools . . . and Winning! Lessons from Houston* (New York: Teachers College Press, 2000), pp. 71–73.

38. The board of education also voted to endorse Chairman Jim Peyser's suggestion that it commit itself to raising the required score in future years.

39. Jeri J. Goldman, "Political and Legal Issues in Minimum Competency Testing," *Educational Forum*, vol. 48 (Winter 1984), pp. 207–16.

40. Goldman, "Political and Legal Issues in Minimum Competency Testing," p. 208.

41. Chris Pipho, "Stateline," *Phi Delta Kappan*, vol. 78, no. 9 (May 1997), pp. 673–74.

42. Darryl Paulson and Doris Ball, "Back to Basics: Minimum Competency Testing and Its Impact on Minorities," *Urban Education*, vol. 19, no. 1 (1984), pp. 5–15.

43. For instance, a study of initial minimum competency testing (MCT) passing rates during 1978–81 in four states with heterogeneous populations (California, Florida, North Carolina, Virginia) showed that black students fared between 10 and 43 percentage points worse than did white students, depending on the subject and the state. Robert C. Serow, "Effects of Minimum Competency Testing for Minority Students: A Review of Expectations and Outcomes," *Urban Review*, vol. 16, no. 2 (1984), pp. 67–75.

44. Martha M.McCarthy, "Minimum Competency Testing for Students: Educational and Legal Issues," *Educational Horizons*, vol. 61 (Spring 1983), pp. 103–10.

45. Pipho, "Stateline," pp. 673–74, esp. p. 673.

46. Stanley J. Vitello, "Handicapped Students and Competency Testing," *Remedial and Special Education*, vol. 9 (September/October 1988), pp. 22–27.

47. Robert C. Serow, "Effects of Minimum Competency Testing for Minority Students: A Review of Expectations and Outcomes," *Urban Review*, vol. 16, no. 2 (1984), pp. 67–75, esp. p. 71.

48. William B. Walstad, "Analzying Minimal Competency Test Performance," *Journal of Educational Research*, vol. 77 (May/June 1984), pp. 261–66.

49. Goldman, "Political and Legal Issues in Minimum Competency Testing."

50. Thomas M. Haladyna, Susan B. Nolsen, and Nancy S. Haas, "Raising Standardized Achievement Test Scores and the Origins of Test Score Pollution," *Educational Researcher*, vol. 20, no. 5 (June/July 1991), pp. 2–7.

51. See Public Agenda, *Questionnaire and Fall Survey Results: National Poll of Parents of Public School Students* (New York: Public Agenda Foundation, 2000).

52. When American Federation of Teachers (AFT) president Sandra Feldman denounced testing proponents at the union's 2001 national convention for failing to provide teachers with the necessary texts and teaching materials, she framed her remarks as a reasonable caution while implicitly advocating an open-ended suspension of coercive accountability measures. The irony is that Feldman's AFT has officially endorsed the use of high-stakes testing for graduation and promotion decisions.

53. See David B. Tyack and William Tobin, "The Grammar of Schooling: Why Has It Been So Hard to Change," *American Educational Research Journal*, vol. 31 (1994), pp. 453–79.

54. The Allen effort was perceived by political opponents as an assault on public schooling. As Virginia Education Association president Rob Jones said in February 1995, "I think there's been a deliberate attempt to make public schools the battleground. People have defamed the public schools for political gain." See Ruth S. Intress, "Education Battle Waged for Money, Control," *Richmond Times-Dispatch*, February 26, 1995, p. A10.

4

Politics, Control, and the Future of School Accountability

TERRY M. MOE

Over the last ten years or so, the movement for school accountability has taken the nation by storm. Its message is a simple one. The public schools should have strong academic standards; tests should be administered to determine what students are learning; and students, as well as the adults responsible for teaching them, should be held accountable for meeting the standards.

This message is an easy sell, especially during a time when improving the public schools is a national priority. So there can be little surprise that reformers pressing for school accountability have found a receptive audience in the American public, and little surprise that policymakers have fallen all over themselves to endorse accountability as a key means of promoting better schools.

In state after state, governments have imposed new curriculum standards, new tests aligned to the standards, new requirements for promotion and graduation, new rules for ranking schools and publicizing test scores, and new systems of rewards and sanctions. And the action is not just at the state level. President Bill Clinton seized on the accountability issue in framing a federal education agenda through the Goals 2000 program, national standards, and national teacher certification. And President George W. Bush, a Republican not otherwise given to federal intervention, followed up by making his No Child Left Behind legislation a centerpiece of his domestic program—imposing, for the first time, a national accountability system of annual testing and performance-based rewards and sanctions.[1]

Accountability is clearly an issue with legs. But can it take us where we want to go? The presumption of the accountability movement is that it can. Yet this is just a presumption backed by common sense, and a thin reed on which to hang billions of dollars' worth of reforms, not to mention the nation's educational future.

So what should we expect from this effort to improve the schools by holding them accountable for their performance? The issue is complicated, and I don't pretend to have all the answers. But I do think there is much to be gained by looking beyond the complexities (or at least not getting distracted by them) and focusing on simple fundamentals. Two are particularly important. The first is that school accountability is an exercise in top-down control. The second is that it is a product of democratic politics. I believe it is mainly by exploring these two basic dimensions of the issue, and by recognizing the distinctive problems associated with each, that we can learn what to expect from school accountability. And whether it can take us where we want to go.

The Problem of Control

The movement for school accountability is essentially a movement for more effective top-down control of the schools. The idea is that, if public authorities want to promote student achievement, they need to adopt organizational control mechanisms—tests, school report cards, rewards and sanctions, and the like—designed to get district officials, principals, teachers, and students to change their behavior in productive ways.

As a general matter, there is nothing unusual about this. Virtually all organizations need to engage in top-down control, because the people at the top have goals they want the people at the bottom to pursue, and something has to be done to bring about the desired behaviors. The public school system is just like other organizations in this respect, and top-down control is routinely exercised with respect to all manner of educational policies, programs, and directives day in and day out. The only thing different about today's accountability movement is that the political authorities are putting the emphasis on student achievement—which they had not done before—and on control mechanisms designed to bring it about.

Principals, Agents, and the Logic of Control

When political scientists and economists think about issues of control (and institutions generally), they usually rely on economic theories of organization, ranging from agency theory to transaction cost economics to information economics to the economics of personnel.[2] Much of this literature is technical and specialized. But its basic ideas are simple, having to do with incentives and information, and they offer useful guidance in thinking about school accountability.

For heuristic purposes, I will frame my discussion with reference to the classic agency model. This model is built around a principal-agent relationship, in which a principal who wants to attain certain goals hires an agent to act on his behalf. This kind of relationship is ubiquitous throughout society. People hire doctors to treat their health problems and mechanics to fix their cars. Employers hire workers to manufacture their products. Legislatures hire public bureaucracies to carry out governmental programs. States hire administrators and teachers to educate children.[3]

As these examples suggest, principal-agent relationships are common because they are beneficial and necessary. Principals of all kinds lack the time or capacity to do everything for themselves. And often their agents have expertise that enables them to do a far better job of pursuing the principals' goals than the principals themselves could do.

There is also a downside to these relationships, however, owing to two basic problems. The first is that the agent inevitably has his own interests—in income, career, leisure, family, ideology, policy, or whatever—that tug him in other directions and give him incentives not to pursue the principal's goals with efficiency and dedication. The second is that the agent tends to have information that the principal does not have. The latter stands to be poorly informed, for instance, about how the agent performs on the job, because many of his actions may not be observable with much precision. Moreover, the principal may have a hard time observing what type of agent he is dealing with—low ability or high ability, lazy or hardworking, trustworthy or not—and cannot readily determine whom to hire, fire, or depend upon.[4]

These information asymmetries put the principal at a disadvantage. It is not just that he does not know certain things about the agent's type or behavior, which is bad enough. It is also that the agent does know these things and can use this private information to his advantage—allowing him (if he wants) to slack off in pursuit of the principal's goals and substitute his own interests in the performance of his job, all the while giving the appearance of being a good agent.

This sets up the basic control problem. What can the principal do, given the problems inherent in their relationship, to get the agent to work as efficiently as possible toward the right goals? The precise solution, not surprisingly, can vary depending on the circumstances. But it generally involves

—the measurement of agent performance;

—the use of screening and signaling devices to reveal information about agent type; and

—the design of compensation schemes, usually involving pay for performance, that brings the agent's interests into alignment with the principal's and gives him incentives to be productive.

In the real world of government and business, these control mechanisms will not work perfectly, and there may be a great deal of slippage between what superiors want and what agents actually do. Indeed, even if the mechanisms are reasonably effective, the simple fact that they are costly to design and enforce means that superiors will have incentives to use them only up to the point at which the costs begin to outweigh the benefits of compliance, allowing some and perhaps a great deal of noncompliant behavior to continue unabated. At some point, noncompliance becomes too expensive to deal with.

In short, then, while there are clearly things the principal can do to get agents to work productively on his behalf, control is imperfect and noncompliance is to be expected. The fact is that his agents have interests that are different from his, they have critical information that he does not have, and he can do only so much to overcome these problems.

School Accountability as a Control Problem

Now let's put this framework to use in gaining perspective on school accountability. State and federal authorities are the principals, whose goal (we'll assume for now) is to promote student achievement and better schools. Their agents are the school administrators and teachers who actually do the educating. Students might be considered agents, too, but I want to focus here on the people who run the schools.

What motivates these people? The answer varies from person to person, but it is a sure bet that teachers and other school personnel—however much they care about children and however public-spirited they may be—have value structures that reach well beyond the goals of the public school system. Like other employees throughout the economy, they care about their own incomes and careers, security, leisure, family, professional norms, and a host of other things. And these values will inevitably come into conflict with what the authorities want them to do, giving them incentives to avoid full compliance. This does not happen because they are bad people. It happens because they are normal people, people whose interests do not line up perfectly with the goals of their superiors.[5]

This said, there are good reasons for thinking that the motivation for noncompliance is especially strong in public education. The fact is, the authori-

ties are faced with a school system that has been in existence for about a century now but has never really been held accountable for student achievement.
This long-standing lack of accountability is heavily reflected in the modern
structure. With few exceptions, for instance, there is no connection between
how much students learn and how much anyone gets paid. Lousy teachers
get paid just as much as terrific teachers, and bureaucrats get their salaries
whether they promote student achievement or not. Virtually all these jobs are
highly secure, and school employees do not have to worry about losing them
if they happen to be bad at what they do. Teachers, who of all employees
have the greatest influence on student learning, are so heavily protected by
civil service and union rules that those who are mediocre or even incompetent are almost never removed from their jobs.[6]

The existing system is also built around delegation to experts. From the
early 1900s on, educational leaders worked hard to convince political authorities and the general public that education is a highly technical business that
needs to be put in expert hands—their own hands—if it is to be carried out
effectively. This strategy worked well, and throughout the last century the
authorities have relied heavily on administrators to guide them on matters of
education policy and operation. While modern times have produced an ava-
lanche of federal and state programs—and rules—that constrain local autonomy, the tradition of deference to experts remains strong. The belief among
administrators is that they should be able to carry out their work as they see
fit. And a variation on the same theme is embraced by teachers, who want to
be regarded as professionals and who want their own expertise respected and
deferred to.[7]

As political authorities attempt to bring accountability to the public
schools, then, they encounter a workplace filled with agents who have had
their expectations and values shaped by the existing system—in which they
have substantial autonomy, their pay and jobs are secure, and they are not
held accountable for their performance. Indeed, it is likely that these properties were part of what attracted many of them to the education system in the
first place, and that those who have stayed for more than several years
(instead of leaving for other careers) are people who have found these properties particularly to their liking.

This is an important point, and it needs to be followed up by another
that, while uncomfortable for educators to face up to, needs to be recognized
in any objective analysis. The follow-up point is that the public school system may suffer from a serious problem of adverse selection—namely, that its
job characteristics have not only attracted certain types of people to work for
the school system, but have actually attracted the *wrong* types and repelled

the right types. It is an established result in the economics of personnel, for example, that an organization that does not reward productive performance will be especially attractive to workers who are less productive (less able, less hardworking), while the more productive workers will seek out opportunities elsewhere, in organizations that recognize their worth and reward them for it. By the same logic, an organization that gives its workers complete job security—in exchange, say, for less pay than they might earn elsewhere—will tend to attract workers who are highly risk-averse and security-conscious, while workers who are more open to risk (because they are more talented or confident or ambitious or innovative) will often find other opportunities more attractive. Thus, to the extent that these forces have been operating within the public school system—and it is difficult to believe they haven't been—the current system is probably filled with teachers and administrators who are the wrong types.[8]

I suspect the adverse selection problem is serious and creates major obstacles to reform. But even if it were not, reformers are still likely to meet with stiff resistance. For even if everyone agrees that student achievement is a laudable goal, the agents clearly have other values that are important to them as well—values nurtured by the current system—and these values are deeply threatened by an accountability reform that erodes their autonomy, shakes up their comfortable arrangements for jobs and pay, and demands that they work differently, work harder, and produce more. Such changes will not be welcome.

Resistance is likely to be all the stronger because teachers, the most numerous and important of all school employees, are represented by powerful unions dedicated to the protection of teacher interests (and union interests as well). Other employees are similarly represented by unions and professional associations. As a result, the resistance of employees to top-down control does not simply arise from the separate, uncoordinated responses of individuals. It also arises from the organized activities of powerful groups: which, like their members, see most aspects of school accountability as undesirable and threatening.

The prospects for control look still worse when we recognize that, as in the classic principal-agent model, there is an information asymmetry here that works to the disadvantage of the authorities. The key factors of interest—how much students are learning, how productive teachers are—are difficult for the authorities to observe, and the administrators and teachers who run the schools have far better information on these scores. They are also repositories of expertise on everything from curriculum to teaching methods to school organization, which are matters the authorities need to understand to make wise decisions.

So, as even these simple considerations suggest, the authorities are up against a control problem of formidable proportions. They do not know how to produce student achievement, nor do they necessarily know student achievement when they see it. But they must try to design a control structure that gets a resistant group of employees to apply their expertise in all the right ways to generate the desired outcomes. Over the last decade, the authorities have sought to do this through regimes of standards, tests, and rewards and sanctions. They are fighting an uphill battle, though, and their prospects for success are not bright.

The basic reasons are already apparent, but let me tie them more specifically to the key components of an accountability system.

STANDARDS. The authorities may want to promote student learning, but what the precise content of that learning should be is unclear (even to experts). It follows that standard setting—the task of measuring the authorities' goals—is hardly an objective process even for well-defined subjects like math and science, not to mention subjects like history and social studies, in which experts regularly go to war over what content is important and how it should be interpreted.[9]

By fiat or compromise, reasonable standards can be settled upon. But there is nothing definitive about them; and because this is so, children may fail according to one set of standards and succeed according to another. So have they succeeded or failed? And have their teachers succeeded or failed in teaching them? These sorts of ambiguities, pervading as they do the very foundations of the accountability system, can only breed trouble for the exercise of control. And they invite manipulation by those with incentives to resist.

TESTS. The next step is to devise tests that measure how well students are meeting the standards. Specialists have been working since the early 1900s on the technology of testing, and a great deal is known about how to do it well. The most familiar objections—that multiple-choice tests cannot measure what students know, that tests are culturally biased—are exaggerated. Many other objections, moreover, are not criticisms of testing per se. Sometimes they are complaints that the wrong kinds of tests are being used (for example, nationally normed achievement tests rather than tests geared to state standards). Sometimes they are complaints that the underlying standards are too vague or do not take into account the full range of important things that schools do. And sometimes they are complaints about how tests are linked to rewards and sanctions. These legitimate issues make accountability more difficult. But they give no reason to think that standardized tests cannot provide useful measures of student achievement.[10]

This said, a flaw in the conventional testing process threatens the validity of the entire enterprise. This is that tests are routinely administered by teachers and local administrators, the very people (aside from students) whose performance is being measured. They have incentives to cheat, and their traditional autonomy in school affairs gives them ample opportunity to do so: by previewing the exams, by feeding kids answers, by doctoring answer sheets, by keeping low-scoring students from taking the exams, and so on. Until the testing process is placed in independent hands, the tests will be subject to self-serving manipulation and their value for accountability undermined.[11]

CONSEQUENCES. While measurement is hardly straightforward, the most serious problems do not arise from measurement itself. They arise from attempts to use the resulting measures (standards, tests) to evaluate school personnel and attach consequences to their behavior. For most organizations, there are two purposes for doing this sort of thing. One is that it provides a basis for hiring productive employees and weeding out or retraining unproductive ones. The other is that it provides employees with incentives to do a good job.[12] Accountability systems are likely to prove disappointing, however, on both counts.

For starters, the authorities inherit a population of agents whose values and expectations have been shaped by the existing system's guaranteed security and lack of emphasis on performance—and for the foreseeable future, they are stuck with these people. Even if the accountability system produced excellent measures of performance that allowed low-productivity workers to be identified, tenure and unions would prevent the authorities from weeding them out. This is a problem of the first magnitude for any accountability system.

Once in place, new compensation schemes and performance pressures may accelerate the voluntary departures of workers who are the wrong types and induce more workers of the right types to sign up. But this will take time. And here, too, current structures get in the way. All states currently require teachers to be certified (or, if hired on an emergency basis, to become certified eventually), but there is no good evidence that certification promotes student achievement. Thus certification drastically limits the pool of potential hires, with no payoff in productivity.[13] Accountability reforms typically do nothing about this; indeed, many reformers believe that stricter certification is called for. The upshot is that the replacement of less productive by more productive workers is likely to be much slower than it would otherwise be—and accountability more difficult.

These problems aside, how well can we expect an accountability system to provide the right incentives? Typically, the best way to generate high-powered incentives is by attaching consequences to performance, and the most obvious way to do this is through some form of performance pay in which teachers and administrators are compensated (at least in part) according to their success in promoting student achievement. Devising a pay-for-performance regime that has the desired results, however, is not easy. Here are a few reasons why.[14]

First, the extent to which pay should be linked to performance depends on how well the latter can be measured. The more uncertain or inaccurate the measures, the more the authorities should rely (in part) on other forms of pay—for example, straight salary coupled with subjective evaluations. The challenge is to strike the right balance, which is difficult.

Second, with performance pay, you get what you pay for. If performance is measured by X, then performance pay will induce employees to produce X even if X turns out to be little related to the organization's goal. This is what testing critics are getting at when they argue that teachers will "teach to the test" without regard for whether students really learn the material.

Third, test scores are heavily influenced by the students' social backgrounds and are not straightforward measures of teacher and administrator performance. If pay-for-performance is to work productively, employees must be held accountable only for their own impacts on student achievement, which requires a more complicated approach to measurement that factors out other influences. There are various ways to do this (through statistical controls, for instance, or value-added scores), but these methods are not straightforward either and raise new problems and controversies. Precise measurement is elusive.[15]

Fourth, test scores tend to rise for several years after a new testing regime is first put in place, but this happens because of growing familiarity with the test, not because students are learning more.[16] Especially during the early years of an accountability system, then, test scores are likely to give a misleading impression of improved performance.

Finally, if organizational goals are multidimensional—in this case, the teaching of academics, but also of tolerance, democratic citizenship, music and art, and so on—then performance pay based on just one of these dimensions (academic achievement) will cause employees to focus all their attention on that one dimension and shift it away from the others. If the authorities value these other dimensions, too, they need to design accountability systems that, while promoting achievement, do not push the schools to ignore everything else.

These problems are daunting enough. But the reality of American education reform raises additional obstacles, because pay-for-performance is never seriously pursued or carefully designed in practice. Instead, the typical accountability system involves rewards and sanctions that are poorly conceived, and whose impacts on employee incentives are not nearly as productive as they might be.[17]

When rewards for good performance are involved, for example, they often go to the school as a whole. As such, they constitute a collective good that, as in any context of team production, gives employees little incentive to work harder. Incentives are diluted even further if, as is often the case, rewards take the form of additional operating funds for the school instead of money that goes into people's pockets.[18]

Sanctions (if any) for bad performance usually involve state intervention or reconstitution. But these are irrelevant to the vast majority of schools and employees and have no impact on their incentives. Furthermore, they are not well suited to solving performance problems even in the rare cases when they are invoked. States can intervene, for example, but they may know less about running the schools than local employees do, and the latter's incentives remain roughly the same: no jobs are lost, and everyone still gets paid for being unproductive. Reconstitution is more threatening, as teachers and principals in the affected schools do "lose" their jobs. But because their jobs are guaranteed within the district, the unproductive employees are simply foisted onto other schools, where they can continue to be unproductive and receive their usual salaries—which is bad for the other schools. Moreover, the "new" employees in the reconstituted schools, probably drawn from elsewhere in the district, continue to be compensated regardless of how well they perform and have incentives that are just as weak as the employees they replaced. In the end, the reconstituted schools may wind up with employees who are higher in average ability, but the rest of the schools will have their average ability levels lowered, and everyone's incentives remain basically the same. This is a strategy of rearranging the deck chairs.

Another favorite approach—sometimes misdescribed as sanctioning—involves singling out low-performing schools and providing them with additional resources and services (such as training) to turn them around. Here, again, the vast majority of schools and employees are unaffected, with no greater incentive to improve. And even in the low-performing schools, there is no positive effect on employee incentives. Indeed, as additional resources and services are desirable to them, any change in incentives could be perverse, with employees essentially being rewarded for their poor performance and having every reason to continue their unproductive ways.

This is not a pretty picture. The belief that the public schools can be held accountable for their performance, and that it can be done successfully through a system of standards, testing, and consequences, may seem to provide a reasonable agenda for improving the nation's schools. But common sense is often a poor guide to public policy, and that is the case here—even if we ignore all the political problems that, as I'll argue below, accountability is likely to run into.

Considered purely as an issue of top-down control, accountability is a very difficult proposition. The authorities face a population of agents who are not of their own choosing, whose jobs are securely protected, who have strong incentives to resist accountability, and whose actions cannot easily be observed. And all this stacks the deck against effective control, particularly given the unimpressive mechanisms the authorities have chosen to rely upon. This does not mean that accountability reforms cannot lead to somewhat better outcomes for schools and students. It simply means that the results are likely to be disappointing.

The Problem of Politics

Reformers face more than a control problem. They also face a political problem, which arises from the simple fact that public schools are agencies of democratic government. As government bodies, everything about their structure and operation, including whether and how they are held accountable, is subject to determination through the political process—and the actors that carry the most weight in that process are not necessarily interested in creating accountability systems that work. That is the problem.

The Political Power of the Agent

Politics gives a profound twist to the usual principal-agent model. The standard assumption is that the principal has certain goals that are given from the outset—student achievement and quality schools, in our case—and that his challenge is to get his agents to pursue these goals productively. Once the relationship is embedded in a political context, however, it no longer makes sense to assume that the principal's goals are exogenously set, nor even that the principal is an independent actor in the relationship. For the principals in a democratic political system are elected officials, and the whole point of politics is to determine which people get to be principals in the first place and what goals they will pursue in office.

What does this twist lead us to expect? The standard view among political scientists is that elected officials are driven primarily by reelection and that, in formulating positions on public policy, they tend to take whatever stands are necessary to gain support from the constituencies that most affect their chances at the polls. The implication is that elected officials often do not choose their policy positions according to what is in the public interest, or even according to what they personally believe. Their policy positions are variables in a political calculus and crafted to maximize their appeal to powerful groups.[19]

There is nothing nefarious about this. Elections are the political system's method of holding public officials accountable; and even though this method—like any other—is an imperfect means of political control, the motivation to gain and keep office contributes to control by encouraging public officials to represent constituencies within the electorate (instead of, say, representing only themselves). So in this sense, the reelection motivation is actually a good thing. The real problem comes about because power in American society is unequally distributed—and this being so, reelection-minded politicians have incentives to favor whatever groups happen to be powerful, even if their interests do not reflect those of the larger society.

This problem is endemic to democracy, and it afflicts virtually all areas of public policy. But it is especially serious in education, because one interest group is by far the most powerful actor in this realm of politics, wielding inordinate influence over the direction and content of policy. I am speaking here of the teachers unions. The teachers unions are a problem, moreover, not simply because they skew public policy toward their own special interests. They are a problem because the special interests they represent happen to be those of the agents.[20]

So here is the situation. Public officials, acting as principals, are responsible for providing a system of public education that meets the needs of ordinary Americans. This requires that they hire agents—teachers and administrators—and impose accountability mechanisms to ensure that the latter do their jobs productively. But the public officials are elected. So the ways they exercise their authority—the policies they support, the goals they seek—are heavily influenced by groups that can wield electoral power. And the most powerful group by far is the group that represents the agents themselves: who have interests quite different from the larger electorate and *do not want to be held accountable* by the authorities who are their formal bosses.

Thanks to politics, then, the familiar control relationship is not what it appears to be. The authorities are in a position to exercise organizational control over their agents within the schools. But the agents, acting mainly through the teachers unions, are in a position to exercise political control over the authorities, and thus to influence whether and exactly how that organizational control gets exercised. As a result, a system of accountability may look like an exercise in top-down control, but it is really a system that has been shaped, perhaps profoundly so, by the self-interest of the very people it is supposed to be controlling. There is every reason to believe, therefore, that it will do a poor job of achieving genuine accountability. Indeed, to the extent that the agents can succeed in wielding their political power, it will be *designed* to do a poor job.[21]

Teachers Unions as Political Actors

Now let's get a better sense what to expect from the teachers unions. First and foremost, they are just unions, and collective bargaining is their core function. It is also the base of their power, for it is through collective bargaining that they get members, resources, and the capacity for political action. These are the fundamentals of their success and prosperity as organizations.

Their most basic interests arise from these fundamentals. Above all else, the teachers unions need to extend the reach of collective bargaining and to do whatever they can to keep members and resources and get more. Other interests follow directly from these most basic ones. For example, the teachers unions find it beneficial to protect their members' jobs, provide their members with higher pay and benefits, expand their formal rights and on-the-job autonomy, increase the demand for teachers, support higher taxes and bigger public budgets, and so on. These interests need have *nothing to do* with what is best for children, schools, or the public interest, and they may often lead teachers unions to take actions contrary to the greater good—by protecting the jobs of incompetent teachers, for example, or by burdening the schools with so many formal restrictions that they cannot be managed.[22]

There is nothing unusual about interest groups pursuing their own interests at the expense of the public good.[23] What makes the teachers unions different is that they wield the kind of power that most interest groups can only dream about. Their grip on the public schools guarantees them some three million members nationwide, massive financial resources, and organizational networks at the national, state, and local levels that are ideal for coordinated political action. Thus equipped, they have everything it takes to be a major force in political campaigns. Their cash is an important source of campaign contributions. But even more important, they can put troops on the ground in virtually every electoral district; and by making phone calls, getting out the vote, and otherwise campaigning for union-friendly candidates, these troops can prove far more potent than money.[24] Throughout American society, no other groups can claim this kind of coast-to-coast coverage and clout.

Indeed, a recent academic study of state-level politics ranked the teachers unions as the single most powerful interest group in the country.[25]

The teachers unions use their power almost exclusively on behalf of Democrats. They normally do everything they can to see that right-thinking Democrats—the most pro-union, pro-government, and antimarket—get nominated and that Democrats defeat Republicans in general elections. They are also forceful in letting Democratic officeholders know what is expected of them: the unions want favorable policies enacted, and they want threatening policies blocked. As vote-seeking politicians, the Democrats have strong incentives to go along.[26] The teachers unions' great power, however, does not allow them to write their own ticket, even with Democrats. They face a few limitations worth pointing out.

—Governors and presidents are less susceptible to union power than legislators are, because they have larger constituencies and are responsive to broader social interests. Executives can be influenced, but they can also be trouble.

—In right-to-work states the laws do not favor collective bargaining, and the teachers unions there have less political clout. This should not be exaggerated, as they are still major players in these states. But they are less able to control public policy.[27]

—Depending on the state and the issue, other powerful groups—from business, for example—may take up positions against the teachers unions. These groups usually have broader agendas than just education, giving them less incentive to reward or sanction politicians on educational grounds. Nonetheless, even Democrats may be cross-pressured in the presence of such opposition and less responsive to union demands.

To these limitations I have to add one more that arises from the American system of checks and balances. New legislation must run a gauntlet of subcommittees, committees, and floor votes in each of two legislative houses, as well as survive executive vetoes (and at the national level, filibusters and holds). This means that, when the teachers unions (or any interest groups) want favorable policies passed into law, they must overcome each and every veto point—while opponents must succeed only once to block. Even for the unions, then, changing public policy is difficult. The deck is stacked in favor of those who want to block, and weaker groups may often be able to stop the unions from carrying out their designs.

Yet the unions can play the blocking game too. And it is here that they are especially well positioned to get their way. In particular, they are usually powerful enough to stop the enactment of reforms that they oppose and thus to protect a status quo—of bureaucracy, collective bargaining, minimal competition, and minimal accountability—compatible with their own best interests. During a time of educational ferment, in which there is widespread pressure for change and improvement in public education, this is the way teachers unions put their power to most effective use. They use it to block change.[28]

The Politics of Accountability, Part I

So it is in the politics of accountability. Reformers are dedicated to holding teachers and administrators accountable for student achievement, but this goal is threatening to union interests—and their incentive is to block.

They are not powerful enough to stop the accountability movement cold. The movement has, after all, achieved legislative successes all across the country, and it has been able to do this because the authorities are eager to respond to *whatever* constituencies can affect their odds of reelection—and there are some who strongly favor school accountability.

A big reason for the movement's prominence is simply that accountability is very popular with the American public, and politicians—including Democrats—clearly see it as something they need to support on electoral grounds. This is particularly true of governors, who, of all public officials, are held responsible for improving the schools. They gain credit when the schools do well, they get blamed when the schools fail, and they are widely expected to "do something" to produce results. Accountability is a popular way of taking action.

Its attractiveness to authorities is all the greater because business groups have taken the lead on school accountability and pushed for reforms that are serious and far-reaching. Concerned about the low quality of the work force and motivated to create more attractive business environments in their communities and states, business groups have seen accountability—which mirrors their own emphasis on managerial efficiency—as a linchpin of school improvement.[29]

The teachers unions, therefore, despite their predominant power, cannot count on dictating the way authorities approach the accountability issue. The authorities face competing pressures from business and the public, and they have incentives to respond to these other constituencies. So what can the unions do? One strategy is to use their power to block any move toward accountability—which, given the relative ease of blocking, would often prove successful. Yet it would not always be successful, given the power and incentives on the other side. And it would not necessarily be wise anyway, because the unions would damage their public image (and ultimately their political clout) by coming across as unyielding opponents of something so broadly popular.

A much better strategy—a favorite of interest groups in all areas of American politics—is to come out enthusiastically in "support" of the popular issue, participate in the design of "appropriate" policies, and exercise power to block the inclusion of anything that is truly threatening. In this way, the teachers unions can appear to be on the right side of the issue, while at the same time ensuring that teachers and administrators are not held accountable in any meaningful sense.

How would such a strategy play out as actual accountability systems are being designed? The answer turns on the nature of union interests and how they are affected by the three key components of modern-day accountability reform: standards, testing, and consequences.

STANDARDS. From the standpoint of union interests, there is nothing threatening about curriculum standards. Standards only become threatening if they are backed by consequences. Thus, if consequences are not involved, or if the unions are confident they can block any such proposals, then they can easily portray themselves as enthusiastic supporters of reform. What they are really supporting is standards without accountability.[30]

Sometimes, however, the unions will be faced with policy packages that link standards to consequences. When this happens, they will take standards more seriously. They will want to see that—as "experts"—they themselves get to play integral roles in shaping the content of the standards.[31] And they will have incentives to see that standards are relatively easy to meet: arguing for passing bars that are comfortably low, and reacting to poor test results by claiming that the standards and passing bars are themselves poorly conceived and need to be changed (by weakening them).[32] It is heavily to their advantage in all this that the notion of standards is subjective and ambiguous to begin with. Because if the unions water down the existing standards, making it easier for students and teachers to avoid consequences, no objective baseline can prove them wrong, and they have lots of room to maneuver.

TESTS. Tests, like standards, are not threatening to the unions as long as they don't give rise to consequences. Until recently, they rarely did. Test results were essentially secret. Scores were used internally by the school system and passed along to the parents of individual students. But there was no public basis for judging how well the schools were doing, and thus little for the unions to fear.[33]

The accountability movement changed all this. Today it is common for states to publicize test scores, and this in itself is a form of consequence—for Americans now have concrete information on school performance, and low scores tend to generate political pressures for improvement that make life uncomfortable for school personnel. The unions do not like this. But because publicizing test scores is so popular and so easy for the authorities to do, they have had a hard time stopping it.

More troubling still from the unions' standpoint, test scores stand to be powerful mechanisms of top-down organizational control. They give the authorities objective measures of performance, and it is on this basis that rewards and sanctions are attached to behavior. A system of testing enables a system of consequences—and a system of control.

The unions, as a result, have strong incentives to oppose testing—or more practically, because testing is popular, to argue that the tests currently in use (whatever they might be) are deeply flawed, need revision, and cannot provide valid measures of anyone's performance, whether student or teacher or administrator. This argument is disingenuous, as they would make it even if the tests were perfect. Fortunately for them, however, some of the arguments they can make about the perils of testing are good ones that deserve to be taken seriously. It is right, for example, to complain when states rely solely on nationally normed tests instead of tests based on their own standards. It is right to say that reliance on a single test, rather than multiple indicators of performance, can be risky and unfair. It is right to say that many factors affect student achievement and that test scores can be misleading unless these things are adequately taken into account (which can be difficult and uncertain). And it is right to emphasize that schools do more than teach academics, and that test scores fail to measure the range of purposes that ought to guide school performance.[34]

Were all these things somehow resolved, however, the unions would still be against testing. When testing is done well, it allows for precise measures of performance and thus for control systems that hold school employees accountable for their performance. The unions want to prevent that from happening. What they can allow themselves to be for, as alternatives, are methods of evaluating student learning that involve subjective judgments on the part of teachers—course grades, assessments of portfolios, assessments of effort. Because student scores on these counts become the basis for evaluating teachers, a system that relies on subjective judgment essentially allows the teachers to determine their own performance evaluations. Not a bad deal if you can get it.[35]

CONSEQUENCES. The unions' prime goal in the politics of accountability is to weaken or eliminate any consequences that might be associated with standards and tests.[36] What they want are accountability systems that look like they are designed to do the job—owing to impressive standards and tests—but lack the consequences for actually holding people accountable. If they get their way, they can have their cake and eat it, too. They can come across as supporters of accountability, but the accountability systems won't work and won't threaten their interests.

Among their highest priorities is ensuring that pay is not linked to performance, and thus that the key mechanism of top-down control is removed from consideration.[37] Most of their members are likely to be averse to performance pay. But the unions also have their own objections, because performance pay creates competition among members, threatens solidarity, and puts discretion in the hands of administrators. The unions want salaries to be set (as they have been for ages) on the basis of seniority and education, which are within reach of all teachers and unrelated to performance in the classroom.[38]

The unions are also against attaching rewards and sanctions to whole schools based on school performance, as this too creates competition (across schools) that the unions seek to avoid. Given a choice, however, they view this approach as preferable to performance-based consequences for individual teachers, for it at least preserves the solidarity of teachers within each school and better protects them from risk.[39]

While the unions would prefer to see no rewards or sanctions at all, they are obviously more opposed to sanctions than rewards. Above all else, *no one should ever lose a job*, and there can be *no weeding out process* by which the school system rids itself of mediocre and incompetent teachers. Other kinds of economic sanctions—pay cuts, reductions in funding—are verboten as well. And so are commonsense policies that might lead to such sanctions: for example, the testing of existing teachers in low-performing schools to ensure that they are competent enough to stay in the classroom.

Should consequences be adopted, unions insist that they take the form of rewards: bonuses for high-performing teachers or, far preferable, bonuses for high-performing schools (with the unions deciding how rewards are distributed among teachers within each school). A union-preferred accountability system, then, would exercise accountability—to the extent it exercises it at all—entirely through a system of positive inducements. There would only be winners. No losers.

This same logic applies to the question of how accountability systems should grapple with the critical problem of low-performing schools. State intervention and reconstitution are both sanction-like approaches that are threatening to union interests. The preferred approach is for low-performing schools to be given greater funding, more assistance with their programs, and more training for their teachers—which are essentially rewards and the kinds of things establishment groups are always lobbying for anyway. Having them included as "consequences" in an accountability system is just a backdoor way of directing more resources to low-performers.

The Politics of Accountability, Part II

What should we expect, then, from the politics of accountability? For starters, we should expect that many authorities will not be motivated to design accountability systems that actually work. Their goals are endogenous to the political process, shaped by the constituencies that can most affect their reelection. And the most powerful are the teachers unions, whose own interests are very much opposed to what reformers are trying to get the authorities to do.

This does not mean that the unions automatically get what they want. Reformers have public support and the power of business on their side, and this gives the authorities—governors in particular—reason to do something in creating systems of accountability. The unions' best strategy is to go along with the political tides and use their considerable clout to block or eviscerate those aspects of accountability that are most threatening to their interests.

Their success will vary, state by state, depending on how conducive the circumstances are to union power. These circumstances may be complicated. But other things being equal (and I emphasize this), the teachers unions should tend to be most successful—and accountability systems weaker—in states where Democrats control the machinery of government, where collective bargaining laws are strong, where business groups are not especially active, and where school performance is positively viewed. The unions should tend to be least successful—and accountability systems stronger—in states controlled by Republicans, where right-to-work laws make union organizing and political action difficult, where business is politically active on education, and where the performance of the public schools is widely criticized.[40]

Across the nation, therefore, we should expect to see a great variety of accountability systems. Some may be little more than symbolic shells, others may be serious systems with real teeth, and most will lie somewhere in between—their properties depending on how much power the teachers unions are able to wield in politics. The modal system, however, is sure to be heavily influenced by union interests, and thus crafted in such a way that the basic requirements of top-down control—all having to do with consequences—are either weakened or thoroughly violated. In particular, we should typically expect to see

—no serious attempt to pay people based on their performance;

—a willingness to give out rewards, but not to apply sanctions;

—the targeting of rewards to whole schools, not to individuals; and

—no mechanisms whatever to weed out mediocre or incompetent employees.[41]

What we should expect to see, in short, are accountability systems that are not built to hold the schools and their employees accountable. They may look like accountability systems. And they may be called accountability systems. But they can't do their jobs very well—because they aren't designed to.

Looking Ahead

My purpose here is not to disparage the school accountability movement. I would be overjoyed if the schools could be held accountable and if student achievement and school quality could be dramatically improved as a result. But wishful thinking is not a sound basis for effective policy. To get where we want to go, we need to understand what we are up against—which requires, at the very least, a commitment to honest analysis that may tell us what we are hoping not to hear.

School accountability faces two fundamental problems, a control problem and a political problem, that undermine its prospects for success. The control problem arises because school employees have their own interests distinct from those of the authorities, as well as information that the authorities do not have, giving them the incentive and the capacity to resist top-down efforts to hold them accountable. The political problem arises because the authorities are elected officials, are responsive to the political power of school employees—exerted mainly through the teachers unions—and thus have incentives not to pursue true accountability anyway.

Both problems are inevitable, and they are not simply going to go away. In the foreseeable future, school employees will continue to have their own interests and information unavailable to the authorities. And elected officials will continue to govern the schools and respond to the power of the teachers unions. The only realistic conclusion is that, for some time to come, we should have low expectations for what accountability systems can achieve.

This does not mean that they should be discarded. We have an education system that for almost a century has not been held accountable for student achievement, whose incentives are almost precisely the opposite of what high levels of productivity require, and whose job characteristics attract employees of the wrong types. An accountability system that emphasizes student achievement, and that even attempts to motivate school personnel along those lines, involves little risk of reducing achievement and offers at least some prospect of improving it, simply because the structure of the current system is so utterly inappropriate.

Some of the obstacles to accountability, moreover, may be somewhat reduced over time. One way to ameliorate control problems, for example, is through better measures of performance, measures that address the reasonable objections of critics and provide more efficacious means of holding people accountable. This is a job for education researchers, and we can expect progress in the future. Researchers can also help figure out how to use these measures, perhaps in combination with subjective evaluations by superiors, to design incentive structures that properly motivate people.[42]

Reform may also benefit from a built-in bonus, which comes about because many accountability systems are likely to be self-improving over time. The reason is that any semiserious form of accountability will make life difficult for unproductive employees, putting them under pressure to work harder and produce results, and they will have at least some incentive to quit their jobs. Similarly, people who are the right types—more able, more geared to productive performance—will find these jobs more attractive than before. The sheer persistence of accountability systems over a long enough period of time, therefore, may change the internal composition of personnel in a good way and lead to better outcomes than a short-term view of the system would suggest.

If we look purely at control issues, then, there are reasons for guarded optimism. Unfortunately, the political problem remains, and it threatens to stop any progress in its tracks. We have to remember that the authorities are not eager to follow the lessons of new research, however much may be learned about the best way to promote accountability, because that is not their goal in the first place. Their goals and decisions are shaped by politics; and to mollify powerful groups, they are happy to adopt accountability mechanisms that they know will not work very well. Research is not going to change that. Politics also affects the extent to which accountability systems can be self-improving through changes in composition: the authorities have strong incentives, as long as the teachers unions are powerful, not to adopt the kind of compensation systems that are attractive to the right types of employees and unattractive to the wrong types. Changes in composition may still occur, but they will be less consequential and take longer than if the authorities actually wanted to make the changes happen.

As all this suggests, politics is the stickier of the two wickets. Absent politics, the control problem might be ameliorated over time. But politics is not absent. And because this is unavoidably so, the authorities—pressured by the unions—can be counted upon to exercise much less control than they have the capacity for, and to take less than full advantage of developments that promise to make their accountability job easier.

When all is said and done, then, the top-down approach to accountability—taken alone—is destined to be a disappointment. The good news, however, is that this is not the only approach to accountability available to us, and it need not be adopted all by itself. While the accountability movement has thus far been transfixed by the top-down model, schools can also be held accountable from below through well-designed systems of school choice. And there is good reason to think that the combination of the two approaches might be much more effective.[43]

When parents are able to choose their kids' schools, whether their choices are purely public (via charter schools) or include private schools as well (via vouchers), the regular public schools are put on notice that inadequate performance has costly consequences: they can lose kids and money. This gives them incentives to perform. And the stronger the competitive threat, the stronger the incentives.

Some of the incentives are felt collectively at the school level and thus are not as potent for individual employees as they might be. But pressures are also transmitted up the chain of authority, for no one responsible for the regular public schools wants the system to shrink and wither as parents run for the exits. These officials have incentives to stop the hemorrhage, and a key way to do this is to make performance much more central to the way schools are organized and employees compensated, hired, and fired. The bottom-up and top-down forces for accountability are thus joined. The competitive pressure from the bottom gives the authorities much stronger incentives to be serious about top-down accountability, and to create better-performing organizations that can keep kids and money from leaving.

Of course, there is a political problem with school choice as well. The unions are fully aware that choice threatens their interests, and they put political pressure on the authorities to oppose it. But choice is popular with parents, a powerful movement is behind it, and the unions are not totally successful in blocking it. Parents have many more choices today than they did ten years ago, and both choice and competition are expanding (especially through the increasing numbers of charter schools). As with today's accountability systems, these choice systems are a pale reflection of what reformers would like to see. But even imperfect choice systems are sources of educational change.[44]

They are also sources of political change—and this, more than anything else, may hold the key to successful reform. For choice undermines the political power of the teachers unions. Were children allowed to leave inadequate public schools for charter or private schools, the vast majority of which are nonunion, life would become more difficult for the teachers unions. They would lose members and resources, their organizing task would become far more challenging, and their basis for political clout would begin to erode. Furthermore, they would have incentives to use their remaining power in a different way. With competition a reality, they would see that the costs and formal rigidities they usually impose on schools would put them at a disadvantage relative to their competitors, giving them incentives to moderate their demands. Indeed, they would see that to keep kids and money—and thus members and resources—they would need to think seriously about accepting accountability mechanisms (such as performance pay) that they usually oppose. This, in turn, would reduce the political constraints on the authorities and give them greater incentives to opt for accountability systems that might actually work.

If the movement for school accountability is to succeed, therefore, reformers need to break out of the mind-set that equates accountability with top-down methods of control, and recognize that—for political as well as organizational reasons—a combination of top-down and bottom-up approaches is likely to prove far more potent. Without such a reorientation, the movement cannot hope to make much progress. But with it, the future of reform may be very bright indeed.

Notes

1. Diane Ravitch, "Testing and Accountability, Historically Considered," in Williamson M. Evers and Herbert J. Walberg, eds., *School Accountability* (Stanford, Calif.: Hoover Institution Press, 2002); and "Quality Counts 2000," *Education Week*, vol. 21, no. 17 (2002).

2. Oliver E. Williamson, "The New Institutional Economics: Taking Stock, Looking Ahead," *Journal of Economic Literature*, vol. 38 (September 2000), pp. 595–613; Robert Gibbons, "Incentives in Organizations," *Journal of Economic Perspectives*, vol. 12, no. 4 (Fall 1998), pp. 115–32; and Canice Prendergast, "The Provision of Incentives in Firms," *Journal of Economic Literature*, vol. 37 (March 1999), pp. 7–63.

3. John W. Pratt and Richard J. Zeckhauser, "Principals and Agents: An Overview," in John W. Pratt and Richard J. Zeckhauser, eds., *Principals and Agents* (Harvard Business School Press, 1985).

4. Here and below, I am simply elaborating the basic logic of the principal-agent model. For an introduction and overview, see Pratt and Zeckhauser, "Principals and Agents"; Gibbons, "Incentives in Organizations"; Prendergast, "The Provision of Incentives in Firms"; and Terry M. Moe, "The Positive Theory of Public Bureau-

cracy," in Dennis C. Mueller, ed., *Perspectives on Public Choice* (New York: Cambridge University Press, 1997), pp. 455–80.

5. For an overview of how employees are generally modeled and understood, see Edward P. Lazear, *Personnel Economics for Managers* (Wiley and Sons, 1998).

6. Myron Lieberman, *The Teacher Unions* (Free Press, 1997).

7. Diane Ravitch, *Left Back: A Century of Failed School Reform* (Simon and Schuster, 2000); and David Tyack, *The One Best System* (Harvard University Press, 1974).

8. On the problem of adverse selection and how jobs with different characteristics tend to attract (and repel) workers of different types, see Lazear, *Personnel Economics for Managers.*

9. Williamson M. Evers, "Standards and Accountability," in Terry M. Moe, ed., *A Primer on America's Schools* (Stanford, Calif.: Hoover Institution Press, 2001).

10. Herbert J. Walberg, "Achievement in American Schools," in Terry M. Moe, ed., *A Primer on America's Schools* (Stanford, Calif.: Hoover Institution Press, 2001).

11. Gregory. J. Cizek, "Cheating to the Test," *Education Next*, vol. 1, no. 1 (Spring 2001), pp. 40–47.

12. Lazear, *Personnel Economics for Managers.*

13. Kate Walsh, "Positive Spin: The Evidence for Teacher Certification," *Education Next*, vol. 2, no. 1 (Spring 2002), pp. 79–84.

14. On the logic—and problems—of linking pay to performance, see Lazear, *Personnel Economics for Managers;* Gibbons, "Incentives in Organizations"; and Pendergast, "The Provision of Incentives in Firms." My discussion simply highlights basic points in the literature.

15. Thomas J. Kane and Douglas O. Staiger, "Volatility in School Test Scores: Implications for Test-Based Accountability Systems," in Diane Ravitch, ed., *Brookings Papers on Education Policy: 2002* (Brookings, 2002), pp. 235–83; and Robert L. Linn, "Assessments and Accountability," *Educational Researcher,* vol. 29, no. 2 (March 2000), pp. 4–15.

16. Linn, "Assessments and Accountability"; Daniel Koretz and others, "The Effects of High-Stakes Testing on Achievement: Preliminary Findings about Generalization across Tests," paper prepared for the annual meeting of the American Educational Research Association, Chicago, Illinois, 1991.

17. For a description of accountability reforms adopted in the states, see "Quality Counts."

18. For a discussion of problems inherent in team production, see Lazear, *Personnel Economics for Managers.*

19. Anthony Downs, *An Economic Theory of Democracy* (Harper and Row, 1957); and David Mayhew, *Congress: The Electoral Connection* (Yale University Press, 1974).

20. Terry M. Moe, "Teachers Unions and the Public Schools," in Terry M. Moe, ed., *A Primer on America's Schools* (Stanford, Calif.: Hoover Institution Press, 2001), pp. 151–84; and Lieberman, *The Teacher Unions.*

21. For a more general argument that government agencies are often designed to be ineffective, see Terry M. Moe, "The Politics of Bureaucratic Structure," in John E.

Chubb and Paul E. Peterson, eds., *Can the Government Govern?* (Brookings, 1989), pp. 267–329.

22. Moe, "Teachers Unions and the Public Schools."

23. Allan J. Ciglar and Burdett A. Loomis, *Interest Group Politics,* 6th ed. (Washington: CQ Press, 2002).

24. Moe, "Teachers Unions and the Public Schools."

25. Clive S. Thomas and Ronald J. Hrebnar, "Interest Groups in the States," in Virginia Gray, Russell L. Hansen, and Herbert Jacob, eds., *Politics in the American States,* 7th ed. (Washington: CQ Press, 1999).

26. Lieberman, *The Teacher Unions*; C. Gregory Moo, *Power Grab* (Washington: Regnery Publishing, 1999); and Maurice R. Berube, *Teacher Politics* (New York: Greenwood Press, 1988).

27. Moe, "Teachers Unions and the Public Schools"; and Lieberman, *The Teacher Unions.*

28. Moe, "Teachers Unions and the Public Schools."

29. Paul T. Hill and Robin J. Lake, "Standards and Accountability in Washington State," in Diane Ravitch, ed., *Brookings Papers on Education Policy 2002* (Brookings, 2002), pp. 199–234; Frederick M. Hess, "Reform, Resistance, . . . Retreat? The Predictable Politics of Accountability in Virginia," in Diane Ravitch, ed., *Brookings Papers on Education Policy 2002* (Brookings, 2003), pp. 69–122; and Michele Kurtz, "Testing, Testing: School Accountability in Massachusetts," Working Paper 1 (Harvard University, John F. Kennedy School of Government, Rappaport Institute for Greater Boston, 2001).

30. Both the National Education Association (NEA) and the American Federation of Teachers (AFT) publicly support standards. The AFT, in particular, has moved aggressively to be a leading voice on this score. But the fact is that both groups are opposed to any meaningful consequences. See National Education Association, "NEA 2001–2002 Resolutions" (www.nea.org [March 18, 2002]); and American Federation of Teachers, *Making Standards Matter* (New York, 2001) (www.aft.org [March 18, 2002]).

31. The NEA, for example, says that "state and local affiliates must participate in the planning, development, implementation, and refinement of standards, conditions, and assessments." It also says that "classroom teachers must be involved in the development of classroom assessment systems and are best qualified to determine the criteria for assessment of students and dissemination of results." See National Education Association, "NEA 2001–2002 Resolutions."

32. No one wants to say they are for weak standards. But the unions are consistently critical of tests that point to low levels of achievement (and thus, implicitly, low levels of performance by their members), and they often take political action to modify the results (allowing more people to pass) by weakening the standards on which they are based. See Hill and Lake, "Standards and Accountability in Washington State"; Hess, "Reform, Resistance, . . . Retreat?"; and Kurtz, "Testing, Testing."

33. Ravitch, *Left Back*; and Ravitch, "Testing and Accountability."

34. For union complaints about testing, see National Education Association, "NEA 2001–2002 Resolutions"; and American Federation of Teachers, *Making Standards Matter.* For their political activities in opposition to testing, see Hill and Lake, "Standards and Accountability in Washington State"; Hess, "Reform, Resistance, . . . Retreat?"; and and Kurtz, "Testing, Testing."

35. Both the NEA and the AFT argue for broader, more comprehensive evaluations of students that go well beyond the usual standardized tests, and these sorts of evaluations inevitably involve subjective judgments by teachers. See National Education Association, "NEA 2001–2002 Resolutions"; and American Federation of Teachers, *Making Standards Matter.*

36. The NEA, for example, says that it "opposes the use of standardized tests when—Used as the criterion for the reduction or withholding of any educational funding. . . . Results are used to compare students, teachers, programs, schools, communities, and states. . . .The results lead to sanctions or other punitive actions. . . . Student scores are used to evaluate teachers or to determine compensation or employment status." See National Education Association, "NEA 2001–2002 Resolutions."

37. The AFT is flatly opposed to merit pay (which is essentially pay for performance), but it has tried to talk a more liberal line on teacher pay lately. What its liberalized position boils down to, though, is that it is willing to get away from the traditional salary schedule somewhat (but not entirely) and have teachers paid in part based on things such as advanced certification, teaching in low-performing schools, and mentoring. These roles and qualifications are potentially open to any teacher and do not depend on the teacher's performance in the classroom or how much the students learn. See American Federation of Teachers, "AFT on the Issues: Merit Pay," (www.aft.org [March 18, 2002]). The AFT affiliate in Cincinnati negotiated a contract in late 2000 that included pay for performance, and pundits around the country pointed to this rare event as evidence that the unions are becoming more flexible. In the spring of 2001, however, the president of the Cincinnati union was voted out of office by a landslide. Subsequently, union members voted—96.3 percent to 3.7 percent—to overturn the performance plan. So much for liberalization. See Education Intelligence Agency, "Cincinnati Federation of Teachers Aborts Pay for Performance Plan," *Communique* (May 20, 2002) (www.eiaonline.com).

38. Moe, "Teachers Unions and the Public Schools"; and Lieberman, *The Teacher Unions.*

39. Here and in the arguments below, evidence that these are the positions the unions tend to take in politics can be found in Hill and Lake, "Standards and Accountability in Washington State"; Hess, "Reform, Resistance, . . . Retreat?"; and Kurtz, "Testing, Testing.

40. It is not an accident that the accountability systems in Texas and North Carolina—both right-to-work states where unions are weaker than elsewhere—are often taken as examples of strong systems that work reasonably well. Pointing to examples like this is a bit risky, however, as a means of documenting my claims about where we ought to find strong and weak accountability systems, because the "other things

being equal" caveat needs to be taken seriously and because even the four factors I mention can interact in a variety of ways. California, for example, has a very powerful union and a Democratic governor, but this governor supported the creation of a fairly strong accountability system (compared with other states). I suspect this is because the state has performed horribly in recent national test rankings, and there is intense public pressure for governmental action. The union did not like it and is still trying to overturn it, but the Democratic governor is hanging tough. In California, then, one factor—horrible performance—seems to have outweighed all the others. Whether this is usually the case, I cannot say. But it would be a mistake to think that accountability can make progress only in Republican states with weak unions.

41. And empirically, in fact, this is what we do see. For an overview of accountability systems, refer to "Quality Counts."

42. For a good discussion of what researchers can contribute to the design of effective accountability systems, see Eric Hanushek and Margaret E. Raymond, "Sorting Out Accountability Systems," in Williamson M. Evers and Herbert J. Walberg, eds., *School Accountability* (Stanford, Calif.: Hoover Institution Press, 2002), pp. 75–104.

43. Chester E. Finn, "Real Accountability in K–12 Education: The Marriage of Ted and Alice," in Evers and Walberg, eds., *School Accountability*, pp. 23–46.

44. Terry M. Moe, "The Structure of School Choice," in Paul T. Hill, ed., *Choice with Equity* (Stanford, Calif.: Hoover Institution Press, 2002), pp. 179–212.

5

Rethinking Accountability Politics

JENNIFER HOCHSCHILD

The 1990s and early 2000s witnessed an array of new policies to promote school improvement and accountability—charter schools, alternative certification programs, systemic reform involving standards and high-stakes tests, a Republican-sponsored law promising to "leave no child behind," state or city takeover of failing school systems, and others. As James B. Hunt Jr., former governor of North Carolina, insisted, "In this new era of accountability, candidates will be judged for their education leadership. They must be knowledgeable about the issues and relentless about results. I predict that the avowed education candidates who fail to follow up platitudes with performance, and who fail to match rhetoric with results, won't be around much longer."[1]

However, this move to electoral accountability for schooling outcomes needs to be explained. Political logic suggests that these reforms should not have occurred. Powerful teachers unions resisted many of them and were ambivalent about others. Parents and citizens were reasonably content with the schools in their community; they saw more problems with students' behavior than with their test scores. Outcomes of schooling in most locations had not deteriorated drastically, so except in inner cities there was no crisis demanding a solution. Elected officials had a long history of remaining far removed from the complicated morass of public schooling. More generally, they are almost always allergic to strict measures of accountability. The

Republican Party has an equally long history of resisting federal involvement in state and local programs, especially schools.

Despite all of these reasons to expect no change or merely token gestures, reforms to promote accountability in the public education system are arguably becoming more widespread and more powerful in their intended and actual impact on American schools. The only proposed reform that has, so far, mostly met defeat in a hostile political environment is vouchers for use by public school students in school districts outside their own or in private or parochial schools.[2] The drive toward standards with accountability may yet fail, for substantive, political, or financial reasons—but so far it has not. This chapter asks why all of this has taken place.

Smoke and Mirrors?

One interpretation of the changes over the past decade is that much less reform has occurred than meets the eye. In this view, laws and regulations promulgating standards with accountability are weaker than they appear to be on paper, charter schools are small and constrained, and alternative programs for teacher certification are mostly symbolic. Alternatively, laws and new programs that started out strong will be greatly weakened as they run into increasing resistance from teachers unions, parents of failing students, some civil rights advocates, and educators disgruntled by too much or the wrong kind of change.

Terry M. Moe predicts this course (see chapter 4 in this volume), and Andrew Rudalevige (chapter 2) and Frederick M. Hess (chapter 3) similarly express uncertainty about the long-term impact of recent reforms. These cautious predictions are entirely plausible. Already some states have postponed deadlines by which tests will determine whether students receive a diploma, or lowered the bar for passing, or excused students who are anticipated to do poorly on a high-stakes exam, or eliminated sanctions against schools or teachers whose students do poorly. In some states charter schools are subject to increasingly assertive oversight. Yet other ways to blunt the force of the accountability movement may be added so that the drive for standards and accountability goes the way of new math or open classrooms.

But the overall trajectory at present is toward stronger, not weaker, policies for holding schools and students accountable. During the 1990s no states withdrew from a system of standards with accountability. In fact, "by 1996, just ten states had active accountability systems, while by 2000 just 13 states had yet to introduce active systems."[3] Almost all states have promulgated standards for core subjects, and most are moving toward stricter measures of accountability for attaining those standards. As Brian A. Jacob says (see chapter 12 in this volume), "Statutes in twenty-five states explicitly link student promotion to performance on state or district assessments. . . . Eighteen states reward teachers and administrators on the basis of exemplary student performance and twenty states sanction school staff on the basis of poor student performance." In many states standards are expanding to cover more subjects, more precision within a subject, more years of school, more students within a given cohort, or all four. Reformers are working to align tests with standards so that students and teachers have fewer excuses for failure. In some states the bar for passing a high-stakes exam has risen. The recent federal law known as No Child Left Behind (NCLB) mandates much more testing of students than was required before 2001 and has more stringent penalties for failing schools than any federal law ever before.

Standards and testing are not the only accountability measures that have expanded since roughly 1990. Many states and districts have passed legislation allowing the takeover or closure of schools that do not show improvement. No states have rescinded laws creating charter schools, and during the 1990s most states created a mechanism for starting them. Many more states have laws permitting alternative routes to teacher certification than did a decade ago. States have taken over schools and school districts. Mayors of many of the largest cities with the worst school systems have succeeded in attaining direct or indirect control over those systems.

These measures appear in the aggregate to be improving what teachers do and what students learn. Eric A. Hanushek and Margaret E. Raymond show that "the summary of estimated effects of introducing an accountability system is simple: Accountability systems appear to lead to significantly better growth in achievement."[4] Another study that disaggregates scores on the National Assessment of Educational Progress (NAEP) by state finds that "state activism has a significant independent effect on teachers' use of classroom practices consistent with a standards-based model of mathematics education. . . . These policy effects on instruction may operate by promoting greater teacher receptivity to reform."[5] In other words, standards with accountability lead to higher test scores, in part because teachers teach differently. In short, the momentum so far is toward greater, not lesser, accountability, with at least some desirable results.

Why Is This Trajectory Surprising?

The closer one looks at the political and societal dynamics that have produced the move toward greater educational accountability, the more surprising it seems. The most likely explanations for such a move do not seem to have much purchase.

Mismatch between Problem and Proposed Solution

To begin with, one might expect widespread reform to emerge in response to a deep and urgent problem. After all, a national commission famously insisted in the early 1980s that "we have, in effect, been committing an act of unthinking, unilateral educational disarmament"; a decade later, a popular book called for an "autopsy" on public education.[6] If schools are that bad and getting worse, reform will soon follow.

This argument, however, has two problems that make it a poor explanation of the accountability movement of the 1990s. First, it is as easy to make the case that American schools have been improving, or are at least stable in the face of a more complicated student population, as to make the claim that they have been worsening over the past several decades. Others have provided strong evidence of worsening; I need not repeat it here. Nevertheless, NAEP scores improved and then stabilized during the past thirty years, especially among black students; dropout rates declined, again especially among black students; students needing special education were increasingly incorporated into mainstream classes.[7] SAT scores rose among both blacks and whites over the past two decades even though more people in both races are taking the test.[8] These results stem partly from the fact that students are enrolling in tougher courses in high school than they used to.[9] College enrollment is up in every racial or ethnic group from several decades ago.[10]

Only schools in poor neighborhoods within inner cities have deteriorated drastically. "For years, it was like storming the Bastille every day," says one urban teacher. During the 1970s and 1980s, the gap in the quality of schools attended by blacks and whites worsened, entirely because poor inner-city schools and schools with fewer than 20 percent white enrollment deteriorated so much. Black students in nonurban schools actually did better during this period, while black students in urban schools were doing worse. Similarly, during the 1990s, the most accomplished quarter of fourth-grade readers improved their test scores on the NAEP, while the least accomplished quarter lost even more ground. The top scorers were mostly white noncity dwellers; the low-scorers were disproportionately non-Anglo boys in poor urban schools.[11]

Measures of accountability have not tracked these patterns of accomplishment or deterioration. The ambiguity in the evidence on the changing quality of schooling across the board implies that one ought to be uncertain about the urgency of reform for all schools. Conversely, the consistency of the evidence of disaster in urban schools suggests that one ought to be passionate about the need for reform in urban schools. Instead, policymakers have shown strong and growing commitment to reform for all schools, regardless of how badly they appear to need it, but not much precisely focused attention or resources directly aimed at the schools that desperately need help.

Citizens' perceptions provide a second reason to be skeptical that change in the quality of American schooling—whether improvement or deterioration—explains the reform movements of the 1990s. Americans are no more or less satisfied with public education than they were thirty years ago, when there was no drive toward accountability. From 1974 (when first asked) through 2002, citizens' grades for the schools in their local community have hovered around a C+. Public school parents always give slightly higher grades than do those with no children in schools. Parents give a solid B on average to the school their oldest child attends, and that grade, too, has not declined. Americans give the worst grade, a C, to the public schools "in the nation as a whole," but this grade, too, is stable.[12] Regardless of whether these ratings are too high or too low, what matters here is the fact that they have not changed. One cannot explain a rising level of educational reform by a flat line of anxiety about school quality.

Americans' Ambivalence about Academic Standards

Americans, in fact, seem thoroughly ambivalent—not to say self-contradictory—when it comes to substantive educational reforms. When people are asked directly about reform, polls show consistent strong support for accountability. Most respondents endorse setting high and systemic standards, testing students, and rewarding or punishing students and staff based on the test results. Enthusiasm is even greater among parents in large cities with many unsuccessful schools, such as Cleveland, Los Angeles, and New York. It is higher among nonwhites than whites. Parents claim to endorse the policy regardless of whether their own child might be held back. In 2000, although 40 percent of Latinos in Texas believed the Texas Assessment of Academic Skills (TAAS) to be biased against minority students, only 30 percent opposed its use as a graduation requirement.[13]

Nevertheless, when given a free choice of what to focus on in possible schooling reforms, Americans pay attention to discipline, safety, extracurricular activities, and the work ethic; they give little attention to performance. Typically, a plurality of respondents (at least 15 percent) agree that "the biggest problem in schools today" is lack of discipline, and another 20 percent or more focus on violence and gangs or on drugs. Five percent or fewer express most concern about the quality of education or standards.[14] Twice as many Americans care that schools teach good work habits as care about advanced mathematics, and almost four times as many endorse teaching the value of hard work as compared with teaching Shakespeare or Hemingway. But not too much hard work: Sixty percent of Americans would rather have their child "make average grades and be active in extracurricular activities" than "get A grades."[15]

Until recently, in fact, Americans worried about too much, not too little, innovation. In 1970 and again in 1982, more parents agreed that local schools' curricula met "today's needs" than thought they needed renovation. At about the same time, more thought local schools were "too ready to try new ideas" than thought they were too dull (their children disagreed). Only in 1997 did a bare majority agree that the curriculum needed to be updated. Policies to promote higher achievement were changing citizens' views instead of responding to them.[16]

In short, when asked about standards and accountability, the public is enthusiastic. When asked about schools, the public gives standards and accountability very low priority. One cannot argue plausibly that school reforms of the past decade were a response to pressure from voters. If they judged by surveys, electorally sensitive public officials would have focused on something else.

Teachers and Teachers Unions

Unions show the same ambivalence as citizens. Albert Shanker pushed the membership of the American Federation of Teachers (AFT), of which he was president, to endorse charter schools in 1988, thus giving the nascent movement its first crucial credibility. Shanker continued to promote substantive school reform and high standards, writing, for example, in 1994 that the "centerpiece" of a report on school reform should be

> an attempt to measure progress toward the goal of improved student achievement and an analysis of what seems to be working and what seems to be failing. . . . The whole point of school reform is to have students learn more. If this doesn't happen, the experiment is a failure, no matter how happy the children, the parents and teachers—and the reformers—are.[17]

Two years later, he described "the key elements" of reform as "safe and orderly schools, rigorous academic standards, assessments based on those standards, incentives for students to work hard in school and genuine professional accountability."[18]

Sandra Feldman carried on the message when she became president of the AFT. As she put it, "Enhanced student achievement, based on high standards and research-proven programs and practices, must be the driving force behind all reform efforts." She argued that schools should be closed or reorganized if they fail, and she endorsed detailed guidelines for "improvement programs and strategies." The larger National Education Association (NEA) was even more closely tied to school reform by the late 1990s. Its president, Bob Chase, gave a "legendary" speech, in the words of *Education Week,* in 1997, insisting that the union's "narrow, traditional agenda" is "*utterly inadequate* to the needs of the future" and pledging to "work . . . to raise and enforce standards for student achievement."[19] Chase reorganized his office and staff to promote student performance and endorsed experiments in peer review and performance-based pay. He was reelected without opposition.

Nevertheless, "when he [Chase] stood up and gave his reform message, there wasn't always a standing ovation." In response to his request for union support of performance-based pay, for example, "the [NEA] assembly not only rejected the proposal, but also strengthened the union's opposition to the idea."[20] Neither candidate to succeed Chase promoted his "new unionism," and the eventual winner dismissed charter schools as a "fad." Both candidates campaigned vehemently against NCLB, calling it variously "another empty phrase" and "little more than Vouchers Lite."[21] Chase's efforts had little discernible impact on the NEA.

Many local teachers unions also consistently fight serious reforms or measures of accountability. In New York, to cite only one instance, "the top echelons of the UFT [United Federation of Teachers], generally regarded as more liberal than the rank and file, usually praise reforms. At the school level, however, union representatives routinely respond to innovations by characterizing changes as violations of the union contract and filing grievances that prevent reforms."[22] The Ohio Federation of Teachers is part of a coalition challenging in court the charter school law in its state.

Unions, unlike school reformers, may be following the wishes of their constituents. Although teachers endorse higher standards in the abstract, very few identify poor curricula or low standards as the biggest problem facing their schools.[23] Almost twice as many (43 percent) superintendents in Ohio ranked teachers as unenthusiastic about proficiency testing as the next highest group, parents.[24] A slim majority of teachers believe that the curriculum in their school needs no improvement; teachers consistently rate local schools much higher than do other Americans and higher than private schools.[25] Four out of five worry about unanticipated consequences of reform; their caution exceeds that of superintendents, principals, school board members, and business leaders. Only 45 percent endorse "tying teacher rewards and sanctions to their students' performance."[26] And over twice as many teachers as members of the public agreed in 1997 that "there is too much emphasis on achievement testing in the public schools."[27] Unions oppose and teachers in polls are evenly split on the issue of alternative certification routes into the classroom.[28]

Teachers unions may be right to resist some reform efforts. And in any case, every professional association from doctors and lawyers through teachers and professors resists external monitoring and sanctions of its members' accomplishments. The substance of unions' positions, however, is not at issue here; what is crucial is that their skepticism or even hostility to reforms promoting accountability deepens the mystery of why such reforms have been steadily gaining ground. The *Economist* in 2002 described teachers unions as "one of the most powerful forces in American politics."[29] If that were the case, the trajectory of the past decade would have been different. Another reason remains to wonder why, from a political standpoint, the education reforms of the 1990s ever happened.

Party Politics

The *Economist* also proclaims that "it is only a small exaggeration to describe the Democratic Party as a wholly-owned subsidiary of the teachers' unions."[30] But that, too, seems wrong; Democratic politicians as well as Republican ones have endorsed strong measures of accountability despite union opposition and public ambivalence. President Bill Clinton strongly supported charter schools, and during his presidency they were authorized and implemented in over two-thirds of the states. President Clinton, like President George H. W. Bush before him, endorsed national tests and standards. Democratic senators and representatives voted overwhelmingly for President George W. Bush's NCLB, and Democratic leaders such as Massachusetts senator Edward M. Kennedy and California representative George Miller were essential to its passage. States with Democratic as well as Republican legislatures and governors are creating programs for alternative certification of teachers and promulgating high-stakes tests. This is not a record of which an all-powerful interest group in opposition, which purportedly controls one party, should be proud.

Political Incentives Not to Impose Clear Measures of Accountability

The puzzle of why measures of accountability have expanded in the face of so many political obstacles grows even stronger when one considers that elected officials have put themselves on the line to produce measurable results among children. Almost everything analysts thought they knew about the history of public schooling, and about political incentives more generally, seems to work against the growth of clear standards with public accountability for achieving difficult outcomes.

As Terry Moe points out (see chapter 4 in this volume), "In state after state, governments have imposed new curriculum standards, new tests aligned to the standards, new requirements for promotion and graduation, new rules for ranking schools and publicizing test scores, and new systems of rewards and sanctions. And the action is not just at the state level." But that is new. Until recently, governors were content to leave educational policy in the hands of obscure and ostentatiously nonpartisan state departments of education and to leave educational programs in the hands of sometimes hundreds of largely autonomous local districts. Mayors in large cities, where schools genuinely are in crisis, are also moving to take direct control of public schooling. That, too, is new; through most of the twentieth-century mayors were content, even eager, to leave this whole arena in the hands of an often-autonomous local district(s) run by a directly elected and frequently nonpartisan school board. Even in cities where mayors appointed members of the school board, the appointments were supposed to be nonpartisan.

Even more surprisingly, the national Republican Party has moved to claim public responsibility for schooling outcomes, despite its historic commitment to stay out of local affairs and the fact that federal dollars cover only 7 percent of schooling costs. After all, the party's presidential campaign platform called for eliminating the Department of Education up until the election of 2000. Most surprisingly of all, leaders of the Republican Party insisted that NCLB require the disaggregation of students' test results, so that it will be clear whether the children whose scores have proven the most intractable and whose parents are not Republican voters—poor children, African Americans, English language learners—actually do better.

As others have pointed out, politicians face a huge principal-agent problem in this arena. That is, the chain of control in public schooling is long and convoluted—from elected officials to school board (whose members may be competitors for their offices), to superintendent, to principal, teacher(s), parents, and, finally, student. No pair of links on that chain has very tight causal bonds; in combination they epitomize "loose coupling." Furthermore, no one doubts that forces outside educators' or politicians' control greatly affect the ability of students to learn and teachers to teach. These forces include children's and their classmates' socioeconomic status, the nature of their neighborhood, the stability and composition of their family, the health and disability status of a child and his or her family, the movement of women into professions other than teaching, the growth of non–English speaking immigrants in many schools, mobility across schools and districts, and more. Some of these forces exercise random but important effects on a child's capacity to reach a set of standards. Most, however, work cumulatively to diminish achievement of poor children in poor communities. Why would any politically sophisticated elected official (that is almost a definitional redundancy) seek responsibility for attaining a clearly measurable outcome that is so difficult to reach and over which he or she has so little control?

They seldom do. R. Douglas Arnold has shown the many ways that elected officials create institutions that permit deniability on contentious issues, maintain maneuvering room on issues with complex causal chains, duck issues on which many constituents have intense and controversial views, and avoid offending powerful constituency groups with deep pockets and highly organized platoons of voters (for example, teachers unions).[31] And yet by mandating standards with accountability, elected officials of all political stripes and at all levels of government have eschewed deniability, narrowed their maneuvering room, and offended a powerful interest group—all for the sake of tackling a contentious and perhaps intractable problem. Why?

The Political Dynamics of Promoting Reform

I have fewer answers than questions, but there must be compelling explanations for events that actually occurred.

Economic and Demographic Imperatives

Possibly politicians are responding to a fear that students are not learning enough to succeed in a changing economy. This argument is well known, so I can be brief. Arguably, new technologies require a more highly educated work force and the nature of work itself is changing, so that workers can no longer rise into the comfortable middle class by dropping out of school and taking a job on the factory floor. As jobs increasingly come to need higher levels of verbal and computational sophistication, employers find it harder and more expensive to train poorly educated new employees, and political actors increasingly worry that poorly educated workers will be a drag on the new economy. Thus, according to this argument, business leaders joined with political leaders and a few far-seeing educators in the 1990s to demand rigorous academic standards with clear assessments for all future workers.[32]

Politicians may also, or instead, be responding to a concern about who those workers will be and where they are coming from. The outstanding demographic impact for the next few decades will stem from the aging of baby boomers and, absent a major change in immigration laws, from increased racial and ethnic diversity in the population, especially among the young. About 13 percent of the American population is now over sixty-five; by 2030, the aged will constitute roughly 20 percent.[33] Because of the growth in the elderly population and the size of the school-aged population, the dependency ratio—the ratio of those of working age to the young and old—is likely to become much higher over the next few decades.[34] At the same time, the Anglo population of the country will decrease from 70 percent in 2000 to about 50 percent in 2050 as the proportions of Asian Americans and Hispanics both double.[35] In at least fifteen states, more than 40 percent of the school-aged population will be non-Anglo by 2015. Latino children already outnumber black children by several million.[36]

As demographer William Frey points out, these changes will have "enormous implications. We're looking down the road at a huge racial generation gap between the old, white baby boomers and these young, multiracial people."[37] This racial generation gap could create serious policy dilemmas if policymakers feel that they must choose between, say, higher budgets for health care for the elderly or higher budgets for schooling for youth. The gap could also lead to severe social division. In addition to polarization between young and old, increased divisions might be seen between Anglo and non-Anglo populations, immigrants and native-born Americans, or ethnic or racial communities.

These dangers can be averted, according to the argument from the demographic imperative, if all children attain a better education. Better-educated workers and fewer unemployable adults will ease the dependency ratio, provide more funds for needed social services for the elderly, and reduce the need for social services for the young. Fully incorporating immigrant children and children of color into the society and economy through the schools will reduce the pull toward polarization both by making Anglos better able to deal with differences and by making non-Anglos less different. In short, recognizing that better schooling for all children will help to solve severe looming problems, political actors, farsighted business executives, and a few educational leaders took action over the past decade to raise standards and insist on accountability.

It would be comforting to use the economic and demographic imperatives to explain the political puzzle that I have been articulating. The logic here is that the nation was facing severe long-term problems that improved education would eventually help to solve, so people took steps to improve education. But any historian knows that political actors are not always farsighted, correct in their visions of the future, or able to put those visions into practice in the face of short-term pressures. Otherwise there would be no—or at least fewer—wars, famines, riots, scandals, and simple mistakes. Anyone who has spent twenty years studying American racial dynamics, as I have, knows that the presence of a deep and troubling problem does not imply that a solution is forthcoming. A more complete explanation is needed for why, given all the obstacles described above, educational reforms of the 1990s took hold.

Issue Expansion

A good explanation will show not just why the reform movement started, given that numerous reform efforts begin, but also why it persisted and even gained momentum in the face of substantial obstacles. One pair of political scientists describes this process as issue expansion, which has several stages. First, "when issues reach the public agenda, . . . political leaders react . . . by doing whatever they can to provide support for specialists who convince them that they have the power to solve a major national problem. Leaders want to be seen as facilitating, not hindering, the work of experts when the public believes that something good may come of it." Next, policymakers "create new institutions to support their programs. . . . These [new] institutions then structure participation and policymaking." Finally, the excitement dies away, replaced by either concern for another problem, frustration with the intractability of this one, or simply fickleness. But "after public interest and enthusiasm fade, the institutions remain, pushing forward with their preferred policies. These institutional legacies of agenda access may structure participation so that a powerful subsystem can remain relatively independent of popular control for decades."[38]

No popular demand was heard for substantive school reform in the 1980s. Many Americans, nevertheless, shared an amorphous but growing concern about "the rising tide of mediocrity" in the schools. More important, voters' opinions generally shifted toward the right end of the political spectrum, generating a growing desire to hold public officials accountable for using tax-payers' dollars efficiently. In some policy arenas, that desire took the form of a move away from public provision of services into markets. (An example is the shift of health care for the poor from public hospitals and local community health services into competitive health maintenance organizations.) But in public education, perhaps because of Americans' commitment to "the ideology of public schooling," increasing public conservatism combined with a vague sense that education was not good enough to generate a focus on more and better performance, mostly within the public arena.[39]

During the 1980s that focus crystallized into rules that increased course requirements and set minimal standards for graduation (see chapter 10 in this volume). It also emerged in calls for moving back to basics in elementary schools and in what eventually became Goals 2000 and the abortive drive by presidents of both parties to develop national standards and tests. A few governors and state legislatures joined in the call for higher standards, perhaps because they thought it could be an unfunded mandate—that is, a requirement by a higher governmental unit that a lower one (or private actor) accomplish some public purpose without additional resources to do so. After all, if legislators could pass laws requiring teachers to make students work harder and learn more, why not?

Once a few political actors prominently demanded higher standards and greater accountability, others joined the movement. The political attractiveness of advocating coherence and high standards proved irresistible to politicians, if only for the pleasure of challenging their opponents to favor incoherence and low standards. That may be too cynical, but regardless of the reason the issue of school quality was prominently on the public agenda by the early 1990s. At that point political leaders began to provide the support needed by specialists who claimed to have solutions to the purported national problem of low achievement, just as the theory of issue expansion would predict.

Part of what is so fascinating about this issue, however, is that neither leaders nor specialists were the people whom one would have initially expected. The specialists were not for the most part educators, who remained largely outside the arena of accountability and reform until late in the process. The specialists were instead state supreme courts, which started demanding adequate schooling as a way to judge how much financial equalization was appropriate, and business leaders who wanted better-trained workers and measurable outcomes for their tax dollars. Other specialists included college professors and professional associations that designed the standards, and commercial test preparers who are creating (and selling) the measures of accountability.

Similarly, the political leaders who moved in to support the specialists were not primarily liberals concerned about the terrible state of inner-city schools. They were, instead, relatively conservative Democratic governors and mayors, perhaps concerned about the impact of the demographic changes that were appearing first in cities, and Republicans seeking to demonstrate their compassion as well as their conservatism. A few liberal civil rights advocacy groups also came to perceive standards with accountability as serving the interests of poor children of color in urban schools, so they united with conservative Democrats and Republicans on this issue.

That combination of actors has, so far, been enough to support the creation of new institutions to develop and maintain reforms. These new institutions are structuring participation and policymaking in the arena of accountability, just as the theory of issue expansion would predict. Every state and most districts have new offices whose purpose is to institutionalize a new repertoire of reforms, ranging from high-stakes tests and curricular coordination and revision, to charter schools, alternative certification programs, or receiverships of the worst-off schools and districts. Mayors of several of the largest cities acquired direct accountability for schools, a major institutional change that will not easily be undone. The mandates of NCLB will also reinforce and expand state- and district-level institutions focused on testing and measurement of outcomes, and they may generate yet more institutions as a result of that measurement.

No one knows how the third stage of issue expansion—the persistence of new policies and institutions once public attention shifts to another problem—will play out. If teachers unions are as powerful as Moe, the *Economist*, and others suggest and if the public is as indifferent to achievement as some surveys indicate, these institutions may be co-opted and hollowed out.[40] In that case, apparent accountability will become a sham. But that has not yet happened, and so far the trajectory remains one of expansion, not contraction. In either case, school reform for accountability persists as a fascinating topic; by the usual political criteria it should not have gotten off the ground, and by the usual educational criteria it should not have met with much success. But it was attempted and arguably is accomplishing its goals.[41] Albert Shanker would have been pleased, even if many of his constituents remain ambivalent.

Notes

1. Public Education Network and *Education Week*, "Accountability for All," *Polling Report*, vol. 18, no. 9 (2002), pp. 1, 7–8.

2. As a consequence, proponents have sought out sympathetic activist conservative courts, where they are meeting with more success. The parallels with liberal supporters of school desegregation almost half a century ago are striking.

3. E. Hanushek and M. Raymond, "Improving Educational Quality: How Best to Evaluate Our Schools?" (Federal Reserve Bank of Boston, 2002) (edpro.stanford.edu/eah/papers/accountability.BostonFed.final%20publication.pdf [July 17, 2003]).

4. Hanushek and Raymond, "Improving Educational Quality," p. 41.

5. Hanushek and Raymond, "Improving Educational Quality"; and C. Swanson and D. Stevenson, "Standards-Based Reform in Practice: Evidence on State Policy and Classroom Instruction from the NAEP State Assessments," *Educational Evaluation and Policy Analysis*, vol. 24, no. 1 (2002), pp. 1-27. More fully, "a state's level of standards-based policymaking exerts a significant positive effect on the use of stan-

dards-based instructional practices within the classroom" (p. 13). This study did not look directly at measures of accountability.

6. National Commission on Excellence in Education, *A Nation at Risk: The Imperative for Educational Reform* (Government Printing Office, 1983); and M. Lieberman, *Public Education: An Autopsy* (Harvard University Press, 1993). See also J. Chubb and T. Moe, *Politics, Markets, and America's Schools* (Brookings, 1990).

7. On worsening, see P. Peterson, "Little Gain in Student Achievement." in P. Peterson, ed., *Our Schools and Our Future: Are We Still at Risk?* (Stanford, Calif.: Hoover Institution Press, 2003), pp. 39–72. On the National Assessment of Educational Progress (NAEP), see National Center for Education Statistics (NCES), *Digest of Education Statistics 2001* (Department of Education, 2002), tables 112, 124. On dropouts, see NCES, *Digest of Education Statistics 2001,* tables 108, 109. On special education, see NCES, *Digest of Education Statistics 2001,* table 53.

8. The proportion of white seventeen- and eighteen-year-olds taking the SAT rose from 18.5 to 22 percent between 1977 and 2000, while the average white's combined SAT score rose from 1036 to 1060. The proportion of African Americans of the same ages taking the SAT rose from 12 to 19 percent over the same period, while blacks' average SAT score rose from 789 to 859. (Calculations done by the author from Bureau of the Census and Educational Testing Service [ETS] data. Test scores control for the recentering done by ETS during this period.)

9. From 1987 to 1998 American students increased the number of courses they took in virtually all subjects. Four times as many blacks and six times as many Hispanics now take a full curriculum as their predecessors did in the early 1980s. Many more students are now studying advanced algebra and chemistry, and here, too, African Americans and Latinos are closing the gap with Anglos and Asians. See Center on Education Policy and American Youth Policy Forum, "Do You Know the Good News about American Education?" (2000) (www.ctredpol.org/archive.htm [July 2, 2003]).

10. NCES, *Digest of Education Statistics 2001,* table 184.

11. Quotation is from L. Olson, "Failing Schools Challenge Accountability Goals," *Education Week,* March 25, 1998, pp. 1, 14. Data on inner-city schools are in M. Cook and W. Evans, "Families or Schools? Explaining the Convergence in White and Black Academic Performance," *Journal of Labor Economics,* vol. 18, no. 4 (2000), pp. 729–54. NAEP results are in K. Zernike, "Gap between Best and Worst Widens on U.S. Reading Test," *New York Times,* April 7, 2001, pp. A1, 10.

12. NCES, *Digest of Education Statistics 2001,* table 22.

13. J. Hochschild and N. Scovronick, *The American Dream and the Public Schools* (Oxford University Press, 2003), p. 97. For some public skepticism, see "Improving Our Schools," *The Polling Report,* vol. 17, no. 15 (2001), pp. 1, 7. On Latinos, see R. A. Dyer, "Most Latinos Back TAAS Exit Exam despite Bias Fears," *Fort Worth Star-Telegram,* July 24, 2000, p. 11.

14. CBS News Poll, January 1999; and all Phi Delta Kappa or Gallup polls on this issue.

15. On work, see Public Agenda, *Assignment Incomplete: The Unfinished Business of Education Reform* (New York: Public Agenda Foundation, 1995), p. 43. On extracurricular activities, see Phi Delta Kappa, *Attitudes toward the Public Schools*, 1996.

16. Phi Delta Kappa, *Attitudes toward the Public Schools*, 1970, 1974, 1982, and 1997.

17. A. Shanker, *Where We Stand: The Chicago Reform* (Washington: American Federation of Teachers, 1994).

18. A. Shanker, "Letter to the Editor," *Education Week*, January 16, 1996.

19. Quotation from Sandra Feldman is at www.aft.org/edissues/rsa/misc/Sfltr.htm [July 2, 2003]; B. Chase, "The New NEA: Reinventing Teacher Unions for a New Era," *American Educator* (1997–98), pp. 12–15 (emphasis in original).

20. Both quotations are in J. Archer, "President Leaves Mixed Record on Pledge to 'Reinvent' NEA: Bob Chase Stepping Down after Two Terms," *Education Week*, June 19, 2002, pp. 10–11; the first is from a National Education Association activist.

21. The comment about charter schools is in B. Keller, "Candidates Stress Experience, Style in Union Contest," *Education Week*, June 19, 2002, p. 11. Reactions to No Child Left Behind are in B. Keller, "NEA Delegates Select Seasoned Union Veteran as Their Next President," *Education Week*, July 10, 2002, p. 10, quoting, respectively, Reg Weaver (the eventual winner) and Denise Rockwell.

22. T. Ross, "Grassroots Action in East Brooklyn: A Community Organization Takes Up School Reform," in C. Stone, ed., *Changing Urban Education* (University Press of Kansas, 1998), pp. 118–38.

23. Phi Delta Kappa, *Teachers' Attitudes toward the Public Schools*, 1996, 1997, and 1998; and Public Agenda, *Given the Circumstances: Teachers Talk about Public Education Today* (New York: Public Agenda Foundation, 1996), pp. 22–25.

24. T. Sutton, "Holding Schools Accountable: The Effects of Top-Down Testing and Management Mandates on Ohio Schools," paper prepared for a meeting of the Midwest Political Science Association, Chicago, 2001.

25. For these views, see Phi Delta Kappa, *Teachers' Attitudes toward the Public Schools*, 1997; Public Agenda, *Educational Reform: The Players and the Politics* (New York: Public Agenda Foundation, 1992), p. 14; Public Agenda, *Given the Circumstances*, pp. 19–20; and Metropolitan Life Survey, *Are We Preparing Students for the 21st Century?* (New York: Metropolitan Life Insurance Company, 2000), p. 112.

26. Public Agenda, *Given the Circumstances*, p. 41; and Public Agenda, *A Sense of Calling: Who Teaches and Why* (New York: Public Agenda Foundation, 2000), p. 44.

27. Phi Delta Kappa, *Teachers' Attitudes toward the Public Schools*, 1997.

28. Public Agenda, *A Sense of Calling*, p. 44.

29. "Lexington: Inching toward Reform," *Economist*, July 6, 2002, p. 34.

30. "Lexington: Inching toward Reform," p. 34.

31. R. D. Arnold, *The Logic of Congressional Action* (Yale University Press, 1990).

32. C. Goldin, "The Human Capital Century and American Leadership: Virtues of the Past," *Journal of Economic History*, vol. 61, no. 2 (2001), pp. 263–92, provides a historical perspective on the relative virtues and vices of the American and Euro-

pean educational systems from the perspective of the economy. She, too, concludes that the "forgiving" American educational system no longer fits the country's economic needs.

33. W. Frey and R. DeVol, *America's Demography in the New Century: Aging Baby Boomers and New Immigrants as Major Players* (Los Angeles, Calif.: Milken Institute, 2000).

34. By one prediction, the dependency ratio in the United States will increase from about 63:100 in 1992 to about 83:100 in 2030. See Bureau of the Census, *Projections of the Total Resident Population by 5-Year Age Groups and Sex, with Special Age Categories*, Middle Series, 2025–2045 (NP–T3-F) (2000). See also E. Toder and S. Solanki, *Effects of Demographic Trends on Labor Supply and Living Standards* (Washington: Urban Institute Press, 1999), pp. 5–10.

35. These figures assume that the racial and ethnic categories now in use will remain meaningful over the next century. That is unlikely, especially if intermarriage continues to grow at the same rate that it has over the past few decades.

36. G. Vernez and R. Krop, *Projected Social Context for Education of Children: 1990–2015* (New York: College Entrance Examination Board, 1999). H. Hodgkinson, *Secondary Schools in a New Millennium: Demographic Certainties, Social Realities* (Reston, Va.: National Association of Secondary School Principals, 2000), surveys the implications of these demographic changes for schools.

37. In Los Angeles County, the "elderly population is still majority white, its working-aged population is only about one-third white, and its child population is predominantly Hispanic and other racial and ethnic groups." See W. Frey, "The New Urban Demographics," *Brookings Review*, vol. 18, no. 3 (Summer, 2000), pp. 18–21. See also M. Skertic, "More Young People Are Multiracial," *Chicago Sun-Times*, March 13, 2001, p. 5.

38. F. R. Baumgartner and B. D. Jones, *Agendas and Instability in American Politics* (University of Chicago Press, 1993), pp. 83–84.

39. The first quoted phrase is in National Commission on Excellence in Education, *A Nation at Risk*; the second is in T. Moe, *Schools, Vouchers, and the American Public* (Brookings, 2001).

40. For such a prediction, see P. Brimelow, *The Worm in the Apple: How the Teacher Unions Are Destroying American Education* (HarperCollins, 2003).

41. Debates continue to rage furiously over whether accountability measures are helping, harming, or having no effect on students. A powerful recent claim of ineffectiveness or even harm is A. Amrein and D. Berliner, *The Impact of High-Stakes Tests on Student Academic Achievement* (Arizona State University, College of Education, Educational Policy Research Unit, 2002). A strong response claiming benefit is M. Raymond and E. Hanushek, *Shopping for Evidence against School Accountability* (Stanford University, Hoover Institution, 2003).

PART 2

The Practice
of School Accountability

6

Lessons about the Design of State Accountability Systems

ERIC A. HANUSHEK AND MARGARET E. RAYMOND

All accountability systems are not alike. They differ in fundamental ways that affect their inherent incentives and potential outcomes. It is easy to conclude that many of the existing systems contain flaws that lead to a variety of undesirable outcomes, particularly in the short run. Yet it is important that discussion moves past whether accountability systems are perfect or not. Evidence of flaws should not be taken as general condemnation of accountability systems but instead should lead to focus on how the structure of accountability and reward systems might be improved.

The basic premise of virtually all proposed school accountability systems is that student performance should be the key element. This change, partially forced by federal legislation, will transform the focus of the past when a majority of states provided rudimentary information about schools in the state, often confined to a few measures of school resources and avoiding any indication of student performance.[1] Even when states have created a hybrid system that combines input and outcome regulatory elements, student outcomes have become a major focus. The appropriate metric for incorporating student outcome information, however, is far from obvious.

The differences across states support a comparative analysis of the structure of the systems and the relationship between structure and performance of the systems over time. Our perspective is that the summary measures of student performance produced by the accountability system are meant to represent the performance of schools and are at least in part intended to introduce incentives for improvement. The question central to this paper is how different accountability measures reflect the quality and performance of schools and whether different accountability systems should be expected to generate improvements in student outcomes.

The Bottom Line

Before analyzing the characteristics of alternative incentive schemes, however, it is useful to take a quick glimpse of currently observable impacts of state systems. Because the number of states that employed accountability systems changed during the 1990s, whether schools in accountability states performed differently from those in other states can be considered.

Accountability systems can have two kinds of consequences: intended and unintended. Fundamentally, accountability systems alter the incentives faced by schools. In the best of worlds, this change would spur states to improve their schools. In the worst, this might induce "bad" outcomes as schools attempted to game the system. For the moment, we concentrate on performance or good aspects.

The impact of existing state systems is illustrated in figure 6-1, which summarizes our estimates of the gains in mathematics that would be expected between 1996 and 2000 for the typical student who progresses from fourth to eighth grade. These expected gains are calculated from regression analyses of scores on the National Assessment of Educational Progress (NAEP). The larger empirical work upon which these estimates are drawn separates the potential impact of parental inputs and school spending from the impact of testing and reporting across states.[2] States were classified according to the type of accountability system they had in place at the time of the NAEP test. (A state could have its classification change between the two years if it adopted an accountability system.) States with "report card" systems display test performance and other factors but neither provide any simple aggregation and judgment of performance nor attach sanctions and rewards. In many ways, these systems serve simply as a public disclosure function. Systems that provide explicit scores for schools and that attach sanctions and rewards are labeled "accountability" systems. The typical student in a state without any formal system would see a 0.7 percent increase in proficiency scores. Reporting systems move the expected gain to 1.2 percent. Finally, states with full accountability systems obtained a 1.6 percent increase in mathematics performance. The performance difference between either reporting systems or accountability systems and no system is statistically sig-

Figure 6-1. *Effect of State Accountability System on National Assessment of Educational Progress Performance*

Percent math gains from fourth to eighth grade

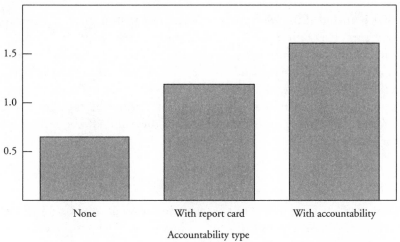

Accountability type

Source: Eric A. Hanushek and Margaret E. Raymond, "Improving Educational Quality: How Best to Evaluate Our Schools?" in Yolanda Kodrzycki, ed., *Education in the Twenty-First Century: Meeting the Challenges of a Changing World* (Federal Reserve Bank of Boston, 2002).

nificant (although the difference between the two systems is not). In short, testing and accountability as practiced have led to gains over that expected without formal systems.

This impact makes clear that the issue is not whether to have accountability but how best to have accountability. What are the alternative approaches to accountability and what is known about their potential impact?

Alternative Accountability Systems

The key to understanding the informational content (and ultimately incentives) of standard accountability systems is to examine the determinants of student performance and how those determinants are displayed and used. Take the simplest model of student achievement that is consistent with prior work on the determinants of achievement:

$$achievement = school + other. \tag{1}$$

Without getting into controversies about testing at this point, the standard approach is to test students during one or more grades to measure achievement. The general idea behind accountability systems is that some aggregation of the tests can be used to assess the contributions of schools—but it is immediately obvious that much will depend on the importance of other things.

What is included in *other*? As is well documented in prior analyses of achievement, many factors outside of the control of schools affect individual student achievement. Students clearly differ in ability, and students get varying input from families and friends. Moreover, measurement of true achievement through common tests is prone to measurement error. Finally, achievement at any particular time is not determined just by current school and other factors. The historical pattern of each of these also affects the current level of achievement. Thus

$$other = ability + family + peers + history + measurement\ error. \qquad (2)$$

Accountability systems use test information for a group of students in each school to present a picture of school achievement. The actual measure of school achievement varies. The simplest measure is the average of test scores for students in a grade or an entire school, although few states end up developing their accountability systems on just school average achievement. Important variants include distributional information such as the percentage of students scoring above some specific level (for example, "passing" or "proficient"). These variants introduce important elements into accountability systems, but, for now, we consider accountability based just on average performance measures.

Cross-Sectional Approaches

The first set of accountability devices begins with the aggregated scores of students in a given year and compares such measures across schools. Virtually all states, whether they provide just report card information or instead develop accountability structures, report average achievement as one of the components of information given. The status model simply takes the average performance of students taking the test in a school as a measure of the outcomes in each school. (While more important later, we do not distinguish at this point between systems built on calculating grade averages as opposed to school averages.)[3] The first point from this is obvious: If the main purpose of the accountability system is assessing the performance of the school, average test score does it imperfectly. The average achievement will incorporate all of the current and historical inputs to achievement including not only schools but also family background and random errors included in *other*. The status model cannot factor out year-to-year changes in student body composition or grade-to-grade changes in instructional design or teacher quality. Thus the simple average score indicates the level of student performance but cannot pinpoint the source of that performance. That these imperfect scores figure into the determination of sanctions and rewards adds to the problem.

This basic confusion between average student achievement and the contribution of schools is well known, and most states report additional information. For example, some states either provide data on family backgrounds (such as rates of free lunch program participation or racial compositions of schools) or describe achievement for reference groups of students judged similar in family backgrounds. These approaches still do not allow an accurate estimation of school performance, because the accountability measures still confound family differences or cohort differences with school impacts. Further, even if *family* factors could be adequately accounted for, these adjusted average scores will not capture the prior factors (that is, *history*) that affect current achievement. Nor do they allow for any measurement errors in performance.

Most of the attention has focused on ways of trying to allow for differences in the nonschool factors, *family*, but existing efforts have simply produced imprecise results, leaving considerable uncertainty about interpretation of scores and little way to separate out the value-added of the school.

In the status change model, the average student achievement of a school is tracked over time. In simplest terms, does the average performance of students increase from one year to the next? The idea is easiest seen in terms of an example. If a grade has a common examination, say third-grade reading, the status change score is the difference in the average scores from one year to the next. The status change model for a school is calculated by aggregating performance across tested grades. We classify this model as cross-sectional, because it compares snapshots of the school scores across years (as opposed to tracking the performance changes for individual students across years).

The status change model is by far the most common approach to assessing what is happening in schools. The change scores factor heavily in reward systems but are manipulated in a wide variety of ways; for example, absolute levels of change, percentage increments of change, and change relative to an external standard. Regardless, the most common interpretation is that this provides a measure of the change in performance of the particular grade or school. Thus, for example, states may have goals or rewards related to the progress that is measured by the status change.

The way to understand this construct is to think of it as providing an estimate of the change across years in value-added of schools ($\Delta school$). It will, however, not be a perfect measure of any school's improvement but will instead contain errors. The approach raises two questions. Does an accountability system based on status change provide biased estimates of performance improvement that systematically diverge in one direction or another? Are the errors so large that they mute any incentives for schools to do better?

The error in measuring change in school performance goes directly back to the underlying determinants of achievement. The status change model necessarily compares two different groups of students, only some of whom are common across years. Thus the status change has two primary components—the object of interest, which is the difference in school quality ($\Delta school$) across the two years, and the difference between the two groups of students in family background and other nonschool factors ($\Delta other$). For some considerations, other differences incorporate any idiosyncratic measurement errors affecting achievement ($\Delta measurement\ error$), and this may have elevated importance. Just like the status model that relies on the level of average achievement, the status change model completely entangles school performance with student background differences and measurement errors. The best interpretation would be that, if variations in quality improvements across schools are large relative to differences in the other factors, changes in grade or school performance would dominate the changes. But, little evidence exists that would support such an interpretation.

It might be tempting to argue that local schools in stable communities have similar family inputs and thus $\Delta other$ will be small. But the U.S. population moves a surprisingly large amount. Only 55 percent of students live in the same house for three years in a row, and this falls to half for disadvantaged students.[4] Moreover, residential mobility is often related to significant changes in family circumstances such as divorce or job loss and change. In growing states the mobility rates increase noticeably from these national averages. The average annual student mobility across schools in Texas, for example, exceeds 20 percent.

The implications of mobility for the accountability approaches are clear. As mobility increases, differences in the backgrounds, preparation, and abilities of the two groups of students over time will influence the difference in aggregate performance in the status change model. Now not only current differences in nonschool factors enter but historical differences also do—and mobility implies that two adjacent cohorts will diverge in terms of the past schools they attended.

While we have concentrated on school averages, it is common to find these cross-sectional approaches taken to individual grades within a school. The basic motivation for doing this is isolating differential performance by parts of schools. In particular, grade change models offer some potential for focusing on school factors when individual cohorts can be tracked over a number of years. Moreover, the use of grade change models becomes particularly important when passing rates or other distinct elements of the student achievement distribution are highlighted. Nonetheless, these grade approaches still suffer from difficulties in separating *school* and *other* factors.

Longitudinal Approaches

Accountability is different when it focuses on the progress of students over time, which we classify as a longitudinal approach. One such approach is the cohort gain model, which tracks the performance of individual cohorts of students as they progress through school. Consider, for example, comparing the scores of third graders in 2001 with those of fourth graders in 2002. With a stable student body (that is, with no in- or out-migration for the school), the historical school and nonschool factors would cancel out (because they influence a cohort's performance both in grade three and grade four). The cohort gain score would then reflect what the school contributed to learning in grade four plus any differences in idiosyncratic test factors or measurement errors across the two grades. The influence of family differences on current achievement growth rates would also remain, so that if, for example, disadvantaged students would be expected to have lower rates of improvement in performance than more advantaged, such differences would remain confounded with school factors. The family background and ability factors that affect the cohort gain calculations are, however, ones that affect the rate of growth of learning, not the level. Thus they would be expected to be relatively small. As a result, the cohort model would generally yield a closer measure of *school* impacts than the status model.

The main concern is how the calculations handle mobility. To the extent that the calculations simply follow the cohort of current students in each grade in each year (for example, fourth graders in 2001 and fifth graders in 2002), in- and out-migration yield the same type of problems discussed previously. The comparisons do not eliminate the differences in nonschool factors across groups, because of changes in cohort composition over time.

A number of options for adjusting cohort gains can provide information that is closer to the true impact of schools. One modification simply excludes students entering during the school year from the average achievement calculations. This modification has three advantages for measuring school quality—students who move typically have less learning gain in the year of the move because of the disruption; they have received less than a full dose of the teaching in their current school but part of the teaching in their prior school;

and one element of potentially large change in nonschool factors is eliminated.[5] With this modification, the cohort model still compares different
groups of students (because those exiting the school between third- and
fourth-grade testing are still included in the earlier achievement calculations
but not the latter). Moreover, because mobility is correlated with family
backgrounds, the achievement measures are likely to be biased by any differences in student mobility rates across schools. The error would nonetheless
be expected to be less than in the no adjustment comparisons.

The influence of mobility suggests an alternative measure for accountability, the individual gain score model. This approach improves on cohort
change models because it analyzes data at the student level and can include
all students with gain scores, not just the students in the original group. If
individual students are followed across grades, any historical influences of
families and nonschool factors wash out, and the average of individual gains
across grades would more closely reflect school quality for the given grade.
Nonetheless, it would still incorporate any current influences of family and
ability on the growth in achievement and any measurement errors in the separate grade tests.[6]

Refinements and Disaggregations

One obvious fact is that the more aggregated the performance information
the less possible it is to pinpoint any causal factors. Thus, for example,
accountability models that aggregate all information to the school level (or,
worse, the district level) make it difficult to pinpoint the source of any high
or low performance. One natural and easy refinement is simply to provide
scores for individual grades instead of aggregating these to the entire school
level. For example, schools with stable teacher forces could use the grade pattern of cohort gains to unravel the contribution of different groups of teachers. Perhaps the ultimate in this regard is the calculation of teacher value-
added as done in Tennessee.[7] These studies, which are legislatively mandated,
provide information to principals and to specific teachers about the student
learning gains over time by individual teachers, although the information is
not made public.

The validity of the different accountability models for constructing school
outcome measures generally relies on a basic stability of underlying nonschool influences and looks at gains in an effort to eliminate the influence of
these other factors. An alternative approach is to adjust for outside influences
directly.

Consider a situation with only two kinds of family influences: good or
bad. If a measure existed of these family influences for different students, a

measure could be created of school accountability by simply averaging achievement separately for all students from a good background and all from a bad background. These separate measures would then provide indications of how well a school did with students in the two categories. More generally, the calculations could be expanded to allow for a range of different family backgrounds, including more than two possible levels and including more than a single dimension. States have actively pursued different approaches such as developing indexes that rely on weighting different student factors (such as proportion eligible for free or reduced-price lunch or average education levels of parents) or using statistical approaches (regression analysis) to adjust scores for alternative measures of family background. This is not to imply that some students cannot learn, but rather that the pacing may differ, and, for incentive purposes, it is important to separate *school* from *other*. Some adjustments for family background, used in conjunction with individual gain scores, offer perhaps the best chance of isolating the effects of school differences. The individual gain calculations focus the measure on current additions to learning, and the family adjustments eliminate the contemporaneous influence of family factors on the rate of learning by students.

As with the simple gain calculations, the effectiveness of these approaches depends on the ability to capture relevant nonschool factors and the ability then to purge the aggregate test scores of things other than school influences.[8] The difficulty in actual application is that normal administrative records typically provide relatively little information about family backgrounds—such as free lunch status and race/ethnicity—and these are crude measures of the relevant family background differences. The paucity of detailed analyses of family effects makes it difficult to assess the impact of alternative specifications and measures of family factors.

Many state systems do not simply report averages of scores but instead weight the scores against preset thresholds to reach judgments about acceptable levels of performance. But this measurement is no different from the averages in terms of identifying the role of schools. The probability that any given school is above or below any benchmark level for aggregate student performance is directly related to various current and past inputs and to the variance of the random errors; that is, the *other* factors affecting achievement.

In an insightful paper, Thomas J. Kane and Douglas O. Staiger note that the variance of average measurement error on a test will be inversely related to the number of students tested (by the standard calculations for the variance of a mean).[9] They go on to show empirically how standard calculations of school success in North Carolina led small schools (with high measurement error variance) to be disproportionately represented among the successful schools. Further, if measurement errors over time are uncorrelated, the probability that any school remains a successful school in subsequent years is very low.

The issues surrounding the variance of test measurement error and its interplay with accountability schemes highlight a set of important trade-offs in designing accountability systems. The first important point is that aggregate achievement scores are error-prone measures of school quality because of the error measures of the underlying tests and because of the other current and historical factors that are outside of the control of the school. Thus, viewed from the vantage point of an accountability system for estimating school quality differences, test scores contain both a random component and an error component arising from systematic but unmeasured differences within schools and historical achievement factors. As a result, even if measurement errors could be eliminated, concerns about obtaining unbiased estimates of the effects of schools would remain.

Clear trade-offs exist. A variety of states are concerned with more than overall performance. They also wish to ensure that high performance reaches distinct subgroups, say by income levels. Clearly, as scores are aggregated across smaller groups of students, the variance of measurement error increases and can directly affect rankings of schools depending on how subgroup information is used.[10]

The implications of measurement error depend on the magnitude of such errors and on the magnitude of other factors affecting performance that might bias the accountability measure. Kane and Staiger suggest alternative approaches to reducing measurement error. These are most relevant for small schools (say, those with fewer than sixty students being aggregated into the score). But their recommendations highlight other choices. They propose aggregating test measures over time. In general this will lessen the impact of measurement errors, but it will also bring into play some of the issues surrounding status models unless they can circumvent errors introduced by differences in current and historical factors for cohorts. Specifically, averaging status scores over years does not eliminate the influence of nonschool factors, which bias any estimate of school quality based just on outcomes.

The Distribution of State Accountability Systems

In the summer of 2001, we conducted extensive interviews of the education department in every state about its accountability system.[11] Considerable attention was devoted to the structure of the system, the calculation of school scores, the choice of metrics, and the strength of any consequences that schools faced based on their scores. Recognizing that the practice is evolving and thus is highly fluid, these choices represent a single snapshot of the incentive structures that states chose to provide to their schools.

Two states at the time of the survey did not have any measurement or accountability system in place. With the Elementary and Secondary Education Act of 2001, we know these states will adopt some system in short order. Seventeen states had report cards at the school or district level. We found that these states provide information about schools but in a manner that precludes much judgment. For example, a single aspect of the school is described such as the number of students scoring in the lower quintile, or schools scores are not compared with an independent standard of performance, or the score does not have any consequences associated with it. The remaining thirty-one states have systems that create a single measure of performance, they have created a scale of judgment about the resulting school scores to determine acceptable and unacceptable results, and they have explicit consequences (sanctions or rewards or both) that schools are exposed to as a result of their score.

The survey of state practices placed states within four categories: status model, status change model, cohort gain model, and individual gain score model. The chief distinction, as described previously, is whether the data are cross-sectional or whether they track individual student achievement changes over time. Table 6-1 displays the states with rating systems by the analytic model used to calculate their school scores. The progression from status to grade-level change to student change is associated with greater precision in the measures and greater detail about the real impacts of school activity.

The chief information conveyed by these data is the prevalence of using cross-sectional score information. This choice generally precludes sorting out the various components of achievement. Moreover, this choice tends to increase the incentives for states to manipulate the testing and to attempt to change scores by means other than improving school quality. Specifically, the accounting systems that track student achievement over time improve the incentives for schools, because the results do a better job of explaining the real state of schools without confounding influences mixed in.

Incentives and Evidence on Effects

Accountability systems have an overall influence on schools in two ways: through defining areas of particular attention for schools and through providing rewards or punishments for improving in those areas. We translate the discussion on the different accountability systems into hypotheses about the

Table 6-1. *Classification of States by the Type of Analysis Model Used in School Rating Systems, 2001*

Cross-sectional approaches		Longitudinal approach	
School status model (or status change)	Grade-level change	Cohort gain	Individual gain score
Alabama	Alaska	New Mexico	Massachusetts
Arkansas	Colorado	North Carolina	Tennessee
California	Delaware		
Connecticut	Florida		
Georgia	Kentucky		
Maryland	Louisiana		
Michigan	Oklahoma		
Mississippi	Rhode Island		
Nevada	Vermont		
New Hampshire	Wisconsin		
New York			
Ohio			
Oregon			
South Carolina			
Texas			
Virginia			
West Virginia			

Source: Stephen H. Fletcher and Margaret E. Raymond, *The Future of California's Academic Performance Index* (Stanford University, Hoover Institution, CREDO, 2002).

incentives introduced and then review the existing evidence. The recent birth of many accountability systems, however, means that the existing evidence is thin in many crucial places.

First, accountability systems focus attention on some details of performance and leave others as irrelevant. A system built solely on test scores, for example, filters out everything except student academic achievement. Similarly, if some subjects are tested and others are not, it is natural to think that attention will go more to the tested areas than the untested areas. And, part of the debate about testing has argued that tests of lower order skills tend to drive out attention of schools to higher order skills.

While these arguments have been widely discussed, little empirical work shows the strength of them. Some general but inconclusive psychometric evidence exists on testing and instruction.[12] More relevant, little work directly links current accountability systems to patterns of time and instruction.

Second, accountability systems increase the exposure of schools in terms of student performance. Incentives attached to exposure come from two separate mechanisms—indirect pressures and directly legislated rewards and consequences.

Any school will prefer higher scores to lower ones, even if no explicit consequences follow. Currently, apparently in the absence of much clear evidence, most parents appear to think that their school is doing a good job.[13] The provision of accountability evidence has the potential for changing this, perhaps sufficiently to overcome the inertial positive regard for local schools. In the absence of direct consequences, one might expect any purely informational incentive to be small relative to organizational pressures to maintain the status quo. Nonetheless, some general evidence on reactions of citizens (in the form of housing prices impacts) to quality information exists.[14] Moreover, early evidence suggests that public disclosure of scores may produce some strong incentives, both in terms of housing prices and other observable outcomes.[15]

The second source of incentives arises from any consequences that might be directly associated with the school scores. The rewards and sanctions built into many state accountability systems motivate schools to change behavior. At the same time, one does not expect these incentives to affect all schools equally. For example, schools that have scores close to a threshold might be expected to alter their behavior more than schools further away from the established critical thresholds. The interrelationship between the choice of school score model, the choice of thresholds, and the location of a given school relative to those thresholds is currently relatively unexplored, but it would be reasonable to speculate that no single design can provide equivalent incentives for all schools.

Cross-Sectional Approaches

Both the status and the status change model confuse the school's influence with other factors. A school can respond in two ways. First, it can adjust teachers, curriculum, and program in an attempt to improve the teaching and learning that occur. This is, however, a difficult long-run proposition. A second shorter-run strategy may result: to become more selective about the student scores that are incorporated into the school scores. The second approach could supplement or possibly replace the first. By weeding out students who are poor performers, the school score can appear to be improving even if nothing different is being done.

Take the example of a third-grade student from a disadvantaged background who arrived at school less well prepared than the others in the school and who progressed at a slower rate each year through the third; that is, he or she falls further behind over time. The status model compares performance of individual classes each year to the prior year's class. Thus, if testing begins in the third grade, the school might exclude this slow student through, say, placement in special education or counseling the student to be absent on the day of testing. If the student is excluded, the average of all remaining students would be higher than otherwise, and the school might also look better in comparison to the third grade in the prior year.

But, consider the dynamics. The next-year comparison of third grades will be worse because the base comparison has been artificially elevated. Moreover, once the student is excluded, a continuing incentive exists to keep him or her out of the testing if subsequent grades are also involved in the accountability system. This continuing incentive puts some restraint into the system, because the school probably cannot increase the exclusion rate year after year. Moreover, given that the potential importance of exclusion rates is widely recognized, the school is always at risk that regulatory changes may make it necessary in the future to bring some previously excluded students back into the accountability system.

The largest effects of exclusion on the school ratings come in the first year of exclusion (when the cumulative effect of low preparation plus slow learning is removed). Nonetheless, some continued accountability benefits accrue to the school from exclusion if the students learn at a slower pace. The status model typically aggregates across grades, so the slower learning pace will be removed from the calculation of the school average for the student's fourth grade and beyond in the example. The key element of this part of the dynamics is how much the rate of learning might be below average, as opposed to the absolute level of deficit that comes into play in the first year of exclusion.

While widespread attention has focused on such things as test preparation and cheating, these seem to be the clearest cases of one-time effects that do not appear after the initial introduction. Specifically, these practices may shift the level of performance in a given year, but, unless their prevalence increases over time, they will not show up in the school gains after the first year. Take, for example, efforts to teach all students how to fill in mechanical scoring sheets for standardized exams. Once students know how to do this—something that might inflate their scores through eliminating errors arising just from coding mistakes—it would not be expected to have any continuing effects on their scores as they progress through the grades. Similarly, any cheating on a given test must be repeated in subsequent years just to stay at the same level, but scores will only improve if the level of cheating is increased over time.

The choice of approach may be assumed to follow rational choice. School officials would select the action that they perceive to have the highest yield, given their planning horizon, budget, and appetite for risk. The preceding discussion highlights the fact that the largest gains from exclusions operate in the first year and that these decline or possibly reverse in subsequent years. Administrators may be myopic or may have short time horizons for their decisions, leading them to overuse exclusions in the first years of an accountability system. Regulatory restrictions are frequently designed in an effort to limit the ability of administrators to increase the use of student exclusions.

A grade-level change version of accountability is used when testing does not cover all grades. If, for example, testing is done only at the fourth grade, the accountability system would feature just that grade. This possibility introduces some additional incentives. Some of the dynamics of exclusions are altered. But also there may be incentives to concentrate attention on the tested grade(s), say by placing the best teachers in the relevant testing grade(s).

Several studies have investigated whether schools appear to react to accountability through exclusions. Brian A. Jacob considers the introduction of test-based accountability for Chicago public schools.[16] He finds that the large increases in test scores after accountability went into effect were accompanied by increases in special education placement and by increased grade retentions. Donald Deere and Wayne Strayer and Julie B. Cullen and Randall Reback also find apparent increases in special education placement with the introduction of accountability in Texas.[17] Prior work in Kentucky by Daniel M. Koretz and Sheila I. Barron suggested no strategic use of grade retentions.[18] Walter Haney suggests that both grade retention and increased dropouts were key to improvements in Texas tests, although both Martin Carnoy, Susanna Loeb, and Tiffany L. Smith and Laurence A. Toenjes and A. Gary Dworkin seriously question this after reanalysis of the data.[19] Any grade retentions are, however, short-run effects that do not provide lasting accountability value except if the placement is educationally valuable. David N. Figlio and Lawrence S. Getzler concentrate on special education placement after the introduction of a state accountability system in Florida.[20] The most persuasive evidence is that placement rates increase relatively over time in grades that enter into the accountability system as opposed to those grades that do not.

Jacob finds that scores also appear to go up more in subjects that enter into the accountability system than in those that do not.[21] This evidence is consistent with analysis in Texas by Deere and Strayer.[22] The interpretation is not, however, entirely clear. Schools appear to be responding to the accountability system, which is what the system is supposed to accomplish. However, one might question whether the weights on different potential outcomes are appropriate. (Zero weight or not paying attention to specific subjects, for example, appears to provide strong incentives to change the pattern of instruction.)

In each case, the analysis considers changes that occur around the time of introduction of an accountability system. The key element of most of this research is using the change in accountability to identify the effects on special education placement rates and the like through finding breaks in the patterns of prior placement. Two things are important. First, very few relevant data are available for these analyses—breaks in trends, perhaps compared with trends of other schools (such as schools outside of Chicago and its accountability system). The validity of the interpretation depends crucially on whether or not other things are changing over time that could also affect the patterns of observed changes. Second, each of these analyses provides information just on the short-run immediate effects. Because the incentives change over time, it is important to understand what happens as these systems continue. Because of the recentness of the introduction of accountability systems, little is know about the long-run dynamics.

Our own national work creates questions about the importance of such exclusions. We consider the pattern of special education placement rates across states from 1996 to 2001.[23] If we simply consider the introduction of accountability systems or the length of time with accountability systems in each state, we find a significant and positive relationship on special education placement. But, if an overall time trend is included to allow for the national increases in special education over this time period, the increased use of exclusions disappears.

Eric A. Hanushek and Steven G. Rivkin investigate the impacts of public disclosure of achievement performance.[24] Specifically, before the Texas accountability system included direct consequences or sanctions for performance, the state made information on disaggregated student performance from the Texas Assessment of Academic Skills (TAAS) available to the public. They find that, in the largest metropolitan area, competition works to push up average scores.

Jay P. Greene analyzes the Florida A+ program that provides exit vouchers to students in failing schools and finds that schools close to being subject to vouchers make unusually large gains.[25] Martin Carnoy reviews this evidence and suggests that the reaction to vouchers that Greene identified was more likely a reaction to information.[26] Carnoy finds that similar studies in North Carolina and Texas investigating what happens to failing schools show similar results—dramatic improvements in the year after identification.[27] This occurs even though those states had no voucher threat.

Kane and Staiger suggest that a portion of the school improvement in North Carolina failing schools may simply result from measurement errors in the examinations.[28] They demonstrate that small schools—where the error variance in aggregate tests will be larger—are much more likely to be found at the extremes of the school score distributions. If the measurement errors are independent over time, schools that realized a large error in one period would expect to receive a smaller one the next period, leading to a reordering of schools in the second year. The researchers do not, however, consider all the potential sources of error of the status model—family differences, teacher and school differences, and measurement errors.

The implications of grade-level versions of accountability have been less studied. Some of the prior work employed differences by grade level primarily as a method of identifying the behavioral effects of the system (comparing a grade included in the accountability system with one not included) as opposed to being a focal point of the analysis. Don Boyd and his colleagues do consider whether teacher placement responds to the specific grades that count.[29] They find that exiting from teaching does not appear related to testing regimes. While they have just indirect measures of quality for the New York State sample (experience and quality of college), they do find some attempt in urban schools to place the more experienced teachers in the grades tested when new teachers entered a school.[30]

Longitudinal Approaches

While cohort gain models are more effective at isolating the school's contribution to performance, they have been implemented in just two states as of fall 2001 (New Mexico and North Carolina). Unlike the status model, the primary incentives in these approaches are to improve student scores by improving teaching and programs. Exclusions could have an effect on measured performance to the extent that they eliminate individuals who would have a lower rate of learning. However, this impact on the accountability score will generally be considerably less than the impact of exclusions on the status model, because it is only achievement growth and not achievement level that is important. In purest form, the group of students being examined is constant over time. Student in-migration is ignored, potentially interacting with district decisions to set school attendance zones and the like. Nonetheless, to date, no evaluations of the effects of cohort gain systems on performance are available. The student-level gain score model follows the progress of individual students and then creates a summary from the net change scores. Of all the models, this approach provides the clearest and strongest incentives for schools to concentrate on the school factors under their control.[31] Because it also focuses on progress, the model can isolate the contribution of individual teachers, although no state makes such information public.[32]

The model provides an inclination and an ability to exclude students who are poor performers. The school will know student-specific performances in the first year of examination and then can follow the students' progress through the second year, presumably providing information by which to pre-judge which students would likely produce negative change scores. By avoid-ing a second-year test, the gain scores for those students cannot be calculated or folded into the school score for two years (that is, neither as the change year nor as the base for the following year).

Craig E. Richards and Tian Ming Sheu provide an early investigation of the South Carolina incentive system.[33] This system, introduced in 1984, was a sophisticated accountability attempt that considered individual student gain scores and adjusted rewards for the socioeconomic status of the student body. They find that the reward system yielded gains, although modest, in performance of students (but did not affect teacher attendance, the other attribute of incentive focus). South Carolina subsequently moved away from this incentive system. Helen F. Ladd investigates the sophisticated gain score incentives in Dallas during the mid-1990s.[34] She finds that performance in Dallas improves relative to other large Texas districts, although the gains come for white and Hispanic students but not black students. Improvements in terms of student dropout rates and on principal turnover also appear.

Deere and Strayer evaluate the impact of Texas incentives on a range of behaviors.[35] They find evidence that schools tend to concentrate on students who are near the passing grade on the TAAS and on subjects that enter into the accountability system. The evidence also suggests some differential exclu-sion from testing. They specifically find some sharp increases in overall exemption rates for special education around the time when these exemp-tions became most important for accountability. (However, while the evalua-tion considers student gains, the Texas incentive system concentrates on over-all pass rates.)

Summary of Evidence

In terms of incentives, the objective of rewarding and punishing schools for their contributions to student learning is met in varying degrees by the alter-natives. Table 6-2 summarizes the hypotheses about the kinds of effects that might be expected under different accountability regimes. We have strong evidence about few of these components, particularly for the longitudinal accountability schemes. The boldface hypotheses in table 6-2 indicate areas

Table 6-2. *Hypothesized Impacts of Accountability*

	Cross-sectional accountability systems	Achievement gain accountability systems
Outcome effects		
Direct response to consequences	SR: muted positive school quality improvements that might be overpowered by other reactions **LR: increasing pressures to improve quality more than SR**	Stronger impact on outcomes than cross-sectional accountability systems, especially in SR but also in LR
Response to public disclosure	Same pattern as effects to direct consequences but less strong	**Same pattern as effects to direct consequences but less strong**
Measurement errors		
Testing effects	Movement toward areas in accountability measure	**Movement toward areas in accountability measure**
Random errors	May lessen incentives for quality improvement	**May lessen incentives for quality improvement; comparison to cross-sectional systems unclear**
Exclusions and selectivity	SR: large incentives to adjust tested population **LR: considerably dampened incentives to alter population**	**SR and LR: relatively modest incentives to alter population, similar to long run in cross-sectional systems**
Other responses		
Teacher decisions and assignment	Higher exit rates of teachers (and principals) with accountability systems	**Higher exit rates of teachers (and principals) with accountability systems**

Note: Boldface implies no existing evidence on hypothesis. SR = short-run or immediate responses; LR = long-run responses.

where we have no systematic evidence. Most accountability systems have been introduced recently, so the history does not give much scope for analysis. The prevalence of bold in the table, particularly about any long-run effects, is unfortunate.

The clearest story is simply that schools do respond to accountability systems. When such systems are introduced, schools appear from observed outcomes to react to the varying incentives.

The most common accountability alternative chosen by states (the status model and its grade-level offshoot) provides information that is far distant from the value-added of each school. One aspect of this is the introduction of incentives to change school scores in ways that are unrelated to their learning outcomes. The largest volume of evidence relates to gaming the system—actions taken in response to incentives but ones not directly related to improving performance. Thus several studies indicate that exclusions from the testing by individual states and districts tend to increase with the introduction of new accountability systems. None, however, says anything about reactions after the initial response. This is unfortunate because most such actions work best in the short run, that is, in the year of their introduction, and would be much less effective in later years. In most cases, the incentives for these types of reactions will decline over time. Moreover, the aggregate picture from looking across states in recent years suggests that general increases in special education placement, perhaps the most frequently named form of gaming, are much more important than specific state reactions to accountability. The impact of special education exclusions does not show up at the state level.

Much less information is available about the range and scope of reactions to improve performance. In most cases studied, the introduction of a performance system does lead to achievement improvements. Moreover, the responses not surprisingly appear more concentrated on the aspects of learning that are measured and assessed as opposed to those that are not. While some people find this to be a negative aspect of the accountability systems, it seems to be just what one would expect. The magnitude of such improvements is nonetheless not easy to characterize. Further, the exact nature of the response—whether emanating from the informational aspects of the systems or from the direct sanctions and rewards—is uncertain.

Our generalization to overall state performance on NAEP suggests that accountability improves learning, not just responses to specific tests. The validity and reliability of NAEP, often called the "nation's report card," are well accepted. It is a test for which students cannot easily be prepped and, because the performance of individual school districts, schools, or students is not reported, there is little incentive to cheat or even to prepare for the test. Given that the test was adopted before the advent of state accountability systems, it also provides a neutral standard for assessing the effects of state policies. Thus improvement there reflects more general learning, not just responses to the specific state testing instruments.

Important for design considerations, little information is available about the comparative effects of the alternative systems. Understanding the differences among accountability systems requires comparing states that employ alternative approaches. It is, however, very difficult to do this. For example, David W. Grissmer and his colleagues interpret estimates of the superior performance of Texas and North Carolina schools on the National Assessment of Educational Progress as resulting from their accountability systems, but no attempt is made to test such a hypothesis formally.[36] Martin Carnoy and Susanna Loeb find that accountability systems that have implications for students and schools ("strong accountability") had faster growth in NAEP math achievement.[37] Moreover, this happens not just for low-achievement students but also for high-achievement students. Nonetheless, their categorization cuts accountability systems in different ways than that previously presented. Our work reported previously finds differences between accountability and report card systems, although the difference is not statistically significant. A distinction in this cannot be made between weak data from the limited number of state observations and true design impacts. Finally, using a different coding for states employing high-stakes tests, we again confirm significant differences in NAEP performance across states that are related to accountability.[38]

Because a number of states will soon be adopting new systems as a result of federal legislation, it is important to know, say, whether more costly and less understandable systems that focus on value-added measurement are significantly better than status models. The bold items in table 6-2 are central to the most significant design issues for state accountability systems.

Implications for Policy and Research

A prime implication of this review is that more extensive and focused analysis is needed before many strong statements can be made about the effectiveness of accountability for raising student performance. While the accountability movement appears to hold significant promise for improvement of schools, its potential has yet to be fully realized. Part of this is a simple reflection of the newness of most state accountability systems.

But part of the uncertainty results from the particular forms of accountability systems that have been adopted. The vast majority of existing systems use performance measures that confuse changes in school performance with other factors that the school does not control—families, student abilities, neighborhood effects, and measurement errors.

Aspects of the confusion have been explored, but current knowledge is skewed. Even though the theoretical discussion indicates that student gain models provide superior precision to cross-sectional models, they remain largely unexplored. Moreover, much of the work to date on cross-sectional models has been useful in identifying unintended consequences or edge cases, but these aspects are likely to be addressed through refinements over time. Further, most of these incentives likely will die out naturally over time. The central features of the systems will eventually be most relevant, and much opportunity remains to fully explore their impact. Additional studies will be needed before these systems can be fully judged as a general policy or whether any success achieved by some approaches can be generalized to others.

The degree of precision in these systems directly affects the strength and clarity of the incentives they create. In addition to knowing if accountability systems create better outcomes, more must be learned about the manner in which schools react. At present, most of these proposed mechanisms for how schools respond are unexplored.

Notes

1. See the discussion in Eric A. Hanushek and Margaret E. Raymond, "The Confusing World of Educational Accountability," *National Tax Journal,* vol. 54, no. 2 (2001), pp. 365–84.

2. The details of these estimates can be found in Eric A. Hanushek and Margaret E. Raymond, "Improving Educational Quality: How Best to Evaluate Our Schools?" in Yolanda Kodrzycki, ed., *Education in the Twenty-First Century: Meeting the Challenges of a Changing World* (Federal Reserve Bank of Boston, 2002). The results pool data on the National Assessment of Educational Progress (NAEP) math gains over both the 1992–96 and 1996–2000 period.

3. For average performance the distinction is unimportant, but a variety of state reward systems are based on such measures as the percentage of students passing a grade-level test. In those, performance requirements or rewards based on separate grades imply different incentives and constraints compared with school-based systems.

4. See the overview and analysis of mobility in Eric A. Hanushek, John F. Kain, and Steven G. Rivkin, "Disruption versus Tiebout Improvement: The Costs and Benefits of Switching Schools," *Journal of Public Economics* (forthcoming).

5. Hanushek, Kain, and Rivkin, "Disruption versus Tiebout Improvement."

6. The cohort gain and individual gain models will yield the same results if both school entrants and school leavers are excluded from the cohort and individual gain calculations. The individual gain still offers the possibility of further disaggregations by, say, income or entering achievement.

7. William L. Sanders and Sandra P. Horn, "The Tennessee Value-Added Assessment System (TVAAS): Mixed-Model Methodology in Educational Assessment," *Journal of Personnel Evaluation in Education,* vol. 8 (1994), pp. 299–311; and William L. Sanders and Sandra P. Horn, "The Tennessee Value-Added Assessment System (TVAAS): Mixed Model Methodology in Educational Assessment," in Anthony J. Shinkfield and Daniel L. Stufflebeam, eds., *Teacher Evaluation: Guide to Effective Practice* (Boston: Kluwer Academic Publishers, 1995), pp. 337–76.

8. We ignore some of the technical problems in doing the analysis and adjustment. For example, the practice of estimating simple regression analyses based solely on family factors can yield potentially misleading adjustments. See Robert E. Klit-

gaard and George R. Hall, "Are There Unusually Effective Schools?" *Journal of Human Resources,* vol. 10, no. 1 (1975), pp. 90–106. See also David W. Grissmer and others, *Student Achievement and the Changing American Family* (Santa Monica, Calif.: RAND Corporation, 1994). Such analysis, which ignores school quality differences, will produce biased estimates of the effects of family background (to the extent that family backgrounds are correlated with school quality differences). These biased estimates will in part incorporate the effects of differences in school quality, the object of the exercise originally.

9. Thomas J. Kane and Douglas O. Staiger, "Volatility in Test Scores: Implications for Test-Based Accountability Systems," in Diane Ravitch, ed., *Brookings Papers on Education Policy 2002* (Brookings, 2002), pp. 235–69.

10. Kane and Staiger, "Volatility in Test Scores."

11. Stephen H. Fletcher and Margaret E. Raymond, *The Future of California's Academic Performance Index* (Stanford University, Hoover Institution, CREDO, 2002).

12. Stephen B. Dunbar and Elizabeth A. Witt, "Design Innovations in Measuring Mathematics Achievement," in National Research Council, ed., *Measuring What Counts: A Conceptual Guide for Mathematics Assessment* (Washington: National Academy Press, 1993), pp. 175–200.

13. Lowell C. Rose and Alec M. Gallup, "The 33rd Annual Phi Delta Kappa/Gallup Poll of the Public's Attitudes toward the Public Schools," *Phi Delta Kappan* (September 2001), pp. 41–58.

14. Sandra E. Black, "Do Better Schools Matter? Parental Valuation of Elementary Education," *Quarterly Journal of Economics*, vol. 114, no. 2 (1999), pp. 577–99; and David L. Weimer and Michael J. Wolkoff, "School Performance and Housing Values: Using Non-Contiguous District and Incorporation Boundaries to Identify School Effects," *National Tax Journal*, vol. 54, no. 2 (2001), pp. 231–53.

15. David N. Figlio and Maurice E. Lucas, "What's in a Grade? School Report Cards and House Prices," Working Paper W8019 (Cambridge, Mass.: National Bureau of Economic Research, 2000).

16. Brian A. Jacob, "Making the Grade: The Impact of Test-Based Accountability in Schools," mimeo (Harvard University, John F. Kennedy School of Government, 2002).

17. Donald Deere and Wayne Strayer, "Closing the Gap: School Incentives and Minority Test Scores in Texas," mimeo (Texas A&M University, Department of Economics, 2001); Donald Deere and Wayne Strayer, "Putting Schools to the Test: School Accountability, Incentives, and Behavior," mimeo (Texas A&M University, Private Enterprise Research Center, 2001); and Julie B. Cullen and Randall Reback, "Tinkering toward Accolades: School Gaming under a Performance Based Accountability System," mimeo (University of Michigan, Department of Economics, 2002).

18. Daniel M. Koretz and Sheila I. Barron, *The Validity of Gains in Scores on the Kentucky Instructional Results Information System (KIRIS)* (Santa Monica, Calif.: RAND Corporation, 1998).

19. Walter Haney, "The Myth of the Texas Miracle in Education," *Education Pol-*

icy Analysis Archives, vol. 8, no. 41 (2000); Martin Carnoy, Susanna Loeb, and Tiffany L. Smith, "Do Higher State Test Scores in Texas Make for Better High School Outcomes?" paper presented at the American Educational Research Association annual meeting, 2001; and Laurence A. Toenjes and A. Gary Dworkin, "Are Increasing Test Scores in Texas Really a Myth, or Is Haney's Myth a Myth?" *Education Policy Analysis Archives,* vol. 10, no. 17 (2002). Carnoy, Loeb, and Smith also find that at least in larger urban areas lower dropout rates are associated with higher student achievement.

20. David N. Figlio and Lawrence S. Getzler, "Accountability, Ability, and Disability: Gaming the System?" Working Paper W9307 (Cambridge, Mass.: National Bureau of Economic Research, 2002).

21. Jacob, "Making the Grade."

22. Deere and Strayer, "Putting Schools to the Test."

23. For details, see Hanushek and Raymond, "Improving Educational Quality." All statistical models include separate state fixed effects to allow for different base propensities to classify students in special education programs. Different variants also include overall school spending patterns.

24. Eric A. Hanushek and Steven G. Rivkin, "Does Public School Competition Affect Teacher Quality?" in Caroline M. Hoxby, ed., *The Economics of School Choice* (University of Chicago Press, 2003), pp. 23–47.

25. Jay P. Greene, *An Evaluation of the Florida A-Plus Accountability and School Choice Program* (New York: Manhattan Institute, Center for Civic Innovation, 2001); and Jay P. Greene, "The Looming Shadow: Florida Gets Its 'F' Schools to Shape Up," *Education Next,* vol. 1, no. 4 (2001), pp. 76–82.

26. Martin Carnoy, *School Vouchers: Examining the Evidence* (Washington: Economic Policy Institute, 2001).

27. Helen F. Ladd and Elizabeth J. Glennie, "Appendix C: A Replication of Jay Green's Voucher Effect Study Using North Carolina Data," in Martin Carnoy, ed., *School Vouchers: Examining the Evidence* (Washington: Economic Policy Institute, 2001); and Amanda Brownson, "Appendix B: A Replication of Jay Greene's Voucher Effect Study Using Texas Performance Data," in Martin Carnoy, ed., *School Vouchers: Examining the Evidence* (Washington: Economic Policy Institute, 2001), respectively.

28. Kane and Staiger, "Volatility in School Test Scores."

29. Don Boyd and others, "Do High-Stakes Tests Affect Teachers' Exit and Transfer Decisions? The Case of the 4th Grade Test in New York State," mimeo (Stanford University, Graduate School of Education, 2002).

30. This evidence is not entirely conclusive about strategic behavior, however. If the grade-level accountability relies just on the levels of achievement in a grade (as all do), schools have an effect that accumulates over time. Thus getting the effect of a good teacher is possible by placing that teacher in the grade being tested or in a prior grade where students would be better prepared for the material in the tested grade.

31. Cohort effects are still uncontrolled to the extent that a specific group of students may be brighter or duller than average (perhaps by design through exclusions).

32. Tennessee produces measures of individual student value-added, but it is not publicly released. See Sanders and Horn, "The Tennessee Value-Added Assessment System (TVAAS): Mixed-Model Methodology in Educational Assessment," *Journal of Personnel Evaluation in Education.*

33. Craig E. Richards and Tian Ming Sheu, "The South Carolina School Incentive Reward Program: A Policy Analysis," *Economics of Education Review,* vol. 11, no. 1 (1992), pp. 71–86.

34. Helen F. Ladd, "The Dallas School Accountability and Incentive Program: An Evaluation of the Impacts of Student Outcomes," *Economics of Education Review,* vol. 19, no. 1 (1999), pp. 1–16.

35. Deere and Strayer, "Closing the Gap"; and Deere and Strayer, "Putting Schools to the Test."

36. David W. Grissmer and others, *Improving Student Achievement: What NAEP State Test Scores Tell Us* (Santa Monica, Calif.: RAND Corporation, 2000). For an analysis of this conclusion, see Eric A. Hanushek, "Deconstructing Rand," *Education Matters,* vol. 1, no. 1 (2001), pp. 65–70.

37. Martin Carnoy and Susanna Loeb, "Does External Accountability Affect Student Outcomes? A Cross-State Analysis," *Educational Evaluation and Policy Analysis,* vol. 24, no. 4 (Winter 2002), pp. 305–31.

38. Margaret E. Raymond and Eric A. Hanushek, "High-Stakes Research," *Education Next,* vol. 3, no. 3 (2003), pp. 48–55.

7

Unintended Consequences of Racial Subgroup Rules

THOMAS J. KANE AND DOUGLAS O. STAIGER

While designing accountability systems for schools, state policymakers have been forced to confront large and long-standing differences in test performance by race and ethnicity. Some states have wielded test-based accountability as a tool with which to try to close the gaps in performance— setting performance goals not only for students overall, but for subgroups of students defined by race and ethnicity as well. As reflected in the legislation's title, the federal No Child Left Behind Act (NCLB) of 2001 aspires to leave no group behind, setting goals for subgroups defined by race/ethnicity, economic disadvantage, disability, and English language learner status. However, as in many other areas of policy design, that which seems reasonable at first glance often has unintended consequences.

In this paper we seek to describe the types of incentives that have been established, to analyze some of the perverse effects these subgroup rules have on schools, to provide preliminary evidence on the impact of such rules on student performance, and to make some suggestions regarding how such rules could be redesigned. Our bottom line is that subgroup rules are counterproductive in test-based accountability systems. Although well intentioned, subgroup rules result in fewer resources and more sanctions targeted on diverse schools simply because of their diversity, and they do not appear

Support from the Andrew W. Mellon Foundation is gratefully acknowledged.

to have any impact on the test score performance of students from minority groups.

Overview of Subgroup Rules

To encourage schools to raise the performance of all youth, seventeen states report performance separately for certain subgroups of students, including minority, low-income, and Limited English Proficient students. In many of these states, schools are held accountable only for their performance overall and do not face separate expectations for each of their subgroups. However, a growing number of states are setting performance targets for schools as well as for subgroups of students within schools.

States have used two basic strategies for incorporating racial subgroups into a school accountability system. First, some states, including Texas, have set a single performance expectation for the absolute level of performance, which applies to schools overall and to subgroups of students within schools. For example, to reach an "exemplary" rating in 2002, schools in Texas were expected to achieve a 90 percent proficiency rate for their school overall as well as for all subgroups, including white non-Hispanic youth, Hispanic students, African American students, and economically disadvantaged students. To reach an "academically acceptable" rating, schools were required to achieve at least 55 percent proficiency rates for all subgroups of students (raised from 50 percent in 2001). Like the Texas plan, the No Child Left Behind Act of 2001 would require all states to establish a single minimum proficiency rate that would apply to all schools as well as to all subgroups of students within schools.

However, given large differences in test performance by race, states using such systems face a trade-off between setting a low standard for proficiency and accepting high failure rates for schools containing students from disadvantaged subgroups. This trade-off is more stark in more integrated states, where a large proportion of schools enroll significant numbers of minority youth. An alternative approach, adopted in California, is to set a uniform standard for the growth in performance and apply the standard to the school overall as well as to all subgroups in the school. One advantage of the latter approach is that it avoids the problem of large differences in baseline performance by race by focusing on changes in performance. However, focusing on annual changes in performance exacerbates other problems—such as those created by the imprecision of test score measures, because a large portion of the change in test scores from one year to the next could be the result of sampling variation and other nonpersistent causes.

Holding All Subgroups to the Same Absolute Standard

The No Child Left Behind Act requires schools to achieve a minimum level of proficiency for their students overall, as well as for each subgroup defined by race/ethnicity, socioeconomic disadvantage, disability status, and English language learner status. The legislation allows states to create their own definition of "proficiency" based upon their own curriculum standards. However, the legislation circumscribes states' flexibility by specifying the manner in which the minimum proficiency rate for schools is to be determined.[1] Once a state defines proficiency, the minimum proficiency rate for each school and subgroup is set at the maximum of the proficiency rate of the 20th percentile school or the proficiency rate of the lowest scoring subgroup. In states with more lenient definitions of proficiency, the minimum proficiency rate will be higher, because the proficiency rate of the 20th percentile school and for all subgroups will be higher.[2] Regardless of the initial proficiency level, the minimum proficiency level must be raised at regular intervals until it reaches 100 percent at the end of twelve years. States setting a high standard, such that a small fraction of students achieve proficiency at the baseline, will be expected to achieve larger improvements over the next twelve years.

In most states, the minimum proficiency rate will be defined by that of the 20th percentile school. It will rarely be equal to the proficiency rate of the lowest scoring subgroup—simply because the 20th percentile school's proficiency rate is likely to be higher. The reason is that the racial gap in performance is large relative to the between-school dispersion in test scores.

The top panel of figure 7-1 reports the black-white differences in fourth-grade math scores on the National Assessment of Educational Progress (NAEP) by state in 2000 plotted against the same differences by state eight years before in 1992. The line in figure 7-1 is drawn at 45 degrees. States with points below the line have experienced a closing of the gap in test scores, while states above the line have witnessed a widening of their racial gap. Both gaps are reported in student-level standard deviations units (31.2 points in fourth-grade math). Two points are worth highlighting in the figure. First, the black-white gap in mean math performance in fourth grade is large. In the year 2000 the gap ranged from 0.6 standard deviations in West Virginia to over 1.2 standard deviations in Michigan. Second, the racial gaps by state are also remarkably stable over time. The states with wide racial gaps in fourth-grade mathematics in 1992 also tended to have wide gaps in 2000. Some closing of the gap occurred between 1992 and 2000. For instance, North Carolina and Texas have been identified as having had particularly rapid closing of the racial gap over time. (Notice the points for both states are

Figure 7-1. *Racial and Ethnic Gaps in NAEP Fourth-Grade Math Scores, 1992–2000*

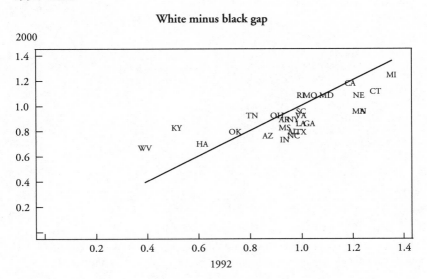

White minus black gap

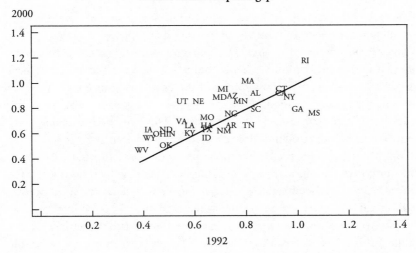

White minus Hispanic gap

Note: NAEP = National Assessment of Educational Progress. Test scores are reported in standard deviation units.

Figure 7-2. *Distribution of Math Scores at the School and Student Level*

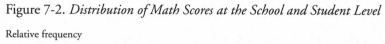

Relative frequency

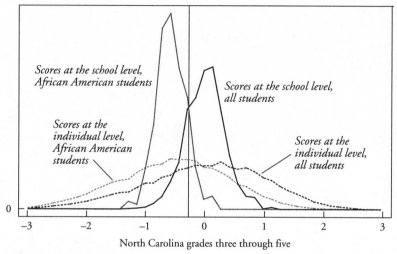

Scores at the school level,
African American students

Scores at the school level,
all students

Scores at the
individual level,
African American
students

Scores at the
individual level,
all students

North Carolina grades three through five

Note: The vertical line corresponds with the 20th percentile from the distribution of school means. Area under each curve sums to one.

below the 45 degree line in the top panel.) However, any improvement has been modest relative to the size of the remaining gap.

The bottom panel of figure 7-1 reports the gap in fourth-grade math scores for Latino students in 1992 and 2000. The gaps are also large, between 0.4 and 1.2 standard deviations. Many of the points are above the 45 degree line, suggesting some widening of the gap in math performance between whites and Hispanics between 1992 and 2000. However, such widening may simply reflect recent immigrant flows into the United States.

Figure 7-2 portrays the distribution of grade three through five math scores in North Carolina at the individual level and at the school level, for African American students and for students overall. The dotted lines portray the distribution of test scores for individual students; the solid lines portray the distribution of test scores when aggregated up to the school level. Even though a difference in mean performance is evident by race, a considerable amount of overlap exists at the individual student level. Even though the mean performance for African American students is 0.5 student-level standard deviations below the statewide mean (0.8 standard deviations below the white mean), 30 percent of individual African American students have test scores above the statewide mean.

However, as portrayed in figure 7-2, moving from the level of the individual student to the level of school means greatly reduces the extent of overlap in the distributions for schools overall and for African American subgroups within schools. The distribution of school means collapses toward the overall mean, while the mean for African American subgroups within schools collapses toward the African American mean. Whereas 30 percent of individual African American students scored above the overall mean, only 2 percent of African American students were in schools where the mean performance of African American students exceeded the statewide mean.

The vertical line in figure 7-2 portrays the mean math score for the 20th percentile school. The 20th percentile school has a mean test score 0.27 standard deviations below the overall mean. However, relatively few African American students—just 12 percent—attended schools where the mean African American student scored above this threshold. In other words, 88 percent of African American students are in schools where the mean for African American students is below the mean for the 20th percentile school. While not reported here, results are similar for Latino subgroups.[3]

The between-school variance in mean test performance is small relative to the racial gap in North Carolina. However, North Carolina is unlikely to be anomalous in this regard. Although it depends upon a number of factors such as the test being used, school size, and the extent of racial integration in a state, the between-school variance in student test scores generally represents between 10 to 15 percent of the variance in student test scores. Similar findings have been reported at least since the analysis by James S. Coleman and his colleagues in 1966.[4] If the distribution of school mean test scores is roughly normal (as a casual inspection of figure 7-2 would confirm) with a variance of 0.10 to 0.15 of the student-level variance, then the 20th percentile is likely to be 0.27 to 0.33 student-level standard deviations below the overall mean—much less than the typical gap in performance between whites and blacks and whites and Latinos. Therefore, although the result may vary somewhat by test and by state, given the magnitude of the racial gaps, the 20th percentile school is likely to have scores considerably higher than the average score for African Americans and Hispanic students.

Anticipating School Failure Rates

The definition of minimum proficiency virtually ensures that 20 percent of schools will have proficiency rates below the minimum initially.[5] However, the proportion of schools failing to meet this new definition of "adequate yearly progress" is likely to be much higher than 20 percent. The reason is that a school is defined as failing if any of the racial subgroups within the school fails to achieve the minimum proficiency rate. Given the definition of minimum proficiency in the law, the vast majority of African American and Latino subgroup mean scores at the school level are likely to fall short. As a result, a vast majority of the schools containing African American or Latino subgroups are also likely to fail.

How many students are likely to be in schools with African American or Latino subgroups? NCLB does not define subgroup status beyond stating that subgroup means could be excluded where "the number of students in a category is insufficient to yield statistically reliable information." Such language is open to interpretation, because no magical sample size exists above which subgroup means are likely to be statistically reliable. In this paper, we apply the definition of subgroup status used by California, requiring any of the categories above to contain at least thirty students and 15 percent of the students in a school or greater than one hundred students, regardless of their percentage representation to constitute an official subgroup. This definition results in somewhat fewer schools with subgroups than the definition currently used in Texas, requiring a subgroup to contain at least 10 percent of the student body and more than thirty students or more than fifty students regardless of the percentage to count.

The proportion of schools containing an African American or Latino subgroup varies widely by state, depending upon the representation of African American and Latino youth in the resident population and the degree of integration. Table 7-1 reports results from the Common Core of Data for the 1999–2000 school year, to provide a rough sense of the proportion of public schools in each state likely to be affected. These data are weighted by school size. Several states, including Idaho, Tennessee, and Washington, did not report complete racial representation data and were dropped. The data in table 7-1 are sorted by the proportion of students in a state that are black or Hispanic.

Several results in table 7-1 are particularly striking. First, a majority of the public schools nationwide (54 percent) contain an African American or Latino subgroup, using the definition of subgroup status described above. Moreover, in the South and West, the percentages are generally much higher. More than 80 percent of the public schools in seven states (California, Delaware, Louisiana, Mississippi, New Mexico, South Carolina, and Texas) and the District of Columbia contain an African American or Latino subgroup. An additional seven states (Alabama, Arizona, Florida, Georgia, Nevada, North Carolina, and Virginia) contain African American or Latino subgroups in more than 60 percent of their public schools. Therefore, given the fact that a majority of the African American and Latino subgroups are

Table 7-1. *Proportion of Students in Public Schools with an African American or Latino Subgroup by State*
Percent

State	Total black or Latino residents	Students in schools with black or Latino subgroups			
		Total	Blacks	Latinos	Whites
District of Columbia	94	97	100	97	49
Texas	54	80	94	96	61
Mississippi	54	86	98	84	71
New Mexico	53	89	96	98	87
California	51	81	94	96	63
Louisiana	50	80	97	86	63
South Carolina	44	86	97	89	76
Florida	43	78	95	94	66
Georgia	42	73	96	82	56
Maryland	40	63	94	85	41
Alabama	40	68	95	61	50
New York	38	50	93	92	20
Arizona	38	65	85	92	50
Delaware	37	90	96	97	86
Illinois	36	48	94	88	23
North Carolina	35	73	95	84	62
Nevada	34	72	91	90	62
Virginia	32	63	92	77	50
New Jersey	32	45	89	86	24
Arkansas	27	48	94	63	32
Colorado	27	49	83	82	35
Connecticut	26	37	87	85	18
Michigan	23	29	91	57	11
Rhode Island	20	29	75	87	13
Massachusetts	19	29	77	83	15
Pennsylvania	19	27	87	78	12
Missouri	19	31	88	45	18
Ohio	18	27	89	59	13
Kansas	18	27	74	70	17
Oklahoma	16	26	76	58	18
Indiana	15	29	90	61	19
Nebraska	15	27	83	69	18
Wisconsin	15	19	86	60	9
Oregon	12	20	51	54	15
Kentucky	11	26	80	54	19
Minnesota	10	17	72	46	8
Utah	10	18	46	57	13
Alaska	9	13	42	25	9
Wyoming	8	8	20	26	7
Iowa	7	11	55	44	8

continued on next page

Table 7-1. *Proportion of Students in Public Schools with an African American or Latino Subgroup by State (continued)*
Percent

State	Total black or Latino residents	Students in schools with black or Latino subgroups			
		Total	Blacks	Latinos	Whites
Hawaii	7	4	37	6	10
West Virginia	5	5	37	6	3
New Hampshire	2	1	6	17	1
North Dakota	2	1	0	10	1
Montana	2	0	2	3	0
South Dakota	2	0	0	0	0
Vermont	2	0	0	0	0
Maine	2	0	5	2	0
Total	34	54	92	91	33

Note: Based upon authors' tabulation of the Common Core of Data for 1999–2000 for public schools, grades three through eight.

likely to fail given the manner in which the minimum proficiency rates are to be calculated, a very large share of the schools in these states are likely to fail to achieve adequate yearly progress.

Second, while 92 percent of African American youth and 91 percent of Latino youth attend a school where black or Hispanic students are sufficiently numerous to constitute a separate subgroup, the proportion of white students likely to be affected varies widely. For example, New York and Alabama have similar percentages of African American and Hispanic students in their public schools, but 20 percent of white youth in New York and 50 percent of the white students in Alabama attend schools with an African American or Latino subgroup. North Carolina and Illinois have similar percentages of black or Latino youth overall, yet white students in North Carolina are nearly three times as likely as white students in Illinois to attend schools containing an African American or Latino subgroup—62 versus 23 percent. The more integrated a state's schools are, the higher the proportion of schools that are likely to be affected by NCLB.

Minimum Proficiency Rates in Texas

The use of the same minimum proficiency rate for schools as well as for subgroups of students within schools is similar in spirit to the accountability system in Texas. However, many more schools are likely to fail under NCLB requirements than the 2 percent of schools rated as "academically unacceptable" in Texas in 2000.[6] The reason is that the minimum proficiency rate

Figure 7-3. *Distribution of Math Proficiency for Schools and Subgroups, 1999–2000 School Year*

Relative frequency

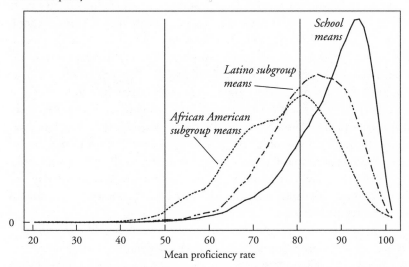

Note: Area under each curve sums to one.

required by NCLB will be much higher than the minimum used in that state in the past. Figure 7-3 portrays the distribution of mean proficiency rates for schools overall and for African Americans and for Hispanic students grouped by school in Texas in the 1999–2000 academic year. Texas used a fairly lenient definition of proficiency, with a median proficiency rate in math of 89.5 percent in 2000. As a result, the 20th percentile school has a proficiency rate in math of slightly higher than 80 percent. This is 30 percentage points higher than the minimum proficiency rate the state used in the 1999–2000 academic year.[7]

The Importance of the Definition of Subgroup Status

Under NCLB, the stakes for schools are potentially high (although it remains to be seen how serious these consequences will be in practice). A school failing to achieve adequate yearly progress for two consecutive years—whether because of its overall mean or because of any of its subgroup means—will be required to submit a school improvement plan. Furthermore, students in the school must be given the choice of attending another school in the district (if that school is not also failing), with the district bearing the transportation expense. In addition, a school failing for three consecutive years will be required to offer vouchers to low-income students to be used for supplemental educational services such as after-school tutoring programs. A school failing for four consecutive years must institute one of several corrective actions, such as implementing a new school curriculum. A school failing for five years is subject to restructuring and must either be converted to a charter school, be turned over to a private operator, or have most or all of its staff replaced.

Therefore, the definition of subgroup status is likely to be an important determinant of success or failure. For instance, in the academic year 1999–2000 in Texas, a racial or ethnic subgroup was required to represent at least 10 percent of the student body and thirty students or at least two hundred students to count as a separate subgroup.[8] To achieve "exemplary" status, a school in Texas was required to have a 90 percent proficiency rate in reading, writing, and mathematics for the school overall and for each subgroup. Given the racial differences in proficiency rates in Texas, relatively few of those schools with an African American or Latino subgroup were able to achieve an exemplary rating.

The impact of the subgroup size threshold is seen clearly in figure 7-4, which portrays the proportion of schools achieving an exemplary rating, by the percentage of their students who were Latino. The graph is limited to the schools that had between three hundred and two thousand students, where the percentage will solely determine subgroup status. The sample was also limited to those schools that did not also have an African American subgroup. Between 40 and 80 percent of such schools with less than 10 percent of their students being Latino achieved exemplary status, whereas only 10 to 20 percent of the schools with more than 10 percent of their students being Latino achieved exemplary status. Moreover, the discontinuity is striking right at the 10 percent threshold. Forty-two percent of schools with 9 percent of their students being Latino were rated "exemplary," while less than 20 percent of the schools with 10 percent of their students being Latino were rated "exemplary." Therefore, given the large racial differences in performance, the designation of minimum size requirements for subgroups of students will largely determine the success or failure of schools near the thresholds.

Requiring Improvements for All Groups

California rewards schools that demonstrate improvement in student performance compared with the prior year. In 2001 California provided over $570 million in aid and teacher bonuses to schools whose improvement in test scores exceeded an annual growth target. All "numerically significant" racial and ethnic subgroups were also required to exceed their growth target

Figure 7-4. *Exemplary School Ratings and Percent Hispanic in Texas*

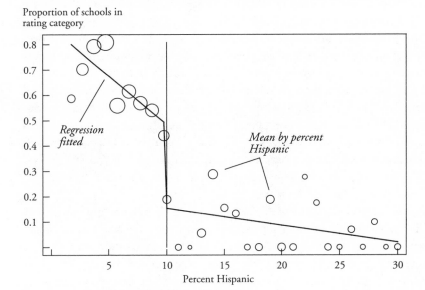

Proportion of schools in
rating category

Percent Hispanic

Note: Size of circles correlates with size of schools.

for the school to receive an award. (The state also provided $100 million in teacher bonuses to schools that were low scoring in 1999 and had achieved the largest improvements by 2000, while also meeting their subgroup targets.) By focusing on improvement in test scores instead of the absolute level of performance for each subgroup, the California approach is intended to level the playing field for schools serving different student populations. However, the imprecision of changes in test scores creates other problems.

Each year California calculates a score (called the Academic Performance Index, or API) for each school and student subgroup. The API score is a weighted average of the proportion of all students in grades three and up scoring in each quintile of the national distribution on the reading, math, language, and spelling sections of the Stanford 9 test. (The weights given to each quintile were 200, 500, 700, 875, and 1000, with an average score in 2000 of about 620.) The annual growth target for each school and subgroup is 5 percent of the difference between its initial API score and the statewide goal of 800. If a school or subgroup started out over 800, it was simply expected to keep its scores above 800. Schools that met their targeted improvements in performance between 1999 and 2000 received $63 per student funding from the Governor's Performance Award program. In addition,

$591 per full-time equivalent teacher was awarded to both the school and teacher (for a total of about $59 per student) through the School Site Employee Bonus program.

To win these awards, a school must achieve not only a minimum improvement in performance at the school level, but also for each numerically significant racial or ethnic subgroup within the school. To be numerically significant, a group must represent at least 15 percent of the student body and contain more than thirty students or represent more than one hundred students regardless of their percentage. Eight different groups could qualify as numerically significant, depending upon the number of students in each group in a school: African American, American Indian (or Alaska Native), Asian, Filipino, Hispanic, Pacific Islander, white non-Hispanic, or socioeconomically disadvantaged students.[9]

By focusing on changes in performance instead of the level of performance, California avoids the problems in NCLB and the Texas system caused by the lower level of performance in African American and Latino subgroups. In contrast to the difference across these groups in the distribution of average test scores (see figures 7-2 and 7-3), the distribution of test score growth is fairly similar across the groups (although the change in performance is more variable for small subgroups).

However, holding schools accountable for changes in subgroup performance introduces another important bias: Annual changes in test scores can be very noisy. The imprecision of test score measures arises from two sources. The first is sampling variation, which is particularly striking in elementary schools. Since the average elementary school has only sixty-eight students per grade level nationally, the amount of variation resulting from the idiosyncrasies of the particular sample of students being tested each year is often large relative to the total variation observed between schools. A second source of imprecision arises from one-time factors that are not sensitive to the size of the sample; for example, a dog barking in the playground on the day of the test, a severe flu season, one particularly disruptive student in a class, or favorable chemistry between a group of students and their teacher. Both small samples and other one-time factors can add considerable volatility to the change in average API scores, particularly for subgroups with relatively small numbers of students. In previous work, we estimate that between 50 and 80 percent of the variation in annual changes in test score measures is the result of one of these two sources of nonpersistent variation in test scores.[10]

The importance of sampling variation in the change in average API scores for a school or subgroup is immediately apparent in figure 7-5. For all elementary schools in California, we plot the difference between API growth

Figure 7-5. *Distribution of Growth in Excess of Target by School Size*

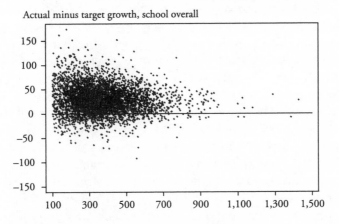

Actual minus target growth, school overall

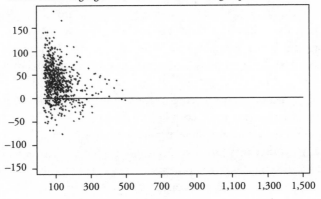

Actual minus target growth, African American subgroups

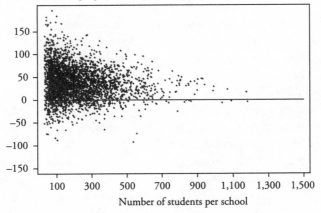

Actual minus target growth, Hispanic subgroups

Number of students per school

and target growth (between 1999 and 2000) against the number of students tested for all students, African American subgroups, and Latino subgroups. Points above the horizontal line at zero in each plot are those schools or subgroups for which API growth exceeded target growth. Figure 7-5 illustrates two facts that are important in the discussion of volatility. First, although the average small school exceeded its growth target by a similar amount as the average large school, small school performance was much more variable because of the noise in API measures based on a small number of students. As a result, both small schools and small subgroups are more likely to have API growth that is below target. A second important fact from figure 7-5 is that the distribution of performance for small subgroups is similar to that for small schools, but because subgroups tend to test a smaller number of students their performance is more volatile and more subgroups fail to achieve their growth target. Thus, for purely statistical reasons, subgroups may be less likely to pass the hurdle for financial awards in California.

Because of the importance of sampling variation in the change in average API scores, many schools will appear to excel in one subgroup but not another. But this is not necessarily the result of disparate improvement. Sampling variation would generate this pattern because fluctuations in one group would be expected to be largely independent of fluctuations in other groups. In fact, the magnitude of improvements for white and minority subgroups in a given school has only a weak correlation. Moreover, schools are about as likely to achieve the target for their minority subgroup but fail for the white subgroup as the other way around. For elementary schools that had a black, white, and Latino subgroup, the probability of exceeding their growth target was about equal for white (83 percent), African American (87 percent), and Latino (90 percent) subgroups, but only 69 percent of such schools exceeded the target for all three groups simultaneously. The probability of exceeding the growth target for any one subgroup but not the other two was similar for whites (2 percent), African Americans (1 percent), and Latinos (3 percent). Moreover, 11 percent of schools exceeded their growth targets for African Americans and Latinos but failed for whites. This was twice the likelihood that they would reach their target for whites and Latinos but miss for blacks, or they would hit the target for whites and blacks but miss for Latinos. In other words, schools were at least as likely (indeed, more likely) to miss the award solely because they failed to hit the target for whites.

When changes in API scores are this noisy, a considerable amount of chance will be involved in whether a school or subgroup exceeds its growth target in a given year. As a result, California's subgroup rules are analogous to a system that makes every school flip a coin once for each subgroup and then

Table 7-2. *Proportion of California Elementary Schools Winning Governor's Performance Awards by Size and Numerically Significant Subgroups*

Schools	Number of numerically significant subgroups				
	1	2	3	4+	Total
Smallest quintile					
Proportion winning	0.824	0.729	0.587	0.471	0.683
Average API growth	(33.4)	(45.6)	(42.2)	(36.0)	(41.2)
Number of schools	204	343	349	51	947
Second quintile					
Proportion winning	0.886	0.769	0.690	0.670	0.749
Average API growth	(29.9)	(42.6)	(42.2)	(43.9)	(40.5)
Number of schools	158	337	358	94	947
Third quintile					
Proportion winning	0.853	0.795	0.708	0.667	0.756
Average API growth	(26.8)	(36.3)	(38.9)	(44.6)	(36.6)
Number of schools	156	308	390	93	947
Fourth quintile					
Proportion winning	0.903	0.823	0.776	0.656	0.799
Average API growth	(28.0)	(41.8)	(39.5)	(40.8)	(38.7)
Number of schools	144	328	379	96	947
Largest quintile					
Proportion winning	0.876	0.776	0.726	0.686	0.755
Average API growth	(29.5)	(37.9)	(36.9)	(40.5)	(37.0)
Number of schools	89	370	387	102	948
Total					
Proportion winning	0.864	0.778	0.699	0.647	0.749
Average API growth	(29.8)	(40.9)	(39.9)	(41.7)	(38.8)
All schools	751	1,686	1,863	436	4,736

Note: Reflecting the rules of the Governor's Performance Award program in 1999–2000, the data reported were limited to elementary schools with more than one hundred students.

gives awards only to schools that get heads on every flip. Schools with more subgroups must flip the coin more times and, therefore, are put at a purely statistical disadvantage relative to schools with fewer subgroups.

This statistical disadvantage is clearly seen in table 7-2, which reports the proportion of California elementary schools winning the Governor's Performance Award by school size quintile and number of numerically significant subgroups in each school. Among the smallest quintile of elementary schools, racially heterogeneous schools were almost half as likely to win a Governor's Performance Award as racially homogeneous schools. Forty-seven percent of schools with four or more subgroups won a Governor's Performance Award as opposed to 82 percent of similarly sized schools with only one numerically significant group. This is particularly ironic given that the more integrated schools had slightly larger overall growth in performance between 1999 and 2000 (36.0 points versus 33.4 points). The statistical bias against racially heterogeneous schools is also apparent among larger schools but is somewhat less pronounced because subgroups in these schools are larger in size and, as a result, their scores are less volatile.

Because minority youth are more likely to attend heterogeneous schools than white non-Hispanic youth, the rules have the unintended effect of putting the average school enrolling minority students at a statistical disadvantage in the pursuit of award money. In California, nearly 30 percent of white students attend a racially homogeneous school with only one subgroup, compared with about 5 percent of African Americans and Latinos. In contrast, most Latinos attend schools with two (47 percent) or three (41 percent) subgroups, while most African Americans attend schools with three (47 percent) or more (21 percent) subgroups. Based only on the number of subgroups in their schools, this makes minority students less likely to be in schools that win awards in California. For example, multiplying the proportion of white students in each type of school (one, two, three, or more than four subgroups) by the probability that each type of school wins an award (from the last row of table 7-2) yields an estimate that 76.5 percent of white students would be in an award-winning school. In contrast, if white students attended schools with multiple subgroups at the same rates as African Americans, only 71.7 percent would be in an award-winning school. Thus 5 percentage points of the difference in rates of award winning for schools attended by African American and white, non-Hispanic youth is solely because of the statistical bias against schools with subgroups. A similar calculation suggests that Latinos are 2.5 percent less likely to be in an award-winning school because of the subgroup bias. The dollar value of these awards was approximately $124 per student. Therefore, a rough estimate would suggest that the subgroup rules in California had the effect of reducing the average award to schools attended by African American and Latino youth by roughly $3 to $6 per student, for a total of more than $6 million per year.[11]

Impact of Subgroup Rules on Minority Achievement

Despite the difficulties, racial subgroup rules may be worthwhile if they are effective in forcing schools to focus on the academic achievement of minority youth. Comparisons of states that do and do not use subgroup rules are inconclusive. For example, Texas closed the racial gap in the NAEP considerably between 1992 and 2000, but so did North Carolina, which does not use racial subgroup rules. In this section, we compare the performance of minority students in schools where they are sufficiently numerous to count as a separate subgroup with the performance of minority youth in schools just below the cutoff for numerical significance. To the extent that schools just below the cutoff are not affected by the subgroup rules, we can use this comparison to evaluate the impact of the subgroup rules on the test performance of minority students. This comparison is not perfect. A school's subgroup status may change year to year; and schools near the cutoff do not know for certain if they qualify for subgroup status until after test scores are reported. As a result, the incentives to focus on minority group achievement may not be so different for schools just below and above the cutoff, but all schools near the cutoff may face intermediate incentives. Nevertheless, if subgroup rules were effective, rising test performance for minority youth would be expected moving from schools below the cutoff to schools above the cutoff.

In Texas, between 1994 and 2000, a racial subgroup did not count separately in the accountability system unless the group contained 10 percent of the students in a school and thirty students or more than two hundred students regardless of their percentage.[12] Therefore, subgroup status depended upon two dimensions—the percentage of all students in the group and the absolute number. To simplify the analysis and limit the determinants of subgroup status to one dimension, we focused on schools with three hundred to two thousand students, where any group that contained more than 10 percent of the students would have counted as a separate subgroup and none of those subgroups representing less than 10 percent of the student body would have contained more than two hundred students.

In California the minimum size requirements for subgroup status are somewhat different. As defined by the Public Schools Accountability Act of 1999, a racial subgroup is not numerically significant unless the group represents 15 percent of the student body and thirty students or one hundred students, regardless of their percentage. As with Texas, to simplify matters, we limited the analysis to those in schools with 200 to 667 students where any group satisfying the 15 percent threshold would have counted separately and any group with less than 15 percent would not have satisfied the one hundred student minimum size for separate subgroup status.

Although the minimum thresholds for numerical significance are necessarily arbitrary, such arbitrariness is fortuitous from the point of view of the evaluation, because we would not expect those schools immediately above or immediately below the thresholds to be systematically different. There may be one exception, however. Because the rules are not a secret, the subgroup rules provide an incentive to schools near the thresholds—particularly those with low-scoring minority youth—to reclassify students by race or to ensure that certain students are not present on the day of testing. If either of these practices were common, we would expect to see an unusual number of schools with minority youth just below the thresholds for numerical significance. While we saw some evidence of clumping of schools in Texas with percentages of African American youth just below the 10 percent threshold, the distribution of percentage Latino was smooth above and below the 10 percent threshold. We did not see any evidence of clumping in California.

Figure 7-6 reports math, reading, and writing proficiency rates for Latino youth in schools with between 1 and 30 percent Latino youth. The sample of schools was limited to those schools that did not also have an African American subgroup, because the performance of Latino students would have been less decisive in determining a school's status. We calculated the mean proficiency rate separately for all schools with a given percentage Latino. In other words, we calculated the proficiency rate separately for schools with j percent Latino students, where j ranged from 0 through 100. The size of the symbols in the graph reflects the number of students in schools with that percentage of Latino students. We also included the regression line that would have been fit by running separate regressions of proficiency on the percentage of Latino youth for those points below 10 percent and for those points at 10 percent and above. As might be expected, the proficiency rates do decline somewhat for Latino youth in schools where Latino youth represent a larger share of the student body—given that the percentage Latino is probably related to the socioeconomic status of the students attending these schools. However, no evidence exists of any rise in proficiency for Latino youth in schools immediately above the threshold for numerical significance. In other words, it does not appear that the performance of Latinos is any better in schools where they constitute 10 percent of the student body and, therefore, do count as a separate subgroup than in schools where they represent 9 percent of the student body and, therefore, do not count as a separate subgroup.

We performed a similar exercise for African American and Latino youth in California in 2001. Because the state does not publish an API index for subgroups that are not numerically significant, we obtained Stanford 9 scaled scores for all subgroups of students consisting of at least ten students. (These scores include the scores of some students who are excluded from the California accountability system. For instance, students who are in the district for less than a year do not count in the API score but were included in the scaled scores we use.) We calculated the mean math and reading scores for African

Figure 7-6. *Hispanic Test Performance and Percent Hispanic in Texas*

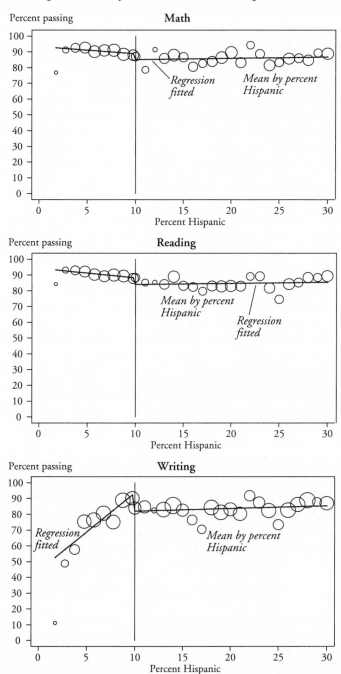

American and Latino youth in schools where they represented j percent of the student body in 2000, where j ranged from 0 through 100. The top two panels of figure 7-7 report mean test scores by single percentage points for schools with 5 to 30 percent African American students. (The minimum percentage required for numerical significance was 15 percent in California.) As with Texas, no evidence is seen of a rise in performance around the subgroup threshold as would have been expected if the subgroup rules were forcing schools to focus on the performance of African American youth. The bottom two panels of figure 7-7 report similar mean scores for Latino subgroups, with no apparent discontinuity at 15 percent. (We have also analyzed the data for the year 2000 with similar results.)

In Texas the strength of the incentive is clouded somewhat by the fact that schools near the threshold may not know whether Latino students will count as a separate subgroup until after the tests are taken. Schools with less than 10 percentage points minority-student enrollment in recent years do face weaker incentives to focus on minority-youth performance than those with 10 or more percent minority enrollment, but the difference at the 10 percent threshold may not be dramatic. In California, however, schools know in the fall what proportion of the students taking the test the prior spring were in each racial and ethnic group, and therefore know which groups are eligible to be subgroups in the coming spring. In figure 7-7, none of those schools with less than 15 percent of a given minority group in 2000 will be held accountable for that group's performance separately in 2001.

The failure to find an impact of the subgroup rules on minority performance is not necessarily evidence that test-based incentives are ineffective in general—only that the racial subgroup rules are not having their intended impact. Some evidence shows that test-based accountability systems do improve test performance overall, although it is not clear whether such test score gains are achieved with broad learning, teaching to the test, or outright cheating.[13] Therefore, holding schools accountable for student test scores may encourage schools to focus on the performance of all students in a school. However, no evidence exists that holding schools separately accountable for the test scores of minority groups encourages schools to focus more heavily on minority-youth performance. It may simply be difficult for schools and teachers to single out one group of students and target their responses by race.

Conclusion

Despite some closing of the gap in performance between whites and blacks between the mid-seventies and the late eighties, such gaps remain large.[14]

Figure 7-7. *African American and Latino Test Performance and Percent in School in California*

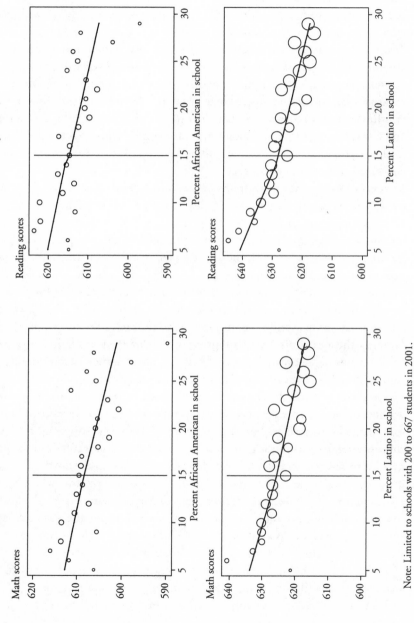

Note: Limited to schools with 200 to 667 students in 2001.

Therefore, raising the academic achievement of minority groups with poor test score performance is an important goal. However, our analysis suggests that the use of subgroup targets in school accountability programs is not the answer. In current accountability systems, subgroup targets cause large numbers of schools to fail (as in NCLB), arbitrarily single out schools with large minority subgroups for sanctions and exclude them from awards (as in Texas), or statistically disadvantage diverse schools that are more likely to be attended by minority students (as in California). Moreover, while the costs of the subgroup targets are clear, the benefits are not. Although these targets are meant to encourage schools to focus more on the achievement of minority youth, we find no association between the application of subgroup targets and test score performance among minority youth. Thus, taken together, the evidence suggests that the use of subgroup targets is counterproductive in test-based accountability systems.

School accountability systems can certainly reduce some of the unintended consequences of subgroup targets by tinkering with the details of their application. For instance, the inequity in California's system could be lessened if, instead of requiring schools to achieve their targets for all subgroups to receive any award, the awards were made proportional to the percentage of students in subgroups achieving their targets. (A school could be provided 75 percent of the award money if the target is reached for the subgroups making up 75 percent of the school's students.) Similarly, NCLB allows states to determine the minimum size threshold for subgroups and to fail only those schools whose subgroup performance lies significantly (in a statistical sense) below their target. This gives states some discretion in determining how binding the subgroup rules will be in practice.

On the one hand, the consequences for those schools more likely to fail as a result of subgroup rules may not be serious enough to warrant tinkering with the subgroup rules. For example, while California's subgroup rules put schools attended by minority students at a statistical disadvantage in winning award money, we do not find that this had any obvious detrimental impact on minority achievement in schools with subgroups. Similarly, while NCLB may result in 50 to 80 percent of schools failing in many states, the consequences for failing schools (at least in the short term)—such as creating a school improvement plan or providing students with school choice—may not be very serious in practice. Moreover, until schools face restructuring after five years of failing to meet adequate yearly progress expectations, states will have the flexibility to apply different corrective actions in schools that fail because of a single subgroup than in schools that fail because of all of their subgroups.

On the other hand, the schools in various states will face very different burdens imposed by NCLB, simply because of the subgroup rules. In the absence of the subgroup rules, an equal proportion—roughly 20 percent—of the schools in each state would fail to achieve adequate yearly progress in the initial years, given the way minimum proficiency is defined at the 20th percentile school. In other words, regardless of how they define proficiency, roughly 20 percent of the schools in a state with few minority students, such as New Hampshire, will fail to achieve adequate yearly progress in the first years—somewhat less if schools succeed in raising performance. However, also without regard to how states define proficiency, the failure rate is likely to be two to four times higher in states in the South and West with large minority populations, because of the subgroup rules. The single most important determinant of the difference in failure rates between states is likely to be the racial composition of their schools. While it is true that submitting a school improvement plan or being required to offer vouchers for supplemental educational services are not overwhelmingly onerous requirements, they will be imposed at different rates in the various states simply because of the racial composition of the states' schools. Moreover, the consequences will become even more severe in five years when schools enter restructuring.

Although there may be room to soften the implications somewhat, identifying ways to tinker with subgroup rules misses the point. Because subgroup targets do not appear to be an effective way to improve the test scores of minority youth in the first place, one could simply eliminate such targets altogether. The fact that North Carolina (which reports subgroup results but does not set subgroup targets) experienced a narrowing in the racial test score gap as test scores rose among all students suggests that an explicit focus on racial and ethnic subgroups may be unnecessary. Test-based accountability systems are intended to shine a harsh light on low-performing schools and raise the stakes for improving student performance. Unfortunately, if a large share of schools are failing to achieve the new standards because of the racial subgroup rules, the law may simply make it easier for the lowest performing schools to be lost in the crowd.

Notes

1. States will still have an incentive to define proficiency at a low level for at least two reasons. First, the minimum proficiency rate must be raised from its baseline level to 100 percent within twelve years. Although a lenient definition of proficiency does not guarantee high passage rates in the first year, the rate of required increase in subsequent years is slower in states with lenient definitions. Second, subgroups that close 10 percent of the gap between their proficiency rate last year and 100 percent in

a single year are counted as having achieved "adequate yearly progress" even if their proficiency rate falls below the expected level. It would be easier for schools to benefit from this safe-harbor provision if their proficiency rate starts out at 80 percent than if their proficiency rate starts at 20 percent.

2. However, after twelve years, the No Child Left Behind Act requires all schools and all subgroups to achieve 100 percent proficiency. Therefore, while a lenient definition of proficiency may not provide many advantages during the first year or two, a lenient definition would be much easier to satisfy in the coming years.

3. Detailed results are in an earlier draft of this paper, which is available from the authors.

4. James S. Coleman and others, *Equality of Educational Opportunity* (Department of Health, Education, and Welfare, 1966).

5. There could be less than 20 percent of schools failing if a large number of schools closed more than 10 percent of the gap between their baseline and the goal of 100 percent proficiency. They would be protected by safe-harbor provisions.

6. As in other sections of this paper, the statistics for school-level characteristics are weighted by school size unless otherwise noted.

7. In 2001 the minimum proficiency rate in Texas was raised slightly to 55 percent.

8. In 2001 the two-hundred-student minimum was lowered to fifty students.

9. A socioeconomically disadvantaged student is a student of any race neither of whose parents completed a high school degree or who participates in the school's free or reduced-price lunch program.

10. Thomas J. Kane and Douglas O. Staiger, "Volatility in School Test Scores: Implications for Test-Based Accountability Systems," *Brookings Papers on Education Policy 2002* (Brookings, 2002), pp. 235–83.

11. This rough approximation was calculated using the number of students with valid scores used in calculating Academic Performance Index scores in California—approximately 300,000 African American students and 1.4 million Latino students.

12. In 2001 the absolute threshold was dropped from two hundred to fifty students.

13. David Grissmer and Ann Flanagan, "Exploring Rapid Achievement Gains in North Carolina and Texas," paper prepared for the National Education Goals Panel, November 1998; Brian A. Jacob, "The Impact of High-Stakes Testing on Student Achievement: Evidence from Chicago," Harvard University, John F. Kennedy School of Government, June 2001; Brian A. Jacob and Steven D. Levitt, "Rotten Apples: An Investigation of the Prevalence and Predictors of Teacher Cheating," Harvard University, John F. Kennedy School of Government, April 2002; and Daniel Koretz, "Limitations in the Use of Achievement Tests as Measures of Educators' Productivity," *Journal of Human Resources,* vol. 37, no. 4 (2002), pp. 752–77.

14. For a summary of the evidence on the racial gap in test performance, see Christopher Jencks and Meredith Phillips, eds., *The Black-White Test Score Gap* (Brookings, 1998).

8

Charter School Achievement and Accountability

TOM LOVELESS

Charter schools rose to prominence in the 1990s with the backing of two powerful reform movements in education, the accountability and choice movements. Supporters argue that charter schools are more accountable than traditional public schools. If charter schools do not perform, they are shut down. One mechanism of accountability involves parental choice. Charter schools' funding is tied to enrollment. A charter school must attract students and please parents, or its main source of revenue disappears. Another mechanism arises from charter schools' renewable license to operate (or charter), which is granted by an authorizing agency—a local school board, university, state department of education, or some other institution. Authorizers act as the state's agents, monitoring charter schools and determining whether the outcomes promised in the schools' charters are met. If a charter school fails to satisfy its authorizing agency, its charter can be revoked.

From 1991 to 2001, while state legislatures were passing charter legislation and charter schools proliferated across the country—from the first few charters in Minnesota in 1992 to approximately twenty-four hundred in 2001—they were also establishing programs to hold all schools, traditional

Thanks to Paul DiPerna and John Coughlan for research assistance and Christopher Avery, Thomas Kane, and Cliff Winston for answering technical questions that arose during the study. All errors are my responsibility.

and charter, accountable for student learning. Charter schools exist in thirty-four states that currently have state testing programs.[1] By December 2006, all states are expected to operate testing and accountability systems under the provisions of No Child Left Behind.[2] Because charter schools and their students are not exempt from these systems, state accountability represents a third way in which charters must answer for their performance. State accountability likely will overshadow accountability to parents and authorizers. Even in schools using multiple measures of student learning, state tests often come to be seen as the authoritative indicator of student achievement.[3] Parents who find out that their charter school has been labeled "failing" by state authorities may consider enrolling their children elsewhere. And such a school would undoubtedly face heightened scrutiny from its authorizing agency. Thus state accountability systems can be reasonably expected to ratchet up the importance of test scores in charter schools.

This paper analyzes achievement data in charter schools with the purpose of assessing how they fare under current state accountability systems and how they may fare under systems inspired by No Child Left Behind. A cautionary note is warranted. This study is not intended to serve as an evaluation of charter schools. Lacking the random assignment of students to charter and noncharter conditions, the analysis of achievement scores cannot adequately control for selection effects—the effect of unobserved differences between students who attend charters and those who do not. Charter schools may be doing a fine job, despite low or declining test scores, or a terrible job, despite excellent or rising scores. Moreover, part of the logic behind the charter school movement is that competition from charters may stimulate improvement among public schools, the very schools against which this evaluation measures their performance. One cannot infer charter schools' desirability as a reform strategy simply by comparing the two sectors.

Despite these limitations, this study is useful. Knowledge of student achievement in charter schools is limited to fewer than twenty studies concentrated in individual states. The current study provides the first national snapshot of charter schools' performance on state tests, the first assessment of charters' standing in relation to several state accountability systems, and the first analysis of how charters will fare under No Child Left Behind.

Research on Charter Schools and Student Achievement

How do students in charter schools perform on tests of academic achievement? The charter school experiment is barely a decade old. Research has been slow to accumulate, because most charters, even today, are relatively new; they lack standardized test score data on which to compare achievement; and the test data from very small charters, which make up a large portion of the total number of charter schools operating, are sketchy at best.[4]

In a recent review of the research on charter school achievement, Gary Miron and Christopher Nelson identified fifteen studies meeting basic quality standards.[5] The studies took place in seven states and the District of Columbia and were conducted by state departments of education, as well as by independent researchers. Miron and Nelson assigned weights to each study according to its methodological strength and the magnitude of effects. None of the studies featured experimental designs with random assignment of students to treatment and control groups. Miron and Nelson summarize the overall results as "mixed or very slightly positive" for charter schools. Positive charter effects were found in some states and negative effects in others. The strongest positive findings were from Arizona; the strongest negative findings, from Michigan.

The mixed results for charter schools were seconded by another summary of the research, this one by Brian P. Gill and a team of researchers at RAND.[6] These reviews were unable to identify policies that states should implement to enhance the academic effectiveness of charters or the policies that states should avoid. On the policy front, Miron and Nelson noted that neither the strength of charter laws (the regulatory freedom granted to charters) nor the stringency of charter oversight (the percentage of charter schools that have been closed by authorizers) seemed to explain why successful charters are more likely to be located in some states than in others.

Four studies have compared test score changes in charters and regular public schools. These studies also offer a mixed verdict. In 2002 a team of researchers in California discovered that charters populated by more than 50 percent of students in poverty had achieved greater test score improvement than traditional schools with similar students. A study in Arizona analyzed the individual test scores of sixty-two thousand students from 1997 to 1999 and found a charter advantage in reading score gains, but not in mathematics. Students' scores fell the first year they enrolled in a charter but then rebounded in the second year. A 1999 study of Michigan charters found that charters' test scores lagged behind those of public schools in fourth grade but were holding their own in seventh grade. And a study in Texas found that the percentage of charter schools qualifying as "low performing" on the state's achievement test increased from 1998 to 2000 while the percentage of traditional schools in the same category declined. The Texas study is the only major evaluation to date that has examined charter school performance in accountability systems.[7]

Data and Methods

Ten states were selected for the study. The states had at least thirty charter schools open in 1999 and tested students in grades four, eight, and ten (allowing for substitution of adjacent grade levels) using the same achievement test in 1999, 2000, and 2001. The ten states yield a total of 638 charter schools that were open in 1999. I did not add charters opening in 2000 or 2001 to the sample so that the number of schools remains fixed during the three-year time frame. Test data on the charters and regular public schools were collected from state departments of education and from websites maintained by state assessment programs. Schools for which test scores or demographic data were unavailable were dropped from the study, reducing the sample to 376 schools. Most of the omitted charters had too few students to report a test score or did not offer the grade level tested by the state.

For each school, a single composite score was computed combining reading and math scores over the three years. Within each state, annual z-scores were calculated for all schools, charter and traditional, standardizing school achievement with a mean of zero and standard deviation of 1.00. Using z-scores is necessary for comparing charter schools across the ten states because the states use different tests and publicly report data on different scales. With the average test score expressed as a z-score of 0.00 in each state, the absolute value of a z-score is the number of standard deviations schools score above or below that average. A z-score of +1.00 is approximately equal to the 83rd percentile, and a z-score of −1.00 is approximately equal to the 17th percentile.

I regressed the z-scores on variables reflecting school racial composition and poverty level, computed residuals to serve as adjusted z-scores, and weighted them by enrollment. These adjusted z-scores are used to compare achievement in charter schools with public schools possessing similar demographic characteristics. Changes in performance level were found by simply subtracting the adjusted z-scores from one year to the next. Demographic data were obtained from the Common Core of Data, a database collected by the National Center for Education Statistics.

A brief comment is necessary concerning the demographic characteristics of charter schools. The Common Core is known to underestimate poverty in charter schools because many charter operators do not participate in the federal free or reduced-price lunch program, which generates the data on poverty found in the Common Core. I computed an alternative estimate by matching charters to regular public schools with the same zip code, then assigning the public school data on free lunch (from the Common Core) to the charter. If more than one public school matched on zip code, I assigned the mean statistic for public schools. Charters without a zip code match retained their original Common Core statistic. The assumption is that schools with the same zip code, on average, draw students from similar households.

The zip code calculation produced a poverty estimate of 35 percent for the charters in the study, undoubtedly more accurate than the Common Core's 26 percent estimate. But the Common Core may be more accurate for large charter schools with significant numbers of poor children. They are the charters most likely to participate in the free lunch program and to collect qualifying information from students' parents. With this in mind, I created a second alternative variable by taking the larger of the zip code and Common Core estimates for each school. This variable raised the estimate of poverty in charters to 38 percent, a figure that is fairly close to the 41 percent reported in RPP International's 1999 survey of charter school principals in the study's ten states. I use this alternative poverty estimate in all of the analyses. That the three estimates—based on zip code, the RPP survey, and the larger of these two variables—converge within a range of 35 percent to 41 percent is somewhat comforting. But the fact remains that accurately determining the number of poor children in charter schools remains a problem with existing databases.

Analysis of Achievement

Table 8-1 displays achievement data from 1999 to 2001. As shown by the three-year composite, charter schools in these ten states scored significantly below regular public schools in the same state serving demographically similar student populations, a deficit of approximately one quarter standard deviation for the entire period (–0.24). Charters start out scoring significantly lower in 1999 (–0.26). They improved their test scores only slightly relative to public schools from 1999 to 2001 (to –0.24), but they did keep pace. Scores in both public and charter schools increased between 1999 and 2001, growth that a z-score, being a measure of relative progress in the two sectors, does not register. Appendix table 8A-1 reports the unadjusted test score gains in their original metric.

What does this mean for charter schools in state accountability systems? In a nutshell, the data on absolute level of achievement in charter schools are negative; the data on changes in performance levels from 1999 to 2001 are neutral. On achievement tests, charters score at lower levels than similar public schools in nine of the study's ten states, with Colorado the exception. In four states—Massachusetts, Michigan, Minnesota, and Texas—the score deficit for charters is statistically significant. The data on changes in test score performance from year to year are more encouraging for charters. In six

Table 8-1. *Achievement of Charter Schools, 1999–2001*

State	1999	2000	2001	Three-year composite	1999–2001 change
Arizona	+0.02	–0.03	–0.13	–0.03	–0.16
(*N* = 51)	(0.12)	(0.12)	(0.12)	(0.11)	(0.17)
California	–0.01	–0.04	–0.03	–0.02	–0.02
(*N* = 97)	(0.07)	(0.07)	(0.07)	(0.07)	(0.10)
Colorado	+0.18	+0.03	+0.25*	+0.18	+0.07
(*N* = 31)	(0.14)	(0.16)	(0.12)	(0.12)	(0.18)
Florida	–0.45	–0.44	–0.28	–0.37	+0.17
(*N* = 29)	(0.23)	(0.26)	(0.22)	(0.22)	(0.32)
Massachusetts	–0.52*	–0.53*	–0.80*	–0.54*	–0.29
(*N* = 21)	(0.17)	(0.16)	(0.19)	(0.16)	(0.25)
Michigan	–0.66*	–0.82*	–0.50*	–0.63*	+0.16
(*N* = 84)	(0.08)	(0.09)	(0.10)	(0.08)	(0.13)
Minnesota	–0.41*	–0.52*	–0.45*	–0.44*	–0.04
(*N* = 16)	(0.20)	(0.15)	(0.19)	(0.16)	(0.28)
Pennsylvania	–0.34	–0.07	+0.29	+0.05	+0.64
(*N* = 11)	(0.24)	(0.16)	(0.44)	(0.27)	(0.50)
Texas	–1.20*	–1.08*	–1.13*	–1.09*	+0.07
(*N* = 25)	(0.33)	(0.44)	(0.36)	(0.33)	(0.49)
Wisconsin	–0.23	–0.20	–0.22	–0.18	+0.02
(*N* = 11)	(0.47)	(0.38)	(0.46)	(0.41)	(0.62)
Average	–0.26*	–0.31*	–0.23*	–0.24*	+0.02
(*N* = 376)	(0.05)	(0.05)	(0.05)	(0.05)	(0.07)

Note: Z-scores, adjusted for socioeconomic status and racial composition, weighted by enrollment.
* $p < 0.05$ on a two-tailed test of z-score = 0.

states, charters logged improvement in test scores that exceeded those of similar public schools, but none of the differences reached statistical significance. In four states, changes in scores from 1999 to 2001 favored traditional public schools, but the differences between the two sectors were again statistically indistinguishable.

Eric A. Hanushek and Margaret E. Raymond in this volume (see chapter 6) discuss the merits of various measures of school performance in accountability systems. They conclude that evaluating changes in test scores of individual students as they move through the various grades at a school is preferred for isolating the effects of schooling from the effects of families, peers, and other nonschool influences on student learning. Yet Hanushek and Raymond also observe that only two states, Massachusetts and Tennessee, rated school performance in 2001 using this method (see table 6-2). Another two states, New Mexico and North Carolina, calculated changes in performance of specific cohorts at schools. The vast majority of states, twenty-seven in

2001, held schools accountable by monitoring test score changes calculated from cross-sectional data, comparable to the data reported in this paper. Ten of these states used changes at particular grade levels. I am reporting changes from 1999 to 2001 for grades four, eight, or ten, with substitution of an adjacent grade (for example, grade seven in Michigan) if dictated by a state's testing program.

Not only was some combination of test score improvement and levels the dominant approach in 2001, but it also will almost certainly continue to anchor accountability systems in the foreseeable future. Although couched in vague language that allows states considerable latitude in implementation, the adequate yearly progress provisions of No Child Left Behind require consideration of both absolute levels (the percentage of students at each school proficient in reading and math) and status change measures (the amount of ground the school must make up annually before 100 percent of students are proficient in 2014). Schools that now serve lower scoring students must accomplish more growth than schools serving students who are already up to standard.

In June 2002 the Department of Education released a survey of the states listing the number of schools failing or in need of improvement. Contrary to several reports in the media, the department did not compile its own list of failing schools. It merely collected the names of schools already identified by the states as "needing improvement" (state departments of education generally avoid the word *failing*) and released a national count by state. Table 8-2 shows the percentage of the current study's charter schools that appeared on these lists as of June 2002. As the table indicates, a larger proportion of the study's charters were failing (18.6 percent) than public schools in the ten states (12.3 percent), not surprising considering the data presented in table 8-1.

Putting a number on the percentage of failing charters nationally is difficult. The 19 percent failure rate reported in table 8-2 exceeds the figure for all charters that were open in 2002 in the ten states examined here. That failure rate is about 7 percent (125 out 1,747), but the figure is misleading. Hundreds of new charter schools opened in these ten states in 2000 and 2001 and could not have produced two consecutive years of declining test scores, which is the criterion used to classify a school as failing. And, a large number of charters did not report test data from 1999 to 2001—and thus were able to escape existing accountability systems—because they served small numbers of children or did not offer grade levels tested by the state. Although much higher, the current study's estimate of 19 percent is a better indicator of how charters will fare under No Child Left Behind. The study's sample only includes charters that would have been eligible for failing

Table 8-2. *Number of Failing Charter Schools, 2001–02*

State	Charter schools			Public schools		
	Number in study	Number failing	Percent failing	Number in state	Number failing	Percent failing
Arizona	51	8	15.7	1,489	346	23.2
California	97	8	8.2	8,238	1,009	12.2
Colorado	31	1	3.2	1,516	152	10.0
Florida	29	2	6.9	2,616	246	9.4
Massachusetts	21	6	28.6	1,858	259	13.9
Michigan	84	35	41.7	3,512	1,518	43.2
Minnesota	16	4	25.0	1,969	78	4.0
Pennsylvania	11	0	0.0	3,172	266	8.4
Texas	25	6	24.0	6,894	121	1.8
Wisconsin	11	0	0.0	2,065	108	5.2
Total	376	70	18.6	33,329	4,103	12.3

Note: Compiled by author from state departments of education websites.

schools lists in 2002. With testing now mandated in every grade from third through eighth, with charter schools' enrollments growing as they mature, and with local political pressure from teachers unions and other advocacy groups to make sure charter schools report a test score for accountability purposes, the number of charters brought under the scrutiny of state accountability systems is certain to increase dramatically.

Furthermore, states have varying definitions of what constitutes a failing school (see appendix table 8B-1 for state criteria). Michigan's standard, labeling 43 percent of schools as failing, is more rigorous than that of Texas, where only 2 percent are labeled as failing. While Michigan has many charter schools, Arkansas and Wyoming (states not included in the present study) list no failing schools, and they only have six charter schools between them. If states in which charter schools are numerous invoke higher standards of performance than states generally—state discretion that is guaranteed under No Child Left Behind—the number of failing charters may appear unduly large when looked at nationally. State variation should be taken into account in the evaluation of charter school performance under accountability systems.

Problems Holding Charters Accountable

Problems loom for incorporating charter schools into state accountability systems: deciding how to evaluate charter schools that explicitly seek out and serve at-risk children, how to interpret test results from new schools during

Table 8-3. *Achievement of Charter Schools Targeting At-Risk Students, 1999–2001*

State	Three-year composite		1999–2001 change	
	At-risk	Non–at-risk	At-risk	Non–at-risk
Arizona	−0.81*	+0.02	−0.13	−0.16
	(0.18)	(0.12)	(0.29)	(0.18)
California	−1.19*	+0.06	0.00	−0.02
	(0.18)	(0.06)	(0.25)	(0.09)
Colorado	n.a.	+0.19	n.a.	+0.07
		(0.12)		(0.18)
Florida	−1.46*	+0.03	+0.06	+0.20
	(0.40)	(0.19)	(0.55)	(0.31)
Massachusetts	n.a.	−0.53*	n.a.	−0.29
		(0.16)		(0.25)
Michigan	−1.28*	−0.59*	−0.41	+0.20
	(0.36)	(0.08)	(0.48)	(0.13)
Minnesota	−1.10*	−0.25	+0.11	−0.09
	(0.34)	(0.14)	(0.46)	(0.28)
Pennsylvania	+0.06	+0.05	+0.41	+0.66
	(n.a.)	(0.30)	(n.a.)	(0.56)
Texas	−0.38	−1.45*	+0.24	−0.01
	(0.70)	(0.38)	(1.21)	(0.54)
Wisconsin	−1.82*	+0.22	+0.58	−0.12
	(0.31)	(0.43)	(0.83)	(0.67)
Average	−1.05*	−0.17*	+0.02	+0.03
	(0.15)	(0.04)	(0.23)	(0.07)

Source: Charter policies were recorded from Center for Education Reform, *The National Charter Schools Directory 2000–2001* (Washington: 2002); and state department websites.

Note: Z-scores, adjusted for socioeconomic status and racial composition, weighted by enrollment.

* $p < 0.05$ on a two-tailed test of z-score = 0.

their first two years of operation, and how to hold small charter schools accountable despite the volatility of their test scores.

At-Risk Charter Schools

Table 8-3 examines whether charters targeting at-risk students are depressing the overall appearance of charters on state tests. The forty-nine charters with an at-risk focus score significantly below other charters (−1.05 versus −0.17), accounting for about 30 percent of the charter school deficit in the entire sample (0.07 of the −0.24 reported in table 8-1). The charters serving at-risk students held their own in raising test scores from 1999 to 2001, with an increase of 0.02. The improvement is comparable to that of regular public schools and of other charter schools without an at-risk focus. It should be interpreted cautiously. The at-risk schools start with such low test scores that a significant portion of subsequent increases may be attributable to regression to the mean.[8] The mean z-score of charter schools targeting at-risk students was −1.16 in 1999, equal to approximately the 13th percentile (not shown in the table).

This pattern highlights the difficulty of holding schools accountable when they serve special populations. Defenders of public schools have made this point for years when challenged by critics to explain the low test scores of public schools. Regular public schools may not seek out and select at-risk students, but they serve thousands of children for whom learning is a struggle. Unless at-risk students are enrolled in special education or limited English speaking programs, their test scores count in the reporting of public schools' scores. The problem is compounded for charters—or any other schools— that primarily enroll at-risk students. The same problem crops up for continuation schools or alternative settings for students who have been expelled or have temporarily dropped out of school. In offering rewards and imposing sanctions, state officials must decide how to treat schools fairly when the schools' primary mission is educating students who are extremely difficult to educate.

Many of the states have few schools specializing in at-risk students, so their impact on state means is muted. The effect appears greatest in two states, Florida and Texas. In Florida, eleven charter schools in the study target at-risk students; eighteen do not. The z-score for at-risk charters is −1.46, placing them among the bottom 7 percent of schools in the state. For non–at-risk charters, the z-score is 0.03, approximately the state average. Both types of charters raised their test scores from 1999 to 2001, but the increases at the non–at-risk schools were larger, 0.20.

In Texas, a strange pattern appears. The schools targeting at-risk students test higher than the non–at-risk schools, −0.38 versus −1.45. After adjustment for racial composition and poverty, the at-risk charters' test scores are statistically indistinguishable from those of the average school in Texas.[9] Even more striking is the fact that the at-risk charters improved by 0.24 from 1999 to 2001. Only six charter schools in the Texas sample target at-risk students, so these findings must be taken with a grain of salt. Moreover, the demographic data for Texas charter schools are undoubtedly flawed. Texas is unique in legislating a separate category for charters serving at-risk students, known as 75 Percent Rule charter schools. These schools must enroll at least 75 percent at-risk students.[10] After combing through state records, Texas researchers were surprised to discover that many of the 75 Percent Rule charters report absolutely no at-risk students attending their schools. However, about one-third of the general open-enrollment schools report more than 75 percent of students at-risk. So what should be made of the performance of Texas charters? Overall, they achieve at extremely low levels. But, notwithstanding deficiencies in the data, something positive may be happening in Texas's charter schools that target at-risk students. They perform reasonably well in terms of absolute test score levels, and, from 1999 to 2001, their test scores increased more than regular public schools serving similar students. In 1999 only a small number of at-risk charters had been established, explaining why so few show up in the current study. It is unwise to draw firm policy guidance until the data problems are solved and a more thorough evaluation is conducted. Nevertheless, my findings do mirror those of the most recent evaluation of Texas charter schools conducted by a consortium of Texas research centers.[11] Texas ultimately may provide examples of charter schools working successfully with students who traditionally underachieve on tests of academic performance.

New School Effect

A study in Arizona detected a first-year effect, in which students' test scores declined the first year they attended a charter school and then rebounded in the second and third years.[12] To investigate this phenomenon, I compared the scores of charters that were new in 1999 ($N = 96$) with charters that had been open before that year ($N = 280$). Figure 8-1 displays the results. A negative new school effect is evident, but it occurs not just in the first year but the first two years that charters take students. In 1999 the new schools started –0.24 z-scores behind existing charters (–0.44 for new schools versus –0.20 for the older schools). They remained approximately the same distance behind in 2000 (–0.54 and –0.23, respectively). And they finally caught up to the older charters in 2001 (both groups at –0.23). By 2001 charter schools that were founded in 1999 and before 1999 look almost the same on achievement tests.

What explains the new school effect? This study's data only allow for speculation. Charters apparently attract low-achieving students. A plausible explanation is that they initially score below students with similar demographic characteristics but, after attending charters for two years, register significant learning gains. And the gains exceed those of students with similar characteristics. This interpretation could be tested by examining test scores of students in the years before transferring from a public school to a charter. But what about older schools? Older charters have flat scores of –0.20, –0.23, and –0.23, suggesting that improvements in performance attributable to

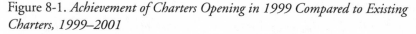

Figure 8-1. *Achievement of Charters Opening in 1999 Compared to Existing Charters, 1999–2001*

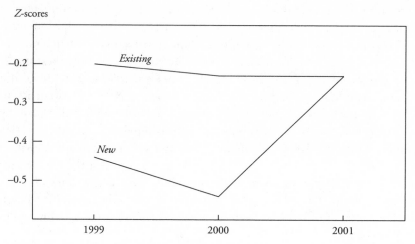

charter schooling dissipate sometime after the third year. Charter competition also could stimulate better performance from the public schools. If the competitive effects of charters kick in around the third year, rising scores for both charters and regular pubic schools would produce flat charter z-scores after the third year. Examining regular public schools' scores before and after charters are established in the same neighborhood would be revealing on that question.

Another reasonable explanation is that scores are depressed from the pressures of starting a new school. The political and organizational obstacles to starting a charter are numerous. A charter school founder must raise funding, secure a building, hire staff, develop curriculum, acquire teaching materials, recruit students, and accomplish myriad additional tasks before opening the classroom doors for the first time. Moreover, most students switch schools to attend charters, and student mobility has been found to depress test scores. New charters may have low test scores for the first two years simply because they are new. Selection into charter schools also could change as charters mature. Unproven schools may only attract those parents desperate enough to take a risk. Wary parents might be more willing to give charters a chance after the schools have established a track record.

Test Score Volatility

Thomas J. Kane and Douglas O. Staiger have documented the difficulty of evaluating small schools in state accountability systems. Small schools' test

Table 8-4. *Mean Absolute Value of Charter School Z-Score Change by Enrollment*

Enrollment	1999–2000	2000–01	1999–2001
11–125 ($N = 64$)	0.68	0.72	0.59
126–250 ($N = 123$)	0.65	0.51	0.59
251–375 ($N = 54$)	0.48	0.48	0.43
> 375 ($N = 135$)	0.30	0.43	0.41

scores are more volatile than those of large schools because changes in a few students' performance—or a shift within the range attributable to random error—has a greater impact on small schools' scores. This phenomenon would especially be expected to affect charter schools because they are substantially smaller than the average public school.[13] The average public school in the nation serves 520 students. The average charter school in the study serves 368 students. (The median charter school has 252 students.)

Table 8-4 disaggregates the schools by enrollment and displays the absolute values of the charters' test score changes. As expected, smaller charters' test scores are more erratic. From year to year, test score changes in schools with fewer than 125 students are about twice as large as in schools with more than 375 students. Combining scores over three years reduces the volatility of smaller schools. This is of heightened importance considering this paper's previous findings. If the test scores of charters are both lower and more volatile than the scores of regular public schools, a disproportionate share of charters would be expected to appear at the bottom of the distribution of scores in any given year and to receive sanctions under state accountability systems. This is particularly true for charter schools specializing in educating at-risk students and for charters in the first two years of operation.

Summary and Discussion

This study analyzed the test scores of charter schools in ten states from 1999 to 2001. The findings suggest that problems loom for charters in state accountability systems and for the states themselves in holding charter schools accountable under provisions of the No Child Left Behind Act. Achievement was significantly lower in charters than in regular public schools, by about one-fourth standard deviation when adjusted for students' racial and socioeconomic backgrounds. However, charter schools registered improvements in test scores from 1999 to 2001 that were comparable to those made by regular public schools. Charters serving at-risk students scored at significantly lower levels than open-admission charters. But these schools were also able to raise their test scores from 1999 to 2001, and the increases were equal to those of both regular public schools and other charters. Charters opening in 1999 scored at lower levels than existing charters for the first two years; then they caught up with older charters by the third year. Foreshadowing the problems that charters may face under No Child Left Behind, the charters in the study are overrepresented on states' 2002 failing schools lists.

Three important considerations temper the pessimism, at least with regard to the quality of education charter schools provide. First, the improving test scores indicate that low achievement in charters may be a temporary condition. Charters probably attract students who were low-achievers before they ever set foot on a charter school campus. A rigorous analysis of changes in individual students' performance would be better able to tease out any selection effects from charter schools enrolling students who are, net of the controls employed here, low-achievers. If charter schools represent a remedial policy intervention—a policy designed to tackle poor academic performance—then initially low test scores are not surprising.

Second, competition from charters may raise achievement in both charters and regular public schools. Caroline M. Hoxby's 2001 study of Arizona and Michigan—two states in the current study—found that charter schools are producing an effect of "all boats rising," with scores rising in traditional schools facing competition from charters. The effect in both states was limited to districts in which charter schools were drawing at least 6 percent of enrollment. Hoxby concluded that public schools can achieve productivity gains when forced to compete for students.[14] Whether "all boats are rising" needs to be explored in additional states.

Third, in seven of the study's ten states, open-admission charters (schools that do not target at-risk students) produce test scores that are statistically indistinguishable from the scores of regular public schools. Charter schools are less costly to operate than regular public schools. If charters can produce the same amount of learning as the average public school, then that is a strong argument in charters' favor.

Nevertheless, this study has uncovered several issues states need to address to integrate charters fully and fairly into accountability systems. Better data must be collected from charter schools, including annual test scores and reliable demographic information. The No Child Left Behind Act mandates annual achievement testing in grades three through eight, so the situation is likely to improve soon. Better information will not only serve the cause of accountability, but it will also allow parents who are considering charter schooling to make more informed decisions.

The two-year new school effect is a constraint that state officials should recognize in building effective accountability systems. No Child Left Behind also requires states to begin some form of intervention after two consecutive years of failing test scores. New charter schools are especially vulnerable to this penalty. If achievement is depressed from the stress of opening a new charter school, a two-year grace period may be advisable before starting the clock on sanctioning new charters. Otherwise, on top of everything else, schools struggling to get up and running will be prematurely placed on watch lists before higher test scores have had a chance to materialize.[15] Some states' accountability systems have moved in this direction. For example, Texas currently exempts charters' first year of test scores from the state's accountability system. No Child Left Behind, however, is silent on this issue as well as on the other two problems uncovered in this study—what to do with charters specializing in educating at-risk students or enrolling small numbers of children. The Department of Education's draft regulations on how No Child Left Behind applies to charter schools are disappointingly vague with regard to the amount of local discretion allowed in holding charter schools accountable.[16]

The third policy implication applies to accountability systems that rely heavily on changes in school test scores. Change models are better than status models in isolating the effects of schools on achievement. Politically, however, change models are vulnerable. The public is unlikely to soon consider a school progressing from the 5th to the 10th percentile as more successful than a school declining from the 95th to the 90th percentile. Moreover, scores of schools are always derived from the scores of students. An accountability system exclusively focused on gains could, theoretically, identify a high school with most of its students headed to Harvard and Yale as failing (if they scored extraordinarily high upon entry) and a school graduating most of its students as functional illiterates as successful (if an even greater proportion could not read when they first entered the school). State systems that hold individual students accountable focus exclusively on the level of a test score, not on gains. In many states, for example, students must demonstrate sufficient knowledge in academic subjects before graduating from high school. Students who make gains but test below the required level are denied diplomas, and students with high test scores graduate even though their test scores may have slipped from the previous year. Accountability systems are unlikely to ever completely ignore the absolute levels of test scores when evaluating school performance.

That raises a final point about politics. Researchers and policymakers should be watchful for how the politics of accountability systems and charter schools evolve in the future. I began this paper by observing that charter schools are a product of both the choice and accountability movements. Charters offer choice advocates an alternative to the traditional public school run by local public districts. They offer accountability advocates the means to prod schools toward better results and the power to close down charters that persistently fail. However, a potential conflict exists between the two ideas. An essential element of choice is that institutions should be free to fashion their own goals and to govern themselves independently in pursuit of outcomes that parents and educators mutually value. Accountability systems intrude on that process. By defining the types of learning that schools will produce—and by establishing a system that measures progress toward those attainments—accountability reduces the autonomy of charter schools. Charter schools with low test scores may be shut down, whether parents like them or not. And students who fail exit exams may be denied a diploma, whether or not parents are satisfied with the education their children have received.

In the case of popular but low-performing charters, one way states could handle the conflict is to ensure that parents who are considering enrolling in the school are informed of the school's academic record. For charters with persistently low test scores, the probationary requirements of No Child Left Behind will kick in, such as requiring tutoring services for low-achieving students. If these schools continue to fail, popular or not, the state will be forced to reconstitute them under new leadership. If the tensions between choice and accountability eventually come to a head, it will probably be over how states should fairly hold charter schools accountable for academic achievement.

Appendix Table 8A-1. *Charter School and Regular Public School Gain Scores, 1999–2001*

State	Test	Metric	1999 score		1999–2000 gain		2000–01 gain		1999–2001 gain	
			Charter	Regular	Charter	Regular	Charter	Regular	Charter	Regular
Arizona	SAT-9	Percentile	49.1	49.3	-1.6	-0.1	+2.8	+2.2	+1.3	+2.1
(N = 51)			(2.6)	(0.5)	(1.4)	(0.3)	(1.3)	(0.3)	(1.3)	(0.3)
California	SAT-9	Percentile	46.5	45.3	+1.7	+3.9*	+2.5	+2.0	+4.1	+5.9*
(N = 97)			(1.9)	(0.2)	(0.8)	(0.1)	(0.7)	(0.1)	(0.8)	(0.1)
Colorado	CSAP	Percent proficient	62.1*	51.4	-6.4	+7.4*	+12.3*	-2.4	+5.9	+5.0
(N = 31)			(4.3)	(0.7)	(2.6)	(0.4)	(2.9)	(0.4)	(2.5)	(0.4)
Florida	FCAT	Scale score	265.9	290.5*	+3.0	+3.5	+10.5*	+5.9	+13.5	+9.5
(N = 29)			(6.7)	(0.5)	(5.0)	(0.2)	(3.5)	(0.2)	(4.1)	(0.2)
Massachusetts	MCAS	Scale score	230.3	232.9	+1.5	+0.6	+2.9	+3.6	+4.4	+4.2
(N = 21)			(1.8)	(0.2)	(0.9)	(0.1)	(0.6)	(0.1)	(0.9)	(0.1)
Michigan	MEAP	Percent satisfactory	41.0	62.2*	-1.6	+1.8*	+5.0*	+0.7	+3.4	+2.5
(N = 84)			(2.3)	(0.4)	(1.4)	(0.2)	(1.6)	(0.3)	(1.6)	(0.3)
Minnesota	BST/MCA	Scale score	810.7	978.6	+68.5	+23.6	-14.0	+14.6	+54.5	+38.2
(N = 16)			(150.1)	(18.9)	(69.3)	(4.1)	(68.1)	(2.4)	(73.0)	(4.3)
Pennsylvania	PSSA	Scale score	1171.6	1304.9*	+15.7	+3.3	+11.4	+2.2	+27.0	+5.5
(N = 11)			(45.8)	(1.8)	(17.6)	(0.8)	(29.6)	(0.8)	(34.2)	(0.9)
Texas	TAAS	Percent passing	75.2	87.6*	-0.2	+1.6	+6.7*	+2.4	+6.5	+3.9
(N = 25)			(3.7)	(0.1)	(3.3)	(0.1)	(3.3)	(0.1)	(2.2)	(0.1)
Wisconsin	CTBS-5	Percentile	57.8	67.3*	+1.8	0.0	+1.0	-0.9	+2.8	-0.9
(N = 11)			(6.1)	(0.3)	(3.6)	(0.1)	(2.6)	(0.2)	(2.7)	(0.2)

Note: SAT-9 = Stanford Achievement Test-9; CSAP = Colorado Student Assessment Program; FCAT = Florida Comprehensive Assessment Test; MCAS = Massachusetts Comprehensive Assessment System; MEAP = Michigan Educational Assessment Program; BST = Basic Skills Test; MCA = Minnesota Comprehensive Assessment; PSSA = Pennsylvania System of School Assessment; TAAS = Texas Assessment of Academic Skills; CTBS-5 = Comprehensive Test of Basic Skills-5.

*p < 0.05 on a two-tailed test of charter = regular.

Appendix Table 8B-1. *How States Determined Failing Schools, 2001–02*

State	Year	Criteria for being identified for improvement
Arizona	1999–2000	Failure to make adequate progress toward either having 90 percent of students scoring "proficient" or above or having no students score "below basic" on the Stanford Achievement Test
California	2000–01	Failure to make adequate yearly progress (AYP) for two consecutive years; AYP: 5 percent schoolwide growth target and comparable growth targets for significant subgroups
Colorado	2001–02	Schools with Colorado Student Assessment Program scores below lowest 2 percent of schools in base year 2000–01
Florida	2000–01	Because no Florida schools received an F in 2000–01, schools that earned a D were identified for improvement; schools score points for percentage of students passing and percentage of students showing improvement, D = 280–320 points; failure to improve reading scores of lowest 25 percent in school results in a reduction of one letter grade
Massachusetts	2000–01	Failure to make expected improvement over two years; schools with high percentage of proficient students are expected to increase scale score 1–3 points; schools with a high percentage of failing students are expected to raise scale score 5–7 points
Michigan	2000–01	Failure to make AYP in at least one of two consecutive years; AYP: close at least 10 percent of achievement gap as reported by the Michigan Educational Assessment Program; achievement gap: (100 percent − percent in highest category) + (percent in lowest category − 0 percent); schools with 75+ percent students in the highest achievement category are considered to have met the AYP requirement
Minnesota	2000–01	Average scale score on Minnesota Comprehensive Assessment below 1420 and missed school-specific growth goal for two consecutive years
Pennsylvania	2001–02	Various local assessment criteria and less than 5 percent of students in bottom two performance categories improving to top two performance categories
Texas	2000–01	Received a rating of "low-performing" or "needs peer review" for two or more consecutive years
Wisconsin	2001–02	Failure to have percent of students scoring at or above "proficient" greater than or equal to 90 percent of the statewide average in base year 1997–98 or failure to show continuous progress according to a sliding scale in which schools at lower levels are expected to make more progress than schools with higher scores

Notes

1. Gary Miron and Christopher Nelson, *Student Academic Achievement in Charter Schools: What We Know and Why We Know So Little* (Columbia University, Teachers College, National Center for the Study of Privatization in Education, 2001).

2. Department of Education, *Consolidated State Application for State Grants under Title IX, Part C, Section 9302 of the Elementary and Secondary Education Act (Public Law 107-110).*

3. Paul Hill and others, *A Study of Charter School Accountability* (Department of Education, Office of Educational Research and Improvement, 2001).

4. Robert V. Antonucci, *1997 Test Results from Massachusetts Charter Schools* (Massachusetts Department of Education, 1997); and Lori A. Mulholland, *Arizona Charter School Progress Evaluation* (Arizona State University, Morrison Institute for Public Policy, 1999).

5. Miron and Nelson, *Student Academic Achievement in Charter Schools.*

6. Brian P. Gill and others, *Rhetoric versus Reality: What We Know and What We Need to Know about Vouchers and Charter Schools* (Santa Monica, Calif.: RAND Corporation, 2002).

7. Lew Solomon, K. Paark, and D. Garcia, *Does Charter School Attendance Improve Test Scores? The Arizona Results* (Phoenix, Ariz.: Goldwater Institute, 2001); Eric Bettinger, *The Effect of Charter Schools on Charter Students and Public Schools* (Columbia University, Teachers College, National Center for the Study of Privatization in Education, 1999); Simeon P. Slovacek, Antony J. Kunnan, and Hae-Jin Kim, *California Charter Schools Serving Low-SES Students: An Analysis of the Academic Performance Index* (Los Angeles: California State University, Charter College of Education, 2002); and University of Texas at Arlington, School of Urban and Public Affairs and others, *Texas Open-Enrollment Charter Schools Fourth-Year Evaluation* (University of Texas at Arlington, 2001).

8. For a discussion of regression to the mean as it affects studies of low-performing students, see Jon Lorence and others, "Grade Retention and Social Promotion in Texas, 1994–99: Academic Achievement among Elementary School Students," in Diane Ravitch, ed., *Brookings Papers on Education Policy 2002* (Brookings, 2002), pp. 13–67. Mean regression accounts for 8.7 of an 18.4-point gain registered by students retained in third grade. Lorrie A. Shephard raises the issue in a commentary on the paper, pp. 56–63.

9. The demographic data for at-risk charters: African Americans, 28 percent; Hispanics, 55 percent; free lunch, 62 percent. For non–at-risk charters: African Americans, 29 percent; Hispanics, 31 percent; free lunch, 45 percent.

10. In the 1999–2000 school year, the number of general open-enrollment charter schools was capped at 120, but state law allowed for an unlimited number of 75 Percent Rule schools. See University of Texas at Arlington, School of Urban and Public Affairs and others, *Texas Open-Enrollment Charter Schools Fourth-Year Evaluation.*

11. University of Texas at Arlington, School of Urban and Public Affairs and others, *Texas Open-Enrollment Charter Schools Fourth-Year Evaluation.*

12. Solomon, Paark, and Garcia, *Does Charter School Attendance Improve Test Scores?*

13. Thomas J. Kane and Douglas O. Staiger, in "Volatility in School Test Scores: Implications for Test-Based Accountability Systems," in Diane Ravitch, ed., *Brookings Papers on Education Policy 2002* (Brookings, 2002), pp. 235–83, found that test score gains almost appear random in California and North Carolina, as did David N. Figlio and Marianne E. Page, "School Choice and the Distributional Effects of Ability Tracking: Does Separation Increase Equality?" Working Paper 8055 (Cambridge, Mass.: National Bureau of Economic Research, 2001), in Florida. For a review of the concerns with value-added accountability systems, see Helen Ladd and Janet Hansen, eds., *Making Money Matter: Financing America's Schools* (Washington: National Academy Press, 1999).

14. Caroline M. Hoxby, *How School Choice Affects the Achievement of Public School Students* (Hoover Institution, Koret Task Force, September 2001); and Caroline M. Hoxby, "School Choice and School Productivity (or Could School Choice Be a Tide That Lifts All Boats?)," paper presented at the National Bureau of Economic Research Conference on the Economics of School Choice, Cambridge, Massachusetts, February 23-24, 2001. See also Bettinger, *The Effect of Charter Schools on Charter Students and Public Schools*, for a different interpretation of the Michigan data—that charters lag in performance.

15. Tom Loveless and Claudia Jasin, "Starting from Scratch: Organizational and Political Obstacles Facing Charter Schools," *Educational Administration Quarterly*, vol. 34, no. 1 (February 1998), pp. 9–30.

16. Department of Education, *The Impact of the New Title I Requirements on Charter Schools: Nonregulatory Guidance* (Government Printing Office, March 24, 2003).

9

The Effects of Accountability in California

JULIAN R. BETTS AND ANNE DANENBERG

Clalifornia has been a relative latecomer to the national trend toward school accountability. In 1998 the state reintroduced a standardized statewide test and began to develop content standards. The third part of the reform was the introduction of an accountability system outlined in the Public Schools Accountability Act (PSAA) of 1999. The PSAA sets out a list of financial awards for schools, staff, and students and sanctions for schools and administrators based on a school's ranking on the Academic Performance Index (API). The API, which is a weighted average of test scores of students at each school, has become the cornerstone of the legislation. Another key element of this system is the Immediate Intervention/Underperforming Schools Program (II/USP, or the Immediate Intervention program), which provides financial assistance to schools that roughly fall in the bottom half of the API distribution.[1]

This paper addresses the most important policy questions surrounding these reforms. First, how have school resources, such as class size and the qualifications of teachers, evolved in response to the accountability reforms? Second, what is happening to achievement in California since these reforms? Third, and perhaps most important given the large variations in student

This research received financial support from the Public Policy Institute of California. We thank Macke Raymond, William Howell, Paul Peterson, and Martin West for helpful comments.

achievement among schools, how effective is the Immediate Intervention/ Underperforming Schools Program?[2]

School Accountability and the Resource Gap between Schools

A central goal of accountability is for students at all schools to perform at high levels. Ironically, however, one potential side effect of school accountability is that the threat of sanctions may induce talented teachers to shy away from the low-performing schools most in need of improvement. We intend therefore to test whether the 1999 accountability law has induced more highly experienced and educated teachers to move away from low-scoring schools.

To do this, we first rank K–6 schools for each academic year between 1995–96 and 2000–01 according to their mean scaled math scores for grade five and divide the schools into quintiles.[3] We then examine whether gaps in selected school and teacher characteristics between the top fifth and bottom fifth of schools have widened or narrowed during this period. For purposes of comparison, we also consider changes in the percentage of students in each quintile receiving free or reduced-price lunch.

Students in low-score schools are clearly less economically advantaged than those in high-score schools. As table 9-1 shows, approximately four to six times as many students are eligible for free or reduced-price lunches in the bottom-scoring quintile of schools as in the top quintile. Moreover, the difference between the low- and high-scoring schools on this measure has increased between 1995–96 and 2000–01.

Low-scoring K–6 schools also have larger shares of novice teachers, teachers with at most a bachelor's degree, and teachers who lack full credentials. Meanwhile, they have smaller shares of teachers who have at least a master's degree. The gaps between low- and high-score schools widened between 1995–96 and 2000–01 for the share of novice teachers, teachers with at most a bachelor's degree, and teachers who lack full certification. The gap in the share of teachers lacking full certification grew by more than 13 percentage points, suggesting that despite efforts to equalize per pupil spending in California, uncertified teachers are concentrated disproportionately at elementary schools with the lowest test scores. In short, the gap in teacher qualifications between low-scoring and high-scoring elementary schools has widened between 1995–96 and 2000–01.

However, these results do not definitively show whether this growth in inequality is attributable to the state's accountability regime or to other factors. We therefore used regression analysis techniques to test whether the gaps in teacher qualifications between these low- and high-scoring schools

Table 9-1. *Average School and Teacher Characteristics of High Test Score Schools and Low Test Score Schools for Grade Five Math, K–6 Schools, 1995–96 to 2000–01*

School or teacher characteristic	1995–96		2000–01		
	1997–98 low-score schools	1997–98 high-score schools	2000–01 low-score schools	2000–01 high-score schools	Gap change 1995–96 to 2000–01
Percent free or reduced-price lunch	81.7	19.7	82.8	16.1	4.7
Average class size	30.4	30.1	22.0	22.4	–0.7
Percent at most bachelor's degree	21.7	10.7	32.2	14.5	6.7
Percent at least master's degree	27.3	34.8	22.6	32.3	-2.2
Percent low experience (0–2 years)	14.2	8.6	19.4	12.5	1.2
Percent lacking credentials	3.0	0.7	20.5	4.9	13.4
Number of observations	738	747	862	866	. . .

Source: Authors' calculations from California Department of Education data sets.

grew more rapidly in the post–PSAA years (1999–2000 and 2000–01) than previously. We find that in most cases a fairly consistent trend is evident over the entire period of widening resource gaps between low-scoring and high-scoring schools.[4] In almost all cases, we find that the passage of the PSAA in 1999 did not widen the resource gaps. In some cases, preexisting trends of widening in the resource gap between the highest API quintile of schools and other schools began to reverse.

Overall, then, the conclusions are clear: Strong evidence exists of steadily widening gaps between the fifth of schools with the highest levels of achievement and lower quintiles of schools between 1995–96 and 2000–01 in teacher education, experience, and credentials. The class-size reduction initiative the state legislature adopted in 1996, the effects of which are also apparent in table 9-1, may be partly responsible for this pattern.[5] However, no evidence supports the notion that the introduction of the PSAA in 1999 exacerbated the trends.

The Immediate Intervention/Underperforming Schools Program

Figure 9-1 shows the cumulative distribution of grade five math test scores for non–Limited English Proficient students across California's schools. The

Figure 9-1. *Cumulative Distribution of Grade Five Math Scores by Year*

Percentiles of schools
(Weighted by number of tests taken)

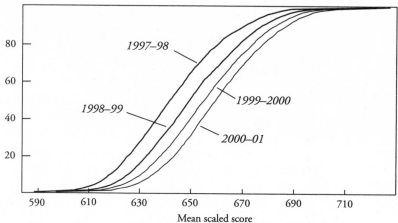

Mean scaled score

Note: Test scores are for non–Limited English Proficient grade five students in K–6 schools. The vertical axis shows the percentage of students scoring at or below the given scaled score.

vertical axis shows the percentage of students attending schools at which average test scores are at or below the scores listed on the horizontal axis. The graph, which is largely representative of patterns in other subjects and grades, shows that the distribution of test scores has shifted upward over time.[6]

However, perhaps a more striking pattern is the dramatic drop-off in test scores among the lowest performing schools. This finding is meaningful, as scores on the test are scaled so that a five-point difference captures the same absolute gap in performance anywhere along the distribution. This *S*-shaped distribution of schools suggests that the lowest performing schools lag considerably behind other schools in the state. Therefore the financial aid and potential penalties directed to these schools arguably constitute the most important part of the PSAA.

The Immediate Intervention/Underperforming Schools Program provides financial assistance to public schools that, roughly speaking, rank in the bottom half of API rankings each year. The first cohort of schools was selected in 1999.[7] Participating schools draft an action plan for reform in year one and implement the plan in years two and three, with an initial planning grant of $50,000 and grants of $200 per student during the implementation years. The first cohort of II/USP schools began their planning phases during the 1999–2000 school year, in conjunction with an external evaluator prescreened by the state. In addition, California began implementing similar

Comprehensive School Reform Demonstration Program (CSRD) grants in the same year with federal money. Below we refer to both types of schools as participants in Immediate Intervention.

In addition to financial carrots, both versions of the Immediate Intervention program include noteworthy sticks. Within twelve months, the district must hold a public hearing to discuss initial progress during the implementation phase. If after twenty-four months the school does not meet its API growth targets, the state may provide one additional year of grants to schools demonstrating some evidence of improvement. But if the school's API score has not improved sufficiently, the school will be subject to a sliding scale of state sanctions, culminating in possible state takeover of the school.

In a state with persistent resource inequalities across schools, this intervention program is notable for devoting additional financial resources to schools that lag behind in the test score rankings. These schools almost always enroll above-average numbers of disadvantaged students. The II/USP program reflects the recognition on the part of the California legislature that additional resources are needed for the lowest performing schools.

Nonetheless, we have many important questions about the efficacy of both the planning and implementation phases of the program. Most important, the question arises of whether the II/USP has started to improve student performance in participating schools. Additional questions relate to concerns that the funds are being distributed too widely, the potentially nonrandom nature in which schools have applied for the program, and the ease with which schools have planned for II/USP funding.

The Effects of II/USP on Achievement Gains

We will attempt to assess the API score growth for schools participating in II/USP between spring 1999 and spring 2001. But it seems almost unfair to expect that II/USP reforms could bear fruit in two years, given that participating schools spend their first year planning the reforms that take root only in the second year. For CSRD schools, there is slightly more hope that we can evaluate the success of the reforms, as the first cohort of these schools began implementing reforms in 1999–2000, instead of 2000–01.

We ran simple models to explain the gains in API scores between 1999 and 2001 for schools that entered the II/USP in 1999–2000 and a sample of comparison schools. Each model included an indicator variable for schools that began to participate in II/USP (including CSRD schools) in 1999–2000 as well as dummy variables for the school's grade-span.

We tested whether, among the sorts of schools that are apt to apply for reform programs such as II/USP, II/USP participation causes the school's

Table 9-2. *Estimated Impact of II/USP Participation on API Gains between 1999 and 2001*

Treatment group	Control group	Coefficient (standard error)
II/USP participants	Eligible II/USP applicants not selected to participate	17.5** (2.4)

Note: II/USP = Immediate Intervention/Underperforming Schools Program; API = Academic Performance Index. Model includes controls for grade-span of school and a dummy variable for II/USP participation beginning in 1999–2000.
** Significant at 1 percent level.

achievement to rise. Table 9-2 shows the coefficient on the II/USP indicator variable in the regression. The first column lists the treatment group; that is, the sample or subsample of II/USP participants included in the regression. The second column lists the control group; that is, the comparison group that provides the benchmark against which the II/USP schools are compared. Notably, our comparison group is schools that not only were eligible for II/USP but also applied and were not selected. This is a valid comparison group because these schools exhibited similar motivation in that they applied but did not win the randomized selection process.

We find II/USP participation to be a positive and highly significant predictor of gains in school API scores over time. The predicted effect, about 17.5 points, represents roughly one-third of the mean gain in API scores for schools in the sample over the period. This is a large effect.[8]

The Self-Selection of Schools into the Immediate Intervention Program

A common criticism of school accountability systems is that schools will game the system. In particular, schools that are likely to gain from participating in voluntary programs with the least effort are the most likely to apply, and these are not necessarily the schools that accountability systems primarily seek to help. To assess this issue, we now examine whether the voluntary nature of participation has caused schools to self-select into the Immediate Intervention program in unintended ways that may undermine the effectiveness of the program.

These potential problems related to self-selection were not inevitable. It is easy to imagine how the Department of Education could have dictated which schools were to participate in the program, by starting at the bottom of the API distribution and working upward until the quota of 430 new schools per year was filled. Instead, a wide swath of schools was deemed eligible. Schools that were in the bottom five deciles of state rankings based on both spring 1998 and 1999 scores were deemed eligible for the first round of the program. Beginning in the 1999–2000 school year and in later years a school became eligible if it ranked in the bottom five deciles for that year and in addition failed to meet the state-imposed target for growth in the API.

This voluntary nature of participation in the Immediate Intervention program potentially creates some severe incentive problems related to which schools volunteer to participate, and whether some schools have an incentive to let test scores slide. Some of the chief possibilities are as follows:

—Schools' API scores can rise or fall between years because of random variations in test scores that are beyond teachers' control. Are schools that had an unlucky year, with atypically low test scores, more likely to apply for the program in the knowledge that they are more likely than average to improve in subsequent years?

A special case of the above argument relates to the number of students in the school. Thomas J. Kane and Douglas O. Staiger argue that smaller schools are more likely than large schools to have unusually high or low test scores in any given year, because of greater random noise in their average test score (see chapter 7 in this volume).[9] Because II/USP schools can dodge the worst penalties by showing improvement in one or two of their first three years, random chance works in the favor of smaller schools. In addition, there is a much more direct reason why smaller schools may be more likely to participate: Principals at such schools may believe that reform is easier to implement when the number of teachers and students is relatively small.

Another incentive mechanism, however, works in the opposite direction. Schools that apply for Immediate Intervention must invest a large fixed cost of time to complete the application and in year one to plan how to spend the dollars that begin to flow in earnest in the second year of program participation. A large school can spread this fixed cost over more students (and teachers) than can a smaller school. Thus simple financial incentives suggest the opposite to what we hypothesized above: Larger schools may be more likely to apply for Immediate Intervention than small schools.

—The API growth targets for each school below the official target of a score of 800 (out of 1000) is 5 percent of the gap between 800 and its previous API score. This means that schools with particularly low performance must increase by more in an absolute sense than do schools that initially had higher scores. II/USP schools must meet their API growth targets within twenty-four months to avoid state sanctions. Does this combination of policies reduce the probability that the worst performing schools will volunteer for the program? This seems to represent a potentially severe problem given

Table 9-3. *Ordinary Least Squares Models of Probability That Eligible Schools Apply for II/USP*

Independent variable	Grade-span		
	K–6	6–8	9–12
API fell	0.053	−0.006	0.057
	(0.031)	(0.12)	(0.049)
Enrollment	−0.075*	0.075*	0.024
(in thousands)	(0.031)	(0.032)	(0.017)
Target API growth	0.015**	0.026**	0.030**
	(0.002)	(0.005)	0.006
Adjusted R^2	0.108	0.101	0.067
Sample size	3,196	899	802

Note: II/USP = Immediate Intervention/Underperforming Schools Program. Numbers in parentheses are standard errors. Years covered are 1999–2000 through 2001–02. Other regressors not shown include a constant and year dummies. API refers to the Academic Performance Index, the state's measure of student achievement. Target API growth is the growth target set by the state for each school.

* Significant at 5 percent level.

** Significant at 1 percent level.

the evidence that the very lowest performing schools fare disproportionately poorly on the state test.

To answer these questions, we ran ordinary least squares models of the probability that a school that was eligible for II/USP in fact applied for the program. We performed these analyses separately for elementary, middle, and high schools. We modeled this probability as a function of whether the API at the school had declined the previous year, total enrollment at the school, and the size of the API growth target set for the school by the state. The first of these controls is a dummy variable set to one if the API score declined in the most recent year, which we take as a proxy for what could well be random noise that affected a school's test scores in that year only. Our earlier hypothesis was that such schools may be particularly apt to apply for the program because the school's administrators rightly believe that test scores will naturally rebound, or regress to the mean.[10]

Table 9-3 shows the results when we model whether a school that was eligible to enter the II/USP in the 1999–2000, 2000–01, or 2001–02 school years applied. Most of the pessimistic hypotheses that we outlined above do not gain support from our regressions. Most important, schools at the bottom end of the API range, which therefore have the largest API growth targets assigned to them, are more, not less, likely to apply to participate in

II/USP. To any policymaker concerned about narrowing the achievement gap across schools, this appears to be good news.

What about the size of the school as measured by enrollment? In only one case did we find support for the idea that smaller schools are more apt to apply, and this was in the model for elementary schools. However, the effect is very small (an increase in enrollment of one hundred students is associated with a 0.75 percent drop in the probability of applying). Moreover, we find the opposite result for middle schools, where larger schools seem more likely to apply. In high schools enrollment also enters positively, but it is not significant statistically. Finally, when we repeated these models by individual years the negative enrollment effect among elementary schools was never statistically significant. We conclude that overall there is little support for the idea that smaller schools are more apt to apply because they realize that their scores are particularly likely to rebound.

The model also tests whether schools that recently experienced a decline in their API score would be more likely to apply for the program if administrators believed that the recent decline was a statistical fluke.[11] As the table shows, no significant link emerges between a recent decline in a school's API and its probability of applying for the Immediate Intervention program.

Overall, we have found little evidence that perverse incentives related to II/USP have created adverse patterns of self-selection among schools eligible for the program. By far the strongest and most consistent pattern was that schools with the lowest APIs, which faced the largest state-mandated targets for growth in the API, were the most likely to apply for the program. This is a welcome sign that schools that need the most help are the most likely to take advantage of program funding.[12]

Is the II/USP Program Sufficiently Focused on the Bottom-Performing Schools?

While the distribution of test scores in figure 9-1 suggests that schools at the very bottom of the test score distribution are most in need of help, the Immediate Intervention program targets limited resources to a broad range of schools—essentially the entire lower half of the API rankings. It would seem to make more sense to concentrate the funding for this program on the schools most truly in need, perhaps those in the bottom one or two deciles of performance. Not only would this improved targeting do more to equalize student achievement, but it would also allow the state to invest proportionately more per student in each of the participating schools.

In this regard, it is useful to compare the state's decile rankings of schools that were eligible, that applied, and that were chosen for the program. Figure 9-2 illustrates these for the 1999–2000 II/USP round. The eligibility criteria

Figure 9-2. *Distribution across API Deciles of Schools Eligible for II/USP, That Applied, and That Were Selected in 1999–2000 Round*

Percent of schools

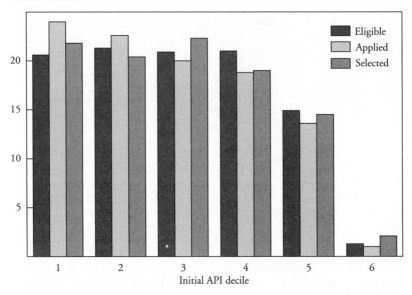

Initial API decile

Note: API = Academic Performance Index; II/USP = Immediate Intervention/Underperforming Schools Program.

led to a relatively even distribution across the bottom four deciles and a drop-off in the fifth decile. In contrast, applicants from the eligibility pool did come disproportionately from the lower deciles. The lottery system through which schools were selected effectively evened out the distribution across deciles as shown. Thus both the rules for eligibility and for selection into the II/USP program tended to draw fairly equal numbers of schools from all of the bottom deciles of school performance.

The disproportionate number of applicants from the bottom API decile was more exaggerated in the 2000–01 application process than in 1999–2000. However, in both that school year and 2001–02, the selection procedure was more representative of the applicant pool than occurred in 1999–2000.[13] This most likely reflects the much smaller eligible pools in the two later years, when in addition to falling in the bottom half of the API rankings a school also had to have failed to meet its API growth target. This reduction in the number of applicants clearly allowed the Department of Education to select schools in a way that more closely represented the applicant mix.

Overall, then, both the eligibility rules and the selection rules, but especially the former, have allowed schools from across the achievement distribution to participate in the program. A more effective way of targeting funds toward the lowest performing schools would have been to select 430 schools each year from the bottom of the API rankings. Ironically, even a simple lottery from among eligible applicants without regard to their initial API ranking would have focused the II/USP funds more narrowly on bottom-performing schools.

Perhaps in recognition of the fact that II/USP may have been distributing financial aid too widely instead of focusing more intensively on the bottom-performing schools, California legislators in 2001 passed Assembly Bill 961, which established the High Priority Schools Grant Program. This program will funnel twice the per capita funding stipulated under Immediate Intervention to schools most in need. The California Department of Education predicts that schools in the bottom decile will be the sole recipients of this additional funding. This innovation represents a partial move to a more dramatic focusing of new dollars on the schools in greatest need.

Early Implementation Studies

II/USP schools undergo a one-year planning cycle. Given the multidimensional problems facing many failing schools, how successful have they been in developing coherent action plans within the space of twelve months? In the case of CSRD schools, they lack any planning period at all, but in return receive an additional year of implementation grants. This could work reasonably well, because the CSRD schools must select from a menu of existing reform approaches, instead of developing a plan from scratch. However, a custom-made plan for an II/USP school might work better than a one-size-fits-all type of reform.

The Department of Education conducted a review of the first-year experiences of II/USP and CSRD schools, based in part on site visits and principal surveys to a subsample of schools. Here we summarize some of the review's key findings.[14] Some principals complained that evaluators were aloof, unprepared, inexperienced, or unaware of the details of the II/USP program. But principals for the most part strongly endorsed the role played by the external evaluators chosen to help each school. For instance, 90 percent of principals responding stated that the external evaluator collaborated closely with the school and 84 percent would recommend their evaluator to other schools.

School site visits and the evaluation of the action plans by the Department of Education suggested less optimistic conclusions. Of the initial action plans submitted, the department rejected 38 percent because they did not meet the stipulations of the II/USP program. Moreover, site visits revealed that both participant schools and their external evaluators complained about the time-line for planning, which in reality was compressed to about four months. In well over half of cases, the site visit teams inferred that schools were relying on the external evaluator to generate a reform plan instead of cooperating actively.[15]

A conference held by the California Education Policy Seminar and the California State University Institute for Education Reform in November 2000 provides additional information on the first year of the II/USP. The comments of external evaluators of the II/USP program generally support the findings of the Department of Education's own evaluation.[16] Notably, the evaluators reported that many of the participating schools genuinely wanted to improve. They generally agreed that progress during the planning phase could have been greater with an extended period of planning time, especially for teachers. Several evaluators also stated that the schools had often made lit-tle progress at implementing reforms in curriculum at the classroom level. In his response to the panel of evaluators, John Mockler, at the time interim sec-retary for education in California, reported on his own reviews of schools' action plans. One of his main concerns was that "there was no discussion of curriculum. And there was very little mention of standards, so it was difficult to tell what the plans were really talking about."

Overall, the qualitative reports suggest some teething pains for the imple-mentation of II/USP and in some schools a lack of focus on the central issues. On the whole, however, participating schools appear to be taking the Immediate Intervention reforms seriously.

Conclusions

This paper extends our initial evaluation of California's school accountability program in two ways. First, we previously identified a widening gap in school resources between low-achieving and high-achieving schools. The current paper extends this analysis over a six-year period to determine whether the growing inequality in school resources, especially related to teachers, has con-tinued well into the post-accountability period beginning with the 1999–2000 school year. Second, the paper studies the Immediate Interven-tion program of financial assistance and potential sanctions that the state has targeted at the lower performing schools. Given the achievement gap between these schools and top-achieving schools, this aspect of the Public School Accountability Act is to many observers the most important compo-nent of the accountability reforms.

We find an overall trend toward fewer highly educated and experienced teachers and more novice and uncertified teachers. We also find that the gaps between low- and high-scoring schools have widened for most measures we examine. These findings remain even after controlling for observable characteristics of students that might affect a school's resources. However, we find no evidence that passage of the PSAA in 1999 exacerbated these trends.

We briefly examine trends in test scores in the state and note a steep and persistent drop-off in student achievement in the lowest performing schools. The plight of low-performing schools provides powerful motivation for our analysis of the Immediate Intervention program, which is targeted at low-performing schools.

The first issue we examined was whether the first cohort of II/USP schools outperformed their peers in terms of student achievement gains between spring 1999, before entry to the program, and spring 2001. When comparing II/USP schools with schools that applied for II/USP but were not randomly selected to participate, we found that the II/USP schools' achievement rose substantially more than did achievement at schools that were not randomly selected. Among the sorts of schools that applied for the program, we find surprisingly strong evidence suggesting that Immediate Intervention works. These results, although promising, are preliminary. Additional work will need to be done in future years to confirm that II/USP has produced gains among participating schools.

The second issue we examined was whether the voluntary nature of II/USP has led to schools gaming the system, in the sense that the schools that are likely to escape the program's sanctions while exerting the least effort are the most likely to apply for II/USP. We tested several variants of this idea and found little evidence of gaming the system. The strongest pattern we identified was that schools with the lowest test scores were the most likely to apply for II/USP, which is heartening given that these are clearly the schools in most need.

Third, we asked whether the state's guidelines for determining II/USP eligibility and for selecting schools from among the applicant pool both worked to spread program funding too widely among the bottom half of schools. We did find evidence that both the eligibility and selection criteria worked to distribute funds across all five of the bottom deciles, and we concluded that the state might consider reforms to target its resources more narrowly toward the lowest performing schools. However, the legislature did pass a bill in 2001 that will provide additional funding for schools at the very bottom of the achievement distribution.

Finally, our review of two qualitative studies suggested that the implementation of II/USP in its first year (1999–2000) ran into several problems. School administrators complained that they had not had enough time to plan how to spend their II/USP grants, and several outside observers stated that the implementation plans devised by schools and their contractors very often sidestepped the key issue of curriculum and how the plan would link to California's subject content frameworks.

Thus the II/USP program, despite some start-up problems and a lack of focus on the schools at the very bottom of the achievement distribution, is off to a reasonably strong start, and we have uncovered preliminary evidence that the program may be helping participating schools substantially.

Overall, the Public School Accountability program is now well under way, and trends in California's schools suggest both a rising tide of achievement and a narrowing in the achievement gap among schools, at least in lower grades and especially in reading.[17] Areas of concern for policymakers should include slow progress in student achievement in the higher grades, the relentless trends that have widened the gap in teacher qualifications between low- and high-achieving schools, and a need to find better targeting of financial resources to the schools that lag furthest behind.

Our paper has not had space to address other technical, financial, and political challenges. On the political side, there is a small but rapidly growing opposition to the state test and the accountability system more broadly, with opponents including the powerful California Teachers Association. Furthermore, in 2001 legislators passed Assembly Bill 961, which provides for alternative penalties—often called soft sanctions—to those in the PSAA. In addition, new legislation proposed in 2002 in Senate Bill 1310 provides more flexibility in imposing sanctions on failing schools in California.[18] However, actions can be taken at district level, such as reassigning principals or converting the school to a charter school (ostensibly under new administration and a largely changed staff), before the state becomes involved. It remains to be seen what these factors might portend for the future path of school accountability in California.

Notes

1. For a more detailed description of the Public Schools Accountability Act (PSAA) of 1999, see Julian R. Betts and Anne Danenberg, "School Accountability in California: An Early Evaluation," in Diane Ravitch, ed., *Brookings Papers on Education Policy 2002* (Brookings, 2002), pp. 123–97.

2. On variation in achievement among California schools, see Julian R. Betts, Kim S. Rueben, and Anne Danenberg, *Equal Resources, Equal Outcomes? The Distri-*

bution of School Resources and Student Achievement in California (San Francisco: Public Policy Institute of California, 2000).

3. For the 1995–96 and 1996–97 school years, when no statewide test was administered, we rank schools using the spring 1998 test scores, while in later years we rank schools based on their test scores in that year.

4. Table 9-1 identified a different set of low-score and high-score schools each year after 1998. Here, we instead keep the makeup of these groups fixed, based on the 1999 Academic Performance Index (API). In addition, we use the overall API, given our evidence that using reading or math scores, two of the most important subcomponents of the API, yields similar trends in resource gaps. We ran regression models for each of the school resource measures listed in table 9-1 as a function of the school's test score quintile, time trends specific to each test score quintile of school, a dummy variable for the period beginning in 1999–2000 (our post–PSAA period), interactions of this dummy variable with the API quintiles, and characteristics that might independently influence the resources the school receives through categorical programs—the percentage of students receiving free or reduced-price lunch, the percentage of Limited English Proficient students, and the enrollment at the school.

5. The class-size reduction initiative immediately gave schools a strong incentive to reduce class size to twenty first in grades one and two and, starting in 1997, in kindergarten and grade three as well. The class-size reduction initiative likely affected the labor market for teachers. As more experienced teachers switched to teaching K–3 with class sizes of twenty or fewer in 1996–97 and later years, school districts had to hunt far afield for new teachers to replace them. Furthermore, minority and low-income students received a disproportionately higher share of the less experienced teachers who entered as replacements. This pattern will tend to widen the resource gap between high- and low-scoring schools, independently of any separate effect of accountability. See Christopher Jepsen and Steven Rivkin, *Class Size Reduction, Teacher Quality, and Academic Achievement in California Public Elementary Schools* (San Francisco: Public Policy Institute of California, 2002).

6. For a detailed analysis of trends in California test scores, see Betts and Danenberg, "School Accountability in California."

7. In fall 1999 any schools performing below the 50th percentile on the Standardized Testing and Reporting (STAR) test in both spring 1998 and spring 1999 were eligible to participate in the Immediate Intervention/Underperforming Schools Program (II/USP), and the state's API determined subsequent cohorts' eligibility. In September 1999 a first cohort of 430 schools of more than three thousand eligible schools was chosen for external evaluation. Second and third cohorts of 430 schools were chosen based on the 2000 API and the 2001 API, respectively. The PSAA text describes a random selection process inside each of fifteen categories (or cells) of schools—deciles one through five for each of elementary, middle, and high schools. However, in reality the selection process depends partially on which schools apply to the program and which schools are already in the program. In theory, all II/USP–eligible schools would eventually enter the program as the eligible pool of schools shrinks each year after a new cohort is chosen.

8. In regression results not shown, we could find no evidence of any difference in improvement rates between Comprehensive School Reform Demonstration Program (CSRD) and regular II/USP schools.

We also estimated a model in which the comparison group was all schools that were eligible to apply, even if they chose not to apply. In this case we found no significant effect of participation in the program. This model appears to have considerable selectivity bias, because eligible schools that did not apply appear to be different from those that did apply.

9. Thomas J. Kane and Douglas O. Staiger, "Volatility in School Test Scores: Implications for Test-Based Accountability Systems," in Diane Ravitch, ed., *Brookings Papers on Education Policy 2002* (Brookings, 2002), pp. 235–83.

10. We also ran probit models to take account of the binary nature of the dependent variable. In addition, we ran simple correlations between whether schools applied to II/USP and each of the explanatory variables to guard against collinearity. Both of these methods suggested similar conclusions to those we report in the main text.

11. For the first year, 1999–2000, we set the dummy for whether the API had declined equal to zero, because schools had been issued an API only once by that point. However, we also include year dummies to account for variations in this variable definition across years. Regressions that include only the later two years of the three years included in table 9-3 produced similar results, as did separate models estimated for each year.

12. We also examined a fourth possible perverse incentive, namely, the incentive that some schools that ranked slightly above the cutoff for II/USP eligibility would have to let their scores slip in the subsequent year to qualify for funding. We found no evidence that this occurred.

13. For the 2000–01 and 2001–02 distributions of these schools, see table 4.2 in the conference version of this paper (www.ksg.harvard.edu/pepg/index.htm [July 30, 2002]).

14. Anne E. Just and others, *Immediate Intervention/Underperforming Schools Program (II/USP): How Low Performing Schools in California Are Facing the Challenge of Improving Student Achievement*, Research Summary (California Department of Education, Division of Policy and Evaluation, May 2001).

15. For a summary of the investigators' analysis of CSRD schools, which was similar overall, see the conference version of this paper (www.ksg.harvard.edu/pepg/index.htm [July 30, 2002]).

16. Kathleen Beasley, *Immediate Intervention/Underperforming Schools Program: First Year Overview* (California Education Policy Seminar and the California State University Institute for Education Reform, November 2000).

17. For detailed documentation on these trends in achievement, see the conference version of this paper (www.ksg.harvard.edu/pepg/index.htm [July 30, 2002]).

18. Jim Sanders noted in a recent *Sacramento Bee* article ("School Takeover Threat Relaxed," May 1, 2002) that it seems unlikely that the state will take over the schools.

PART 3

The Promise
of Student Accountability

10

The "First Wave" of Accountability

THOMAS S. DEE

The No Child Left Behind Act, signed into law by President George W. Bush in January 2002, mandates the development of test-based student assessments and holding schools accountable for their academic performance relative to their state's minimum threshold.[1] This bipartisan legislation will promote, and shape, the accountability systems that have been introduced in almost every state over the last several years. The accountability policies recently adopted at the state level have taken several forms, including the publication of "report cards" and ratings for schools, teacher evaluations coupled with merit pay, and the legal authority for states to control or close failing schools.[2] An increasing number of states also hold students directly accountable by withholding grade promotion or high school graduation for low performance on tests. The impetus for output-based accountability has grown out of the widely held perception that the long-standing focus of prior reforms on educational inputs and processes has been relatively unproductive. In particular, proponents of accountability policies argue that reliable information is not available on how to systematically use educational programs and resources to improve student outcomes. According to this line of reasoning, the idiosyncratic nature of educational production implies that output-based incentives provide a more reliable method for enhancing productivity.[3] However, as suggested by the title of the recent federal legislation, another clear intent of accountability programs has been to close the performance gap between advantaged and disadvantaged students, in particular the gap between white and minority students.

Critics of these policies suggest that explicit standards may exacerbate that performance gap, particularly in the absence of other systemic reforms related to local control, teacher training, and available resources.[4] Another major concern with standards-based reforms is that they may promote an undesirable narrowing of teaching styles and student curricula.[5] A recent national survey of public school teachers suggests that those concerns could be well founded. While a majority of surveyed teachers (87 percent) supported establishing higher standards, nearly 70 percent also thought that their teaching overemphasized testing to the detriment of learning in other important areas.[6] A large majority of these teachers also opposed using state tests as the sole basis for grade promotion and graduation. Nonetheless, some early indications also show that the states making the strongest recent gains in measured student achievement have been those that aggressively implemented new standards and assessments. However, the proper interpretation of the recent experiences within particular states has been the subject of considerable controversy, and many of the new state policies have been implemented too recently to be evaluated with currently available data.[7]

The premise for this paper is that useful insights into these controversies may be gained by looking back to consider the consequences of earlier state-level standards. Over the last twenty-five years, almost every state introduced stricter, state-level standards for high school graduation in response to highly publicized concerns about student effort and the quality of public schools. The key first-wave reforms consisted of a test-based performance standard, minimum competency testing (MCT), and a process standard—course graduation requirements (CGRs) that mandated the amount of academic credits that must be earned in core academic areas. Though the adoption of these reforms occurred with much fanfare, surprisingly little study has been conducted since then of their consequences. In this chapter, I describe these reforms and what is currently known about their implications for student outcomes. I also present new evidence on how these reforms influenced a variety of student outcomes (for example, educational attainment, labor market experiences, high school curricula) in empirical specifications that address the possible shortcomings of prior evaluations. I conclude by discussing what this broad set of results may contribute to our understanding of the currently evolving state and federal experiments with standards-based reform.

The First Wave of Education Reform

Much of the ongoing public interest in reforming public education can be traced to the mid-1970s and the widely discussed evidence that student test scores and the quality of public schooling were in decline.[8] In particular, critics of that period emphasized that a high school diploma, once a significant and hard-earned, personal accomplishment, had been debased through the abuses of social promotion and the tolerance of low academic standards.[9] Politicians at the state level proved highly responsive to these concerns and began enacting a variety of new standards and regulations now known as the first wave of education reform.[10] The earliest manifestation of these centralized reforms was the widespread adoption of a test-based performance standard: minimum competency testing. Beginning in 1975 nearly every state introduced new MCT programs designed to assess students' basic skills.[11] Most of these programs were simply intended to identify low-performing students and to direct them to sources of remediation. However, several of these states also mandated that students pass a minimum competency test to graduate with a standard diploma. By 1992 the graduating high school seniors in fifteen states were required to pass such a test.[12] Typically, students would first sit for these exams in the ninth or tenth grade and have multiple opportunities for retests. The conventional wisdom regarding these test-based diploma sanctions has been that they were "legislated as a lion but implemented as a lamb" (see chapter 3 in this volume).[13] Specifically, the MCT standards typically required that students demonstrate basic math and reading skills at only an eighth- or ninth-grade level. Furthermore, in response to failure rates on initial tests that were deemed politically unacceptable, these standards were sometimes lowered. As a consequence, the ultimate pass rates among high school seniors were extremely high.[14] However, whether MCT has had a more substantial influence on dropout rates is an open empirical question because the attrition of discouraged students may make the ultimate pass rates misleading. Furthermore, a full consideration of MCT policies should also consider their effects on other outcomes that are relevant to all students (for example, student curricula and labor market experiences).

The adoption of first-wave reforms accelerated more dramatically in the early 1980s after the publication of several panel reports, which were highly critical of public education. The most widely discussed of these reports, *A Nation at Risk*, emphasized the need for higher expectations and standards for high school graduates.[15] In particular, the report alleged that the combination of a "cafeteria-style curriculum" and "extensive student choice" meant that too many students pursued a diffuse and unchallenging course of study. The report recommended that states respond with new high school graduation standards mandating a minimum amount of course taking in core academic areas. The report specifically recommended a "New Basics" curriculum requirement consisting of four years of English and three years each of social studies, science, and mathematics.[16] Again, politicians proved highly responsive to the strong public interest in these policies. By 1992 nearly every state had increased its course graduation requirements in the four core academic areas.[17] However, in all but three states (Florida, Louisiana, and Pennsylvania), the new CGRs fell short of the "4/3/3/3" standard recommended by *A Nation at Risk*.

Standards and Student Achievement

The fundamental motivation for these two first-wave reforms (MCT and CGRs) was simply to promote student effort and learning, making high school diplomas worth the paper they are written on. Are new educational standards likely to have beneficial effects on student achievement? Commentators on this issue have disagreed sharply. Proponents of higher standards make the straightforward claim that the "incentive effects" of such policies will raise the level of achievement among those students who would pass under a weak standard and choose to increase their effort to meet the new standard.[18] Julian R. Betts and Robert M. Costrell also suggest that those students whose prior levels of effort would clearly imply failing or passing both standards (that is, those at the top and bottom ends of the ability distribution) will not have any incentive to change their behavior. However, they also recognize that the incentive effects for some students who marginally passed under weaker standards will promote discouragement and reduced effort. They recommend targeted policies to attenuate these losses.

However, the potential benefits of higher standards are not necessarily limited solely to those marginal students who choose to increase their effort. For example, John H. Bishop discusses how a high, external standard can limit the "nerd harassment" and peer pressure that encourages high-ability students to shirk educational effort.[19] Standards may also generate broader educational gains through general increases in educational expectations and school productivity. Furthermore, even those students who fully anticipate dropping out of high school may be compelled in the short term to greater educational effort through curricular mandates such as course graduation requirements. The "sorting effects" of higher standards may also lead to passive labor market rewards.[20] Specifically, if educational attainment functions as a signal of unobserved individual ability, higher standards could increase the attractiveness to employers of all students by increasing the average level of ability among both dropouts and graduates.

The critics of standards-based reform emphasize the many negative consequences associated with the expected reductions in educational attainment. Furthermore, they note that the reductions in educational attainment are disproportionately likely to be among those whose poor socioeconomic backgrounds make it unusually difficult to meet new standards. In particular, several observers suggest that higher standards will exacerbate the troublesome performance gaps between black and white students.[21] The consequences of higher standards for the racial gap in educational performance may be driven by more than simple differences in socioeconomic backgrounds. Higher standards and high-stakes testing may also harm minority students if they generate "stereotype threat": academic underperformance due to the risk of confirming negative stereotypes.[22]

However, the critics of standards also suggest that these reforms will have other, pejorative effects that harm all students. For example, the introduction of high-stakes testing such as minimum competency tests may lead to a narrowing of teaching styles and curricula (that is, "teaching to the test") that comes at the expense of substantive learning.[23] Furthermore, the establishment of minimum competency tests and stricter course graduation requirements may suggest to students that learning for its own sake is not worthwhile. In particular, these standards may encourage otherwise high-achieving students to avoid challenges and simply choose the path of least resistance to satisfying their requirements.[24] The authors of *A Nation at Risk* made a similar allegation, suggesting that minimum competency tests were inadequate because they would become maximum standards and lower expectations for high-ability students.

Evidence from the 1990 PUMS

These disagreements suggest that fundamental, policy-relevant issues about the educational consequences of higher standards can be informed only by empirical evidence. Given this, one might expect that the first-wave reforms have been subjected to exhaustive empirical evaluation. Surprisingly, relatively little empirical evidence exists about the consequences of these policies that would allow for sorting through these conflicting theoretical predictions. Furthermore, what evidence is available is often directly contradictory.[25] One possible explanation for these conflicting results is that almost all of the prior empirical studies have effectively relied on cross-sectional comparisons of students who reside in states with different policies.[26] Educational outcomes vary considerably across states, reflecting a variety of cultural, socioeconomic, and political determinants that are often inherently difficult for researchers to measure directly. These unobserved but state-specific determinants of educational achievement are also likely to be associated with each state's propensity to adopt high school graduation requirements such as MCT and CGRs. This implies that the results of cross-state comparisons may be sensitive to the presence of additional control variables and subject to biases of an unknown direction.[27] A second drawback of prior empirical studies is that they have not directly addressed claims about whether these graduation standards would be particularly harmful or beneficial to minority students. In this section, I present new evidence that addresses both of these concerns by relying on individual-level data from the 1990 Public Use Micro-Data Sample (PUMS).

Data and Specifications

The 1990 PUMS consists of approximately twelve million respondents (5 percent of the population) who completed the long-form questionnaire to the decennial census. One useful feature of the PUMS is that the large number of PUMS respondents implies increased statistical precision and, in particular, a better ability to detect race-specific responses to the new graduation standards. My extract from the PUMS data consists of the 1,348,766 white (non-Hispanic) and black respondents who were age eighteen between 1980 and 1988 and born in one of forty-nine states.[28] Two of the outcome variables defined for each respondent identify educational attainment, a binary indicator for high school graduation (mean = 0.858) and another for college entrance (mean = 0.519).[29] I limited the sample to those who were at least eighteen by 1988 because of the biases that could be generated by state-specific trends in the "incomplete spells" of high school completion and college entrance among cohorts who were younger at the time of the census interview.[30] The other dependent variables reflect the labor experiences of each PUMS respondent. One is a binary indicator for employment participation (mean = 0.745), which is defined for all respondents.[31] The other is the natural log of average weekly wages, which is only defined for 1,143,352 respondents. This wage variable is the ratio of pre-tax wage and salary income reported for the previous calendar year and the corresponding number of weeks worked (mean = 327).

Another particularly useful feature of the PUMS is that it provides data from different birth cohorts within each state. This allows me to construct before-and-after comparisons of students within the same states, instead of relying exclusively on cross-state comparisons. My research method effectively begins by comparing individuals of different ages within each state, some of whom attended high school before the first-wave education reforms were implemented and others who attended afterward—and were thus required to take minimum competency exams and more courses in academic areas to graduate. To eliminate the influence of age and other national trends, my methodology also compares the changes within states that introduced first-wave reforms (treatment states) with the contemporaneous changes in states that did not (control states). More specifically, these types of comparisons are effectively made by relying on estimates from the following multiple-regression model:

$$Y_{ist} = \beta X_{ist} + \gamma Z_{st} + \mu_s + \nu_t + \varepsilon_{ist}, \tag{1}$$

where Y_{ist} is the dependent variable and the matrix, X_{ist}, includes observed, individual-level traits. In most models, these controls simply include binary indicators for race and gender. However, in the models for labor market outcomes, these controls also include measures of educational attainment (that is, separate dummy variables for high school graduates, those with some college, and those with bachelor's degrees) and a dummy variable for whether the respondent attended school within the last year.[32] The terms μ_s and ν_t represent fixed effects specific to each state of birth and year of birth. The term ε_{ist} is a mean-zero random error.[33]

The matrix, Z_{st}, includes the observed determinants that were specific to the birth cohorts within each state. These variables include the two independent variables of interest: dummy variables that reflect the state MCT and CGR policies in effect for each birth cohort at age eighteen. One dummy variable simply indicates whether a minimum competency test was required for that particular graduating class. The second dummy identifies whether the state had a high, academically focused CGR in effect for that graduating class. A high CGR is defined here as a required high school curriculum that includes at least three Carnegie units in English, two in social studies, one in science, and one in mathematics.[34] These and other state-year controls were matched to the respondents by their state of birth and year of birth. One noteworthy limitation of the PUMS data is that relying on state of birth may introduce measurement error because some children have moved to different states by the time they reach high school. However, the attenuation bias implied by such measurement error suggests that the reported estimates can be interpreted as lower bounds on the true effects.[35]

The identification strategy embedded in this model makes a potentially important contribution to the understanding of the consequences of first-wave reforms because it removes the possible biases resulting from unobserved state-level determinants. The model effectively does this by comparing the cohort differences in the treatment states before and after the introduction of new standards to the contemporaneous cross-cohort changes in the control states. I present some evidence on the empirical relevance of relying on within-state versus cross-state comparisons by comparing the results of models that do and do not include the state fixed effects, μ_s. I also present some heuristic evidence on this specification issue through the use of a simple counterfactual in which I estimate the effect of a state policy that should not have large and statistically significant effects on educational attainment. To the extent that a particular specification suggests that this policy did have large and statistically significant effects, the existence of specification error is suggested.[36]

In the preferred specifications, which include state fixed effects, the possible sources of omitted variable biases are the unobserved determinants of Y that are also related to the timing of new standards within states. The matrix, Z_{st}, addresses this concern by including other regression controls that vary by state and year. For example, new state standards were sometimes part of omnibus education bills that included other policy changes such as increased spending. To control for the possible effects of school spending, some models include, as an independent state-level variable, real expenditures on K–12 public schools per student in average daily attendance when the respondents were sixteen to seventeen years old. For example, respondents who were eighteen in 1980 were matched to the school expenditures in their state during the 1978–79 school year. Another state-year control in most models is the state unemployment rate when the respondent was seventeen years old. This variable is expected to have a positive effect on educational attainment because it reduces the opportunity costs associated with remaining in school.[37] David Card and Thomas Lemieux present evidence that the natural variation in the size of a particular birth cohort's population can also influence educational attainment.[38] At the college level, this could occur if temporary increases in cohort size are not fully matched by an increased supply of enrollment space at local colleges and universities. At the secondary level, increased cohort size may reduce the benefits of remaining in school by lowering school quality.[39] Therefore I also include a measure of cohort size based on the natural log of the U.S. Census Bureau's estimate of eighteen-year-olds in the respondent's state of birth at age eighteen. I also include a measure of the real costs of postsecondary tuition based on the in-state rate at "lower-level" state colleges and universities when the respondent was seventeen years old.[40] Finally, as a control for within-state changes in socioeconomic background, I also matched all respondents to the poverty rate in their states when they were seventeen years old.

Results

In table 10-1, I present the estimated effects of MCT and CGR policies on educational attainment across a variety of specifications. These results demonstrate that the estimated effects of the first-wave reforms on educational attainment are sensitive to controlling for unobserved state fixed effects. For example, the models that exclude state fixed effects but include the other state-year controls suggest that MCT significantly reduced the probability of graduating from high school and attending college. These results also suggest that CGR policies had no statistically significant effects on either measure of educational attainment. However, the models that include state fixed effects and the other state-year controls imply that MCT had small and statistically insignificant effects on both outcomes. These models also suggest that higher CGRs reduced the probability of graduating from high school by a statistically significant 0.48 percentage points. An effect of this size represents a 0.6 percent reduction in the mean probability of graduating from high school, or, alternatively, a 3 percent increase in the mean probability of dropping out. Another way to frame the size of this estimate is to note that high school completion rates among eighteen- to twenty-four-year-olds increased from 82.8 percent in 1972 to 86.5 percent in 2000. My results suggest that in states that adopted high curricular standards these average gains were attenuated by approximately 14 percent.

Several dimensions of the results in table 10-1 suggest that the inferences from the models with state fixed effects are more reliable. First, F-tests indicate that the state fixed effects are jointly significant determinants of educational attainment. Second, in models that exclude state fixed effects, the key results are highly sensitive to the presence of the other state-year controls. For example, similar to prior studies, the first model implies that MCT significantly increased the probability of attending college. However, after introducing the other controls, this estimate becomes negative and significant. This type of sensitivity suggests the difficulty of relying on proxies for the determinants of educational achievement across states. Third, the sensitivity of these evaluation results to the introduction of state fixed effects does not appear to reflect any loss of sampling variation or statistical precision. Specifically, some of the cross-state models suggest that MCT and CGRs had effects roughly 2 percentage points in size. However, in the preferred specification (column 5 of table 10-1), the standard errors are sufficiently small that effects of that size can be rejected at conventional levels of statistical significance.

Table 10-1. *Linear Probability Models for Educational Attainment*

Independent variable	Estimated effects					
High school graduate						
Minimum competency test	0.0001	−0.0187***	−0.0165***	−0.0013	−0.0014	−0.0015
	(0.0065)	(0.0033)	(0.0031)	(0.0020)	(0.0020)	(0.0020)
High course graduation requirement	−0.0051	−0.0027	−0.0020	−0.0055**	−0.0048**	−0.0048**
	(0.0041)	(0.0024)	(0.0023)	(0.0025)	(0.0022)	(0.0022)
Any state executions at age eighteen?	...	...	−0.0126***	...	...	0.0004
			(0.0041)			(0.0019)
College entrant						
Minimum competency test	0.0244**	−0.0240***	−0.0211***	−0.0054*	0.0002	0.0009
	(0.0113)	(0.0056)	(0.0054)	(0.0028)	(0.0030)	(0.0030)
High course graduation requirement	−0.0197***	−0.0058	−0.0047	−0.0079*	−0.0028	−0.0028
	(0.0075)	(0.0046)	(0.0045)	(0.0048)	(0.0033)	(0.0033)
Any state executions at age eighteen?	...	...	−0.0170***	...	...	−0.0026
			(0.0064)			(0.0024)
State fixed effects?	No	No	No	Yes	Yes	Yes
State-year controls?	No	Yes	Yes	No	Yes	Yes

Source: Author's calculations based on the 1990 Public Use Micro-Data Sample (PUMS), state-year controls for state graduation requirements, the unemployment rate, the natural log of cohort size, the poverty rate, real K–12 expenditures per pupil, and real postsecondary tuition.

Note: The PUMS extract consists of the 1,348,766 white (non-Hispanic) and black respondents who were born in one of forty-nine states (Nebraska excluded) and who were age eighteen between 1980 and 1988. All the models include fixed effects for race, gender, and year of birth. Heteroscedastic-consistent standard errors, adjusted for state-of-birth by year-of-birth clustering, are reported in parentheses.

* Statistically significant at 10 percent level.
** Statistically significant at 5 percent level.
*** Statistically significant at 1 percent level.

A final way to provide some ad-hoc evidence on the reliability of cross-state versus within-state comparisons is through the use of a simple counterfactual. To the extent that empirical evaluations relying on cross-state comparisons generate reliable results, conditional on the other controls, irrelevant state policies should have small and statistically insignificant effects on educational attainment. However, to the extent that an irrelevant policy appears to have a large and statistically significant effect, it suggests the existence of biases driven by the unobserved, state-specific determinants of educational outcomes. The results in table 10-1 present such evidence by reporting the estimated effects on educational attainment of having any state executions at age eighteen. The models without state fixed effects suggest that capital punishment generates large and statistically significant reductions in the probability of high school completion (1.3 percentage points) and college entrance (1.7 percentage points).[41] However, in the models that rely on the within-state variation in executions, these estimates are much smaller, more precisely estimated, and statistically insignificant.

In table 10-2, I present the key evaluation results from the preferred specifications that include both the state and year fixed effects and the state-year controls. I also report the estimated effects of these first-wave reforms from separate models for white males, white females, black males, and black females. All of these models suggest that the first-wave reforms had statistically insignificant effects on the probability of entering college. The absence of any effects on college entrance is plausible because these high school graduation requirements are less likely to be binding for the relatively high-achieving students on the margin for attending college. However, the results also indicate that these reforms had fairly large and statistically significant effects on the probability of completing high school and that these effects varied considerably by race and gender. In particular, the estimates suggest that higher CGRs significantly reduced the probability of completing high school for white males and blacks but not for white females.[42] Notably, the reform-driven reductions in educational attainment were particularly large among blacks (roughly 2 percentage points). These estimated reductions are roughly four times larger than those for white males. Similarly, the results suggest that the only large and statistically significant effect of introducing MCT was among black males who experienced an estimated 1.26 percentage point reduction in the probability of completing high school. The estimated effects of these first-wave reforms are also fairly large relative to the recent growth in educational attainment among blacks. Between 1972 and 2000, the high school completion rate of eighteen- to twenty-four-year-old blacks increased from 72.1 percent to 83.7 percent.

Table 10-2. *Estimated Effects of Minimum Competency Tests (MCT)
and High Course Graduation Requirements (CGR) on Educational Attainment
by Race and Gender*

| | Dependent variable | | | | |
| | High school graduate | | College entrant | | |
Sample	MCT	CGR	MCT	CGR	Sample size
All respondents	−0.0014	−0.0048**	0.0002	−0.0028	1,348,766
	(0.0020)	(0.0022)	(0.0030)	(0.0033)	
White males	0.0025	−0.0053**	0.0049	−0.0026	585,376
	(0.0033)	(0.0025)	(0.0045)	(0.0040)	
White females	−0.0022	−0.0005	0.0007	−0.0017	588,611
	(0.0026)	(0.0032)	(0.0035)	(0.0035)	
Black males	−0.0126**	−0.0211**	−0.0024	−0.0161	81,799
	(0.0055)	(0.0087)	(0.0073)	(0.0111)	
Black females	0.0010	−0.0203***	0.0044	−0.0188	92,980
	(0.0054)	(0.0070)	(0.0070)	(0.0015)	

Source: Author's calculations based on the 1990 Public Use Micro-Data Sample (PUMS), state-year controls for state graduation requirements, the unemployment rate, the natural log of cohort size, the poverty rate, real K–12 expenditures per pupil, and real postsecondary tuition.

Note: The PUMS extract consists of the 1,348,766 white (non-Hispanic) and black respondents who were born in one of forty-nine states (Nebraska excluded) and who were age eighteen between 1980 and 1988. All the models include the state-year controls and fixed effects for race, gender, state of birth, and year of birth. Heteroscedastic-consistent standard errors, adjusted for state-of-birth by year-of-birth clustering, are reported in parentheses.

** Statistically significant at 5 percent level.
*** Statistically significant at 1 percent level.

The evidence from table 10-2 is largely consistent with the concerns sometimes raised by critics of standards-based reforms.[43] The introduction of high school graduation standards led to reductions in educational attainment that were particularly concentrated among black students. These effects could stem from a race-specific phenomenon such as stereotype threat. Regardless, these results suggest that the largest impact of higher standards will be upon those students whose socioeconomic background puts them at high risk for academic failure. However, a full evaluation should also consider the implications of these reforms for labor market experiences. Attention to the labor market consequences of these policies also has a strong intuitive appeal given that local business leaders concerned with the quality of their work force were often instrumental in the adoption of first-wave reforms. Higher standards may benefit students (even those who drop out) by inducing increased educational effort that is rewarded in the labor market (an incentive effect). There may also be distributional consequences of these

Table 10-3. *Estimated Effects of Minimum Competency Tests (MCT) and High Course Graduation Requirements (CGR) on Employment Participation and Wages by Race and Gender*

	Dependent variable			
	Employed		Log wages	
Sample	MCT	CGR	MCT	CGR
All respondents	−0.0053*	0.0081**	0.0088	−0.0074
	(0.0031)	(0.0035)	(0.0060)	(0.0070)
White males	0.0012	0.0106***	0.0094	−0.0075
	(0.0033)	(0.0041)	(0.0069)	(0.0078)
White females	−0.0095**	0.0011	−0.0073	−0.0041
	(0.0031)	(0.0044)	(0.0066)	(0.0070)
Black males	0.0164**	0.0339***	0.0108	−0.0279
	(0.0069)	(0.0101)	(0.0148)	(0.0177)
Black females	−0.0025	0.0182*	0.0169	−0.0251
	(0.0080)	(0.0104)	(0.0133)	(0.0166)

Source: Author's calculations based on the 1990 Public Use Micro-Data Sample (PUMS), state-year controls for state graduation requirements, the unemployment rate, the natural log of cohort size, the poverty rate, real K-12 expenditures per pupil, and real postsecondary tuition.

Note: The PUMS extract consists of the 1,348,766 white (non-Hispanic) and black respondents who were born in one of forty-nine states (Nebraska excluded) and who were age eighteen between 1980 and 1988. Log wages are only defined for 1,143,352 respondents. All the models include the state-year controls, individual-level controls for educational attainment, and student status and fixed effects for race, gender, state of birth, and year of birth. Heteroscedastic-consistent standard errors, adjusted for state-of-birth by year-of-birth clustering, are reported in parentheses.

* Statistically significant at 10 percent level.
** Statistically significant at 5 percent level.
*** Statistically significant at 1 percent level.

reforms to the extent that higher standards increase the prestige of being a high school graduate and correspondingly reduce the stigma associated with being a dropout (a sorting effect).

Table 10-3 presents new evidence on these issues by reporting the estimated effects of the first-wave reforms on employment participation and log wages for the full PUMS sample and for samples defined by race and gender. These models include state and year fixed effects, the state-year controls, and additional individual-level controls for educational attainment and student status. Unlike the prior cross-sectional evaluations, these results suggest that both reforms had small and statistically insignificant effects on wages for all groups. However, the results also suggest that the first-wave reforms had some statistically significant effects on employment participation. For example, a minimum competency test significantly reduced the probability of employment for white females by 0.95 percentage points.[44] But most of the reform-driven changes in employment were positive. The existence of employment gains and the simultaneous absence of significant wage effects indicate that the labor market gains may largely reflect improved signaling and not productivity gains among students. The reform-driven changes in employment also appear to vary considerably by race. For example, the estimates in table 10-3 indicate that higher CGRs increased the probability of being employed by roughly 1 percentage point for white males and by 3 percentage points for black males. The introduction of MCT also increased the probability of employment for black males by a statistically significant 1.64 percentage points but had a smaller and statistically insignificant effect among white males. One useful way to underscore the magnitude of these race-specific policy effects is to note that, in these data, white males were roughly 19 percentage points more likely to be employed than black males. Because the employment gains attributable to each first-wave reform were roughly 2 percentage points larger for black males than for white males, states that implemented one of them closed the black-white employment gap by roughly 11 percent.

The results in tables 10-2 and 10-3 suggest that new CGRs were a meaningfully binding standard that had educational and labor market consequences for almost all students. In contrast, the effects of MCT were more limited. These results are consistent with the anecdotal evidence suggesting that minimum competency tests were "implemented as a lamb" in response to political realities. The results also suggest that, when binding, higher standards of either type had decidedly mixed distributional consequences. They reduced educational attainment, particularly among black students. However, they also generated some labor market rewards in the form of increased employment probabilities that were also concentrated among black students. How can these gains and losses be compared? One possibly useful point of reference is the expected wage associated with being a high school graduate or a dropout. A rough calculation based on these data suggests that high school graduates receive an expected wage premium equal to approximately 33 percent of a dropout's average wage, w_d.[45] This implies that those who dropped out of school in response to the higher standards suffered substantive consequences. Their loss of this wage premium was offset only somewhat by a 0.0081 increase in the probability of employment as a dropout. However, for those who would have dropped out or graduated without regard to the changed graduation requirements, there were unambiguous labor market gains because they were significantly more likely to be employed.

Another possible useful way to frame these costs and benefits is to ask how these reforms might change the expected wage for someone who was uncertain about whether he or she would be a high school graduate or not. For such a person, the expected cost of higher CGRs is related to the reduced probability of enjoying the 33 percent wage premium of high school graduates. This expected cost equals $0.0016w_d$ (that is, 0.0048 x 0.33). The expected benefit of a higher CGR is related to the increased probability of being employed (0.0081) at an expected wage equal to $1.155w_d$.[46] This expected benefit equals $0.0094w_d$. Therefore, the expected wage benefits of a higher CGR exceed expected wage costs by a factor of roughly 6 (0.0094/0.0016).[47] This suggests that a risk-neutral person might prefer a regime with higher standards to one without and that the net effects of the higher standards on expected wages are positive. However, these back-of-the-envelope calculations do not constitute a full cost-benefit analysis. In particular, the comparisons ignore distributional consequences as well as the other social losses that may be associated with reform-induced reductions in educational attainment (for example, those related to health, criminal, and civic behaviors).

Standards and Educational Processes

The evidence suggests that first-wave reforms sometimes reduced educational attainment and also generated some improvements in the probability of employment. These labor market consequences of stricter graduation standards could, in most cases, simply reflect passive sorting effects. However, they could also indicate some reform-induced increases in educational effort, which were subsequently rewarded in the labor market (that is, incentive effects). In this section, I provide some empirical evidence on the second possibility by examining how the first-wave reforms influenced several educational process measures: the amount of academic course taking among individual high school students. Academic course taking among public high school graduates did increase significantly during the eighties across students of varying demographic traits.[48] These increases were particularly large in mathematics and science. For example, the average number of Carnegie units among public high school graduates in 1982 and 1994 increased 27 percent in mathematics and 38 percent in science.[49] Some studies have suggested that the new CGRs were at least partially responsible for these increases. For example, Stanley Legum and others find that the high school graduates in states with higher CGRs have higher levels of academic course taking.[50] Similarly, William H. Clune and Paula A. White, in a study of four states, found that academic course taking among graduates increased after the introduction of more demanding CGRs.[51] However, two specification issues may bias these inferences about the effectiveness of first-wave reforms. One is that the appearance of policy-induced increases in academic course taking could simply be the result of the increased dropout rate (table 10-2) instead of genuine increases in academic effort. A second concern is that the identification strategies, which rely exclusively on either cross-state or time-series comparisons, may lead to substantively biased inferences.[52] The evaluations presented here provide new evidence on these issues by examining estimates from models that include eventual dropouts and that control for unobserved state and year fixed effects.

These evaluations also provide new evidence on some important concerns raised by critics of standards-based reform. Specifically, they suggest whether higher educational standards might have unintended and pejorative effects on educational processes. For example, the models for academic course taking presented here provide some evidence on whether the creation of minimum standards led to high-performing students reducing their curricular effort in the core academic areas.[53] I also discuss evidence on how such effects differed for high- and low-performing students and whether the first-wave reforms narrowed student curricula by reducing Carnegie units in the visual and performing arts. And I consider how these reforms may have influenced the intellectual engagement of students as measured by changes in time spent reading for pleasure, watching television, and doing homework.

Data and Specifications

The data for these evaluations were created by pooling observations from two major longitudinal studies fielded by the National Center for Education Statistics: the sophomore cohort from High School and Beyond (HS&B) and the National Education Longitudinal Study of 1988 (NELS). These surveys provide student-level data from before and after the time when most first-wave reforms were implemented. More specifically, HS&B and NELS provide nationally representative samples of tenth-grade students from 1980 and 1990, respectively.[54] Because each of these studies had a transcript component, they also include data on the Carnegie units earned in particular subject areas in addition to survey questions on students' use of time.[55] My extract from these surveys consists of white non-Hispanic and black respondents who were tenth graders in 1980 (HS&B) and 1990 (NELS) and includes eventual dropouts. The combined sample size with available transcript data consists of 18,134 observations (9,331 from HS&B and 8,803 from NELS).[56]

The econometric specification I used for models based on these data is similar to the preferred specification from the previous section. The independent variables of interest reflect the state high school graduation requirements in effect for the graduating classes of 1982 and 1992, respectively. The other independent variables include state and year fixed effects, individual-specific variables, and variables specific to each state-year cell. The individual-level controls include single dummy variables for race, gender, and age (born before 1964 for HS&B respondents and before 1974 for NELS respondents). These controls also include four dummy variables for the highest level of parental education, five dummy variables for family composition, and four dummy variables for quartiles of socioeconomic status (including one for a missing socioeconomic status index). I matched each respondent to the relevant graduation requirements and other state-year controls by exploiting the state identifiers in the restricted-use versions of these surveys.[57] The state-year controls again include 1981 and 1991 data on real public school spending per capita, the state unemployment rate, the poverty rate, and the real postsecondary tuition level. I also matched each respondent to the size of his or her state-year cohort: 1982 and 1992 data on the natural log of the eighteen-year-old population in the state.

Results

In table 10-4, I present estimates of how first-wave reforms influenced the amount of academic credit earned in the four core subject areas. These results uniformly suggest that the introduction of MCT reduced course taking in these academic areas. However, these estimated reductions are statistically significant only in the sciences and mathematics. The estimated effects in these two subjects are roughly equal to 5 percent of the dependent means. The reductions in curricular effort could reflect lowered motivation among students who clearly exceeded the testing standards or a possibly unintended reallocation of school and teacher resources toward lower performing students. But there could be an additional ambiguity to these results as presented because these effects might simply be explained by students who were induced into dropping out (table 10-2), thereby taking fewer courses. However, other evidence suggests that these effects reflect real policy-induced reductions in curricular effort among conventional students. For example, the introduction of MCT only appeared to increase the probability of dropping out among black males (table 10-2). But the reductions in course taking associated with MCT were more uniform across demographic traits and were particularly large for female students. Furthermore, the introduction of MCT also led to large and statistically significant reductions in calculus credits, a margin only relevant for high-achieving students.[58]

In contrast to the MCT results, the evidence in table 10-4 suggests that higher CGRs had the desired effect of generating substantive increases in the

Table 10-4. *Estimated Effects of Minimum Competency Tests (MCT) and High Course Graduation Requirements (CGR) on Carnegie Units by Academic Subject*

Academic subject	Dependent mean	Independent variable		
		MCT	1–2.99 units required in subject	3+ units required in subject
English	3.7	−0.067	0.032	0.329***
		(0.056)	(0.051)	(0.051)
Social studies	3.1	−0.088	−0.015	0.133
		(0.084)	(0.098)	(0.101)
Science	2.4	−0.135**	0.092*	0.393***
		(0.055)	(0.052)	(0.084)
Mathematics	2.7	−0.127**	−0.020	0.110*
		(0.050)	(0.046)	(0.059)

Source: Author's calculations based on High School and Beyond (HS&B), the National Education Longitudinal Study of 1988 (NELS), state-year controls for state graduation requirements, the unemployment rate, the natural log of cohort size, the poverty rate, real K–12 expenditures per pupil, and real postsecondary tuition.

Note: The HS&B and NELS extract consists of the 18,134 white (non-Hispanic) and black respondents (Nebraska excluded) who were in tenth grade in 1980 (HS&B) or 1990 (NELS). All the models include the state-year controls, individual-level controls for race, gender, age, parental education, family composition, socioeconomic status quartile, and state and year fixed effects. Heteroscedastic-consistent standard errors, adjusted for state-year clustering, are reported in parentheses.

* Statistically significant at 10 percent level.
** Statistically significant at 5 percent level.
*** Statistically significant at 1 percent level.

credits earned in these core areas. In particular, a high CGR (three or more Carnegie units required in a particular subject) led to increased credit in each academic subject.[59] For example, a high CGR in science increased credits earned by 0.393 relative to the reference category of a weak or nonexistent CGR (less than one Carnegie unit required in subject). This estimated effect is roughly equal to 16 percent of the mean science credits. However, the estimated effect of a high CGR on social studies was statistically insignificant as were the much smaller estimated effects of weaker CGRs (1–2.99 Carnegie units required). Nonetheless, these results suggest that new CGRs did contribute substantively to the academic upgrading of high school curricula over this period, particularly in English and the sciences. For example, the estimated effect associated with a high CGR in science is equal to roughly 60 percent of the average growth in science credits over this period.

Overall, the results in table 10-4 suggest that MCT sometimes had negative effects on curricular outcomes while the effects of higher CGRs were often positive. However, one of the difficulties of interpreting the CGR results is that they define the policies' effects for the average student. The introduction of higher CGRs could conceivably have had very different effects among high- and low-performing students. In particular, the results in table 10-4 could be misleading because the introduction of higher CGRs may have simultaneously reduced academic course taking among the low-performing students induced into dropping out. However, that does not appear to be the case. The introduction of higher CGRs appears to have increased academic course taking among those at risk for dropping out. Specifically, similarly specified models indicate that higher CGRs increased the probability of having at least one Carnegie unit in these academic subjects (particularly English and the sciences).[60] Other concerns about student-level standards involve whether they narrow student curricula in undesirable ways or reduce the intellectual engagement of students. To address the first issue, I used similarly specified models to estimate the effects of the first-wave reforms on student involvement in the visual and performing arts (as measured by Carnegie units) and on student participation in school musical activities (that is, the school band, orchestra, or chorus). For both outcomes, the estimated effects of the first-wave reforms were imprecisely estimated and statistically indistinguishable from zero. However, I found that the first-wave reforms did influence proxy measures of intellectual engagement: the amount of time students spent reading for pleasure, watching television, and doing homework. In particular, a higher CGR was associated with large and statistically significant reductions in the amount of time spent reading for pleasure and doing homework and corresponding increases in television use.[61]

Lessons from the First Wave

The ongoing debate about the design and desirability of standards-based reform hinges critically on how such policies may influence a variety of outcomes among students with different backgrounds. In this chapter, I provided new evidence on those issues by examining the effects of the earlier state-level standards on several outcome and process measures. These results demonstrated that the first wave of student-level standards appears to have had many of both the positive and negative effects suggested by commentators on both sides of these issues. For example, these reforms led to reductions in educational attainment that were particularly large for black students. Furthermore, minimum competency testing led to some apparent reductions in curricular effort while higher course graduation requirements had negative effects on the amounts of time students spend watching television, doing homework, and reading for pleasure. However, these reforms also increased subsequent employment probabilities. And higher CGRs were partly responsible for the substantial academic upgrading of high school curricula that occurred over this period. In light of this mixed evidence, what can these prior state-level experiences contribute to the current discussions about standards?

A productive, though modest, initial step may be to consider what these results would suggest, to a proponent of standards-based reform, about how those standards should be designed. In particular, the first-wave reforms provide an interesting basis for comparison because they included both a test-based standard (MCT) and a process standard (CGRs). The results presented here suggest that advocates of standards-based reform may prefer the ultimate effects of process standards to those of a test-based standard. More specifically, minimum competency testing had relatively few of the desired effects on educational attainment and early labor market experiences (tables 10-2 and 10-3). The results are consistent with the widely held perception that test-based standards were often weak because of political pressures and the relatively easy and veiled manner in which they could be subsequently lowered. In contrast, newly introduced course graduation requirements created more binding, new standards for students and they were also largely immune to subsequent political redesign.

The evidence from student-level transcripts provides additional support for the relative attractiveness of process standards. More specifically, the results in table 10-4 indicate that CGRs contributed directly to the academic upgrading of the high school curriculum over this period. In contrast, this evidence also suggests that the introduction of MCT lowered their curricular effort, particularly in the sciences and mathematics. The one caveat to the comparative attractiveness of CGRs is that their benefits may be attenuated by changes in teacher expectations (for example, how much homework is assigned) and changes in how students allocate their time. Furthermore, whether these comparative, first-wave results have much external validity for ongoing efforts to develop test-based accountability is clearly open to conjecture. But, at a minimum, the early state-level experiences with minimum competency testing provide an important, cautionary tale.

The implications of the results presented here for the broader debate over whether standards are a desirable type of education reform must be based on more subjectively normative grounds. For example, an advocate of a Rawlsian social welfare function would almost certainly look with favor on such reforms because they increase the employment probability of those who would have dropped out of school anyway. However, others with a more utilitarian perspective may be less willing to accept small employment gains for many students at the cost of significant welfare losses among those encouraged by new standards to drop out of high school. Those welfare losses encourage advocates of standards-based reform to recommend the simultaneous adoption of targeted efforts to assist those who may be newly at risk of dropping out. Similarly, critics of standards also suggest that, if standards are to be implemented, they should be accompanied by increased capacity building in the form of higher teacher salaries, teacher training, and local control of schools.

However, such approaches to attenuating the difficult trade-offs implied by higher standards may provide a deceptively facile solution. In particular, a fundamental motivation for instituting standards in the first place has been the controversial claim that educational inputs cannot be targeted in ways that systematically promote student achievement. So, recommendations to help somehow the students harmed by standards bring a return to the notoriously difficult research questions about which programs or expenditures might be effective.

The experiences within some of the states that adopted first-wave reforms suggest no one should be too sanguine about their ability (or willingness) to craft solutions that soften these difficult trade-offs. For example, consider the first-wave reforms that were introduced in the two states with the largest public school enrollments. The state of California instituted a new course graduation requirement (first effective for the graduating class of 1987) as part of the Hughes-Hart Educational Reform Act of 1983 (Senate Bill 813). This legislation was a comprehensive school reform package that combined a new state CGR with $800 million in new funds targeted at more than eighty other initiatives including higher starting salaries for teachers and a teacher mentoring program.[62] Similarly, the state of Texas introduced minimum competency testing in 1984 (first effective for the graduating class of 1987) as one component of an extensive package of school reforms (House Bill 72). These reforms included a variety of other complementary initiatives such as increased starting salaries for teachers, a teaching career ladder, management training for principals and superintendents, and a "no pass, no play" restriction on extracurricular activities.[63] Some districts in Texas also responded to MCT by developing summer school initiatives targeted at those at risk for dropping out because of the new standards.[64] These examples indicate that many students who faced new state-level graduation standards were also supported by a contemporaneous mix of other financial and regulatory changes. The extra efforts made by the reform states imply that the difficult trade-offs identified in this study are a relatively intractable feature of introducing higher student-level standards. This interpretation suggests that ongoing public discussions about the desirability of highly centralized standards should explicitly address how those trade-offs might be valued. Furthermore, these discussions should also consider how the diverse set of policy effects presented here might compare with those of alternative proposals such as the second-wave reforms that stress decentralization and local control.

Notes

1. Erik W. Robelon, "An ESEA Primer," *Education Week*, January 9, 2002, pp. 28–29.

2. Lori Meyer and others, "The State of the States," *Education Week*, January 10, 2002, pp. 68–70.

3. Eric Hanushek and Margaret E. Raymond, "The Confusing World of Educational Accountability," *National Tax Journal*, vol. 54, no. 2 (2001), pp. 365–84.

4. Richard J. Murnane and Frank Levy, "Will Standards-Based Reforms Improve the Education of Students of Color?" *National Tax Journal*, vol. 54, no. 2 (2001), pp. 401–15.

5. Alfie Kohn, "Fighting the Tests: A Practical Guide to Rescuing Our Schools," *Phi Delta Kappan*, vol. 82, no. 5 (2001), pp. 349–57; and Murnane and Levy, "Will Standards-Based Reforms Improve the Education of Students of Color?"

6. Kathryn M. Doherty, "Poll: Teachers Support Standards—With Hesitation," *Education Week*, January 11 2001, p. 20.

7. Lynn Olson, "Finding the Right Mix," *Education Week*, January 11, 2001, pp. 12–20; Jay P. Greene, "The Texas School Miracle Is for Real," *City Journal*, vol. 10, no. 3 (2000) (www.city-journal.org/html/10_3_the_texas_school.html [July 9, 2003]); and Peter Schrag, "Too Good to Be True," *American Prospect*, vol. 11, no. 4 (January 3, 2000) (www.prospect.org/print/V11/4/schrag-p.html [July 9, 2003]).

8. Before this, the most extensive public discussions of education reform were occasioned by the *Sputnik* launch in 1957.

9. See, for example, W. James Popham, "The Case for Minimum Competency Testing," *Phi Delta Kappan*, vol. 63, no. 2 (1981), pp. 89–91.

10. These top-down reforms consisted of state-level standards and regulations that influenced teachers (for example, licensing and salaries) and schools (for example, curriculum and length of school day) as well as students (for example, graduation requirements). In contrast, the subsequent, second wave of reform stressed decentralized improvements such as school-based management, teacher professionalism, and school choice. See, for example, Ahmet Saban, "Emerging Themes of National Educational Reform," *International Journal of Educational Reform*, vol. 6, no. 3 (1997), pp. 349–56. The second-wave reforms are sometimes viewed as a response to the failure of the first wave. See, for example, John Chubb and Terry Moe, *Politics, Markets, and America's Schools* (Brookings, 1990).

11. Chris Pipho, "Minimum Competency Testing in 1978: A Look at State Standards," *Phi Delta Kappan*, vol. 59, no. 9 (1978), pp. 585–88.

12. The enactment of this requirement was often delayed for several years to provide students with adequate notice, to allow the states to test and develop their assessments, and to allow schools to adjust curricula in response to court challenges (for example, *Debra* v. *Turlington* in Florida). I identified the existence and effective date of minimum competency testing (MCT) requirements for graduation by drawing on several sources, including Brian A. Jacob, "Getting Tough? The Impact of High School Graduation Exams," *Educational Evaluation and Policy Analysis* (forthcoming); John H. Bishop and Ferran Mane, "The Impacts of Minimum Competency Exam Graduation Requirements on High School Graduation, College Attendance, and Early Labor Market Success," *Labour Economics*, vol. 8, no. 2 (2001), pp. 203–22; and publications from the Education Commission of the States and Lexis-Nexis searches of state newspaper accounts.

13. See James S. Catterall, "Standards and School Dropouts: A National Study of Tests Required for High School Graduation," *American Journal of Education*, vol. 98, no. 1 (1989), pp. 1–34.

14. Robert C. Serow, "Effects of Minimum Competency Testing for Minority Students: A Review of Expectations and Outcomes," *Urban Review*, vol. 16, no. 2 (1984), pp. 67–75.

15. National Commission on Excellence in Education, *A Nation at Risk: The Imperative for Educational Reform* (Government Printing Office, April 1983).

16. The amount of credit for a course is typically defined in terms of Carnegie units, which represent a standardized amount of time spent studying a subject over a full academic year. One unit represents successful completion of a class, which averages fifty minutes per day, five days per week, for 180 school days. See Dean R. Lillard and Philip P. DeCicca. "Higher Standards, More Dropouts? Evidence within and across Time," *Economics of Education Review*, vol. 20, no. 5 (2001), pp. 459–73. *A Nation at Risk* also recommended a one-half Carnegie unit of computer-related courses and two of a foreign language for college-bound students.

17. State-year data on course graduation requirements (CGRs) were drawn from several sources, most of which were published by the Education Commission of the States.

18. Julian R. Betts and Robert M. Costrell, "Incentives and Equity under Standards-Based Reform," in Diane Ravitch, ed., *Brookings Papers on Education Policy 2001* (Brookings, 2001).

19. John H. Bishop, "Nerd Harassment, Incentives, School Priorities, and Learning," in Susan Mayer and Paul Peterson, eds., *Earning and Learning* (Brookings, 1999).

20. Betts and Costrell, "Incentives and Equity under Standards-Based Reform."

21. Serow, "Effects of Minimum Competency Testing for Minority Students"; Murnane and Levy, "Will Standards-Based Reforms Improve the Education of Students of Color?"; and Meredith Phillips and Tiffani Chin, "Comment," in Diane Ravitch, ed., *Brookings Papers on Education Policy 2001* (Brookings, 2001).

22. Claude M. Steele, "A Threat in the Air—How Stereotypes Shape Intellectual Identity and Performance," *American Psychologist*, vol. 52, no. 6 (1997), pp. 613–29;

and "Stereotyping and Its Threats Are Real," *American Psychologist*, vol. 53, no. 6 (1998), pp. 680–81.

23. Murnane and Levy, "Will Standards-Based Reforms Improve the Education of Students of Color?"

24. Philips and Chin, "Comment."

25. See, for example, Norman Frederiksen, *The Influence of Minimum Competency Tests on Teaching and Learning* (Princeton, N.J.: ETS Policy Information Center, March 1994); Lillard and DeCicca, "Higher Standards, More Dropouts?"; Bishop and Mane, "The Impacts of Minimum Competency Exam Graduation Requirements"; John H. Bishop and others, "The Role of End-of-Course Exams and Minimal Competency Exams in Standards-Based Reforms," in Diane Ravitch, ed., *Brookings Papers on Education Policy 2001* (Brookings, 2001), pp. 267–345; Thomas B. Hoffer, "High School Graduation Requirements: Effects on Dropping Out and Student Achievement," *Teachers College Record*, vol. 98, no. 4 (1997), pp. 584–607; Jacobs, "Getting Tough?"; William H. Clune and Paula A. White, "Education Reform in the Trenches: Increased Academic Course Taking in High Schools with Lower Achieving Students in States with Higher Graduation Requirements," *Educational Evaluation and Policy Analysis*, vol. 14, no. 1 (1992), pp. 2–20; and Stanley Legum and others, *The 1994 High School Transcript Study Tabulations: Comparative Data on Credits Earned and Demographics for 1994, 1990, 1987, and 1982 High School Graduates* (Department of Education, 1997).

26. One exception is the difference-in-difference comparisons reported by Frederiksen, *The Influence of Minimum Competency Tests on Teaching and Learning*. Another is Lillard and DeCicca, "Higher Standards, More Dropouts?" (p. 467, model 4), who find that higher CGRs increase the probability of dropping out. However, they do not address the effects of MCT in these fixed effect models.

27. For example, one plausible conjecture is that the states most willing to adopt higher standards are those with an unobserved propensity for higher academic achievement. However, it is similarly plausible to suspect the opposite—that the states with an unobserved propensity for lower student achievement would adopt higher standards more aggressively.

28. Steven Ruggles and others, *Integrated Public Use Microdata Series: Version 2.0* (University of Minnesota, Historical Census Projects, 1997). I excluded respondents born in Nebraska because that state does not use Carnegie units in defining its graduation standards. I identified the year in which each respondent was eighteen by the respondent's age on enumeration day (April 1, 1990).

29. College entrants are those whose highest reported educational attainment was "some college, no degree" or higher. Unfortunately, the Public Use Micro-Data Sample (PUMS) does not distinguish high school graduates from general equivalency diploma (GED) completers. However, to the extent that higher standards generated a reduction in this measure of high school completion, there was not a wholly offsetting increase in GED completion. Furthermore, this sample includes students who attended private schools. However, their inclusion is arguably appropriate because students may switch schools to avoid the consequences of stricter standards.

30. Joshua D. Angrist and William N. Evans. "Schooling and Labor Market Consequences of the 1970 State Abortion Reforms," in Solomon W. Polachek, ed., *Research in Labor Economics* (Stamford, Conn.: JAI Press, 1999), pp. 75–113.

31. Those who report that they are not in the labor force are defined as unemployed to avoid omitting discouraged workers. However, the exclusion of these respondents does not substantively alter the subsequent results.

32. The school attendance variable is meant to control for the fact that those respondents still in school over the last year would have had limited labor market experiences. This specification is similar to those used by Bishop and Mane, in "The Impacts of Minimum Competency Exam Graduation Requirements," on high school graduation, college attendance, and early labor market success. However, I also estimated purer reduced-form versions of this model that excluded the measures of educational attainment and school attendance. The results were similar to those reported here (table 10-3).

33. I report Huber-White heteroscedastic-consistent standard errors, which assume clustered effects specific to each state-of-birth by year-of-birth cell. Also, I found that probit models for the binary dependent variables generated similar results.

34. Some studies represent state CGR policies by the total number of Carnegie units required. However, this measure may more accurately reflect the focus of reform efforts (for example, *A Nation at Risk*), which was to promote course taking in core academic areas.

35. Also, I found that the results were similar in models that matched respondents to the state-year variables by their state of residence five years before the census.

36. Specifically, I estimate, in models with and without state fixed effects, the effects on educational attainment of whether there were any state executions at age eighteen. One virtue of using state executions for this counterfactual is that considerable variation exists over this period both within states and across states. An increasing number of states began executions in 1984.

37. Beverly Duncan, "Dropouts and the Unemployed," *Journal of Political Economy*, vol. 73, no. 2 (1965), pp. 121–34.

38. David Card and Thomas Lemieux, "Dropout and Enrollment Trends in the Postwar Period: What Went Wrong in the 1970s?" in Jonathan Gruber, ed., *An Economic Analysis of Risky Behavior among Youths* (University of Chicago Press, 2001).

39. David Card and Thomas Lemieux find that cohort size is associated with significant increases in pupil-teacher ratios.

40. Card and Lemieux, "Dropout and Enrollment Trends in the Postwar Period"; and Thomas Kane, "College Entry by Blacks since 1970: The Role of College Costs, Family Background, and the Returns to Education," *Journal of Political Economy*, vol. 102, no. 5 (1994), pp. 878–911.

41. The execution of criminals could have an influence on educational attainment because the prosecution of these cases can be a meaningful drain on public resources. However, this reduced-form effect should be small and these models control for real school spending per pupil.

42. The PUMS definition of a high school graduate includes GED completers, so these results may understate the true reform-induced reduction in high school completion.

43. Murnane and Levy, "Will Standards-Based Reforms Improve the Education of Students of Color?"

44. Because MCT did not significantly influence educational attainment among white females, the employment reduction could reflect a lowering of educational effort. The results in the next section provide some suggestive evidence that this may be so by evaluating the effects of these reforms on individual process measures drawn from transcript data and survey questions.

45. The wage regression indicates that the wages of high school graduates are 18 percent higher than those of dropouts. The mean probability of employment among dropouts is 54 percent. The regression model for employment participation suggests that high school graduates are 20 percentage points more likely to be employed. Therefore, the implied premium in expected wages is $0.33w_d$ (that is, 0.74 x 1.18 – 0.54).

46. Given the stated uncertainty about whether the observer will be a dropout or not, the expected wage is based on the probabilities of being a graduate or a dropout (0.86 and 0.14, respectively) and the wage premium for graduates (18 percent). However, these calculations generate similar results if it is assumed that the observer receives only w_d.

47. For black males and females, the policy-induced gains in expected wages are also several times larger than the corresponding losses.

48. See Thomas D. Snyder and Charlene M. Hoffman, *Digest of Education Statistics 2000* (Department of Education, 2001), table 138.

49. Snyder and Hoffman, *Digest of Education Statistics 2000*, table 138.

50. Legum and others, *The 1994 High School Transcript Study Tabulations.*

51. Clune and White, "Education Reform in the Trenches."

52. For example, a pre-reform/post-reform time-series comparison may attribute to higher CGR increases in academic course taking that stem from other time-varying determinants (for example, the growing college wage premium in the 1980s).

53. These reduced-form evaluations do not isolate the structural mechanism for such effects. For example, the evidence that MCT reduced course taking in science and mathematics could reflect a reduction in motivation among more able students or a policy-induced reallocation of school and teacher resources.

54. My National Education Longitudinal Study (NELS) extract does not include all NELS respondents because some of the base-year sample (that is, those in eighth grade in 1988) were not in tenth grade at the time of the 1990 follow-up. However, to be representative of high school sophomores, the extract does include respondents who freshened the sample: tenth graders who were not in eighth grade in 1988.

55. Each course taken by a student was assigned one of the more than twenty-two hundred unique codes associated with the Classification of Secondary School Courses (CSSC). For details of each transcript study, see Legum and others, *The*

1994 High School Transcript Study Tabulations; and Steven J. Ingels and others, *National Education Longitudinal Study of 1988: Second Follow-up Transcript Component Data File User's Manual* (Department of Education, 1995).

56. The sample sizes for the nontranscript outcomes are over nineteen thousand. The lower sample size for course-taking data largely reflects the fact that the schools of some NELS respondents were not surveyed for transcripts. Respondents from Nebraska were also excluded because the state does not use Carnegie units in defining its graduation standards.

57. The restricted use version of High School and Beyond (HS&B) does not directly identify each high school student's state. I identified the states of HS&B schools through a crosswalk of the HS&B data on the 1980, 1981, and 1982 state unemployment rates and published numbers.

58. These results are presented in detail in an earlier conference draft of this chapter, Thomas S. Dee, "Standards and Student Outcomes: Lessons from the 'First Wave' of Education Reform," Harvard University, John F. Kennedy School of Government, June 10, 2002.

59. The reference category is a weak or nonexistent CGR (less than one Carnegie unit required in subject).

60. See the conference draft of this paper for details. These results imply that any subsequent labor market gains associated with higher CGRs could reflect incentive effects as well as sorting effects.

61. See the conference draft of this paper for details. Some ambiguity exists in interpreting these results. It could reflect the direct effect of imposing minimum requirements on student perceptions of the value of learning. However, other issues related to the implementation of new CGRs contribute to these results as well. For example, teachers may assign less homework after increases in state CGRs. Nonetheless, these results suggest that CGR-induced increases in academic course taking were attenuated by undesirable changes in how students allocate their time.

62. Larry Cuban, "School Reform by Remote Control: SB 813 in California," *Phi Delta Kappan*, vol. 66, no. 3 (November 1984), pp. 213–15; and Chris Pipho, "States Move Reform Closer to Reality," *Phi Delta Kappan*, vol. 68, no. 4 (December 1986), pp. K1–K8.

63. Pipho, "States Move Reform Closer to Reality."

64. Edith L. Archer and Judith H. Dresden, "A New Kind of Dropout: The Effect of Minimum Competency Testing on High School Graduation in Texas," *Education and Urban Society*, vol. 19, no. 3 (May 1987), pp. 269–79.

11

No Child Left Behind, Chicago-Style

ANTHONY S. BRYK

While the rhetoric of No Child Left Behind has come center place in national educational policy, it has been at the heart of Chicago's reform since the mid-1990s. In the spring of 1995, the Illinois General Assembly passed its second major bill in less than a decade affecting the Chicago public schools (CPS). While leaving in place most of the school-level provisions in Chicago's 1988 decentralization reform, the School Reform Act of 1995 turned over virtually complete administrative control of the school system to the mayor of the city of Chicago. It created a small Reform Board of Trustees, directly appointed by the mayor, and authorized a new role of chief executive officer who is also appointed by the mayor. More generally, all senior appointments in the school system are now routinely vetted through the mayor's office. The 1995 reform act granted strong school accountability provisions to the new school system leaders, including author-

This report draws heavily on both published research and analysis work in-progress at the Consortium on Chicago School Research. I am deeply indebted to both the Steering Committee and the codirectors of the consortium. Their concerns about the progress and problems in Chicago's reforms, as well as their comments about my research in-progress, have strongly influenced my thinking about these matters. The paper presented here, however, represents my personal work. No endorsement by the Steering Committee, other consortium codirectors, or research staff should be assumed. While I am indebted to the contributions of many, I alone am responsible for any errors of argument or fact that might reside here.

ity to place schools on probation and to close and reconstitute schools. The legislation moved several major sources of funds into a block grant and greatly increased the flexibility afforded the system in its budgeting and accounting procedures. It also forbade a teacher strike for eighteen months and delimited the provisions subject to collective bargaining, including the right of the CPS to privatize services.

Paul Vallas, chief executive officer of the CPS, and Gery Chico, president of the Reform Board of Trustees, guided the day-to-day operations of the Chicago schools under this new regime. Both had been trusted senior officials in Mayor Richard Daley's city administration; both were appointed in the summer of 1995 to their new CPS posts; and both stepped down from their school system posts in late spring of 2001, marking the end of phase II of reform in Chicago.

This new leadership team brought a remarkable burst of energy to the CPS. A $350 million fiscal crisis was seemingly resolved in a matter of days. Shortly thereafter, the teachers union, which had been badly beaten in the 1995 legislative session downstate, quickly agreed to a long-term contract that included a significant salary increase. A major salary increase for principals followed shortly thereafter. Next came a consolidation of some two dozen labor agreements that finally brought long-term labor peace to the CPS. These quick changes set a very positive tone—a new direction—for a school system that had been plagued by fiscal instability and labor unrest for over a decade. Also before the opening of schools in September 1995, Vallas and Chico launched a major campaign to improve the school system's physical plant. What began initially as a building cleanup initiative, expanded quickly into an unprecedented commitment to renovate existing buildings and construct new facilities.

The Emergence of No Child Left Behind, Chicago-Style

By late spring of 1996, system leaders were finally ready to turn their attention to an academic reform agenda. Phase I of reform, from 1989 through the 1995–96 academic year, had banked heavily on democratic localism as a lever for change.[1] A major transition was now marked as a high-stakes test-driven accountability initiative began to take shape. Accompanied by powerful political rhetoric, complete with vivid images of helicopters hovering over the U.S. Embassy as Saigon was abandoned, Chicagoans were told that this time no one would be left behind. Over the course of the next twelve months, system leaders staked out an expansive, complex, interrelated set of initiatives intent on improving student achievement.

The fullest force of this educational plan was felt in the elementary schools where high-stakes promotional gates were introduced for students at grades three, six, and eight. Under Chicago's End of Social Promotion Policy, any student who failed to achieve a minimum reading or math score on a norm-referenced assessment, the Iowa Tests of Basic Skills (ITBS), could be required to attend summer school. These students were retested in August, and if they still failed to achieve the test cutoff score, they could be retained in grade. Over the first two years of this initiative, some fifty thousand third, sixth, and eighth graders attended mandatory summer school and more than twenty thousand of these students were eventually retained in grade the following academic year.[2]

Accompanying this was a high-stakes accountability initiative aimed at schools. Over the course of the next five years, 147 elementary schools with low ITBS scores were placed on probation. A probation manager was appointed to each of these schools to oversee the school's improvement plan and use of its discretionary resources. The authority of local school councils was restricted, and principals could be replaced if they were judged by central office leaders to be blocking reform. Perhaps most significantly, probation schools operated under the threat that they would be subject to reconstitution if they did not improve. While no elementary schools were reconstituted during this time period, seven low-performing high schools were.[3]

The introduction of these high-stakes initiatives was supported by three basic mechanisms to directly improve student learning. The first, and most important, expanded instructional time through the mandated summer programs and through an extended day initiative. Second, the CPS invested heavily in a scripted instructional curriculum, which was required in the summer programs and left optional for use by schools during the academic year. This curriculum, which was carefully aligned to the ITBS, consisted of detailed day-by-day lesson plans and homework assignments. Third, probation schools were provided with an external partner who offered a range of school services including professional development for teachers. While this afforded probation schools some much needed assistance, the overall intensity and scope of these efforts remained modest.[4]

In sum, the system primarily placed its bets on improving student learning through sanctions (that is, required summer school and grade retention for students; probation and the threat of reconstitution and possible job loss for teachers and principals) intended to encourage greater effort, coupled with more instructional time aligned with the ITBS.

Chicago's Larger Reform Context

The phase II reforms came on the heels of an earlier piece of state legislation, enacted in 1988, which introduced an unprecedented level of decentralization into the Chicago public schools. In essence, the 1995 School Reform Act was laid on top of the original Chicago School Reform Act of 1988. Specifically, the 1988 reform created local school councils (LSCs) composed of a majority of parent and community representatives along with two teachers and the school principal. Principals are selected by LSCs and work under four-year performance contracts. They may be replaced by a majority vote of their LSCs after four years. Teachers are hired by principals at the school building level and can be appointed without regard to seniority considerations. Substantial discretionary resources are allocated annually by individual schools according to a school improvement plan and budget developed by the principal and approved by the LSC. Although the state and federal funds in this category were capped by the CPS in 1995 and have remained flat since, the typical elementary school in Chicago still allocates about a half million dollars each year for its discretionary programs.

Chicago has now embarked on a new phase in a decade-plus effort at reforming its schools. In the summer of 2001 Mayor Daley appointed a new school system administration. Michael Scott, as president of the Reform Board of Trustees, and Arne Duncan, as chief executive officer, now head the CPS. The rhetoric of high-stakes accountability based on ITBS results abated immediately. The new CPS leadership quickly began a literacy improvement program, expanded the school accountability indicators to include a focus on trends in students' learning gains as well as overall status, created a new infrastructure between the district and schools to support instructional improvement, and initiated a comprehensive strategic planning process aimed at deepening the long-term human and programmatic resources to support further school improvement.

I present here a synthesis of evidence concerning the changes in academic productivity in Chicago elementary schools during the high-stakes accountability reform of phase II and compare these results to the progress recorded during phase I.[5] In so doing, I also illustrate the difficulties in making accurate assessments of this sort from the kinds of public data typically found in annual school system reports. Under its phase II reforms, Chicago emphasized the idea of "working harder and longer." I conclude by summarizing the results of several recent studies which suggest that more attention is now needed on "working smarter."

Figure 11-1. *Trends in Chicago Elementary School Achievement in Reading and Math, Iowa Tests of Basic Skills*

Percent at or above norm

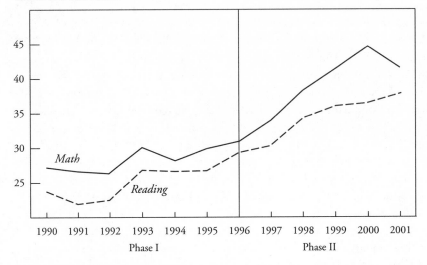

Source: Chicago public schools tabulations, systemwide data.

Improvement in Academic Productivity under Phase I and II

I begin with an examination of the annual test score reports released by the CPS. The media, and many policy analysts as well, regularly use data of this sort in making judgments about the success or failure of various educational policy initiatives. I then proceed to detail a more appropriate value-added perspective for assessing changes in school productivity and present descriptive evidence based on this.

A Casual Look: Impressive Improvements in Student Learning during Phase II

Figure 11-1 presents the test score trends for 1990 through 2001 in elementary reading and mathematics achievement as reported by the Chicago school system. The CPS routinely reports its results in the metric of "percentage of students at or above national norms." Elementary school test scores bottomed out for the CPS in reading in 1991 and mathematics in 1992, and they have been rising ever since. This rate of improvement appears to accelerate post-1996 with the introduction of the high-stakes accountability initiatives, suggesting that an incredible reform success story was at work.

A Closer Look at These Simple Trends

In the post-1996 period, however, many other changes were occurring in the CPS, in addition to any genuine improvements in the academic productivity of schools. Each of these would manifest itself as a short-term positive burst to the bottom line of annual test score reports.

1. The introduction of an end of social promotion initiative had an immediate short-term impact on annual test score reports. Retained students are now counted against a lower grade. As a result, test scores in the next higher grades (four, seven, and nine under Chicago's policy) immediately shot up.[6]

2. The CPS changed its rules in 1997 and again in 1999 for the reporting of test scores for students in bilingual programs. In 1997 only students who had more than three years of bilingual education were counted (previously the rule had been two years). In 1999 the CPS raised the exclusion rule again to more than four years. Because bilingual students tend to score poorly when first tested in English but improve rapidly, deferring their entry into the accountability reports also causes the reported test scores to rise.[7]

3. The CPS experienced a changing demographic profile during the mid- to late 1990s as Latino enrollments grew by about 3 percent per year and the proportion of African American enrollment declined by a corresponding amount. When Latino students do eventually enter the accountability reports, they tend to have higher test scores than African American students and their scores subsequently grow at a somewhat faster rate. As a result, as Latinos make up a larger portion of the school system, overall test scores should go up, even absent any changes in school productivity.[8]

4. An increasing number of children, especially at grades six, seven, and eight, have been referred to special education as a result of failing to meet the promotional gate and being retained in grade. Thus a derivative consequence of the introduction of the promotional gates is that an increasing number of historically low-achieving elementary students are no longer included in the annual testing reports. The cumulative effects of points 2 and 4 can be seen in the changing test score inclusion rates for the CPS over the last ten years. In 1992, 83.2 percent of Chicago's elementary students were tested and included in the annual report. By 2001 the inclusion rate had dropped to 74 percent.[9]

5. Beginning in 1996–97, the CPS effectively moved the ITBS testing program later in the academic year by starting the school year earlier. They never adjusted, however, the criterion for judging what it means to be at grade level from 0.8 (that is, eight months into the academic year) to 0.9 (that is, nine months into the academic year). The reporting metric of "per-

centage of students at or above national norm" is sensitive to small movements in the scoring threshold. Although I have not estimated the exact magnitude of this effect, clearly it provides some positive boost to the annual test score reports.

6. The CPS repeatedly used the same three forms of the ITBS since they were first introduced in 1993. This was not much of a problem up through 1996 as testing occurred only once a year and no form had been used more than twice.[10] The frequency of testing, however, increased dramatically under high-stakes accountability. A student caught at a promotional gate could be tested five times over fifteen months, cycling multiple times through the same three tests. The possibility of improved scores simply through familiarity with the test questions, no less outright cheating, grows under such circumstances (see chapter 12 in this volume).

To be sure, a reasonable rationale can be offered for each of the system policy changes. No evidence exists that CPS leadership was deliberately gaming the system to mislead the public about the efficacy of its reform initiatives. The only point here is that the data in figure 11-1 are clearly misleading for purposes of drawing inferences about the improvements in student learning that resulted from the introduction of the high-stakes accountability reform.

In an effort to provide a better indicator of overall test score trends, the Consortium on Chicago School Research began in 1999 to publish its own annual ITBS test score brief. Samples from these are presented in figures 11-2 and 11-3. These data, which are reported in the average grade equivalent achieved by each age group of students, indicate that, while systemwide test scores did improve during phase II, the improvements occurred at a slower rate and varied by grade and student-age level.[11] While thirteen-year-olds (approximately grade seven) continued to show improvements up through the spring of 2000, the test score trends for nine-year-olds flattened out beginning in 1998. As discussed further below, these age cohort differences have important implications for evaluating the efficacy of the phase II reforms.

A Value-Added Perspective

It is tempting to use the adjusted test score trends presented in figures 11-2 and 11-3 as the basis for judging school improvement. While these data are better than the simple annual statistics reported by CPS, drawing inferences about changing productivity over time still remains fraught with errors. A school system may be adding much to student learning, but if the school district has a continuous influx of weakly prepared students, annual test score

Figure 11-2. *Trends in ITBS Grade Equivalents, Nine-Year-Olds*

Grade equivalent

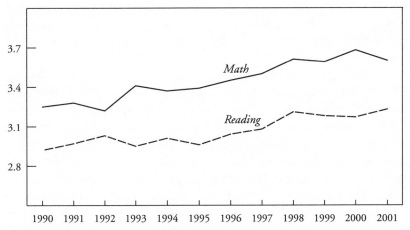

Source: Consortium on Chicago School Research tabulations based on individual student data; Todd Rosenkranz, *2001 CPS Test Trend Review: Iowa Tests of Basic Skills, Research Data Brief of the Academic Productivity Series* (Chicago: Consortium on Chicago School Research, 2002).

Figure 11-3. *Trends in ITBS Grade Equivalents, Thirteen-Year-Olds*

Grade equivalent

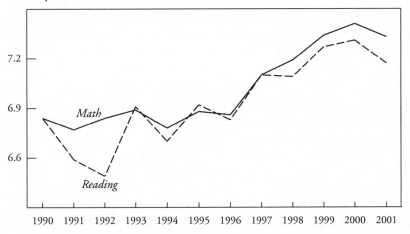

Source: Consortium on Chicago School Research tabulations based on adjusted individual student data; Todd Rosenkranz, *2001 CPS Test Trend Review: Iowa Tests of Basic Skills, Research Data Brief of the Academic Productivity Series* (Chicago: Consortium on Chicago School Research, 2002).

reports may miss these positive effects.[12] On the other side of the ledger, if a district begins to attract better students or manages to lose some of its weaker students, its achievement scores are likely to improve even without any real change in organizational productivity. This is an inherent weakness in status change models for assessing productivity improvements (see chapter 6 in this volume).

Concerns of this sort lead to a key principle. To make a valid inference about changes in the performance of a school, two questions need to be answered: How much are children learning during the period in which they are enrolled in a school (or district)? Are these learning gains improving over time?

This perspective focuses attention on assessing trends in student learning gains instead of student status over time. That is, if genuine productivity improvements are occurring, a school or district's contribution or the value-added to students' learning should be increasing over time.[13] To be clear, improving school productivity does not necessarily mean high test scores. If a school or district enrolls a large proportion of weakly prepared students, the school or district may be contributing a great deal to their learning (that is, high productivity), but overall test scores can still remain low because of student mobility among schools and districts.

Figures 11-4 and 11-5 display the trends in ITBS learning gains in the CPS from 1994 through 2001 in reading and mathematics, respectively.[14] Judging these gains is complicated because the CPS rotated test forms from year to year and the norming tables were not always well equated across the various forms and levels used.[15] The most valid analyses of learning trends result from comparing years when a pair of test forms was used in the same sequence. This occurred for the gains reported in 1993–94, 1995–96, and 2000–01. In each instance, form K was used in the base year followed by form L the next year. (These are the black bars in figures 11-4 and 11-5.) Another common form-pair sequence occurred in 1996–97 and 1998–99, when form L was administered in the base year (that is, 1996 and 1998, respectively) followed by form M.

Notice that at all grade levels the 1996 gain exceeds the 1994 gain by 10 to 15 percent on average. This indicates that the second half of the phase I reforms, the period from 1993 through 1996, was marked by significant across-the-board improvements in academic productivity in both reading and mathematics. In contrast, the 2001 gains in reading appear generally flat as compared with 1996 (grades four and five are down slightly, grades six and eight are up slightly, and grades three and seven are flat). The mathematics results in 2001 are even more pronounced, where the 2001 gains are less than

Figure 11-4. *Trends in Reading Gains, in Grade Equivalents,*
Iowa Tests of Basic Skills

Grade equivalent

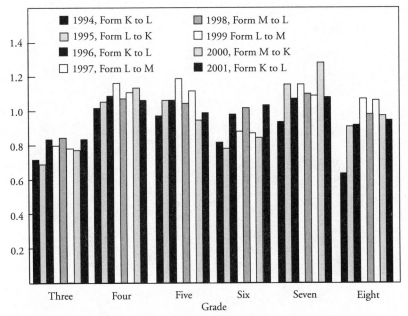

Source: Consortium on Chicago School Research tabulations; and Todd Rosenkranz, *2001 CPS Test Trend Review: Iowa Tests of Basic Skills, Research Data Brief of the Academic Productivity Series* (Chicago: Consortium on Chicago School Research, 2002).

in 1996 for all grades except grade three. The results from the common test-form sequences in 1997 and 1999 offer further corroborating evidence in this regard. The 1999 gains are lower for all grades in reading and for all grades, except third, in mathematics.

Figure 11-6 provides an overall summary of the changes in academic productivity in the CPS for both reform phases. As the decentralization reform began, students in Chicago were gaining 0.86 years of learning for a year of instruction in reading and 0.82 years for a year of instruction in mathematics.[16] By the end of the phase I reforms, these indexes had risen to 0.97 and 0.90, respectively. This translates into a 12.5 percent productivity increase in reading and a 9.5 percent increase in mathematics learning from 1990 through 1996.[17] By the end of the phase II reforms five years later, academic productivity had increased by 2 percent more in reading and about 3 percent more in mathematics. Although modest in size, these are improvements above and beyond those recorded in phase I.

Figure 11-5. *Trends in Math Gains, in Grade Equivalents,*
Iowa Tests of Basic Skills

Grade equivalent

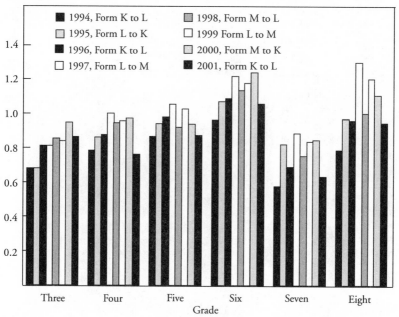

Source: Consortium on Chicago School Research tabulations; and Todd Rosenkranz, *2001 CPS Test Trend Review: Iowa Tests of Basic Skills, Research Data Brief of the Academic Productivity Series* (Chicago: Consortium on Chicago School Research, 2002).

Putting these results in more substantive terms, a child entering grade one in the CPS in 2001 would be expected to gain over the course of the next eight years about 0.2 years more learning in both reading and math as a result of the high-stakes accountability initiatives. The accumulated value-added to the same student's learning from the phase I reforms is closer to a full extra year of learning in both subjects.

Reconciling These Results with Other Reports

The results presented here represent the best estimates of the underlying improvements in school productivity during phase II. These enduring effects of high-stakes accountability are different from the total improvements in test scores experienced by those students who were enrolled in the CPS during the period 1996–2001. A close inspection of figures 11-4 and 11-5 reveals that the largest single-year learning gains occurred in 1997 for a majority of the grades in both reading and math. In fact, the average sys-

Figure 11-6. *Summary of ITBS Gain Trends over Time*

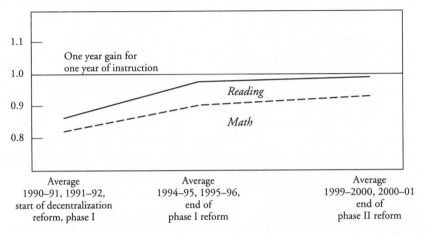

Source: Consortium on Chicago School Research tabulations of individual student data from the Chicago public schools.
Note: ITBS = Iowa Test of Basic Skills.

temwide achievement gains in 1997 actually exceeded a year of learning (1.04 precisely) for a year of instruction in both subjects. This suggests that the CPS experienced a one-time burst in student learning in the year that the high-stakes accountability initiative was announced. However, as the subsequent instructional initiatives associated with these CPS policies rolled out—the extensive summer school and after-school programs, the scripted curriculum, and the retention in grade of low-achievers—no further productivity improvements were recognized. In fact, the annual learning gains declined some post-1997, resulting in the final numbers found in figure 11-6.

A simple estimate of the total improvements in student test scores attributable to phase II can be derived by accumulating the actual student learning gains in the years post-1996 (see figures 11-4 and 11-5), and then comparing this with the base level of learning gains recorded at the end of phase I (see figure 11-6). Absent a high-stakes accountability effect, CPS students would be expected to continue to gain on average 0.97 years of learning in reading and 0.90 years in math in the post-1996 period. Any improvements above and beyond this represent new effects attributable to phase II reforms.

Accumulating these phase II effects amounts to 0.17 extra years of learning in reading and an extra 0.37 years in mathematics. (In an effect size metric, these five-year effects translate into approximately 0.12 for reading and 0.30 for math.)[18] About half of these effects appear attributable to the underlying productivity improvements in phase II estimated above. The remainder is likely associated with a variety of other short-term, one-time factors. The pushing back of the testing program later into the academic year probably added a bit here. Evidence also exists that students increased their effort during testing, which added another bit to the reported test scores.[19] And finally, evidence shows that cheating, on the part of teachers and school administrators, also increased post-1997.[20]

The productivity estimates for phase II differ sharply from the apparent effects present in the status report trends in figures 11-2 and 11-3. They can also differ from those reported in studies that use adjusted cross-cohort status comparisons as the basis for drawing inferences about the impact of the phase II reforms.[21] A key factor producing these differences is how analyses of the 1996 to 2001 data treat the value-added accruing to student learning as a result of the earlier academic productivity improvements during phase I. Even absent any phase II effects, students post-1996 would now receive larger school effects than were experienced by earlier cohorts (for example, pre-1994). Thus the annual test score would be expected to continue to rise in subsequent years because of the enlarged value-addeds that schools would now be making to student learning. These increments, resulting from earlier productivity improvements, will continue to push up the annual test score reports until a full cohort of students has moved fully through the elementary school system post-1996.

The data presented in figures 11-2 and 11-3 offer corroborating evidence in this regard. Absent a new burst in productivity during phase II, the improvements in test scores, resulting from phase I effects, should slow first in the lower grades and then eventually also slow in subsequent years in later grades. This has happened in Chicago. The improving achievement trends for nine-year-olds in both reading and mathematics flattened out beginning in 1998. In contrast, for thirteen-year-olds, the first evidence of slowdown did not appear until 2001.

Trends in White, Black, and Hispanic Achievement

Since the publication of the seminal volume by Christopher Jencks and Meredith Phillips summarizing the evidence on the size and causes of the minority gap in student achievement, increased attention has focused on how schools affect not only average achievement levels but also the performance of distinct subgroups within the overall student population.[22] One might wonder how Chicago has done in this regard. Because most of the phase II reforms were targeted at the city's most disadvantaged students, these reforms might be judged somewhat differently if they effected a significant reduction in the minority achievement gap, even though they only marginally moved the overall bottom line.

In the Chicago context, this issue translates primarily into a concern about the achievement of African American students, given that they compose the majority of the school system's enrollment, they historically have had the lowest test scores, and schools with predominately African American enrollments (more than 85 percent) were less likely to improve under the phase I decentralization reforms. In addition, these students and schools were the de facto principal target of both the end of social promotion and school probation initiatives during phase II. African American students were much more likely, for example, to be required to attend summer school and subsequently retained in grade than any other racial/ethnic group.[23] Similarly, of the 147 elementary schools placed on probation from 1996 through 2001, 75 percent were predominately African American schools.

As the decentralization reform began, African American students were gaining 0.14 less per year of instruction in both reading and mathematics than white students; Hispanics were gaining 0.05 less per year of instruction than whites in both subjects. During phase I, the learning gains for African American, Hispanic, and white students tracked over time along lines parallel to the overall system trend displayed in figure 11-6. Each subgroup improved by approximately the same amount in both reading and mathematics. Although all subgroups improved during this period, no closing of the initial learning gaps for African American or Hispanic students occurred.[24]

The results differentiate somewhat more during phase II. By 2001 the gap in reading learning gains for African American students as compared with whites increased to 0.18 less per year of instruction. Counterbalancing this was a slight decrease in the black-white gap in mathematics learning to 0.12 per year of instruction. Hispanics fared somewhat better during phase II even though neither these students nor their schools were especially targeted for high-stakes accountability.[25] By 2001 the Hispanic-white gap in reading remained at 0.05 and the gap in mathematics narrowed to 0.02 years of learning per year of instruction.

Thus, even though the high-stakes accountability reforms were largely aimed at African American students and their schools, no special productivity improvements occurred for this subgroup. Relatively speaking, they fared about the same under the high-stakes accountability reform of the late 1990s as they had under the decentralization reform of the early half of the decade.

The End of Social Promotion and the Impact on Productivity

Previous consortium studies have documented impressive short-term improvements in student achievement associated with the introduction of the end of social promotion initiative. These reports suggest that the promotional gates created incentives for students and teachers to focus more attention on the learning of basic skills in reading and mathematics and resulted in significant improvements in achievement. Similarly, the introduction of the summer school program produced large learning gains for participating students.[26] Why do these effects not manifest themselves more in the overall learning gain trends presented above?

A full and complete explanation requires more investigation. Longitudinal evidence is now available on one of the major components of the end of social promotion initiative, the effects of summer school, which helps to shed some light here.

The Chicago public schools initially reported some very large gains, ranging typically from a half to a full year of learning or more—depending on the subject (reading or math) and the grade level (three, six, or eight)—from a six-week summer program. Such results, if true, would be astounding. The data reported by the CPS consisted of the simple observed gains from the May to August testing for those students who were required to attend summer school. Because the selection into the program depended almost entirely on the May test scores, the CPS reports are subject to a classic regression to the mean artifact. That is, many students who just happened to perform unusually poorly in May were required to attend summer school. The test scores of these students would be expected to rise in a subsequent test administration even if there were no program effect. Chance alone dictates that they will do somewhat better the second time around.

In response, consortium researchers developed an adjusted estimate of the summer school effect using students' longitudinal achievement data.[27] From each student's longitudinal test data, Melissa Roderick and her colleagues computed an expected end-of-grade test score to compare with their end of summer school performance. By using this predicted end-of-grade test score (instead of the observed score that was used for selection into summer school), they were able to separate out a true summer school effect from the regression artifact resulting from the selection process. As expected, the adjusted estimates of the value-added to student learning as a result of summer school were substantially smaller, by a factor of about one-half, than the original CPS reports. Even at these reduced sizes, however, the effects remain substantively important.

However, when these students were tested two years later, a different picture emerged. Consortium researchers performed a regression discontinuity analysis to examine the two-year residual effects of summer school participation.[28] This analysis compares the long-term achievement trajectories of students just above and just below the test score cutoff used for mandatory summer school. The analysis focuses on the achievement growth for these two groups from two pre-policy years, 1993 and 1994, and contrasts this with those from 1997 and 1998. The results indicate that, two years after summer school, most of the original summer school effects had disappeared. The residual effect at the end of grade five for those students who attended summer school in grade three was about 0.05 of a year of learning. For those students who attended summer school in grade six, the residual effect discerned in grade eight was about one-tenth of a year of learning. Moreover these estimates may be positively biased in that the students retained at grades three and six had to be excluded from the analysis.[29]

Multiple possible explanations exist for this pattern of effects, and sorting out among the competing hypotheses warrants further study. Some might argue that the summer effects were illusory, resulting from a "teaching to the test." Roderick and her colleagues, however, offer several good reasons to believe that the summer school effects were genuine but that subsequent instruction did not build on this and so they dissipated over time. Specifically, the authors document many positive attributes of the summer school program: substantially reduced class size, efficient use of instructional time, adequate instructional materials, and intensive instructional supervision. Moreover, both student and teacher survey reports offer very positive accounts about the summer school experience as compared with their regular school year experiences. All of this is highly consistent with significant summer learning gains.[30]

The Next Round of Reform in Chicago

Where then does all this leave us?

"It's Instruction, Stupid!"

Reminiscent of Bill Clinton's campaign for the presidency in 1992 (with its refrain, "It's the economy, stupid"), many Chicago reformers have gradually come to see that the quality of instruction and the factors instrumentally linked to it (that is, standards, assessment, curriculum, professional development, and more generally the quality of human resources) must be central to the next phase of school reform. As was proclaimed in the lead story line for the February 2001 issue of the city's independent school reform publication, *Catalyst,* a broadly held consensus has formed around this concern, and the CPS has now given it a central priority.

On balance, some might be guarded about the possibilities of further improvements in the CPS because students are currently achieving almost a year of learning for a year of instruction on norm-referenced standardized tests. How much more can realistically be expected, some might ponder, given the highly disadvantaged nature of the school systems' population (that is, 90 percent of the students come from low-income families)? Results from the studies summarized below, however, offer good reasons for rejecting this view. The findings from three independent investigations are clear. Many students in very disadvantaged neighborhood schools already make considerably larger learning gains, and many more could as well if they had similar instructional opportunity.

Quality of the intellectual work in classrooms matters. The first evidence on this point comes from a longitudinal study by Fred Newmann and his colleagues of the academic work of more than five thousand students in four hundred classrooms in nineteen disadvantaged neighborhood elementary schools.[31] The study involved gathering a sample of the instructional tasks in mathematics and writing that teachers assigned to students in third-, sixth-, and eighth-grade classrooms. An independent group of Chicago teachers (not from the schools involved in the study) were asked to score the intellectual demands made by each task using an established set of rubrics for authentic intellectual instruction.[32] The scorers were blind to the names of the schools and the specific teachers' classrooms. In addition, a random subset of the tasks was rescored blind each year as a check on rater reliability. The researchers combined the individual task scores into an overall measure of the intellectual demand in each class and then related these measures to the learning gains recorded by students on both the Iowa Tests of Basic Skills in reading and mathematics and to student scores from the Illinois Goals Assessment Program (IGAP) in reading, writing, and mathematics. Controls were introduced in the analysis for preexisting differences between classrooms on student demographics in addition to prior test performance.

Newmann and others found very large differences in learning gains between the one hundred classrooms they studied that had the most intellectually demanding instruction as compared with the one hundred classrooms with the least challenging instruction. Even though both kinds of classrooms exist in the same schools, students in classes where authentic intellectual work was assigned could easily learn 50 percent more over the course of a year than their schoolmates across the hall. Gains of 1.25 years for a year of instruction were average in such classrooms.

Independent corroboration from a study of improving and nonimproving predominately African American elementary schools. The Center for Urban School Policy at Northwestern University undertook a comparative retrospective study of five matched pairs of very disadvantaged, predominately African American elementary schools. The paired schools came from the same or similar neighborhoods with one school in each pair having substantially improved its reading achievement over an eight-year period; the other had not. Researchers found that in schools with larger gains in standardized reading scores "teachers taught to greater (intellectual) depth than their counterparts in schools with little or no test score gain. A strategy of teaching directly to the test was less effective in boosting achievement levels than teaching for depth and understanding."[33]

Insights gained from a study of effective summer schools. The design of Chicago's summer school program represents a near ideal natural experiment for examining teacher effects. Considerable efforts were made by CPS to leave little to chance in attempting to teacher-proof instruction. The curriculum was organized as detailed, minute-by-minute lesson plans and student work assignments. All necessary materials were prepackaged and introduced to teachers before the start of summer school. Class size was reduced, and extraneous activities that might interfere with regular instruction were minimized.[34] Finally, extensive teacher monitoring was put in place in an effort to assure that teachers did the program. It is hard to envision, at least in a big urban school district, a more sophisticated effort to directly control classroom practice.

Nevertheless, Roderick and others still found large variations across classrooms in student learning.[35] Because class size, materials, time, and the prevalence of external monitoring were all carefully controlled, and because the students were also homogeneous as a result of the rules controlling selection into the program, these residual classroom differences are almost pure teacher effects. Based on direct observations, the researchers classified instruction into three broad categories: nonimplementation of the required curriculum; routine, mechanical use of the mandated lesson plans; and tailored instruction with teachers using the required materials but also modifying and supplementing this instruction as they judged necessary. Effects, ranging from an extra 0.2 to 0.3 years of learning, were found in classrooms with tailored instruction as compared with settings with rote use of required materials or program nonimplementation. Comparing this quality instruction effect with the average summer school effect in Chicago indicates that quality teaching can almost double the amount of student learning that occurs.

These results suggest clear limits as to what can be achieved through reforms that do not directly confront the limitations in teachers' capacity to engage more ambitious instruction. Efforts such as reduced class size and more instructional time are low-hanging, albeit expensive, fruit. They can be introduced quickly into schools and will likely produce some positive effects. The big effects that remain to be harvested, however, require attention to teachers' knowledge and skills and capacity to engage and sustain disadvantaged urban students in more challenging academic work.

Thus the summer school study by Roderick and her colleagues confirms the general findings from Newmann and others. Disadvantaged students can demonstrate impressive learning gains when given an opportunity to engage quality instruction. Reforms aimed in this direction have potential for profound effect on the overall level of student learning, dwarfing both the decentralization and accountability effects estimated above.

These improvements may not come easily. Were the latter true, quality instruction would be much more commonplace than is now the case. Nonetheless, such instruction is occurring with sufficient prevalence so that it is reasonable to assume that it could become more widespread if policies were enacted to support and encourage this. The work on high-performance learning communities by Richard F. Elmore, Lauren Resnick, M. K. Stein, and others offers considerable guidance as to what this might look like from the perspective of state and district-level reform.[36] Other consortium research on instructional coherence provides closely related guidance for leading instructional change at the individual school building level.[37]

Conclusions

Chicago's phase II reform was not some superficial, underresourced initiative like many urban school improvement efforts. The system put substantial fiscal resources into the plan and spent considerable political effort in building public support and professional engagement around the work. As system leaders received feedback around problems in the initiative, they made important administrative rule modifications. While it is hard to characterize the grade retention policy as evidence-based, many other aspects of the initiative, including the use of summer school, reduced class size both in summer school and for retained students, and the alignment of curriculum and assessment fit that bill.

Nonetheless, when the day is done, the evidence assembled here leads to one overall conclusion. While some individual students and schools benefited, little evidence exists of a major overall improvement in the academic productivity of the Chicago public schools during phase II. While published system reports of test scores and some other indicators may suggest dramatic changes, most of these differences evaporate upon closer scrutiny. A number of forces converged—some systematically planned, others by happenstance— to drive up test scores in the second half of the 1990s. Ironically the effects of the decentralization reform from phase I, which was much maligned by system leadership during phase II, was probably the single biggest source of the much heralded system successes during the late 1990s.

In sum, the research reported here documents that the results of the high-stakes accountability reform implemented under No Child Left Behind, Chicago-style, were modest at best. The initiative did galvanize public attention around the learning of all students and challenged school professionals to take this goal more seriously. Moreover, it certainly did help to pave the way for a subsequent phase III of reform that now focuses directly on instruction and the broad array of school and system-level factors that contribute to its improvement. Although none of this is trivial, one would hope that other ways could be found to move more expeditiously in this direction.

Finally, a sobering methodological conclusion is embedded in all of this work. Because most policy pundits and even some serious policy analysts often draw their conclusions based on a casual inspection of public data such as found in figure 11-1, even disinterested individuals can easily be misled and draw erroneous conclusions about the actual efficacy of any reform initiative. Add to this the powerful shaping forces that one's prior beliefs and professional roles bring to any policy conversation and a recipe for disaster begins to form.[38]

Urban school system reforms are typically complex undertakings with multiple elements, planned and otherwise, changing at the same time. Assessing effects, even with access to good data and sophisticated analytic tools, as has been the case in Chicago, remains an uncertain undertaking. Different analysts, such as Brian A. Jacob and I, can easily come to somewhat different conclusions. The overarching lesson is the need to maintain some humility about what is known and some caution in the forcefulness with which arguments are made, based on this evidence, about what should happen with regard to the education of other people's children.

Notes

1. For a detailed description of Chicago's phase I decentralization reform, see G. Alfred Hess, *School Restructuring, Chicago Style* (Newbury Park, Calif.: Corwin, 1991); G. Alfred Hess, *Restructuring Urban Schools: A Chicago Perspective* (New York:

Teachers College Press, 1995); and Anthony S. Bryk and others, *Charting Chicago School Reform: Democratic Localism as a Lever for Change* (Boulder, Colo.: Westview Press, 1998).

2. The administration of the policy was more complex than was reported in the public media. Certain groups of students, primarily in special education and those enrolled in bilingual programs, were excluded from the policy. In addition, district officials granted some waivers from the policy, especially around grade retention. For more details on the policy, its implementation, and its short-term effects, see Melissa Roderick and others, *Ending Social Promotion: Results from the First Two Years* (Chicago: Consortium on Chicago School Research, 1999); and Melissa Roderick and others, *Update: Ending Social Promotion; Passing, Retention, and Achievement Trends among Promoted and Retained Students, Data Brief* (Chicago: Consortium on Chicago School Research, 2000).

3. In the spring of 2002, three elementary schools were designated for closing and reopening as Renaissance schools—in essence a reconstitution plan. For further details on the high school reconstitutions in Chicago, see G. Alfred Hess Jr., "Accountability and Support in Chicago: Consequences for Students," in Diane Ravitch, ed., *Brookings Papers on Education Policy 2002* (Brookings, 2002), pp. 339–87.

4. For a thorough analysis of the state of professional development opportunities in the Chicago public schools (CPS) during the phase II reform, see Mark A. Smylie and others, *Teacher Professional Development in Chicago: Supporting Effective Practice* (Chicago: Consortium on Chicago School Research, 2001). They report that only a quarter of Chicago's teachers judge their professional development opportunities to be of high quality. While somewhat more positive reports were found in probation schools, the overall quality of professional development in Chicago was viewed as weak.

5. Because of the limits of space in an edited volume of this sort, my account here focuses only on findings about elementary schools (grades K–8). Fortunately, a good summary of the results of high-stakes accountability in Chicago's high schools exists elsewhere. See Hess, "Accountability and Support in Chicago." Hess's findings are generally corroborated in an independent series of reports recently released by the consortium. See Elaine M. Allensworth and Shazia Rafiullah Miller, *Declining High School Enrollments: An Exploration of Causes; Report of the State of Chicago Public High Schools: 1993 to 2000 Series* (Chicago: Consortium on Chicago School Research, 2002); Shazia Rafiullah Miller, Elaine M. Allensworth, and Julie Reed Kochanek, *Student Performance: Course Taking, Test Scores, and Outcomes; Report of the State of Chicago Public High Schools: 1993 to 2000 Series* (Chicago: Consortium on Chicago School Research, 2000); and Shazia Rafiullah Miller and Robert M. Gladden, *Changing Special Education Enrollment: Causes and Distribution among Schools; Report of the State of Chicago Public High Schools: 1993 to 2000 Series* (Chicago: Consortium on Chicago School Research, 2000). The results reported in these studies on CPS high schools are consistent with the findings presented here on the impact of phase II reforms at the elementary level.

6. For a documentation of this effect and appropriate adjustments for it, see John Q. Easton and others, *Annual CPS Test Trend Review, 1999* (Chicago: Consortium on Chicago School Research, 2000).

7. On this point, see John Q. Easton and others, *Annual CPS Test Trend Review, 2000* (Chicago: Consortium on Chicago School Research, 2001).

8. For race/ethnicity trends in student performance on the Iowa Tests of Basic Skills (ITBS) in Chicago, see Todd Rosenkranz, *2001 CPS Test Trend Review: Iowa Tests of Basic Skills, Research Data Brief of the Academic Productivity Series* (Chicago: Consortium on Chicago School Research, 2002).

9. Rosenkranz, *2001 CPS Test Trend Review.*

10. The forms used in 1993 and 1994 were reused for the second time in 1995 and 1996. Beginning in 1997, these two forms, plus a third form, were administered on a rotating basis by the system up to four times each year through 2001.

11. The Consortium on Chicago School Research series reports average test score trends by age group, not percent at national norms by grade level. By focusing on age cohorts, it controls for grade retention effects (that is, problem 1 identified above). The consortium indicator is in essence the students' average achieved status for a given number of years of schooling. The indicator series also maintains a common definition over time for the inclusion of bilingual students in response to problem 2, and it attempts to do the same thing with regard to special education students (problem 4) to the extent that test data are available but not included in the CPS reports. In addition, threshold statistics, such as the percent at national norms, are insensitive to changes in the academic performance of students who are either very low or very high achieving. A simple average of all the test scores is preferable for these reasons. The average achievement statistic also provides some buffer on problem 5 as well. For a further discussion of potential inferential artifacts embedded in threshold indicators, see Anthony S. Bryk and others, *Academic Productivity of Chicago Public Elementary Schools* (Chicago: Consortium on Chicago School Research, 1998). No controls are introduced in this consortium indicator for changing demographics across the CPS over time or for possible testwiseness or test cheating effects (problems 3 and 6, respectively.)

12. Rob H. Meyer, "Value-Added Indicators of School Performance," in E. Hanushek and D. W. Jorgensen, eds., *Improving the Performance of America's Schools* (Washington: National Academy Press 1996), pp. 197–223, reports on a systematic study of efforts to judge school improvement from only cross-sectional data. Meyer demonstrates that, in some cases, average annual test score reports for a school could indicate declining student achievement even though the school is having a very positive impact on the children it has the opportunity to educate. A school with many highly mobile new immigrant students is a prototype case in this regard.

13. The basic logic of the evidence presented in this chapter was first developed as part of a technical project to assess individual school productivity changes during phase I of Chicago's reform. See Bryk and others, *Academic Productivity of Chicago Public Elementary Schools.* A parallel report on developments under phase II of reform

is now in preparation. The analytic models use longitudinal student-level data to develop empirical Bayes estimates of the valued-added to student learning in each grade for each school each year. Trends in these value-added estimates over time represent the most precise evidence about changing school and district productivity. The analytic models are a specific example of the strategy recommended by Eric A. Hanushek and Margaret E. Raymond, in chapter 6 in this volume, of using an individual gain score model as the basis for school accountability measures.

In the interest of simplicity of presentation in this chapter, I rely mainly on the gain score data to illustrate my points. The trends in these descriptive statistics are consistent with those found in the model-based longitudinal analyses. These findings are also consistent regardless of whether these data are analyzed in the grade equivalent or in an item response theory metric. Although the latter has some favorable technical properties, again in the interest of simplicity of presentation, the norm-referenced metric is relied on primarily here.

In the original Bryk and others, *Academic Productivity of Chicago Public Elementary Schools,* my colleagues and I had access only to students' test records. Students were included in a school's report if their test scores in consecutive years had the same school identification. As a result, only about 60 percent of the students entered into any given analysis. Subsequently, we gained access to CPS administrative history files, which have direct information about student enrollment. In our more recent analyses, we include any student who is enrolled in a school as of October 1 and is tested in that school the following spring. This raises our inclusion rates above 80 percent. The maximum possible attainable rate is about 90 percent, because each year about 5 percent of the students eligible for testing fail to record a valid score and a student must have data from two consecutive years to be included. The remaining 10 percent are excluded because they transfer during the academic year or are administrative recording errors, which interfere with a proper data match.

14. These are based on all of the individual student-level data available. In other analyses, only students who were enrolled for the first time in a grade were considered to control for possible cumulative effects associated with the end of social promotion initiative. The same pattern of results occurs in the reduced data set. Although Brian A. Jacob raises an important general concern in this regard in chapter 12 in this volume, no evidence was found that it materially affects the results presented here.

15. See Bryk and others, *Academic Productivity of Chicago Public Elementary Schools.*

16. Because of the noise introduced in the gain score trends by the CPS use of different test forms over time, I have presented here average gains from two consecutive years. This averaging washes out much of the noise in the data series. In the actual model-based analyses in Bryk and others, *Academic Productivity of Chicago Public Elementary Schools,* extensive controls for year-to-year form effects are introduced through use of locally equated Item Response Theory measures. Again, the descriptive results presented here are consistent with the model-based findings.

17. Chicago public schools did not operate under a test-driven high-stakes reform during phase I. Although the School Reform Act of 1988 aimed to raise student

achievement, no explicit rewards or sanctions were applied based on the annual ITBS test score reports. Instead, the reform encouraged broad-based school restructuring, which admittedly might take several years to effect. Under such low-stakes circumstances, standardized test score trends represent a more reliable indicator of changes in overall effectiveness. That is, if a school truly improves, some signs of it should be seen in these data.

18. Computing these is complicated by the fact that the pooled within school student-level standard deviation varies by grade level and test form, and these effects are a complex average across both. For purposes of these calculations, I have used a standard deviation 1.4 and 1.2, respectively, for reading and mathematics, which is what might typically be found in grade six ITBS data.

19. Brian A. Jacob, in "Accountability, Incentives, and Behavior: The Impact of High-Stakes Testing in the Chicago Public Schools," Working Paper 8968 (Cambridge, Mass.: National Bureau of Economic Research, June 2002), has analyzed students' item-level test score results. He demonstrates that, following the introduction of the high-stakes reforms, students became much more likely to complete the test instead of leaving a string of blank responses at the end. Because no penalty is imposed for guessing on the ITBS, even a random bubbling of responses as time is running out is likely to improve a student's test score.

20. See Brian A. Jacob and Steven D. Levitt, "Rotten Apples: An Investigation of the Prevalence and Predictors of Teacher Cheating," *Quarterly Journal of Economics* (forthcoming). These results are best read as estimating a lower bound for the actual incidence of cheating. Jacob and Levitt's simulations indicate that, while they had high statistical power to detect extensive cheating by teachers, more modest amounts of classroom cheating were likely to go undetected. In addition, their analysis focuses on only one form of cheating, the bubbling of extra answers for children (or erasing and correcting answers). They did not estimate, for example, the prevalence of allowing students extra time during testing, or explicit prepping of children on the exact items that might appear on the test, or numerous other creative ways that one could cheat once incentives to do so exist.

I assume that each of these factors has primarily a one-time effect. For example, if students increased their testing effort in 1997 because of the accountability stakes, this would appear in their estimated learning gain that first year. This effort effect, however, is now part of the base achievement for computing the next year's gains. Students would have to further increase their efforts for the enlarged gain recorded in 1997 to continue to appear. The same is true for cheating. The only way that cheating effects continue to drive up the learning gains would be if the scope of the cheating grew over time. Similarly, the effect on learning gains associated with lengthening of the academic year (before testing) occurs only in the year that the policy is introduced. After that, this, too, is in the base for subsequent computations.

21. These problems affect all efforts to draw inferences from cross-cohort data regardless of whether extensive covariate adjustment models are used (see Jacob, "Accountability, Incentives, and Behavior") or individual growth curve modeling strategies [see Melissa Roderick, Brian Jacob, and Anthony Bryk, "Evaluating

Chicago's Efforts to End Social Promotion," in L. Lynn and C. Heinrich, eds., *Governance and Performance: New Perspectives* (Georgetown University Press, 2000); and Melissa Roderick, Brian A. Jacob, and Anthony Bryk, "The Impact of High-Stakes Testing in Chicago on Student Achievement in Promotional Gate Grades," *Educational Evaluation and Policy Analysis*, vol. 24, no. 4 (Winter 2002), pp. 333–57]. Neither approach explicitly represents the differences across cohorts in the accumulated value-added to learning that may be experienced. This can be seen clearly by examination of equations (1) and (3) in Eric A. Hanushek and Margaret E. Raymond, "Lessons for the Design of State Accountability Systems," the conference version of chapter 6 in this volume. Traditional statistical modeling strategies are principally concerned with controlling for the cross-cohort differences in background characteristics that affect student learning [that is, the X's in equation (1)]. Even if it is assumed that different cohorts have identical students including identical prior achievement levels, and so the X effects subtract out in the cross-cohort comparisons, the cohorts are still not equivalent because each will have been exposed to a different history of school effects [that is, the accumulated δ_{iGt} in equation (1)]. The later cohorts in the Chicago data accumulate larger increments, δ_{iGt}, to their learning as a result of the gradual increasing effectiveness of the phase I reforms. Moreover, even in the absence of new productivity improvements from phase II, the subsequent δ_{iGt} for later cohorts would be expected to be larger than for earlier cohorts. Thus, even absent a new treatment effect, later cohorts would now be expected to outperform their earlier counterparts.

22. See Christopher Jencks and M. Phillips, eds., *The Black-White Test Score Gap* (Brookings, 1998).

23. See Roderick and others, *Ending Social Promotion.*

24. This is based on tabulations provided by the Consortium on Chicago School Research. Closely related evidence can be found in Easton and others, *Annual CPS Test Trend Review, 2000*; and Rosenkranz, *2001 CPS Test Trend Review.*

25. Interpreting these results is complex because many Hispanic students during phase II were not subject to the social promotion policy and their test scores were not included in the annual accountability reports. Their relative improvements during the later 1990s merit further investigation.

26. For a general review of the finding on the introduction of the end of social promotion initiative, see Roderick and others, *Ending Social Promotion*; and Roderick and others, *Update*. See also Melissa Roderick and Mimi Engel, "The Grasshopper and the Ant: Motivational Responses of Low-Achieving Students to High-Stakes Testing," *Educational Evaluation and Policy Analysis*, vol. 23, no. 3 (2001), pp. 197–227. For a more detailed technical discussion of the academic-year incentive effects, see Jacob, Roderick, and Bryk, "The Impact of High-Stakes Testing in Chicago on Student Achievement in Promotional Gate Grades." The results on student learning gains, presented in this line of research, also use cross-cohort status comparisons for purposes of assessing effects. As a result, they, too, are subject to the modeling biases associated with differences in the accumulated prior reform effects.

27. See Melissa Roderick, Mimi Engel, and Jenny Nagaoka, *Ending Social Promotion: Results from Summer Bridge* (Chicago: Consortium on Chicago School Research, 2003). See also Melissa Roderick, Brian Jacob, and Anthony S. Bryk, "Summer in the City: Achievement Gains in Chicago's Summer Bridge Program," in G. D. Borman and M. Boulay, eds., *Summer Learning: Research Policies and Programs* (Mahwah, N.J.: Lawrence Erlbaum Associates, forthcoming.)

28. See Roderick, Engel, and Nagaoka, *Ending Social Promotion.*

29. Students retained at the end of summer made small or no gains as a result of the summer school program. Because these students recognized virtually no summer school effect to begin with, it is very unlikely that any significant residual effect occurred. Because these students were subject to both summer school and retention effects, with the latter dependent on the former, Roderick, Engel, and Nagaoka, in *Ending Social Promotion,* were unable to separate the individual component effects for these students in their analysis.

30. These Chicago summer school results are also consistent with the findings of a metanalysis of summer school effects conducted by Harris Cooper and others, *Making the Most of Summer School: A Meta-Analysis and Narrative Review*, monographs of the Society for Research in Child Development 65, No. 260 (Malden, Mass.: Blackwell, 2000).

31. Fred Newmann, Anthony S. Bryk, and Jenny Nagaoka, *Authentic Intellectual Work and Standardized Tests: Conflict or Coexistence?* (Chicago: Consortium on Chicago School Research, 2001).

32. See Fred M. Newmann and Associates, *Authentic Achievement: Restructuring Schools for Intellectual Quality* (San Francisco: Jossey-Bass, 1996).

33. G. Alfred Hess, *Examining Achievement Differences in Predominately African American Elementary School,* report of the Center for Urban School Policy (Northwestern University, 2001).

34. On the problems that can occur in this regard in urban schools, see Bets Ann Smith, *It's About Time: Opportunities to Learn in Chicago's Elementary Schools* (Chicago: Consortium on Chicago School Research, 1998).

35. See Roderick and others, *Ending Social Promotion.*

36. See Richard F. Elmore, "The Role of Local School Districts in Instructional Improvement," in S. H. Fuhrman, ed., *Designing Coherent Education Policy: Improving the System* (San Francisco: Jossey-Bass, 1993), pp. 96–124.; Richard Elmore and Deanna Burney, *Investing in Teacher Learning: Staff Development and Instructional Improvement in Community School District # 2, New York City* (New York: National Commission on Teaching and America's Future, 1997); L. D'Amico and others, *Examining the Implementation and Effectiveness of a Districtwide Instructional Improvement Effort,* paper presented at the annual meeting of the American Educational Research Association, Seattle, 2001; and Amy Hightower and others, eds., *School Districts and Instructional Renewal* (New York: Teachers College Press, 2002). See also David K. Cohen and Heather C. Hill, *Learning Policy* (Yale University Press, 2001).

37. Fred Newmann and others, "Instructional Program Coherence: What It Is and Why It Should Guide School Improvement Policy," *Educational Evaluation and Policy Analysis*, vol. 23, no. 4 (2001), pp. 297–321.

38. See, for example, Stanley S. Litow's effusive comments about the efficacy of high-stakes accountability in reaction to the rather negative assessments of its impact in Chicago on high schools offered by Hess in "Accountability and Support in Chicago." Stanley S. Litow, "Comment," in Diane Ravitch, ed., *Brookings Papers on Education Policy 2002* (Brookings, 2002), pp. 374–79.

12

A Closer Look at Achievement Gains under High-Stakes Testing in Chicago

BRIAN A. JACOB

I n January 2002 President George W. Bush signed into law the No Child
Left Behind Act of 2001, ushering in a new era of educational accountability. School reforms designed to hold students and teachers accountable for
student achievement are already in place throughout the country. Statutes in
twenty-five states explicitly link student promotion to performance on state
or district assessments. At the same time, eighteen states reward teachers and
administrators on the basis of exemplary student performance and twenty
states sanction school staff on the basis of poor student performance. Many
states and districts have passed legislation allowing the takeover or closure of
schools that do not show improvement.[1]

Advocates of test-based accountability claim that such policies will motivate students and teachers to work harder, cause parents to become more
involved in their children's education, and force school administrators to
implement more effective instruction. Pointing to Chicago, North Carolina,
and Texas, they argue that test-based accountability can substantially improve
student learning. Critics of test-based accountability respond that such policies lead to a host of undesirable outcomes, including a narrowing of the curriculum and a shift away from low-stakes subjects and untested skills. They
also worry that accountability will foster behaviors designed to game the system, such as placing low-ability students in special education where they will
either not be tested or receive special accommodation on the exams. Perhaps

the most serious criticism of high-stakes testing is that it leads to inflated test scores that do not truly reflect students' knowledge or skills and therefore cannot be generalized to other outcome measures.

In 1996 the Chicago public schools (CPS) became one of the first large, urban school districts to implement high-stakes testing, introducing a comprehensive accountability program that incorporated incentives for both students and teachers. Beginning in 1996, Chicago schools in which less than 15 percent of students met national norms in reading were placed on probation. If student performance did not improve in these schools, teachers and administrators were subject to reassignment or dismissal. At the same time, the CPS took steps to end social promotion, the practice of passing students to the next grade regardless of their academic ability. Students in third, sixth, and eighth grades were required to meet minimum standards in reading and mathematics to advance to the next grade (see chapter 11 in this volume). In previous research, I found that the accountability policy in Chicago led to a substantial increase in student achievement.[2] However, others have argued that the achievement gains in Chicago may have been inflated by excessive test preparation or cheating and therefore do not reflect real gains.

Did High-Stakes Testing Lead to Higher Test Scores?

In previous research, I found that the accountability policy in Chicago led to a substantial increase in student achievement.[3] Anthony S. Bryk (see chapter 11 in this volume), however, contends that the test score improvements witnessed in Chicago may have been caused by a variety of factors other than the accountability policy. How can the apparently disparate findings from the two studies be reconciled?

Figure 12-1 shows that observed math and reading scores on the Iowa Tests of Basic Skills (ITBS) increased substantially in Chicago during the 1990s. As Bryk points out, however, a number of factors might explain this pattern other than the accountability policy—for example, changes in student composition, a shift in the distribution of students across grades, changes in exclusion rates, and so on. My research attempted to account for all of these factors. To control for the fact that retention has changed the distribution of students across grades, I limited my analysis to students who were in a particular grade for the first time (that is, those students who had not been retained), which in practice is roughly equivalent to grouping students by age as Bryk suggests. To account for demographic shifts in the student population, I controlled for an extremely rich set of student and neighborhood characteristics. I also conditioned on students' prior achievement.

Figure 12-1. *Observed versus Predicted Achievement Levels in Chicago, 1993–2000*

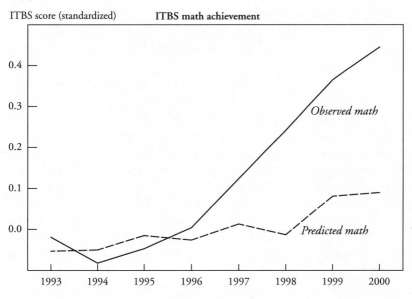

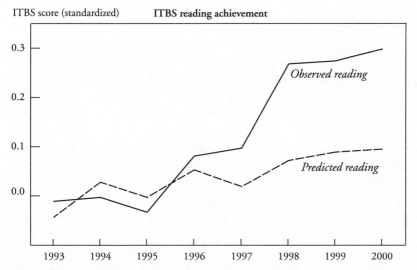

Notes: ITBS = Iowa Tests of Basic Skills. The sample includes third-, sixth-, and eighth-grade students from 1993 to 2000, excluding retainees and students whose scores were not reported. Scores are standardized separately for each grade using the 1993 student-level mean and standard deviation. The predicted scores are derived from an ordinary least squares regression on pre-policy cohorts (1993 to 1996) that includes controls for student, school, and neighborhood demographics as well as prior student achievement and a linear time trend.

This not only controls for demographic changes in the student population that cannot be picked up with the variables described above, but also helps to distinguish the effect of the accountability policy from that of earlier reform efforts. Finally, I accounted for preexisting trends in student performance in the district, measuring the impact of the accountability policy as the deviation from this trend.

After accounting for these factors, one can predict what student achievement in Chicago would have looked like in the absence of the accountability policy. The difference between the observed and predicted trends represents the impact of the reforms. Figure 12-1 shows that the magnitude of the effect was equivalent to 0.20 to 0.30 standard deviations, an extremely large improvement as educational programs are concerned. To check these findings, I conducted a series of sensitivity analyses in which I re-ran the estimates using a variety of different specifications and samples. For example, to isolate form effects, I limit the analysis to years in which identical forms were given such as 1994, 1996, and 1998 (form L) and 1993, 1995, and 2000 (form K). While the exact estimates vary slightly across these various specifications, in all cases I find that the accountability policy has a statistically significant and educationally meaningful effect on ITBS scores.

Finally, I explored an issue not raised by Bryk—the possibility that achievement gains in Chicago may have reflected broader trends taking place at the state or federal level. To determine whether this was the case, I compared the achievement trends in Chicago with a control group that was likely to have experienced similar economic and policy changes: other large, urban districts in the Midwest such as Indianapolis, Gary, Cincinnati, St. Louis, and Milwaukee. I found that achievement in Chicago increased dramatically in the late nineties even in comparison with trends in these districts. This provides additional support for the contention that accountability was responsible for the increasing achievement in Chicago.

How then can one reconcile the results of the two studies? The crucial difference between the two analyses involves the way in which prior achievement is measured. Bryk uses a one-year achievement gain as the primary outcome measure. He does this not only to control for changes in student composition or preparation that should not be attributed to the current school regime, but also because he believes (justifiably) that annual achievement changes capture an important aspect of school productivity.

While these are both legitimate objectives, I believe that the emphasis on one-year achievement gains creates several problems at both the analytical and conceptual level. First, when one looks at cohorts after the first year of the accountability policy (that is, cohorts from 1998 to 2001), the student's initial or incoming achievement score will have been attained under the high-stakes regime. This means that any improvements realized in the initial or early years of accountability would not show up in Bryk's analysis of the later cohorts.[4] To avoid this problem, I controlled for student achievement three years before the introduction of the accountability policy, which essentially involves looking at three-year value-added gains as opposed to one-year value-added gains. In assessing the achievement level of a student in the 1999 cohort, for example, I controlled for the student's achievement in 1996, the year immediately before the introduction of the policy. This provides a measure of the overall impact of the policy.

It is certainly reasonable, however, to ask how the effect of the accountability policy has changed since its implementation in 1996. For example, one could imagine that the policy had a large initial effect stemming from the publicity that faded in later years. Conversely, one might imagine that the effect of the policy increased after several years, as teachers and administrators learned ways to more effectively support low-achieving students or as more resources became available for at-risk students. Bryk addresses this question when he compares the annual learning gains of, for example, the 1997 cohort with the 2000 cohort.

Although the question is important, answering it is difficult because the social promotion policy has changed the composition of students in many grades and differentially influenced student incentives across grades. Starting in 1996–97, many low-achieving students in grades three, six, and eight were not promoted to the next grade. In 2001 the social promotion policy changed, requiring administrators to take into account more subjective measures of student achievement in making retention decisions. This means that the earlier and later cohorts under the accountability policy (for example, the 1997 cohort versus the 2000 cohort) most likely contained very different groups of students. Hence, when one compares the annual learning gains for these two groups, it is extremely difficult to know whether any differences stem from changes in the effectiveness of the accountability policy or simply are a result of the fact that these students were different to begin with, so that they would have experienced different learning gains regardless of the accountability policy.

An additional concern with focusing on annual achievement gains involves the implicit expectations of success that this approach establishes. The goal of most educational reform is to improve the level of student achievement or, alternatively, to shift the rate of achievement growth to a higher level, so that student achievement levels increase over time. By focusing on changes in the growth rate, I worry that an expectation is implicitly being created that success requires improvement that not only continues but also becomes more rapid each year and continues indefinitely. While this may be desirable and feasible for several years, particularly in extremely low-achieving systems with considerable room for improvement, it is clearly unsustainable in the long run.

While my analysis suggests that the accountability policy had a substantial, positive impact on ITBS scores in Chicago, this is not to say that the high-stakes testing in Chicago was a panacea. Some evidence suggests that achievement has leveled off in recent years and that the policy has had several unintended consequences such as increasing special education placements and off-grade retention.[5] And, perhaps most important, some have questioned whether the achievement gains are real.

Were the Achievement Gains in Chicago Real?

One of the most common critiques of high-stakes testing in Chicago and other cities or states is that the improvement in student performance is more apparent than real. That is, the rising test scores do not reflect actual increases in student knowledge and skill. This is often called *test score inflation*. Although the notion of score inflation does embody some legitimate concerns, the term is poorly understood and often misinterpreted.

What Is Test Score Inflation?

To understand what people mean when they claim that test scores are inflated or achievement gains are not real, one must first understand something about educational testing. Achievement tests are samples of questions from a larger domain of knowledge. They are meant to measure a latent construct, such as knowledge of mathematics or the ability to read and comprehend written material. The important point is that the score on the test itself is not as important as the inference that can be drawn from the score (that is, what the test score reveals about the student's set of knowledge and skills). In most cases, the score and the inference are thought of as identical. If a student scores high on an exam, he or she must know a considerable amount of math, reading, geography, and so on. However, this might not be true. In the case of cheating, for example, a high score does not necessarily reflect true understanding.

When one hears that high-stakes accountability leads to inflated test scores, it means that the test scores are no longer a good indicator of the overall student skills and knowledge and, by extension, the achievement gains are misleading because they may not reflect a more general mastery of the subject. A number of reasons can be cited for why test score inflation could occur. While cheating is undoubtedly the most egregious example, test preparation is perhaps the most common. When teachers focus instruction on particular topics and skills that are commonly measured on the high-stakes exam, students may make substantial improvements on the exam because of their improvement on items that test these specific understandings, instead of a general improvement in the larger subject area.

The notion of test score inflation, therefore, relates to what social scientists sometimes refer to as generalizability. Researchers have found considerable evidence of test score inflation throughout the country during the past two decades. In 1987 J. J. Cannell discovered what has become known as the "Lake Wobegon effect"—the fact that a disproportionate number of states and districts report being "above the national norm."[6] This phenomenon was documented in several studies, one of which concluded that teaching to the test played a role in these results.[7] Similarly, R. L. Linn and S. B. Dunbar found that states have made smaller gains on the National Assessment of Educational Progress (NAEP) than their own achievement exams. This finding suggests that the gains on the state exams do not generalize to the NAEP, which is considered an important benchmark of student learning in the United States.[8]

Less evidence is available on whether accountability programs lead to inflated test scores. However, research on Kentucky and Texas suggests that achievement gains realized under a state test-based accountability program did not fully generalize to student performance as measured by the NAEP. D. M. Koretz and S. I. Barron found that students in Kentucky improved more rapidly on the state's exam, the Kentucky Instructional Results Information System (KIRIS), than on other assessments.[9] Between 1992 and 1994, for example, KIRIS scores in fourth-grade mathematics increased by about 0.60 standard deviations in contrast to NAEP scores, which increased 0.17 standard deviations. Moreover, the NAEP gains were roughly comparable to the national increase and not statistically different from gains in many other states. Stephen P. Klein and colleagues conducted a similar analysis of Texas, comparing performance trends on the Texas Assessment of Academic Skills (TAAS) and the NAEP in the 1990s.[10] The researchers in this case found that TAAS scores increased by considerably more than NAEP scores. For example, in fourth-grade reading, TAAS scores for black students increased by roughly 0.50 standard deviations while NAEP scores only increased by 0.15 standard deviations.

Concern about Test Score Inflation

The generalizability of achievement gains is certainly an important issue, but should it be the sole concern when examining student performance? Even if an accountability program produced true, meaningful gains, no one would expect gains on one test to be completely reflected in data from other tests because of the inherent differences across exams. Even the most comprehensive achievement exam can cover only a fraction of the possible skills and topics within a particular domain. For this reason, different exams often lead to different inferences about student mastery, regardless of whether any type of accountability policy is in place. For example, simply by changing the relative weight of algebra versus geometry items, the NAEP influences the black-white achievement gap.

Yet in discussing how to interpret test score gains, even testing experts such as Daniel M. Koretz occasionally slip into language that seems to neglect the value of gains in particular areas. "When scores increase, students clearly have improved the mastery of the sample included in the test. This is of no interest, however, unless the improvement justifies the inference that students have attained greater mastery of the domain the test is intended to represent."[11] Does this mean that if children truly improve their ability to add fractions, interpret line graphs, or identify the main idea of a written passage, this is of no interest?

Most people would agree that these improvements, while limited to specific skills or topics, are important. This suggests an alternative criterion by which to judge changes in student performance, which I will describe, for lack of a better phrase, as meaningfulness. In this framework, achievement gains on test items that measure particular skills or understandings may be meaningful, even if the student's overall test score does not fully generalize to other exams.[12] For achievement gains to be meaningful, they must result from greater student understanding and they must be important in some educational sense. Because the idea of whether test score improvements are meaningful is imprecise, it is perhaps best illustrated by counterexample.

Test score gains that result from cheating on the part of students or teachers would not be considered meaningful because they do not reflect greater understanding on the part of students.[13] In previous research, I, along with S. Levitt, have examined the incidence of teacher cheating in the Chicago public schools and how it changed after the introduction of the accountability policy.[14] Based on an examination of unexpectedly large achievement gains and unusual item response patterns, we found that the prevalence of cheating increased by 30 to 40 percent after 1996, although the absolute magnitude of cheating was so small that it can explain only a small part of the overall test score gains.

Similarly, most people would not consider increases in performance owing to an improvement in testing conditions as meaningful. In a study of accountability in Florida, David N. Figlio and Joshua F. Winicki found that low-achieving Virginia schools provided unusually high-calorie lunches to students on days when standardized tests were administered, presumably to increase awareness and concentration during the exams.[15] Such sugar-induced gains would not be considered meaningful.

A less clear-cut example involves student effort. Various studies have shown that accountability policies lead students to take standardized exams more seriously, either by working harder during the school year, or concentrating harder during the exam, or both. While working harder clearly represents meaningful gains, concentrating harder may not. One could argue that teaching students to try hard in critical situations is a useful thing. But the observed improvements in student performance would represent greater effort, not greater understanding.

Finally, achievement gains that are limited to a particular question format to such an extent that the knowledge appears to reflect simple memorization may not be meaningful. A classic example of this situation comes from a study of New Jersey state assessment in the 1970s. L. A. Shepard found that when students were asked to add decimals in a vertical format, the state passing rate was 86 percent, but when they were asked to perform calculations of the same difficulty in a horizontal format, the passing rate fell to 46 percent.[16] For subtraction of decimals, the passing rates were 78 and 30 percent, respectively. The author suggests that this differential was due to the fact that schools had traditionally taught students decimal arithmetic in a vertical format, and the students did not understand the concept well enough to translate it to a different format. If this were the case, one might conclude that the achievement represented by the vertical scores was not meaningful.

This example, however, also demonstrates the difficulty inherent in such judgments. One might argue that the format differences represented by vertical and horizontal arithmetic entail real differences in required skills and difficulty. Horizontal problems require a student to understand place value well enough to know to center on the decimal point instead of right-justifying the decimals when rewriting the problems vertically (in their mind or on paper).[17] In addition, this example illustrates the fine line between generalizability and meaningfulness. Discounting the view that solving problems in a horizontal format entails different skills than solving problems in a vertical format, one would expect the ability to add or subtract fractions to generalize from vertical to horizontal format to be considered meaningful.

Evidence of Test Score Inflation in Chicago

One of the ways that people have investigated score inflation in high-stakes testing scenarios is to compare student performance trends across exams.[18] If the test score gains on the high-stakes exam are not accompanied by gains on other achievement exams, then the gains may not be generalizable and would thus be considered inflated.

In Chicago, elementary students have traditionally taken two exams. For many years, the district has administered the Iowa Tests of Basic Skills to students in grades three to eight. The ITBS is one of several standardized, multiple-choice exams used throughout the country (others include the Stanford Achievement Test and the Comprehensive Test of Basic Skills). Under the Chicago accountability policy, student promotion and school sanctions were determined solely by the student performance on the ITBS, making it the high-stakes exam. During the time period, Chicago elementary students took another standardized, multiple-choice exam administrated by the state, known as the Illinois Goals Assessment Program (IGAP).[19] Before 1996 the IGAP was arguably the higher-stakes exam because results appeared annually in local newspapers, although no direct consequences for students or schools were tied to the IGAP.[20] After 1996 the IGAP clearly became the low-stakes exam for students and teachers in Chicago in comparison with the ITBS.

ITBS performance in Chicago grew very slightly from 1990 to 1996 and then increased dramatically starting in 1997. In contrast, IGAP scores have increased steadily since around 1993, but no significant jump in achievement followed the introduction of the accountability policy.

What can be inferred from these trends? On the one hand, if student achievement is simply compared at the beginning and end of the decade, then the finding is that improvement on the two exams was roughly equivalent and the achievement gains could be largely generalizable. On the other hand, if how achievement in the late 1990s changed is considered in relation to the preexisting trends on each exam, then the finding is that the accountability policy had a large effect on ITBS scores but little if any effect on IGAP scores. The ITBS gains in Chicago thus were driven largely by test score inflation.[21]

At least two significant difficulties, however, arise in drawing either conclusion from the data. The first problem is that the ITBS and IGAP are different in both content and format. In mathematics, the ITBS places more emphasis on computation while the IGAP appears to give greater weight to problem-solving skills. The computation items that are on the IGAP are often asked in the context of a word problem. The general format of the reading comprehension sections on the two exams is similar—both ask students to read passages and then answer questions about the passage—but the IGAP consists of fewer, but longer passages, whereas the ITBS contains a greater number of passages, each of which is shorter. Perhaps more important, the questions on the IGAP may have multiple correct responses in comparison to the ITBS, which has only one correct response. The fact that the two exams displayed different trends before the introduction of the accountability policy suggests that they measure somewhat different concepts.

The natural solution is to adjust the ITBS and IGAP scores to account for such content differences. For example, one might attempt to estimate what the IGAP scores would have been if the exam had the same type and number of questions as the ITBS. Suppose that the IGAP exam contained two questions involving fractions and two questions involving decimals whereas the ITBS contained three fraction questions and only one decimal question. If students always answer fraction questions correctly and always answer decimal questions incorrectly, then the observed ITBS and IGAP scores would be 0.75 and 0.50, respectively. However, if the IGAP score is adjusted by assuming that the IGAP has the same composition of questions as the ITBS, students would do equally well on both exams.

In practice, this type of adjustment is probably only feasible in mathematics where test items can be categorized with relative precision.[22] To perform this type of exercise, one would need to know the exact item types and distribution of questions for both exams as well as the individual item-level results for at least one exam (and preferably both). Unfortunately, the information on the item distribution and on item results is available for the ITBS, but not for the IGAP.[23]

A second difficulty involves student effort. Students undoubtedly began to increase test-day effort for the ITBS after 1996. It is unclear how, if at all, effort levels changed on the IGAP. One might imagine that effort increased somewhat given the new climate surrounding testing. However, one might imagine that effort has declined insofar as teachers and students now view IGAP scores as largely irrelevant. If student effort on the ITBS increased at the same time as effort on the IGAP decreased, one would expect more rapid achievement growth on the ITBS even if exams were identical or learning were completely generalizable.

This situation in Chicago illustrates the limitations of using cross-test comparisons more generally.[24] Given the differences in composition between the two exams along with possible changes in student effort over the time period, it is extremely difficult to determine what one should expect to see under the best of circumstances where the learning gains were truly meaningful. Alternative strategies thus need to be explored for understanding the generalizability and meaningfulness of improving performance.

Achievement Gains under High-Stakes Testing in Chicago

One way to explore the generalizability and meaningfulness of achievement gains is to examine how changes in student performance varied across individual test items.

Improvement by Skill Area and Topic

The ITBS assesses student understanding in a variety of areas. The math section measures understanding of five broad areas: number concepts, estimation, problem solving, data interpretation, and computation. The computation portion consists of straightforward arithmetic problems—with no words or context—covering whole numbers, decimals, and fractions. The data interpretation section requires students to read and analyze information from various types of graphs, charts, and figures. The problem-solving items are essentially word problems that generally involve arithmetic but may involve more complicated concepts as well. The estimation problems are a mix of standard rounding items along with word problems that require students to have a good sense of appropriate order of magnitude in different situations. Finally, the section on number concepts measures understanding of a wide variety of skills and topics, including geometry, algebra, probability, and measurement. Questions in this section might include any of the following: basic addition of fractions, interpretation of a number line, operations with negative and positive numbers, identification of various shapes, calculation of area and perimeter, and the probability of drawing different color balls from an urn. In a broad sense, one might understand the computation and number concept sections as measuring basic skills while the other sections contain less straightforward questions that tap more complex skills or abilities.

Questions in the reading section are broken into three broad categories with many subcategories in each. The first category measures the ability to understand factual information in the passage, including the literal meaning of words used in the passage. The second group tests the ability to evaluate meaning, which refers to tasks such as identifying the author's purpose or viewpoint, determining the main idea, interpreting nonliteral language, and understanding the structure and style of the passage. The third category measures student ability to draw inferences, including skills such as inferring

Table 12-1. *Relationship between Test-Based Accountability and Achievement by Item Type*

Subject and item type	Proportion of students answering the type of item correctly in		Percentage point gain	Percent gain
	1994	1998		
Math				
Number concepts	0.497	0.568	0.071	0.142
Estimation	0.440	0.494	0.053	0.121
Problem solving	0.465	0.508	0.043	0.093
Data interpretation	0.478	0.534	0.055	0.115
Computation	0.516	0.584	0.068	0.132
Reading				
Construct evaluation meaning	0.491	0.545	0.054	0.110
Construct factual meaning	0.456	0.507	0.051	0.112
Construct inferential meaning	0.490	0.544	0.054	0.110

Notes: Sample consists of students in grades three, six, and eight for the first time who were tested and included for reporting purposes.

the feelings, motives, and traits of characters in a story, predicting likely outcomes, applying information, and drawing conclusions.

In earlier work, I found that on average students made substantially larger gains in computation and number concepts than in the other three areas (that is, data analysis, estimation, and problem solving). To illustrate this, table 12-1 presents descriptive statistics of ITBS achievement by item type and subtype for students in 1994 (under low stakes) and in 1998 (under high stakes). Achievement here is characterized by the proportion of students answering an item correctly. Looking first at the five broad item categories, students improved 7.1 percentage points on items involving number concepts and 6.8 percentage points on items involving computation. In contrast, students gained only 4.3 percentage points on problem-solving items and roughly 5.5 percentage points on data interpretation and estimation questions. Looking within categories at student performance on more detailed item types (not shown here), within computation students seemed to make the largest gains on fraction questions. Within some of the less arithmetic-based sections—estimation, problem solving, and data interpretation—students seemed to make the most improvement in the most straightforward or simplest types of problems. Within data interpretation, for example, students made the largest gains on questions requiring them to simply read amounts from charts or graphs. Within estimation, students made larger gains on items involving standard rounding than on items involving order of magnitude or compensation.

Overall, these results suggest that math teachers may have focused on specific content areas in response to the accountability policy, which would suggest that the math gains might not generalize well to other performance measures. Given the considerable weight placed on mathematical computation and number concepts in the ITBS, perhaps along with the relative ease of teaching these skills, it may not be surprising that teachers chose to focus on these areas. However, this means that if students take an alternative exam that does not place as much weight on these skills, such as the IGAP or the NAEP, they are not likely to score at the same level as they did on the ITBS. The result is that the ITBS math gains may not fully generalize to other achievement measures, leading to the claim that the ITBS scores are inflated.

In contrast, in reading students made comparable improvement in all three areas, suggesting that the improvement in reading performance may be more generalizable. The bottom panel of table 12-1 shows descriptive statistics for reading performance by item type. Students gained a little over 5 percentage points on all items. When one looks at the most detailed item categories, a noticeable pattern does not emerge. While these aggregate results provide some insight, the accountability policy affected students and schools differently based on prior achievement levels. In particular, considerable concern has arisen that the lowest performing schools have responded to the policy by simply focusing on test preparation. In the same vein, others have worried that teachers in all schools have helped the lowest performing students to prepare for the test but little else. If this were true, one would expect the patterns of test score gains across items to differ for low- versus high-performing students and schools. For example, one might expect the gains in mathematical computation to be even larger in the lowest performing schools.

It is thus useful to explore how the pattern of item gains varies across students and schools. To do so, I estimate regression models showing the relationship between item type and achievement gain. The dependent variable in these models is the proportion of students who answered an item correctly in a particular year. The relevant unit of analysis in these models is the item times year. The key independent variables are the interactions between year and item type. The sample includes students in grades three, six, and eight in 1994, 1996, and 1998. The sample is limited to these cohorts because they took an identical form of the exam, allowing the most consistent comparison of item types over time. I consider only those students who were tested and whose scores were included for official reporting purposes, which excludes

Table 12-2. *Relationship between Item Type and Achievement on the ITBS Math Exam under High-Stakes Testing*

	Dependent variable = proportion of students answering the item correctly					
	Student prior achievement			School prior achievement		
Independent variable	Low	Medium	High	Low	Medium	High
High stakes	0.026	0.018	0.031	0.023	0.012	0.000
	(0.018)	(0.013)	(0.020)	(0.014)	(0.014)	(0.022)
Math computation * high stakes	0.025	0.033	0.025	0.027	0.025	0.016
	(0.011)	(0.010)	(0.016)	(0.009)	(0.009)	(0.014)
Number concepts * high stakes	0.020	0.030	0.025	0.024	0.023	0.016
	(0.011)	(0.009)	(0.015)	(0.008)	(0.009)	(0.013)
Estimation * high stakes	0.005	0.012	0.004	0.002	0.000	0.005
	(0.016)	(0.014)	(0.023)	(0.013)	(0.013)	(0.020)
Data analysis * high stakes	0.005	0.016	0.011	0.003	0.005	0.008
	(0.017)	(0.015)	(0.025)	(0.013)	(0.014)	(0.021)
R^2	0.925	0.952	0.848	0.957	0.959	0.888

Note: ITSB = Iowa Tests of Basic Skills. The sample consists of all tested and included students in grades three, six, and eight in years 1994, 1996, and 1998. The units of observation are item * year proportions, reflecting the proportion of students answering the item correctly in that year. Fixed effects for grade, main effects for item difficulty, item difficulty * 1998, and item position are included in the models but not shown here. The omitted category includes items that focus on problem-solving skills.

some bilingual and special education students. The sample is further limited to students who were in the particular grade for the first time, thereby excluding all retained students.

Table 12-2 shows the results for mathematics. Each column shows the results for a separate regression model with the columns corresponding to the sample of students used in the estimation. Standard errors are shown in parentheses under the coefficient estimates. Columns 1 to 3 show the results for low-, medium-, and high-achieving students, respectively. The prior achievement measure is based on an average of the student's math and reading score three years earlier, with the exception of third graders where second grade scores are used. Students scoring in the bottom quartile of the national distribution are considered low-achieving; those scoring in the second quartile are considered moderate-achieving; and those scoring above the 50th percentile are classified as high-achieving.[25] Because problem-solving items are the omitted category, the estimates in the first row are interpreted as the achievement gain for these items. The data in column 1 show that under the high-stakes testing regime low-achieving students were 2.6 percentage points more likely to correctly answer math questions tapping problem-solving skills than they were before the introduction of the accountability policy. The coefficient of 0.025 on the interaction variable computation times high stakes indicates that on average these low-achieving students improved 2.5 percentage points more on computation items than on problem-solving items, meaning that the overall improvement on computation items was 5.1 percentage points. Low-achieving students made similar gains on questions involving number concepts. In contrast, the gains on estimation and data analysis items were comparable to those on problem-solving items. Columns 2 and 3 show a generally similar pattern for moderate- and high-achieving students. Hence, regardless of prior achievement level, students appear to have improved more in math computation and number concepts than on other skill areas.

Columns 4 to 6 show how these results vary across different types of school achievement. The measure of prior school achievement is based on the percentage of students scoring at or above national norms on the ITBS reading exam in 1995.[26] Schools with less than 20 percent of students meeting norms are defined as low-achieving; those with 20–30 percent meeting norms are defined as moderate-achieving; and those with at least 30 percent meeting norms are defined as high-achieving. One can see that low- and moderate-achieving schools made greater overall gains than high-achieving schools under the accountability policy. This is consistent with the incentives generated by the policy, which placed low-achieving schools on probation. Regardless of prior achievement level, however, all schools appear to have improved more in computation and number concepts. While low-achieving schools improved in other areas such as problem solving and data analysis, higher achieving schools made little if any improvement in these areas.

Table 12-3 shows the regression results for reading. Two patterns stand out. First, high-achieving students and schools made smaller gains than their peers. For example, low-achieving students were roughly 4 percentage points more likely to correctly answer items on the reading exam following the introduction of the accountability policy whereas high-achieving students were no more likely to do so. Second, in contrast to mathematics, students made comparable gains across items. Regardless of prior achievement level, students and schools showed similar improvement on items measuring factual, inferential, and evaluative understandings.

In summary, the preceding item-level analysis suggests that observed gains in student achievement in Chicago as measured by the ITBS may generalize

Table 12-3. *Relationship between Item Type and Achievement Gain on the ITBS Reading Exam under High-Stakes Testing*

| | Dependent variable = proportion of students answering the item correctly | | | | | |
| | Student prior achievement | | | School prior achievement | | |
Independent variable	Low	Medium	High	Low	Medium	High
High stakes	0.046	0.022	0.001	0.044	0.035	0.012
	(0.022)	(0.021)	(0.032)	(0.016)	(0.031)	(0.028)
Construct factual meaning * high stakes	−0.006	−0.006	0.000	−0.002	0.001	0.003
	(0.014)	(0.012)	(0.019)	(0.010)	(0.010)	(0.017)
Construct inferential meaning * high stakes	−0.004	0.002	0.006	0.000	0.003	0.005
	(0.013)	(0.011)	(0.018)	(0.009)	(0.009)	(0.016)
R^2	0.888	0.937	0.835	0.948	0.954	0.860

Note: ITBS = Iowa Tests of Basic Skills. The sample consists of all tested and included students in grades three, six, and eight in years 1994, 1996, and 1998. The units of observation are item * year proportions, reflecting the proportion of students answering the item correctly in that year. Fixed effects for grade, main effects for item difficulty, item difficulty * 1998, and item position are included in the models but not shown here. The omitted category includes items that tap the construction of evaluative meaning.

to other measures of reading performance but may be less likely to generalize to other measures of math performance.

Can Guessing Explain the Achievement Gains?

The preceding analysis sheds some light on the generalizability of gains, but it alone does not help in determining whether the gains were meaningful. To shed light on this question, I investigate whether the achievement gains appear to have been driven by guessing. If this factor explains a large portion of the improvement, one might worry that student test-day efforts were driving the test score increases, in which case one might view them as less meaningful. This analysis will not prove that the gains were in fact meaningful.

Because no penalty is imposed for guessing on the ITBS (total score is determined solely by the number correct), the simplest way for a student to increase his or her expected score is to make sure that no items are left blank. Before the introduction of the accountability policy in Chicago, a surprisingly high proportion of students left one or more items of the ITBS exam blank. For example, table 12-4 shows that in 1994 only 58 and 77 percent of eighth-grade students completed the entire math and reading exams, respectively. (The higher completion rates in reading are likely because it is consid-

Table 12-4. *Relationship between Test-Based Accountability, Test Completion, and Guessing, by Student Ability*

	Math			Reading		
Category of student ability	1994	1998	Percentage point change	1994	1998	Percentage point change
All students						
Fraction of items completed	0.968	0.979	0.011	0.966	0.987	0.021
Fraction correct divided by fraction completed	0.466	0.520	0.054	0.508	0.558	0.050
No blanks	0.577	0.632	0.055	0.773	0.834	0.061
No final blanks	0.722	0.817	0.095	0.857	0.917	0.060
Guessing	0.171	0.234	0.063	0.043	0.083	0.040
Low-ability students (0–25 percentile)						
Fraction of items completed	0.960	0.973	0.013	0.956	0.973	0.017
Fraction correct divided by fraction completed	0.371	0.402	0.031	0.397	0.425	0.028
Guessing	0.148	0.227	0.079	0.034	0.086	0.052
Moderate-ability students (26–50 percentile)						
Fraction of items completed	0.970	0.980	0.010	0.969	0.982	0.013
Fraction correct divided by fraction completed	0.483	0.516	0.033	0.532	0.556	0.024
Guessing	0.203	0.259	0.056	0.051	0.090	0.039
High-ability students (51–99 percentile)						
Fraction of items completed	0.981	0.986	0.005	0.984	0.991	0.007
Fraction correct divided by fraction completed	0.650	0.680	0.030	0.717	0.733	0.016
Guessing	0.173	0.212	0.039	0.049	0.069	0.020

Note: Sample consists of all tested and included first-time eighth-grade students in 1994 and 1998. The prior achievement categories are based on the average of math and reading score in fifth grade, with the percentiles referring to percentiles on a national distribution. Guessing is measured by a series of identical, incorrect items in the last three questions on the exam (for example, AAA, BBB, CCC, or DDD).

erably shorter than the math exam, which consists of three separate subsections.) Most students did not leave many items blank. On average, students answered 97 percent of the questions on both exams.

As one would expect, test completion rates increased sharply under the high-stakes testing regime. The number of eighth graders who completed the entire math exam (that is, left no blank items) increased from 58 percent in 1994 to nearly 63 percent in 1998, an increase of 5.5 percentage points. Prior achievement here is measured as above. All of the patterns are replicated across the prior achievement groups. Not surprisingly, the greatest impact was for low-achieving students, largely because nearly all higher-achieving students had always finished the exam before high-stakes testing.

How much of the increased test completion was attributable to guessing versus trying to solve the problems? While it is impossible to determine with certainty whether a student guessed on any particular question, the pattern of responses across items provides some evidence. If students fill in a string of identical responses for the final questions on the exam (for example, AAA or CCC), it seems likely that the student simply meant to guess on these items. Because students may guess in a variety of other ways, however, the prevalence of identical responses at the end of the exam will understate the true level of guessing. Table 12-4 shows that the instances of strings with identical responses at the end of the exam increased from 17.1 to 23.4 percent between 1994 and 1998, an increase of roughly 37 percent. Guessing in reading increased by 93 percent. Not surprisingly, bottom quartile students showed the largest increases in guessing.

What percentage of the observed achievement gains in Chicago can be explained solely on the basis of the increase in guessing? If the increased test scores were due solely to guessing, the percent of questions answered might be expected to increase, but the percent of questions answered correctly (as a percent of all answered questions) would likely remain constant or perhaps even decline. The percent of questions answered has increased, but the percent answered correctly has also gone up, suggesting that the higher completion rates were not entirely the result of guessing. A more detailed analysis suggests that, at most, guessing can only explain 5 to 15 percent of achievement gains across grades and subjects.[27]

These results suggest that the achievement gains realized after the introduction of the accountability policy in Chicago are not simply from guessing. Early research has suggested that, while cheating appears to have increased in the late 1990s, the magnitude of the increase could explain only a tiny fraction of the overall achievement gains.[28] These results provide preliminary evidence that the achievement gains may be meaningful.

Conclusions

As states seek to implement the mandates of NCLB, educators will increasingly face the task of interpreting test score gains in the context of test-based accountability. Because of differences in content and emphasis across exams, gains on one test should not be expected to generalize completely to another test. Perhaps the most important question is whether the test score gains on any particular exam are meaningful—that is, whether they reflect a true increase in some set of student knowledge or skills. By carefully examining how achievement gains vary across items on a high-stakes exam, one may reach a better understanding of the performance changes under an accountability program.

Item-level analysis of test score gains in Chicago during the 1990s reveals several findings. First, the large observed math test score gains came disproportionately in the areas of computation and number concepts, areas that measure knowledge of basic skills more than complex thinking. This suggests that the improvement in math achievement may not generalize to other achievement measures that emphasize problem solving or more complex skills. In contrast, the improvements in reading appear to be spread relatively evenly across item types, suggesting that the gains may be more generalizable in this subject. Second, while guessing increased following the introduction of accountability, it alone can explain only a small fraction of the observed test score changes. This clearly does not prove that the test score gains in Chicago were meaningful, but it does eliminate one concern that has been raised in regard to increases in achievement.

While many questions about test-based accountability remain unanswered, researchers and policymakers must look beyond aggregate measures of student performance if they are to truly understand the impacts of these policies. At the same time, policymakers must be more careful in discussing test score inflation, distinguishing between concerns of generalizability and concerns of meaningfulness. As states and school districts begin to implement NCLB, it will be increasingly important to understand the nature of improvements in student performance.

Notes

1. "Quality Counts 2002," *Education Week*, vol. 21, no. 17 (2002), pp. 74–77.
2. B. Jacob, "Accountability, Incentives, and Behavior: Evidence from School Reform in Chicago," NBER Working Paper 8968 (Cambridge, Mass.: National Bureau of Economic Research, 2002).

3. Jacob, "Accountability, Incentives, and Behavior."

4. Economists and statisticians refer to these initial measures as endogenous.

5. The policy also led to relatively greater increases in math and reading performance as compared with science and social studies, which, while perhaps intended, may be criticized by some.

6. J. J. Cannell, *Nationally Normed Elementary Achievement Testing in America's Public Schools: How All Fifty States Are Above the National Average* (Daniels, W.Va.: Friends for Education, 1987).

7. Cannell, *Nationally Normed Elementary Achievement Testing in America's Public Schools;* R. L. Linn, M. E. Graue, and N. M. Sanders, "Comparing State and District Test Results to National Norms: The Validity of the Claims That 'Everyone Is Above Average,' " *Educational Measurement: Issues and Practice,* vol. 9, no. 3 (1990), pp. 5–14; and L. A. Shepard, "Inflated Test Score Gains: Is the Problem Old Norms or Teaching the Test?" *Educational Measurement: Issues and Practice,* vol. 9, no. 3 (1990), pp. 15–22.

8. R. L. Linn and S. B. Dunbar, "The Nation's Report Card Goes Home: Good News and Bad about Trends in Achievement," *Phi Delta Kappan,* vol. 72, no. 2 (October 1990), pp. 127–33.

9. D. M. Koretz and S. I. Barron, *The Validity of Gains on the Kentucky Instructional Results Information System* (Santa Monica, Calif.: RAND Corporation, 1998).

10. D. M. Koretz and others, "The Effects of High-Stakes Testing: Preliminary Evidence about Generalization across Tests," paper prepared for "The Effects of High Stakes Testing" symposium, chaired by R. L. Linn, at the annual meetings of the American Educational Research Association and the National Council on Measurement in Education, Chicago, April 1991. This is one of the earliest studies examining score inflation in two state testing programs where accountability policies were introduced in the 1980s. In this study, researchers administered one of two independent tests to a random selection of elementary classrooms—a commercial multiple-choice test comparable to the high-stakes exam used in the states or an alternative test constructed by the investigators to measure the same content as the high-stakes test. A parallel form of the high-stakes test, designed by the publisher, was also administered to an additional randomly selected group of classes. Results from the high-stakes exam and the parallel form were compared to assess the effect of motivation while results from the two independent exams and the actual exam were compared to examine the generalizability of learning. The researchers found considerable evidence of score inflation, particularly in math. One particularly interesting finding was that scores dropped sharply when a new form of test was introduced and then rose steadily over the next several years as teachers and students became more familiar with the exam.

11. D. M. Koretz, "Limitations in the Use of Achievement Tests as Measures of Educators' Productivity," *Journal of Human Resources,* vol. 37, no. 4 (Fall 2002), pp. 752–77.

12. Koretz, in "Limitations in the Use of Achievement Tests as Measures of Educators' Productivity," emphasizes this distinction as well.

13. While cheating may seem unusual, documented cases of such cheating have recently been uncovered in California, Massachusetts, New York, Texas, and Great Britain. See T. Tysome, "Cheating Purge: Inspectors Out," *Times Educational Supplement*, August 19, 1994, p. 1; D. Lindsay, "Whodunit? Officials Find Thousands of Erasures on Standardized Tests and Suspect Tampering," *Education Week*, October 2, 1996, pp. 25–29; Regina Loughran and Thomas Comiskey, *Cheating the Children: Educator Misconduct on Standardized Tests,* report of the City of New York Special Commissioner of Investigation for the New York City School District (December 1999); Claudia Kolker, "Texas Offers Hard Lessons on School Accountability," *Los Angeles Times,* April 14, 1999; D. Hofkins, "Cheating 'Rife' in National Tests," *Times Educational Supplement*, June 16, 1995, p. 1; John Marcus, "Faking the Grade," *Boston Magazine*, February 2000; and Meredith May, "State Fears Cheating by Teachers," *San Francisco Chronicle*, October 4, 2000, p. A-1.

14. B. Jacob and S. Levitt, "Rotten Apples: An Investigation of the Prevalence and Predictors of Teacher Cheating," *Quarterly Journal of Economics* (forthcoming).

15. David N. Figlio and Joshua F. Winicki, "Food for Thought? The Effects of School Accountability on School Nutrition," Working Paper (University of Florida, 2002).

16. L. A. Shepard, "Should Instruction Be Measurement-Driven?: A Debate," paper presented at the annual meeting of the American Educational Research Association, New Orleans, April 1988; and L. A. Shepard, "The Harm of Measurement-Driven Instruction," paper presented at the annual meeting of the American Educational Research Association, Washington, April 1988.

17. I thank an anonymous referee for pointing this out.

18. Koretz and Barron, *The Validity of Gains on the Kentucky Instructional Results Information System;* Stephen P. Klein and others, "What Do Test Scores in Texas Tell Us?" Issue Paper 202 (Santa Monica, Calif.: RAND Corporation, 2000); and Jacob, "Accountability, Incentives, and Behavior."

19. The Illinois Goals Assessment Program (IGAP) was revised in 1999 and renamed the Illinois Student Assessment Test (ISAT).

20. In 1995 the state began a policy of placing schools with low IGAP scores on a state watch list. In practice, this had no real consequences for schools.

21. While troubling for other reasons, the fact that ITBS gains outpaced IGAP gains following the introduction of the accountability policy provides further evidence that the performance was driven by the high-stakes testing regime. If the achievement improvements during the later 1990s were simply a residual effect of earlier reform efforts, one would expect them to affect ITBS and IGAP scores equally.

22. Even in mathematics, the process of categorizing test items can be extremely difficult and subject to error. In reading, where passage length and difficulty play a large role in the difficulty of the questions and the exams differ in terms of response format (single versus multiple correct responses), this task is likely impossible.

23. For test security reasons, the Illinois State Board of Education does not disseminate individual item-level information or precise descriptions of the test items.

24. Perhaps the most fundamental difficulty with this strategy is that it requires the existence of two or more achievement exams covering the same subjects and given to the same grades, administered before and after the introduction of the accountability policy. Chicago had administered two relatively comparable exams for several years before the policy. Yet the differences described above still make interpretation difficult. Unfortunately, when states administer multiple exams, they often explicitly administer them to different grades or in different subjects, to minimize the amount of testing experienced by any one group of students. For the same reason, many districts phase out older exams when newer accountability exams are introduced.

25. The results are not sensitive to the precise way in which student achievement is defined.

26. The results are not sensitive to the precise way in which school achievement is defined.

27. Tables available from author upon request.

28. Jacob and Levitt, "Rotten Apples."

13

Central Exit Exams and Student Achievement: International Evidence

LUDGER WÖßMANN

Virtually all education systems examine students' educational achievement, but the way this task is conducted varies widely. A pivotal feature of examination systems is whether exams are designed, carried out, and graded by individual teachers or whether they are conducted by an entity external to schools. In external-exam systems, every student takes the same tests, which become an intrinsic part of the school system. The exams are designed to classify student performance based on an external standard, not relative to other students in the same class. While often referred to as central exams, "central" need not necessarily mean that the exams are administered by the national government; it can also refer to centralization at some

Financial support for the construction of the TIMSS-Repeat micro-database by the Program on Education Policy and Governance (PEPG), Harvard University, under a grant from the John M. Olin Foundation is gratefully acknowledged. The hospitality of both the PEPG and the National Bureau of Economic Research during spring 2002, which enabled me to write this paper, is highly appreciated. I would also like to thank Caroline Hoxby and Kathryn Schiller for their constructive discussion of the paper at the conference, John Bishop for his kind provision of data on central exit exams in most of the countries analyzed, Eugenio Gonzalez of the TIMSS International Study Center for helpful clarifications on the TIMSS-Repeat data, Andreas Ammermüller for research assistance in the construction of the TIMSS-Repeat database, and Marty West for many helpful comments on several versions of this paper.

regional level or to a widely used system of exams administered by a private company. What is crucial is that they are truly external, so that neither teachers nor students know in advance the specific questions contained in the exams. To improve performance, it is necessary to teach, or respectively learn, the curricular standards on which the exams are based.

The incentives that students, teachers, schools, administrators, and parents face differ substantially between external-exam systems and teacher grading. This paper studies the effects of external exams on the prevailing incentives by looking at the specific case of exit exams administered at the end of secondary education, instead of external exams given at several grade levels during secondary education. Such central exit exams are largely ignored in the No Child Left Behind legislation, with its focus on testing in grades three to eight. While the exit exams generally require a minimum score for graduation, they also establish many different thresholds for performance that can be differentially rewarded by parents, institutions of higher education, and potential employers. This distinguishes them from the kind of minimum competency tests studied by Thomas Dee (see chapter 10 in this volume).

The empirical analysis of this paper assesses the impact of central exit exams on students' academic performance using new international evidence from two large cross-country comparative studies of student performance, the Third International Mathematics and Science Study (TIMSS) and TIMSS-Repeat. These studies include performance data in both math and science for about 450,000 individual students from fifty-four countries, as well as background data on families, school resources, and institutional settings for individual students, teachers, and schools. This rich micro-database allows the estimation of how students perform in education systems with and without central exams and of whether the extent of school autonomy, teacher influence, and parental involvement have different consequences in education systems with and without central exams.

The virtue of using international comparisons to estimate the effect of central exams on student performance is that it exploits the institutional variation that exists between countries—a kind of variation that does not occur within most countries.[1] And while much of the previous cross-country research was performed at the country level and was thus unable to account for differences in local features within the school systems, the individual student data used in this paper make it possible to look at the interactions of central exams with local features, thereby indicating how central exams work in different local settings.[2]

Central Exams as an Accountability Device
to Mitigate Agency Problems

Accountability systems are often defined narrowly as systems that "reward and punish schools by allocating funding according to whether the school meets certain performance criteria."[3] In this paper, I define accountability systems more broadly as any device that attaches consequences to measured educational performance. That is, the two common features of accountability systems are that they measure students' educational achievement directly and that they attach consequences to measured performance. These consequences may be positive (rewards) or negative (sanctions), they may be implicit or explicit, and their target may be any educational stakeholder—be it districts, schools, teachers, or students. While good performance would generally be rewarded, poor performance may lead either to sanctions or to more positive consequences such as additional assistance, usually with some sacrifice of local control or the threat of future sanctions attached. Proponents of accountability systems hope that attaching consequences to student outcomes will motivate educational stakeholders to increase their effort, thereby improving educational productivity.

Why should accountability systems be necessary in education systems in the first place? The answer is that a network of principal-agent relationships prevents accountability from being automatically secured. A principal-agent relationship is created whenever a principal who desires a certain outcome hires an agent to act on his behalf, as when a parent contracts with the head of a school to oversee his child's education. The first generic feature of such relationships is asymmetric information: The agent is simply better informed about his own behavior and the effort required to accomplish his assigned task than is the principal. Efforts to monitor the agent's behavior are generally costly and only partially effective, constraining the principal's ability to hold the agent accountable. For example, teachers and parents cannot know precisely how much effort a student puts into learning. Likewise, heads of schools and parents cannot perfectly monitor teachers' preparation of lessons and behavior in the classroom.

The second common feature of principal-agent relationships is that the agent and the principal have different interests. For example, students may be more interested in leisure than their parents would want them to be; heads of schools and teachers may be more interested in their own finances and workload than parents and administrators would prefer. Together, incomplete monitoring owing to asymmetric information and divergent interests lead to

Figure 13-1. *Monitoring in the School System*

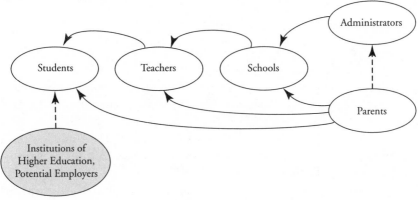

the possibility of opportunistic behavior on the part of the agent—that is, the agent will further his own interests instead of the principal's.

Figure 13-1 provides a stylized diagram of educational stakeholders and the monitoring relationships among them. Students, the focal point of the whole system, are most directly monitored by their parents and by their teachers. The fact that their performance will ultimately be evaluated by employers and institutions of higher education may introduce an additional, less direct layer of monitoring for farsighted students. Teachers, meanwhile, are monitored by the heads of their schools and by the parents of the students whom they teach. Schools in turn are monitored by the government agencies responsible for education and by the parents of the students attending them.[4]

Central exams can provide the principals in this network of agency relationships with information that is not available in education systems without central exams, facilitating the monitoring of agents' behavior. The different principals may use this information to impose performance-based consequences on their agents, helping to align agents' incentives with the goal of the education system, namely increasing the educational performance of its students. In theory, the existence of central exams should affect the behavior of all educational stakeholders, establishing several mechanisms through which central exams may affect how school systems work and, ultimately, how students perform academically.[5] The beneficial effects of central exams on educational performance should be especially substantial when tasks are involved that include a large potential for opportunistic behavior; that is, when both informational asymmetries and differences of interest between principals and agents are large.

The International Micro-Database of TIMSS and TIMSS-Repeat

The empirical evidence in this paper draws on two large international comparative studies of student achievement, the Third International Mathematics and Science Study of 1995 (TIMSS-95) and its replication in 1999 (TIMSS-Repeat).[6] The target population of TIMSS-95 at the middle school level were the two adjacent grades with the highest share of thirteen-year-old students, or seventh and eighth grade in most countries. TIMSS-Repeat was conducted only at the higher of these two grades. Within each participating country, a random sample of schools was selected, and one class within each target grade was randomly chosen and tested in both math and science, yielding a representative sample of students within each country.

Both studies were conducted by the International Association for the Evaluation of Educational Achievement (IEA), an independent collaboration of national research institutes and governmental research agencies. The development of the test contents was a cooperative process involving national research coordinators from all participating countries. This, together with the fact that all participating countries endorsed the curriculum framework and that substantial efforts were made to ensure high-quality sampling and testing in all countries, should make the student performance tested in the TIMSS tests comparable across countries. To ensure the comparability of results, both studies conducted a test-curriculum matching analysis that restricted the analysis to items definitely covered in each country's curriculum. This had little effect on the overall achievement patterns.[7]

In addition to testing students in math and science, the two studies collected contextual information in three background questionnaires: a student questionnaire, a teacher questionnaire, and a school questionnaire. Students answered questions about their demographic characteristics and home background. The math and science teachers of each tested class answered questions about their personal characteristics and classroom environments. Heads of schools answered more general questions about the school's administration and governance.

The set of participating countries differed between the two studies. Of the thirty-nine countries for which complete data sets had been available for TIMSS-95, sixteen did not repeat the assessment in 1999. Thus fifteen of the thirty-eight countries participating in TIMSS-Repeat were new to the international assessment. This change allows for a test of the robustness of previous findings obtained using TIMSS-95 data on a substantially altered set of countries.

Table 13-1 shows the countries participating in TIMSS-95 and in TIMSS-Repeat. The first two columns report the size of the student samples in each country in TIMSS-95 and TIMSS-Repeat, respectively. The average sample size across all participating countries was 6,834 students in TIMSS-95 and 4,751 students in TIMSS-Repeat. The subsequent columns report the average performance in math and science of the countries participating in TIMSS-95 and TIMSS-Repeat. For most of the countries that participated in both studies, the difference between the performance levels achieved in 1995 and 1999 was small and statistically insignificant.[8]

The two micro-databases used in this paper, based on the two TIMSS studies, include rich student-level data for representative samples of students from all the participating countries.[9] Drawing from the background-questionnaire data contained in the databases, the analysis in this paper uses seventeen variables to control for students' family background, thirteen variables to control for resource endowment and teacher characteristics, and eighteen variables to control for the institutional setting of the education system.[10] To enable an even higher statistical precision in the estimation, the two databases are also pooled into one large TIMSS data set containing information on 447,089 students.

The TIMSS micro-databases were merged with data on the existence of central school-leaving exams in the participating countries (or regions within the countries), with all forms of curriculum-based external exit exam systems (CBEEES) considered.[11] The measure does not recognize university entrance exams, as these are usually not taken by all students and do not constitute an integrated part of the school system. The exam data used in this paper are based on reviews of comparative-education studies and educational encyclopedias, interviews with representatives of the national education systems, government documents, and background papers. The data are presented in the final columns of table 13-1. When central-exam systems were present in some parts of a country but not in others, the value indicates the share of students in the country facing central exams.[12]

International Evidence on Central Exit Exams and Student Performance

This section presents reduced-form estimates of the impact of central-exam systems on student performance, which reflect the total impact caused by all

Table 13-1. *Descriptive Statistics: Number of Students, TIMSS Test Scores, and Central Exams*

| | Students | | TIMSS-95 | | | | TIMSS-Repeat | | Central exams | |
| | | | Seventh grade | | Eighth grade | | Eighth grade | | | |
Country	TIMSS-95	TIMSS-Repeat	Math	Science	Math	Science	Math	Science	Math	Science
Australia	12,812	4,018	498	504	530	545	525	540	0.81	0.81
Austria	5,698	...	509	519	539	557	...	...	0	0
Belgium (Flemish)	5,662	5,259	558	529	565	550	557	534	0	0
Belgium (French)	4,849	...	507	442	527	471	...	...	0	0
Bulgaria	...	3,272	...	...	...	...	510	518	1	1
Canada	16,572	8,770	494	499	527	531	531	534	0.51	0.51
Chile	...	5,907	...	...	...	...	394	421	0	0
Colombia	5,299	...	369	388	385	411	...	...	0	0
Cyprus	5,827	3,116	446	420	474	463	477	462	0	0
Czech Republic	6,671	3,453	523	533	564	574	520	537	1	1
Denmark	4,354	...	465	439	502	478	...	...	1	1
England	3,538	2,916	477	513	506	553	496	542	1	1
Finland	...	2,920	...	...	...	...	520	537	1	1
France	5,898	...	492	452	538	498	...	...	1	0
Germany	5,744	...	485	500	509	531	...	...	0.35	0.35
Greece	7,921	...	440	449	484	497	...	...	0	0
Hong Kong	6,745	5,179	564	495	588	522	582	529	1	1
Hungary	5,978	3,183	502	518	537	554	531	554	1	1
Iceland	3,727	...	459	462	487	494	...	...	1	0
Indonesia	...	5,848	...	...	...	...	401	433	1	1
Iran	7,416	5,301	401	436	428	470	423	448	1	1
Ireland	6,201	...	500	495	527	538	...	...	1	1
Israel	1,403	4,193	...	...	522	525	466	470	1	1
Italy	...	3,328	...	...	...	...	479	495	1	1

Japan	10,271	4,745	571	531	605	571	579	551	1	1
Jordan	...	5,052	...	...	607	...	428	451	1	1
Korea, Republic of	5,827	6,114	577	535	607	565	587	551	1	1
Kuwait	1,645	...	...	...	392	430	...	...	0	0
Latvia	4,960	2,845	462	435	494	485	504	500	0.50	0.50
Lithuania	5,053	2,361	428	403	477	476	481	486	1	1
Macedonia	...	4,023	...	...	...	...	447	458	0	0
Malaysia	...	5,577	...	...	...	...	519	492	1	1
Moldova	...	3,711	...	...	...	...	468	458	1	1
Morocco	...	5,402	...	...	...	...	336	319	1	1
Netherlands	4,076	2,943	516	517	541	560	538	544	1	1
New Zealand	6,866	3,613	472	481	508	525	491	511	1	1
Norway	5,732	...	461	483	503	527	...	...	1	0.30
Philippines	...	6,601	...	...	...	...	349	344	0	0
Portugal	6,753	...	423	428	454	480	...	...	0	0
Romania	7,471	3,425	454	452	482	486	471	472	1	0
Russian Federation	8,160	4,332	501	484	535	538	526	530	1	1
Scotland	5,666	...	463	468	499	518	...	...	1	1
Singapore	8,285	4,966	601	545	643	607	603	568	1	1
Slovak Republic	7,101	3,492	508	510	547	544	533	535	1	1
Slovenia	5,603	3,109	498	530	541	560	531	533	1	1
South Africa	...	8,146	...	...	...	...	278	246	1	1
Spain	7,595	...	448	477	487	517	...	...	0	0
Sweden	8,855	...	477	488	519	535	...	...	0.50	0.50
Switzerland	11,717	...	...	...	...	...	...	...	0	0
Taiwan	...	5,772	...	...	...	...	584	572	1	1
Thailand	11,627	5,732	495	493	522	525	469	482	1	1
Tunisia	...	5,051	...	...	...	...	446	428	1	1
Turkey	...	7,841	...	...	...	...	430	432	1	1
United States	10,967	9,028	476	508	500	534	503	515	0.07	0.07

Note: TIMSS = Third International Mathematics and Science Study.

conceivable mechanisms—be it altered behavior of parents, administrators, schools, teachers, or students.

Basic Results from TIMSS and TIMSS-Repeat

The quantity of interest in this analysis is the coefficient α on central exams in a regression of student performance on a host of explanatory variables:

$$T_{ilsc} = \alpha E_c + B_{ilcs}\beta_1 + R_{lcs}\beta_2 + I_{lcs}\beta_3 + \eta_c + \nu_{sc} + \varepsilon_{ilsc}, \qquad (1)$$

where T_{ilsc} is the TIMSS math or science test score T of student i in class l in school s in country c. These test scores have been divided by the standard deviation of the test scores of all students to facilitate interpretation of coefficients and enable comparisons with other studies using different tests.[13] E_c are central exams, measured at the country level. B_{ilcs} are a set of variables reflecting background characteristics of the student and his or her family, R_{lcs} are measures of resource endowment and teacher characteristics, and I_{lcs} are variables depicting other institutional features of the school system such as the centralization of other features of the school system, school autonomy, teacher influence, and parental involvement. The latter two sets of variables are mostly measured at the classroom or school level. The error term has a country-level component η, a school-level component ν, and a student-level component ε.[14]

Table 13-2 reports the coefficient on central exams in both math and science, separately for the TIMSS-95 test, the TIMSS-Repeat test, and the combined data set that pools the results of both tests.[15] Students in countries with central-exam systems scored 40.9 percent of a standard deviation higher on the TIMSS-95 math test than students in countries without central-exam systems, controlling for effects of family background, educational resources, and institutional environment. Similarly, the advantage for students in countries with central exams was 47.0 percent of a standard deviation in the TIMSS-Repeat math test. In the pooled math regression, the lead was 42.7 percent of a standard deviation. In science, students in countries with central-exam systems scored 39.7 percent of a standard deviation higher in TIMSS-95 and 35.9 percent higher both in TIMSS-Repeat and in the pooled analysis. All these coefficients on central exams are statistically significant at the 1 percent level. Thus the findings based on the TIMSS-Repeat test, with its differing set of participating countries, confirm previous findings derived from TIMSS-95 that central exams seem to exert a substantial positive impact on the educational performance of students.[16] Even the sizes

Table 13-2. *Impact of Central Exams on Student Performance*

Exam	TIMSS-95	TIMSS-Repeat	Pooled	Pooled, with regional controls
Math				
Central exams (coefficient)	0.409**	0.470**	0.427**	0.286*
(standard error)	(0.135)	(0.135)	(0.098)	(0.132)
Number of students (unit of observation)	266,545	180,544	447,089	447,089
Number of countries	39	38	77	77
R^2	0.238	0.362	0.285	0.363
Science				
Central exams (coefficient)	0.397**	0.359**	0.359**	0.417**
(standard error)	(0.099)	(0.129)	(0.083)	(0.108)
Number of students (unit of observation)	266,545	180,544	447,089	447,089
Number of countries	39	38	77	77
R^2	0.205	0.326	0.256	0.317

Note: Dependent variable: Third International Mathematics and Science Study (TIMSS) international math/science test score. All regressions control for forty-eight family, resource, teacher, and institutional control variables. Clustering-robust standard errors are in parentheses. All standard errors reported in this table take countries as the level of clustering.

*Significant at the 5 percent level, based on clustering-robust standard errors.

**Significant at the 1 percent level, based on clustering-robust standard errors.

of the effect of central exams as estimated with the two data sets are statistically indistinguishable.[17]

It is informative to analyze how much of the international variation in student performance is due to the existence versus lack of central-exam systems in the different countries. In the pooled regression, adding the central-exam variable to all the other explanatory variables increases the explained proportion of the total variation in student test scores (the R^2) by 2.4 percentage points in math (from 0.260 to 0.285) and by 1.9 percentage points in science (from 0.237 to 0.256). The total cross-country variation is only part of the total cross-student variation—34.1 percent in math and 28.5 percent in science. Relative to this cross-country share of the test score variation, the proportion of the variance additionally explained by central-exam systems is 7 percent of the total cross-country variation, both in math and in science. That is, about 7 percent of the international variation in math and science performance can be attributed to the existence of central-exam systems.

An alternative way to evaluate the substantive significance of central exams is to compare the magnitude of their estimated effect to the effect sizes estimated for other policy reforms. For example, Alan B. Krueger found for the Tennessee Project STAR that reducing class size in primary schools by seven to eight students (from about twenty-three to about sixteen students) led to an increase in test scores of about 0.22 standard deviations.[18] This estimate of the impact of reduced class size on student performance is at the upper bound of what other studies have found and may be biased upward.[19] But even if Krueger's estimate is taken at face value, the estimated impact of central exams is two-thirds larger in science and twice as large in math. Furthermore, reducing class size by one-third would increase educational spending proportionally. By contrast, in a cross-country regression of per student educational expenditure on central exams and other potential determinants, the point estimate on central exams is statistically insignificant and slightly negative, suggesting that gains in effectiveness of resource usage might overcompensate any direct cost of central-exam systems.[20] Thus implementing central-exam systems does not seem to increase overall educational spending. Considering the size of their performance impact and their cost-effectiveness, central-exam systems would seem like an attractive policy alternative.

More detailed analyses of the impact of central exams on student performance yield a number of additional interesting results. Central exams might be expected to have the most direct impact on performance in the year leading to the exam. But especially in the case for exit exams, their impact should also extend into lower levels, because they tend to test all the knowledge learned in secondary school and to exert signaling effects that change incentives during the whole school life of a student. The measure of central exams in this analysis indicates whether a school system has exit exams at the end of upper-secondary school. Student performance is tested in seventh and eighth grade. Thus the reported results that the central exit exams improve student performance in lower-secondary school suggest that they do send incentive signals down to lower grades. As the impact of school-leaving exams should become more salient the closer students are to taking them, the effects on student performance should also become stronger in higher grades. Using the TIMSS-95 data in which students from both grade levels were tested, the impact of central exit exams on student performance can be shown to be stronger in eighth grade than in seventh.[21]

Including interaction terms of central exams with family background variables also reveals differences in the impact of central exams for students with different family backgrounds. The interaction terms between central exams and indicators of whether the students and parents were born in the country are statistically significantly negative. That is, central exams seem to dampen the effect on performance of the country of birth of students and their parents, so that immigrants seem to benefit more from central-exam systems than native-born students. Likewise, central exams decrease the effect of parental education, so that under a system of central exams, it seems to matter less from which parental background a student comes. Thus, especially in math, the disadvantage of coming from a less beneficial family background seems to be reduced by central exams, suggesting that central-exam systems work toward equalizing opportunities for students from different family backgrounds.

Analyzing the impact of central exams on the performance of students from different performance quartiles shows that students from all performance quartiles perform better under a central-exam system than under a system without central exams. While both poor- and high-performers gain from the existence of a central-exam system, some evidence exists that the improvement in math performance for high-performing students is larger than that for poor-performing students.

The Potential for Bias in the Estimates

One potential disadvantage of the type of cross-country analysis conducted above is the possibility of bias resulting from omitted variables. If, for example, the countries with central-exam systems also share other characteristics that make them high-performers, central exams may appear to be more effective than they are. Among the features that vary across countries and that might in principle bias the coefficient on central exams in cross-country regressions, four in particular come to mind: the overall degree of centralization of the education system, other institutional settings of the school system, the homogeneity of a country's population, and cultural differences.

The extent to which central exams reflect the general centralization of a school system can be checked by including control variables for centralization. Thus the regressions reported in table 13-2 include two measures of the general centralization of the school system, namely the centralization of the curriculum and of textbook approval. The coefficient estimates on these two controls are consistently positive, but much smaller than the estimate on central exams and often statistically insignificant.[22] More important, including these variables does not substantially change the estimated effect of central exams, suggesting that the influence of the latter is independent of any effects of the general centralization of the school system. Using the share of educational funds controlled by the central government (comparable data on which are available for Organization for Economic Cooperation and Development countries) as an alternative control variable for educational centralization also does not notably change any of the estimated effects of central exams. Centralized financing has a statistically significant negative coefficient in most specifications. Thus the coefficient estimate on central exams does not seem to capture the effect of a generally centralized school system.

Likewise, the regressions of table 13-2 include many additional institutional features of the school system as explanatory variables, such as school autonomy in different areas of decisionmaking and teacher and parental influence, which should control for the most important potentially biasing influences by other country features and incentive environments. The change in the estimated effect of central exams when these observed institutional features are omitted proves to be small. Including a measure of ethnolinguistic fractionalization as a proxy for the homogeneity of a country's population also leaves the substantive results on central exams unchanged.[23] Given that none of these additional control variables, which might have been thought to bias the central-exam coefficient, makes a difference for the estimated central-exam effect, concerns about potential bias stemming from omitted variables might be dampened.

Some people argue that much of the international variation in student performance may be influenced more by fundamental cultural differences than by specific policies. As far as such cultural differences are related to the existence of central-exam systems, the estimates of the coefficient on central exams will be biased. One way to assess the potential for omitted-variable bias from this direction is to include regional (continental) dummies as additional control variables. By controlling for any differences that might exist between regions, such an estimation considers only the within-region variation in central-exam systems and performance. As concerns about cultural differences generally arise in cross-regional comparisons—for example, in terms of Asian versus European values—but should not be as large within regions, estimates of the impact of central exams that control for regional differences should not be substantially biased by cultural differences.

The last column for each subject in table 13-2 presents results of including a set of regional dummies, with the regions being Western Europe, Eastern Europe, North America, South America, Oceania, Asia, Middle East, Northern Africa, and South Africa.[24] In both subjects, the estimated effect of central exams remains positive and statistically significant. The estimate is smaller when the regional dummies are included in the case of math and larger in the case of science. In neither subject is the difference in the coefficient estimate on central exams between the regression with and without regional dummies statistically significant.[25] Thus the comparison of the base estimation to the within-regional estimation also leaves the case for substantial omitted-variable bias rather weak. The conclusion to be drawn from the different findings is that the potential size of any bias seems small in most cases and that it is not clear whether any potential bias is downward or upward. Therefore the case against interpreting the base estimates as reasonably accurate estimates of the actual impact of central exams on student performance is weak.

How Central Exams Change the Working of the Education System

The basic analytic strategy to examine how central exams exert their effects through various mechanisms is to test whether various institutional features of the school system that relate to the behavior of schools, teachers, and parents have different effects on student performance in systems with and without central exams. This evidence provides some indication on which stakeholders in the education process are most influenced by central-exam systems.

Altered Effects of School Autonomy

The changes in incentives have implications for how other features of the school system affect educational outcomes. Specifically, the decentralization of decisionmaking should have different impacts in systems with and without central exams. When schools are autonomous, they have ample leeway in their behavior. Whenever large room for opportunism exists on a decision—that is, when information asymmetries as well as differences in interests between schools and parents or administrators are both large—the extent of monitoring is vital for determining whether autonomous decisions will be carried out in the interest of student learning or not. Without central exams, schools with substantial autonomy may act in ways inconsistent with furthering student achievement without penalty, as their detrimental behavior cannot be observed. With central exams, by contrast, the results of such opportunistic behavior will be observed, forcing schools to operate in a manner more conducive to student performance.

Intrinsic to the educational process is that informational asymmetries are large in virtually all areas of educational decisionmaking. However, the extent to which schools' own interests run counter to the interest of furthering student knowledge will depend on the specific task, or area of decisionmaking, in question. Schools might be expected to have a strong self-interest running counter to student learning whenever money is involved in the decision, as it is only natural to try to increase the personal payoff for a given level of work (or, conversely, to reduce the level of work for a given payoff). Devices that hold agents accountable should have their largest beneficial impact in this group of tasks. By contrast, schools' own interests may be well in line with student learning in such decisionmaking areas as the choice of textbooks or supplies, as it is not obviously in the interest of schools to use poor supplies. In these tasks, the scope for opportunistic behavior is limited, and the need for accountability systems is correspondingly small.

Whether school autonomy is beneficial also depends on the extent to which decentralized knowledge is important for a given task. In many decisionmaking areas, local decisionmaking is likely to be better informed because it can draw on the decentralized knowledge that is available to schools, but not to any central entity. The extent to which decentralized knowledge is important again depends on the decisionmaking area in question. For example, the best way to transfer educational contents to students may vary among schools in different locations, making local discretion regarding the most suitable teaching techniques and supporting equipment vital. By contrast, decentralized knowledge concerning the body of knowledge that students should be taught may not surpass the expertise that a central agency can acquire when employing several curricular experts.

These two considerations, severity of opportunism and importance of local knowledge, jointly determine the expected net impact of school autonomy in a given area of decisionmaking on students' educational achievement in systems without and with central exams. Figure 13-2 summarizes these relationships. If, on the one hand, no danger of opportunism exists in a task, the impact of school autonomy will be equivalent in systems without and with central exams. It will be conducive to student learning when local knowledge is important to the task (cell [N2a]), and it will have no impact on student performance when no specific local knowledge is involved [N1].[26] The one exception to the equivalence between the two systems in the absence of opportunism is when central exams limit the leeway within which schools can decide and when at the same time local behavior beyond this leeway would be superior [N2b]. In this case, central exams might reduce the extent to which school autonomy is beneficial for achievement.

If, on the other hand, the potential for opportunistic behavior is large, decentralized decisionmaking will have substantially different effects in systems without and with central exams. If there are no central exams and local knowledge is not vital [O1], the possibility of opportunistic behavior will make school autonomy strongly detrimental to student learning. As schools' incentives are focused on student learning when central exams are in place, the negative impact of local behavior will be eliminated. When local knowl-

Figure 13-2. *The Impact of School Autonomy on Achievement without and with Central Exams*

Opportunism / Local knowledge		Severe		No	
		Without central exams	With central exams	Without central exams	With central exams
Not important		[O1] $--$ $\rightarrow$ 0		[N1] 0 $\rightarrow$ 0	
Important	Within limits set by central exams	[O2] [a] $-$ $\rightarrow$ $++$		[N2] [a] $+$ $\rightarrow$ $+$	
	Beyond limits set by central exams	[b] $-$ $\rightarrow$ $+$		[b] $++$ $\rightarrow$ $+$	

Note: $--$ = very detrimental; $-$ = detrimental; 0 = no impact; $+$ = conducive; $++$ = very conducive. Within each cell, the impact to the left of the arrow is for systems without central exams and the impact to the right of the arrow is for systems with central exams.

edge is important for a task [O2], the negative impact of school autonomy in systems without central exams is lessened to some extent, although the detrimental effect of opportunism may still overcompensate the positive influence of local knowledge. But once opportunism is curbed through central exams, decentralized decisionmaking can be expected to lead to superior outcomes as it can draw on superior local knowledge. In short, changing the way in which decentralization affects outcomes is one mechanism through which central exams may affect educational performance, and they should be especially helpful whenever opportunism can be curbed.

As in the case of school autonomy, decentralization of decisionmaking authority to individual teachers should have different effects in systems with and without central exams. Teacher autonomy in tasks where local teacher knowledge might help informed decisions but where the scope for opportunism is substantial should change from being detrimental to student learning without central exams to being conducive under a central-exam system. An example of substantial scope for opportunistic behavior by teachers may be tasks involving money for supplies.

The scope for opportunistic behavior is also substantial when teachers as a group influence what is taught in class. Interest groups are generally formed to advance a group's interests relative to the interests advanced by other groups. In education, this may mean that teacher interest groups will place their own interests over the cause of improving student performance. When teachers have group influence at the school level, central exams may again work as a device that focuses their incentives on academic achievement. Instead of watering down the curriculum taught in the school, group influence of schoolteachers may focus on improving teaching methods in a system of central exams that monitors their behavior and externally sets the contents that are meant to be covered in class. However, if teachers form interest groups at the central level where the central exams are set, the existence of a central-exam system may strengthen the negative effects of the actions of teacher groups—such as countrywide teacher unions—as these now can easily influence the standards of the whole education system. Thereby, central-exam systems may be more susceptible to teacher unions' furthering of teachers' idiosyncratic interests over the interest of student achievement.

The Impact of School and Teacher Autonomy

The question of whether institutional features have a different effect on student performance in systems with and without central exams is addressed empirically by including interaction terms between these institutional features and central exams. Thus the equations estimated in this section take the form

$$T_{ilsc} = \alpha E_c + I_{lcs}\beta_1 + (E_c I_{lcs})\beta_2 + B_{ilcs}\beta_3 + R_{lcs}\beta_4 + \eta_c + \nu_{sc} + \varepsilon_{ilsc}, \qquad (2)$$

where the only change relative to equation (1) is the inclusion of interaction terms $(E_c I_{lcs})$ between central exams and the different institutional variables as additional explanatory variables.

Figure 13-3 depicts selected examples of the interaction between central exams and local autonomy in several areas of decisionmaking corresponding to different cells in figure 13-2. All estimates in figure 13-3 are based on regressions using the math data set that pools the TIMSS-95 and TIMSS-Repeat tests.[27] Each of the four pictures reports the performance of students in four situations: students in systems without central exams whose school or teacher does not have autonomy in the specific decisionmaking area depicted by the picture; students without central exams but with local autonomy; students with central exams but without local autonomy; and students with central exams and with local autonomy. The estimates are presented in percent of a standard deviation in test scores, and the lowest performing of the four categories in each picture has been set to zero.[28]

The first decisionmaking area analyzed is whether schools have autonomy over their budgets. This measure is based on a background-questionnaire item answered by the heads of schools who report whether formulating the school budget is primarily a school responsibility in their specific schools.

Figure 13-3. *Central Exams and the Effects of School and Teacher Autonomy*

A. Does school have budget autonomy?

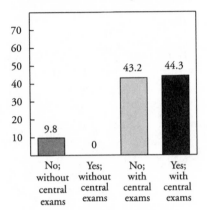

B. Does school have salary autonomy?

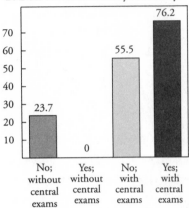

C. Do individual teachers influence curriculum?

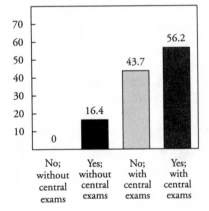

D. Do class teachers choose textbooks?

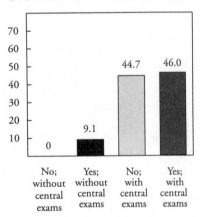

Arguably, this is a case corresponding to cell [O1] of figure 13-2. The scope for opportunistic behavior on the part of the school seems substantial in budgetary questions, as schools would seem to have other interests than purely furthering student performance when it comes to the money available to them. Furthermore, the scope for better-informed decisionmaking at the school level relative to some external level might be small in budgetary matters, as external agencies may even have superior knowledge in this area. Thus one might expect that giving schools autonomy over formulating their own budget is detrimental for students' academic performance when no system of central exams is in place that helps in holding schools accountable for their decisions. However, once central-exam systems are in place to hold schools accountable, giving them budgetary autonomy might not lead to the detrimental opportunistic behavior.

The results depicted in panel A support this reasoning. In school systems without central exams, students performed 9.8 percent of a standard deviation better when their school did not have autonomy over the budget, suggesting that budgetary autonomy enables opportunistic behavior of schools when no central exams are in place. Students in schools with budgetary autonomy in central-exam systems performed 43.2 units better than students in a situation with school autonomy and without central exams, or 33.4 units better than students without school autonomy and without central exams. Notably, no significant difference appears in student performance between schools with and without budgetary autonomy once a central-exam system is in place. This may suggest that central exams curb the opportunistic behavior of schools and that no difference exists in how informed budgetary decisions are between school-based or external decisionmakers. Alternatively, the negative impact of whatever opportunism is left in spite of the improved monitoring as a result of central exams could be almost perfectly offset by any potential positive impact stemming from superior local knowledge. In either case, the detrimental effect of school autonomy in budgetary matters that exists in school systems without central exams is not existent in central-exam systems. This suggests that schools respond to the altered incentive environment by behaving more favorably to students' educational performance.

While school autonomy makes no difference to student performance in situations where opportunism is curbed and local knowledge is not important, it should have positive effects on student performance if opportunistic behavior is checked and local knowledge is important to the task in question (cell [O2] in figure 13-2). This seems to be the case in the task of determining teacher salaries (figure 13-3, panel B). In systems without central exams, students in schools that have autonomy in determining teachers' salaries perform worse than students in schools that do not have salary autonomy. This might reflect that schools again behave opportunistically in this decisionmaking area when money is involved, as long as they cannot be held accountable for their behavior. In systems with central exams, by contrast, students in schools with salary autonomy perform better, not worse, than students in schools without salary autonomy. That is, the effect of school autonomy is reversed once central exams are in place. It seems that, in salary decisions, heads of schools know better than any external agency which teacher worked hard and deserves a bonus or pay raise and which teacher does not. Again, the evidence on salary autonomy strongly suggests that schools seem to change their behavior once central exams enable monitoring of educational outcomes.

The last two pictures of figure 13-3 deal with the influence of individual teachers in decisionmaking areas where local knowledge seems to be important, but where the scope for opportunistic behavior seems limited. The evidence presented in panel C is based on a background-questionnaire item answered by the heads of schools on how much influence each teacher individually (as opposed to teachers collectively and to other educational stakeholders) has in determining the curriculum that is taught. The picture contrasts schools where individual teachers had a considerable amount of influence on the curriculum to schools where teachers had no, little, or only some curricular influence. Both in systems with and without central exams, students in schools where individual teachers had much influence on the curriculum scored significantly better than students in schools where they did not. The difference between systems with and without central exams in the advantage of schools with teacher influence is not statistically significant. This suggests that curricular influence of individual teachers is an example of cell [N2a] in figure 13-2. There does not seem to be much scope for opportunistic behavior on the part of individual teachers in this area, individual teachers' knowledge on how to teach the curriculum seems to be substantial, and central exams do not seem to limit the positive impact of teacher autonomy. However, performance in central-exam systems is still substantially superior to performance in systems without central exams, a differential impact that presumably works through other mechanisms.

Panel D presents evidence on teacher autonomy in the choice of textbooks, based on a background-questionnaire item answered by the math teachers on how much influence they have on the specific textbook to be used. Students whose teacher reported considerable influence on textbook choice scored better than students of teachers without much textbook influence in systems without central exams. By contrast, in systems with central exams there was no statistically significant difference between teachers with and without autonomy in the choice of textbooks. This may reflect the situation of cell [N2b] in figure 13-2, where there is not much scope for opportunism (the choice of a poor textbook would probably hurt the teachers themselves as much as the students), where the local knowledge of teachers is important on which textbook might be best for their students, and where central exams to some extent limit teachers' capabilities to make the best choices.

The most obvious pattern in all pictures of figure 13-3 is that student performance is substantially better when central exams are in place. The change

Table 13-3. *Interaction Effects of Central Exams with Other Institutional Settings*

Institutional settings	Math		Science	
	Coefficient	Interaction with central exams	Coefficient	Interaction with central exams
Central exams	0.390*	...	0.042	...
	(0.197)[a]		(0.209)[a]	
School responsibility				
School budget	−0.071**	0.080**	−0.121***	0.163***
	(0.028)	(0.035)	(0.026)	(0.034)
Purchasing supplies	0.070**	−0.057	0.165***	−0.072
	(0.033)	(0.050)	(0.030)	(0.054)
Hiring teachers	0.218***	−0.207***	−0.013	0.064**
	(0.027)	(0.033)	(0.019)	(0.025)
Determining teacher	−0.279***	0.497***	−0.073***	0.280***
salaries	(0.037)	(0.042)	(0.026)	(0.031)
Teachers' influence				
Class teacher has strong influence on				
Money for supplies	−0.260***	0.304***	−0.062*	0.129***
	(0.053)	(0.065)	(0.036)	(0.045)
Kind of supplies	0.033	−0.040	0.054***	−0.030
	(0.029)	(0.038)	(0.020)	(0.029)
Subject matter	−0.120***	0.085***	−0.041**	−0.013
	(0.024)	(0.028)	(0.017)	(0.022)
Textbook	0.116***	−0.117***	0.061***	−0.096***
	(0.032)	(0.037)	(0.018)	(0.026)

continued on next page

in school and teacher behavior reflected in the different impact of school and teacher autonomy between systems with and without central exams seems to be one of several mechanisms through which this superior performance comes about. Furthermore, the positive impact of central exams is especially apparent in decisions where opportunistic behavior can be curbed, and this is especially the case wherever financial resources are involved, such as budgetary and salary decisions.

Table 13-3 presents evidence on including a complete set of interaction terms between central exams and other institutional features of the school system as in equation (2) for the pooled TIMSS-95 and TIMSS-Repeat data. The first column of each subject reports the coefficient estimates β_1 on the

Table 13-3. *Interaction Effects of Central Exams with Other Institutional Settings (continued)*

Institutional settings	Math Coefficient	Math Interaction with central exams	Science Coefficient	Science Interaction with central exams
Strong influence on curriculum				
Teacher individually	0.161***	−0.057**	0.150***	−0.082***
	(0.021)	(0.028)	(0.018)	(0.025)
Subject teachers	−0.054**	0.034	−0.056***	0.083***
	(0.025)	(0.032)	(0.021)	(0.028)
Schoolteachers collectively	−0.158***	0.073***	−0.160***	0.152***
	(0.021)	(0.028)	(0.019)	(0.026)
Teacher unions	−0.063	−0.319***	−0.040	−0.349***
	(0.053)	(0.086)	(0.052)	(0.093)
Students' incentives				
Scrutiny of testing	0.037***	−0.013*	−0.008*	0.017***
	(0.006)	(0.007)	(0.005)	(0.006)
Homework	0.012	0.017**	−0.046***	0.062***
	(0.007)	(0.009)	(0.010)	(0.015)
Parents' influence				
Uninterested parents limit teaching	−0.098***	−0.075*	−0.017	−0.177***
	(0.035)	(0.042)	(0.028)	(0.039)
Interested parents limit teaching	−0.198***	0.201***	−0.102**	0.171***
	(0.054)	(0.061)	(0.041)	(0.052)
Number of students (unit of observation)		447,089		447,089
Number of schools (primary sampling units)		12,175		12,175
Number of countries		77		77
R^2		0.294		0.264

Note: Every two columns headed "Coefficient" and "Interaction with central exams" together report the results of one regression. "Coefficient" reports the coefficient on the variable labeled in each row, while "Interaction with central exams" reports the coefficient on the interaction term between central exams and the variable labeled in the row. Dependent variable: Third International Mathematics and Science Study (TIMSS) international math/science test score. The regressions control for thirty-two family, resource, teacher, and centralization control variables. Clustering-robust standard errors are in parentheses (schools as level of clustering unless noted otherwise).

a. Standard error has countries as the level of clustering.

* Significant at the 10 percent level, based on clustering-robust standard errors.

** Significant at the 5 percent level, based on clustering-robust standard errors.

*** Significant at the 1 percent level, based on clustering-robust standard errors.

different institutions I, and the second column reports the estimates β_2 on the interaction term EI between each institution and central exams of the same regression. The results of table 13-3 show that the pattern of results presented in figure 13-3 is robust against the inclusion of other institutional interactions, and that the pattern in science is similar to the pattern in math.[29]

In addition to the interaction effects discussed in figure 13-3, school autonomy in purchasing supplies has a positive effect on student performance that is somewhat smaller in central-exam systems than in systems without central exams, reflecting cell [N2b] in figure 13-2. The pattern for school autonomy in hiring teachers is less clear, with the effect in math being positive in systems without central exams but about zero with central exams, and an opposite finding in science. Teacher autonomy over money for supplies has a negative impact on student performance when no central-exam system is in place but a positive impact with central exams, reflecting the case of opportunism and important local knowledge of cell [O2] in figure 13-2. Teachers' influence on the money for supplies seems to get well channeled once central exams introduce accountability. Teacher autonomy in the choice of the subject matter to be covered in class has a negative impact on student performance that is substantially lowered in math when central exams are in place. This suggests a large scope for opportunism on the part of the teachers to determine their own workload in this decisionmaking area (cell [O1] of figure 13-2 for math).

Teacher influence may be especially prone to opportunistic behavior when exerted by teachers as an interest group. Accordingly, in systems without central exams, teacher influence on the curriculum is detrimental to student performance once it is exerted by teachers of the same subject as a group, by teachers collectively for the school, or by teacher unions. In the case of teachers grouping together within a school (teachers of the same subject and all schoolteachers collectively), this negative effect is substantially mitigated when central exams are in place, reflecting a situation comparable to cell [O1] of figure 13-2. The negative influence of teachers acting as unions to influence the curriculum, however, is even more detrimental in systems with central exams than in systems without central exams. This suggests that central-exam systems are especially susceptible to the group interests of teachers once these are pursued at the system level, as their interests might then water down the design and implementation of the central-exam systems.

The Impact of Regular Testing and Homework

Teachers often use devices to monitor students' efforts to increase their performance. Two such devices are regular testing of students' educational progress and the assignment of homework to have students practice their knowledge. In central-exam systems, the impact of such devices on student performance might be altered in two ways. First, teachers' incentives are aligned with student performance because of their own increased monitoring by parents and heads of schools, which should increase teachers' efforts to focus these devices on ensuring high student performance. Second, as students themselves get better monitored, their own effort should increase and get better focused on educational achievement.

The scrutiny of testing is measured discretely by teachers' responses on how many hours per week they normally spend outside the school day preparing or grading student tests or exams. Similarly, homework assignment is measured discretely in hours per week based on teachers' reports on how often and for how many minutes they usually assign homework. In math, both scrutiny of testing and homework have positive effects on student performance both in systems with and without central exams (table 13-3). The effect of testing is slightly smaller with central-exam systems, which might reflect that teacher testing comes in addition to central-exam testing in central-exam systems while it is the only way of testing in systems without central exams. By contrast, the positive effect of homework assignment is doubled in central-exam systems. In science, both monitoring devices have a slightly negative effect on student performance in systems without central exams. The effect is turned into a positive one once central exams are in place.

This shows that monitoring devices such as regular testing and homework assignment do not seem to further student performance strongly as long as agents' incentives are not aligned with the goal of increased student performance. If this is not the case, the design and content of these devices do not seem to be well focused, a problem that is especially severe with subjects whose content may be less coherent in the absence of explicit standards (for example, science as compared with math). Given the alignment of incentives with student performance in central-exam systems, teachers' and students' efforts in the design of and performance on tests and homework seem to get better focused on enhancing students' educational achievement.

The Impact of Parental Influence

All effects discussed so far may be linked to changes in the behavior of parents who are able to increase the monitoring of educational achievement once they have the information generated by central exams. This positive effect of central exams should be especially salient with parents who are strongly concerned with their child's educational progress, but not as much with parents who are less concerned about their child's education. Two meas-

Figure 13-4. *Central Exams and Parental Involvement*[a]

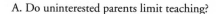

A. Do uninterested parents limit teaching?   B. Do interested parents limit teaching?

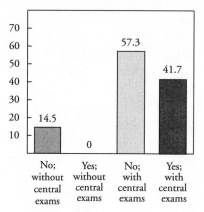
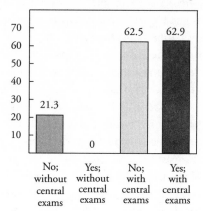

a. Parental involvement according to teacher reports.

ures contained in the TIMSS teacher background questionnaires may help to shed some light on this differential impact. First, teachers reported to what extent, in their view, parents uninterested in their children's learning and progress limit how the teachers teach their class. Second, teachers reported whether their teaching is limited by parents interested in their children's progress.

The math performance of students in the different situations is depicted in figure 13-4.[30] Students whose teachers reported that their teaching was not substantially limited by uninterested parents performed better than students whose teachers reported that their teaching was limited by uninterested parents, irrespective of whether a central-exam system was in place (figure 13-4, panel A).[31] The results are different for the involvement of parents who are interested in their child's progress, however. In systems without central exams, students whose teachers reported that their teaching was limited considerably by interested parents again performed worse. But in central-exam systems, students whose teachers reported that interested parents limited how they teach their class performed just as well as students whose teachers did not say so. That is, even though teachers judged the intrusion of interested parents as limiting their teaching, student performance did not suffer from this limitation.

In science, the negative impact of uninterested parents was even more negative in systems with central exams than in systems without central exams (table 13-3). For interested parents limiting teaching, the negative effect in systems without central exams is turned around to be positive when central exams are in place. Even though teachers complained that their teaching was limited by the involvement of interested parents, the performance of students was furthered by this parental intervention.

While the involvement of interested parents may limit student performance in systems without central exams because parents do not have well-founded information on which to base their interventions, central-exam systems seem to ensure that interested parents have the information necessary to intervene properly. Parents uninterested in their child's educational progress do not seem to make use of this information, and their lack of interest hurts the child's performance. But it seems that the involvement of interested parents can never go all the way to being detrimental when central exams are in place, even when teachers might judge it to be so. While no data are available to estimate the effect of the involvement of interested parents when it is approved by the teachers, this likely would be even superior for teaching and learning.

Conclusion

The international evidence based on TIMSS-95 and TIMSS-Repeat confirms that central exams are a powerful accountability device. Student performance in math and science is substantially higher in school systems with central exams than without central exams, and this is true for students from all performance quartiles and family backgrounds. Parents, administrators, schools, teachers, and students all appear to respond to the changed incentive environment created by central exams by placing additional emphasis on educational achievement. Parental involvement becomes more informed and effective. The opportunistic behavior of schools and teachers is curbed, so that local autonomy in many decisionmaking areas becomes an attractive feature of a school system. And the efforts of teachers and students are better attuned with the goals of the education system as represented in the exam content.

When considering what the United States in particular can learn from this evidence, it is useful to consider how central exams work in systems with a high level of local autonomy. The U.S. school system is to a large extent locally controlled and funded and lacks a centralized system of wage bargaining, contracting, or teacher assignment. The results reported here suggest that central exams are especially capable of bringing out the positive aspects of local autonomy, while mitigating its negative consequences. In some cases, central exams also seem to limit the ability of local decisionmakers to make appropriate decisions. However, such limitations are far outweighed by their positive incentive effects.

The relative merits of central exams as an accountability device may be compared with other accountability systems, such as teacher merit pay or school-based (as opposed to student-based) accountability systems. Much discussion is found in the literature about which educational stakeholders should be targeted by accountability systems. Much of the current U.S. discussion on educational accountability seems to favor rewards for high-achieving schools, sanctions for failing schools, or both. For example, Helen F. Ladd argues that "subject to some important qualifications related to funding and capacity, schools are an appropriate unit for accountability purposes and have clear advantages compared to other possible units of accountability, such as school districts, individual teachers, and students."[32] In contrast to this recommendation, central-exam systems primarily target the individual students who take the central exam.[33] However, the arguments and evidence presented in this paper show that the incentives created by central-exam systems extend far beyond the individual student. With central exams providing the information necessary to monitor educational outcomes, all stakeholders are more likely to face consequences for their behavior. Thus central exams not only have the direct effect of changing students' incentives, but they also work indirectly to change incentives all the way up the agency ladder spanning from students over teachers and schools to administrators. As all these stakeholders respond to incentives, their behavior becomes more closely aligned with furthering students' educational performance.

The practical merits of other accountability systems are less clear. Performance-related pay for teachers has generally been deemed a failure when practiced in the American public school system.[34] Likewise, several recent studies have hinted at substantial implementation problems facing school-based accountability systems that rely on value-added measures of performance. For example, value-added measures of a school's performance at a particular grade have been shown to vary substantially in ways unrelated to school performance, both because of ability differences in the student sample and one-time factors.[35] In addition, even the more sophisticated value-added measures of school effectiveness currently implemented, which follow the performance of students from year to year, have been shown to fail to thoroughly account for resource differences and measurement error in the test score data.[36] Because measurement errors are amplified when the data used are based on changes instead of levels, this problem is especially severe for value-added measures. However, one would not want to base schools' performance assessments on level measures of their students' performance, which is strongly determined by the students' social background. Thus both school-based accountability systems based on value-added measures and on level measures of performance could lead to distorted incentives and arbitrary performance evaluations for schools. By contrast, student-based central-exam systems, which are based on level measures of performance, are less prone to arbitrariness and create incentives that induce each student to get the best possible performance out of his or her ability and social background. The incentive effect will be working for students of all ability levels if the central exams establish multiple thresholds for performance that have meaningful rewards tied to them, instead of simply establishing minimum competencies (see chapter 10 in this volume).

Despite their apparent connotation of centralizing decisionmaking, central-exam systems may require less central regulation and allow more flexibility at the local level. For external-exam systems to exert their beneficial incentive effects, no central person or agency is required to have detailed knowledge of the educational production process in every school. Central administrators may in practice lack the necessary information to intervene in a beneficial way—and the solutions for different failing schools may differ depending on backgrounds, customs, and local experiences. Instead of trying to micromanage schools by central regulators, external exams change the system so that the incentives of all stakeholders are better aligned with the goals of the system. If adequately motivated to improve performance and equipped with valid performance information, local stakeholders may be better equipped than any central agency to evaluate accountability and thus to reward or punish performance. Given the implementation problems of accountability systems that rely on central regulation, evaluation, and intervention, the relative merits of external-exam systems as an accountability device make them a highly attractive policy.

Notes

1. See Ludger Wößmann, *Schooling and the Quality of Human Capital* (Berlin: Springer, 2002).

2. For examples of country-level studies, see John H. Bishop, "The Effect of National Standards and Curriculum-Based Exams on Achievement," *American Economic Review*, vol. 87, no. 2 (1997), pp. 260–64; and Jong-Wha Lee and Robert J. Barro, "Schooling Quality in a Cross-Section of Countries," *Economica*, vol. 68, no. 272 (2001), pp. 465–88.

3. David N. Figlio and Marianne E. Page, "Can School Choice and School Accountability Successfully Coexist?" in Caroline M. Hoxby, ed., *The Economics of School Choice* (University of Chicago Press, 2003), pp. 49–66.

4. In prolonging this chain of monitoring relationships, the educational administration might be viewed as being monitored by parents in its constituency and by the

government, which in turn is monitored by the electorate, which in part is made up of parents. In a sense, parents might be seen as coming nearest to something like an ultimate principal in this network of principal-agent relationships in education.

5. For a more detailed discussion of the different mechanisms through which central exams affect behavior in the education system, see Ludger Wößmann, "How Central Exams Affect Educational Achievement: International Evidence from TIMSS and TIMSS-Repeat," Research Paper PEPG/02-10 (Harvard University, Program on Education Policy and Governance, June 2002), pp. 9–16.

6. The Third International Mathematics and Science Study (TIMSS) has been renamed the Trends in International Mathematics and Science Study, as assessments are meant to be conducted on a regular basis every four years.

7. For details on the content areas covered in the math and science tests, on specific test items, sampling and implementation procedures, questionnaire development, translation verification tests, data collection, quality control procedures in all steps of the study, data processing, and test score scaling in TIMSS-Repeat, see the TIMSS documentation contained in Ina V. S. Mullis and others, *TIMSS 1999 International Mathematics Report: Findings from IEA's Repeat of the Third International Mathematics and Science Study at the Eighth Grade* (Boston College, 2000); Michael O. Martin, Kelvin D. Gregory, and Steven E. Stemler, eds., *TIMSS 1999 Technical Report* (Boston College, 2000); and Eugenio J. Gonzalez and Julie A. Miles, eds., *User Guide for the TIMSS 1999 International Database* (Boston College, 2001). For details on TIMSS-95, see Ludger Wößmann, "Schooling Resources, Educational Institutions, and Student Performance: The International Evidence," *Oxford Bulletin of Economics and Statistics*, vol. 65, no. 2 (2003); and the references therein.

8. See Mullis and others, *TIMSS 1999 International Mathematics Report*.

9. Wößmann, "Schooling Resources, Educational Institutions, and Student Performance," contains a detailed description of the construction and content of the TIMSS-95 database used in this paper, which combines the TIMSS-95 performance data in math and science with data from the different background questionnaires for each individual student and includes imputed values for missing values of questionnaire data. The TIMSS-Repeat database was constructed for the purposes of this paper, as described in Wößmann, "How Central Exams Affect Educational Achievement," appendix.

10. For a complete list of these control variables, see Wößmann, "How Central Exams Affect Educational Achievement," table A1a.

11. For more details on the definition and characteristics of curriculum-based external exit exam systems, see Bishop, "The Effect of National Standards and Curriculum-Based Exams on Achievement"; and John H. Bishop, "Are National Exit Examinations Important for Educational Efficiency?" *Swedish Economic Policy Review*, vol. 6, no. 2 (1999), pp. 349–98.

12. Unfortunately, not much information is available about the specifics of the different central-exam systems in the different countries, for example, whether performance information is publicly available or whether there are regular central exams

during secondary education. The evidence presented in this paper can produce only estimates of the general effect of whether there is central examination at all or not, so that the coefficient on central exams should be interpreted as a measure of the impact of central-exam systems and everything else that goes with them.

13. However, the standard deviation of test scores in an international setting may be larger than the standard deviation of scores on tests undertaken within individual countries.

14. This structure of the error term is implemented by using clustering-robust regression techniques that allow any degree of correlation among the error terms within each cluster to obtain consistent estimates of standard errors in the presence of an hierarchical data structure [see Brent R. Moulton, "Random Group Effects and the Precision of Regression Estimates," *Journal of Econometrics*, vol. 32, no. 3 (1986), pp. 385-97]. For variables measured at the country level—such as central exams—the standard errors reported in the tables use countries as the clustering unit, reflecting the fact that the number of independent observations on this variable is not the number of students, but only the number of countries. For all other variables, measured at the student, classroom, or school level, the standard errors reported in the tables use schools as the clustering unit, as schools constitute the primary sampling unit (PSU) in TIMSS. All regressions are weighted least squares estimations that use the TIMSS sampling weight of each student as their weights. The weighting ensures that the proportional contribution of each stratum in the sample to the coefficient estimates is equal to the one that would have been obtained had there been a complete census enumeration [see William H. DuMouchel and Greg J. Duncan, "Using Sample Survey Weights in Multiple Regression Analyses of Stratified Samples," *Journal of the American Statistical Association*, vol. 78, no. 383 (1983), pp. 535–43], and it ensures that each country gets the same weight within the international estimation.

15. Complete results tables are reported in Wößmann, "How Central Exams Affect Educational Achievement," appendix. In the pooled regressions, a control for the study year (TIMSS-95 versus TIMSS-Repeat) was never statistically significant and was consequently dropped from the estimations.

16. Bishop, "The Effect of National Standards and Curriculum-Based Exams on Achievement"; Bishop, "Are National Exit Examinations Important for Educational Efficiency?"; and Wößmann, "Schooling Resources, Educational Institutions, and Student Performance."

17. When the impact size is allowed to differ between the two tests in the pooled regression by including an interaction term between central exams and a dummy for the TIMSS-Repeat test, the difference in the size of the estimate is statistically insignificant both in math and in science.

18. Alan B. Krueger, "Experimental Estimates of Education Production Functions," *Quarterly Journal of Economics*, vol. 114, no. 2 (1999), pp. 497–532.

19. See Eric A. Hanushek, "Some Findings from an Independent Investigation of the Tennessee STAR Experiment and from Other Investigations of Class Size Effects," *Educational Evaluation and Policy Analysis*, vol. 21, no. 2 (1999), pp.

143–63; and Caroline M. Hoxby, "The Effects of Class Size on Student Achievement: New Evidence from Population Variation," *Quarterly Journal of Economics*, vol. 115, no. 4 (2000), pp. 1239–85.

20. Similarly, Caroline M. Hoxby, "The Cost of Accountability," Working Paper 8855 (Cambridge, Mass.: National Bureau of Economic Research, 2002), shows that the cost of the accountability programs implemented in several U.S. states that include comprehensive external testing is minuscule.

21. For detailed results on differing impacts by grade, as well as by performance quartiles and family background, see Wößmann, "How Central Exams Affect Educational Achievement," pp. 27–29.

22. Detailed results and further discussions of potential biases are reported in Wößmann, "How Central Exams Affect Educational Achievement."

23. The measure of ethnolinguistic fractionalization is defined as the probability that two randomly selected persons from a given country will not belong to the same ethnolinguistic group, as reported in Paolo Mauro, "Corruption and Growth," *Quarterly Journal of Economics*, vol. 110, no. 3 (1995), pp. 681–712. It is never statistically significantly related to student performance in the regressions.

24. Only three of the eight coefficient estimates on the regional dummies are statistically significant in either subject. There is no statistically significant difference in the math and science performance between Western Europe, North America, South America, and Oceania, after controlling for central exams and for the family, resource, and institutional variables considered in this study.

25. Based on Hausman tests, the standard error of the difference of –0.142 in math is 0.089, and the standard error of the difference of 0.058 in science is 0.069.

26. If central knowledge is superior in a task, then rendering schools autonomy in this task might even be detrimental to student achievement.

27. While the regressions on which the pictures in figure 13-3 are based control for the whole set of family, resource, and institutional controls, they do not control for interaction terms between central exams and other variables. As shown in Wößmann, "How Central Exams Affect Educational Achievement," the estimate of the genuine effect of central exams gets imprecise once a whole set of interaction terms is introduced. Excluding other interaction terms allows for basing the size of the bars depicting the impact in central-exam systems on reasonably exact, statistically significant estimates of the general effect of central exams.

28. All estimates reported in figure 13-3 are statistically significantly different from zero.

29. To determine the combined impact of central exams and an institutional characteristic, the coefficient estimates on central exams, on the institutional coefficient, and on their interaction term have to be summed. Wößmann, "How Central Exams Affect Educational Achievement," tables 7a and 7b, shows that the results are also robust against additionally including interaction terms between central exams and student and family background characteristics.

30. As was the case in figure 13-3, the regressions on which figure 13-4 are based control for family, resource, and institutional controls, but not for interaction terms between central exams and other variables.

31. In the specification of the estimation equation that controls for all other institutional interaction effects (table 13-3), the negative impact of uninterested parents with central exams is even worse than without central exams.

32. Helen F. Ladd, "School-Based Educational Accountability Systems: The Promise and the Pitfalls," *National Tax Journal*, vol. 54, no. 2 (2001), p. 386.

33. See Eric A. Hanushek, "Publicly Provided Education," in Alan Auerbach and Martin Feldstein, eds., *Handbook of Public Economics*, vol. 4 (Amsterdam: Elsevier, 2002).

34. See Richard J. Murnane and David K. Cohen, "Merit Pay and the Evaluation Problem: Why Most Merit Pay Plans Fail and a Few Survive," *Harvard Educational Review*, vol. 56, no. 1 (1986), pp. 1–17; and Dale Ballou, "Pay for Performance in Public and Private Schools," *Economics of Education Review*, vol. 20, no. 1 (2001), pp. 51–61.

35. Thomas J. Kane and Douglas O. Staiger, "Improving School Accountability Measures," Working Paper 8156 (Cambridge, Mass.: National Bureau of Economic Research, 2001); and Figlio and Page, "Can School Choice and School Accountability Successfully Coexist?"

36. Helen F. Ladd and Randall P. Walsh, "Implementing Value-Added Measures of School Effectiveness: Getting the Incentives Right," *Economics of Education Review*, vol. 21, no. 1 (2002), pp. 1–17.

Contributors

Julian R. Betts
University of California, San Diego

Anthony S. Bryk
University of Chicago

Anne Danenberg
Public Policy Institute of California

Thomas S. Dee
Swarthmore College

Eric A. Hanushek
Stanford University

Frederick M. Hess
American Enterprise Institute

Jennifer Hochschild
Harvard University

Brian A. Jacob
Harvard University

Thomas J. Kane
University of California, Los Angeles

Tom Loveless
Brookings Institution

Terry M. Moe
Stanford University

Paul E. Peterson
Harvard University

Margaret E. Raymond
Stanford University

Andrew Rudalevige
Dickinson College

Douglas O. Staiger
Dartmouth College

Martin R. West
Harvard University

Ludger Wößmann
Institute for Economic Research, Germany

Index

Academic Achievement for All Act (Straight A's program; *1999*), 32, 33, 38, 39, 41

Academic Performance Index (API; Calif.). *See* California

Accountability and accountability movement: approaches to, 9–10, 12–14, 15, 17–18, 19, 26–27, 86, 215–16, 318–19; compromises, 66, 70, 71–72, 73–74, 95–98, 108; as a control problem, 83–90, 96, 100; criticism of, 269–70; effects and incentives of, 71–72, 74–75, 87–90, 99, 100, 147, 198, 215; "gaming" the system, 202–05, 209, 269; goals of, 198, 294; high-stakes accountability, 57–68, 71–75; NEAP and, 5; history and future of, 3–8, 15, 108–09, 118–20; outcome and output accountability, 59, 215; politics of, 8–12, 56–68, 69, 73, 74, 75, 80, 90–99, 107–08, 109–12, 114–20; practice of, 12–14, 56–57, 58, 60, 69–71, 74–75, 76n9, 80–81; public views of, 111; school choice and, 101, 177; standards-based approaches, 57–58, 71–75, 86, 95, 116, 215–16; subgroup rules and targets, 153, 174; teachers unions and, 10–11, 85, 91, 94–98; tests and, 10, 57–58, 60, 66, 75, 86–87, 95–96, 172, 175, 182, 269, 275. *See also* Chicago; North Carolina; Texas; *individual states*

Accountability systems: achievement in, 129–30, 139–44; central exams, 294–319; definition of, 294; distribution of state systems, 136–37, 138t; effects of, 128–29, 137–47; grade-level accountability, 143; political issues, 191–92; school incentives and responses, 137–47

Accountability systems—methods and models of analysis: alternative accountability systems, 129–36;